The Garland Library of War and Peace

The Garland Library of War and Peace

Under the General Editorship of

Blanche Wiesen Cook, *John Jay College, C.U.N.Y.*

Sandi E. Cooper, *Richmond College, C.U.N.Y.*

Charles Chatfield, *Wittenberg University*

The First Book of World Law

A Compilation of the International Conventions to Which the Principal Nations Are Signatory with a Survey of Their Significance

by

Raymond L. Bridgman

with a new introduction for the Garland Edition by

Warren F. Kuehl

Garland Publishing, Inc., New York & London

1972

Garland Publishing Inc.
24 West 45 St., New York, N.Y. 10036

Library of Congress Cataloging in Publication Data

Bridgman, Raymond Landon, 1848-1925, comp.
The first book of world law.

(The Garland library of war and peace)
1. Treaties--Collections. I. Title. II. Series.
JX151.B7 1972 341'.026 79-147597
ISBN 0-8240-0358-6

Printed in the United States of America

Introduction

Raymond Bridgman (1849-1925), a Boston journalist, wrote extensively between 1903 and 1914 to convince mankind that the organization of the world into a political body was only a matter of time. Bridgman believed that a chain of events in the form of growing cooperation, both political and non-political in nature, would achieve this desired end. In another book of his reprinted in the Garland Library, World Organization, *Bridgman presented the nature of the organization he preferred, one with executive, legislative, and judicial departments with sufficient power to perform effectively.*

The First Book of World Law, *which appeared in 1911, represents Bridgman's efforts to persuade people that such a development represented no startling change. The political organization of the world began, Bridgman argued, with rather insignificant efforts on the part of the individuals at first to confer and later to unite regarding mutual interests. The behavior of men and nations as exemplified by this growing spirit of cooperation could be seen in the wealth of international conventions regarding agriculture, weights and measurements, economics, communications, health, moral problems, and trade as well as in conferences and societies to promote peace through arbitration, disarmament and an international court of justice.*

The progress of the world in this direction, he claimed, left the earth with only a few political decisions on the part of governments to achieve world unity. By noting the existence of commissions, conventions, and other accords and by recording their structure and operating procedures, Bridgman sought to convince readers that a dynamic transformation had already occurred which had to be accepted as inevitable. The First Book of World Law *thus recorded what men had already established and, more importantly, what they had developed in the way of procedures, standards, and customs. Bridgman distinguished such rules from international law, which dealt primarily with official customary developments. International lawyers had long insisted that a law of nations could be determined by compiling the evidence of common standards of behavior on the part of governments, and through a study of treaties, conventions, accords, and practices they had sought to record a set of acceptable rules. Bridgman acknowledged the correctness of their approach but insisted that they would be writing the Second Book of World Law. He was concerned with a more tangible factor, the behavior of men and nations as revealed by the actual evidence of their cooperation through formally organized efforts. This, he believed, was a truer indicator of customary law than that pursued by the lawyers.*

The ample documentation in his chapters showing such cooperation made Bridgman's volume a more conventional treatise on international law than he thought it was, since legal scholars employed the same technique in their efforts to codify rules of behavior among nations. But Bridgman was a reporter and editor, not an attorney, and his knowledge of international law was not extensive or sophisticated. He seemed unaware that his method of a brief survey of developments followed by the text of conventions was the commonplace methodology of the legal scholar.

Bridgman also did not note that his approach represented no novel idea. He reflected a rather widespread belief among internationalists of that time in an evolutionary hypothesis. They viewed the world as moving inexorably toward union and sought to document this claim by tracing the growing evidences of cooperation. The Hague Conferences of 1899 and 1907 seemed to substantiate their assumption as did the vast number of international societies which had emerged in the previous half-century.

The importance of these bodies, both private and public, had already been noted by the time Bridgman's book appeared. An Office Centrale des Institutions Internationales had been founded at Brussels, which had sponsored a World Congress of International Associations in 1910. The following year P. H. Eijkman established the Foundation for the Promotion of Internationalism at The Hague to serve as a clearinghouse for such bodies with special emphasis upon scientific ones. Eijkman listed over one hundred twenty-five of the latter as already in existence.

In 1913, the Foundation reported that six hundred fourteen international societies had been created, a fact which may have stimulated the writing of a dissertation at Columbia University by John C. Faries, published in 1915 as The Rise of Internationalism. *Faries described the historical evolution of political and non-political agencies and international conferences and noted the common world concerns these revealed. Nicholas Murray Butler of Columbia and the Carnegie Endowment for International Peace had already coined his oft-quoted phrase, the "international mind," to describe this phenomenon, and further evidence existed in the form of friendship societies and the exchange of students and professors. By 1913 Hendrick C. Andersen, an eccentric Scandinavian-American sculptor, developed an elaborate proposal for a World Center in the form of a new international city which would serve as the home and communications center for the growing number of organizations. Andersen assumed, as did Bridgman, that a new relationship of men and nations was developing which reflected the universality of mankind.*

While Bridgman did not elaborate in his book upon this vast network developing, he reflected these common assumptions. The fallacy of their logic appeared in the summer of 1914 when it became evident that the cement provided by such "first" world laws was insufficient to prevent the disintegration of the international community. The inevitability thesis as well as the evolutionary hypothesis seemed less valid thereafter.

This book, published by Ginn and Company and promoted by the World Peace Foundation and the American Peace Society at a modest price, apparently found a receptive audience. Unfortunately, most of those persons who read it did so to strengthen views previously held. It may have brought a few pacifists into the ranks of the internationalists, but it appears to have had little impact upon the public in general.

This may help to explain why Bridgman apparently abandoned his efforts on behalf of an international organization around 1914. In the last decade of his life, until 1925, he no longer promoted this cause with vigor. Yet for nearly fifteen years he devoted himself to winning men and women to the cause of world organization, and he thus stands as one of the foremost internationalists of the twentieth century.

Warren F. Kuehl
University of Akron

THE FIRST BOOK OF WORLD LAW

A COMPILATION OF THE INTERNATIONAL CONVENTIONS TO WHICH THE PRINCIPAL NATIONS ARE SIGNATORY, WITH A SURVEY OF THEIR SIGNIFICANCE

BY

RAYMOND L. BRIDGMAN

PUBLISHED FOR THE WORLD PEACE FOUNDATION
GINN AND COMPANY, PUBLISHERS
1911

911.8

The Athenæum Press
GINN AND COMPANY · PROPRIETORS · BOSTON · U.S.A.

PREFACE

Two reasons stand forth why the time demands such a book as this. One is historical. In the progress of events certain international conferences have been held. In the beginning those conferences were for the purpose of settling some specific subject of international complication. Latterly they have looked higher than the specific to the general. At the second conference at The Hague, that of 1907, there was distinctly before the minds of the delegates the prospect of future conferences upon broad lines, sufficient to include all of the nations with organized governments; and out of that development promises to come the organized political unity of mankind. A work covering the ground which this covers, or similar ground, is a necessity in keeping up with the development of the times. Though no person perhaps will wish to read it all, any more than he wishes to read all of his encyclopedia, yet any person who wishes to be well informed upon the political progress of the world must have the main facts at his command and be familiar with the specific lines of progress. Certain things have been done; certain records have been made in history; certain principles have been established in the progress of humanity. To be ignorant of these things is as unthinkable for all who keep informed upon human growth in civilization and organization, as ignorance of progress in physics is unthinkable on the part of a specialist in that department.

Of even more importance as a motive for action is the political reason. When gunpowder was applied to war, warfare entered sharply upon a new era. In like manner, and with almost equal sharpness, a new era has opened in the relations of nations. No man is in his correct environment who does not recognize the truth and adjust himself to it. The second conference at The Hague, following that of 1899, which established the Hague court of arbitration, and characterized by the establishment of an international prize court, which promises to be the historical germ of the world's judiciary, was followed by the London Conference of 1908–1909, attended by delegates of ten of the leading nations of the earth, called for the purpose of promoting true judicial methods in case of naval warfare. These gatherings have inaugurated, beyond reverse, a new era. The propositions for arbitration and for a true system of world courts are officially and practically before the world. Henceforth a new standard of official speech and action is imperative for all men in public life, in all nations. Whatever any statesman's personal views regarding the present practicability of disarmament or of checking military expenditure, he is inexcusable if he does not officially, as earnestly and as often as official occasion permits, urge upon the people within his influence the importance of working for the attainment of the ideal standard of international justice through legal methods, as opposed to the old injustice of the robber-might of strong nations and the horrors of war. Otherwise it is a fair judgment that he prefers slaughter to justice and personal glory to the peace and prosperity of all.

The spirit of world progress is more active, more insistent, and more severely critical than ever before. When men say that there is no progress, that the world is still in the bloody and barbaric era of international war, the spirit points to the Hague court of arbitration and charges the apologists with willful blindness, if not even willful falsehood, for the facts are too well known to permit mistake. When they say that the sword is the ultimate arbiter, she points to the world judiciary, now coming out of its germ, and commands them to make the most of the light and the opportunities they have. When they profess their fear of national, race, religious, or commercial conflict, she replies that they are false to what is highest and most natural in the modern man, — that fraternity among labor organizations, among scientific associations, and among business bodies is spreading to all parts of the earth, to promote intercourse and commerce, and that the solidarity of mankind is a growing motive, stronger than ever before. Every public official, therefore, is under the strongest obligations, by the very fact of his position, to spread the spirit of peace and justice; and every official who uses his high position and power to encourage ideas of armament and of conflict, without recognition of the higher plane of action, fails miserably to rise to the duty and opportunity of the times.

CONTENTS

THE FIRST BOOK OF WORLD LAW

CHAPTER I

BEGINNINGS OF WORLD ORGANIZATION

This book follows logically the author's little book entitled "World Organization." In that book demonstration was made of the existence of an unwritten world constitution, with mighty forces operating upon all parts of the human race. Already the nations have begun, officially, by duly appointed delegates, to express this world constitution. Already so many of the nations that they may reasonably be regarded as representatives of the human race have joined in the formation of a Declaration of Rights and Relations pertaining to the entire human race as a unit. Already the records of the world, as shown in "World Organization," contain mention of action which implies, not in the exact words, yet in the exact sense, recognition of the following articles of such a Declaration:

ART. I. All men are kindred; therefore the nations must be humane.

ART. II. All men are social; therefore intercommunication must be universal, reliable, and inexpensive.

ART. III. Each part of the world needs all the other parts; unimpeded exchange of the world's goods promotes world prosperity; therefore obstacles to such exchange must be removed.

ART. IV. Mankind advances most rapidly by coöperation; therefore national pride and prejudice must be discarded in order that nations may work together.

ART. V. World movements must be regulated by world intelligence; therefore the will of the whole must be supreme over all the parts.

ART. VI. Every part of mankind is of right entitled to freedom; therefore every power which attempts to enslave men must be destroyed.

ART. VII. The illness of one is the peril of all; therefore all must be vigilant for the health of each and of all.

ART. VIII. Mankind is intellectual and moral, not brutal; therefore differences between nations must be settled by reason and right, not by force.

Further than this, demonstration has also been made that the nations have begun, officially, by duly accredited delegates, the formation of that part of the world constitution which relates to the frame of government. In substance, though not in these exact words, the nations have already adopted these three articles: (1) there shall be a legislative department; (2) there shall be a judicial department; (3) there shall be an executive department.

Next in order, historically, from this point, must come the collection of the legislation already accomplished by the will of the world, or the First Book of World Law. For more than a generation true world law has been growing. In some instances, conspicuously in the case of the Universal Postal Union, the will of all the world has found official expression. In most instances the will has been only that of the leading nations of the world. In the case of the part, the process has been the same as in the case of the whole. Since the process is in its early stages of development, and since it is the same in method for the part as for the whole, it is reasonable to include in the body of world law certain propositions which have been affirmed officially by groups of the principal nations, but not by all nations.

Within a comparatively short time the organization of all mankind into a political unit has advanced rapidly. During the few years of the present century this advance has been so marked as to be highly encouraging to those who have been promoting it directly. By those who made the beginnings of true world legislation, the quality of their memorable service does not seem to have been understood. Certainly the world did not, at the time, appreciate the historic importance or character of their action in nourishing the germs of true world legislation, — meaning by world legislation the official expression of the will of the nations in definite form. But now that world legislation has undoubtedly been enacted, and now that the world legislature, in germ, is already here, rising into the self-consciousness of mankind as an actual existence, we can look back and see certain international gatherings in a very different light from that in which they appeared to the participants and spectators. They did not know when the dawn of the new era began out of the night of the past; but we, in the sure light of the present, which they did not enjoy, can not only say positively that the light now shines, but that certain phenomena of the past, not rightly understood then, were certainly rays of the dawn, prophetic of the noonday glow of the accomplished political unity of all the nations of mankind.

It is right and reasonable to say that the world legislature is here, because the will of all the world has been expressed by the means of the Hague conferences in formulating and submitting propositions which have been ratified by the nations. Those ratified propositions are the will of the world, officially and formally expressed through the different nations. In the recommendation by the Second Hague Conference that a third be called, there was in the consciousness of those official representatives of all the nations of the world a perception that they were promoting a mighty world movement which was sweeping all the nations of the earth into a political unity. The First Hague Conference was called primarily to deal with the armaments of the nations. The second was called primarily to settle questions left unsettled by the first. The third was recommended to be called primarily because of the mighty world impulse, plainly felt by the second conference, toward organizing the world and toward the political unity of the race.

With this dawn of the self-consciousness of the race a new era in the world's history began. It is not too much to affirm that this new era is the most important political era the human race has ever seen. These two gatherings at The Hague in 1899 and 1907 are now seen to have been true germs of the legislative department of the world. Yet they had their precedents, their roots, in many more or less similar gatherings before then, so that it is impossible to say that the beginning of the movement had its time and place here or there, otherwise than in the very nature of the human race as a unit from the beginning of its existence.

Frederick W. Holls, a delegate from the United States to the Hague peace conference of 1899, in his book, "The Peace Conference at The Hague," says (p. 352):

> The gathering at The Hague was the lineal descendant, so to speak, not of the innumerable peace congresses held in various quarters of the globe, but of the diplomatic assemblies called for the purpose of solving a present problem and of furnishing guarantees, more or less permanent, for peace between the Powers represented, beginning with the conferences of Münster and Osnabrück in 1648, including those of Utrecht in 1713, of Paris in 1763, and, above all, the Congress

of Vienna in 1815, and that of Berlin in 1878. The vital distinction between these gatherings and the peace conference at The Hague is that all of the former were held at the end of a period of warfare, and their first important object was to restore peace between actual belligerents; whereas the peace conference was the first diplomatic gathering called to discuss guarantees of peace, without reference to any particular war, — past, present, or prospective.

Only one qualification is to be made upon this judgment, — that it does not go far enough back for the beginning of the series. To the trained mind of Mr. Holls there was such similarity of quality between the gatherings which made the treaties of Westphalia, Utrecht, and Paris, and the Hague conference of 1899, that they belong in the same class. He is clearly right from one point of view, but that point hardly rises to the height of world legislation. Those early gatherings, making treaties for the peace of Europe, were merely preparing the road for the march of the body of world legislators who were destined, in the fullness of time, to enjoy the fruit of their earlier wisdom and to lead the way to still higher international action.

Before taking up the evolution of the world will which has already become world law through the official action of the nations, it is pertinent, for the sake of noting how the organized political unity of the world is advancing, to add that the germ of a true world judiciary department is found in the recommendation for an international prize court, which was submitted to the nations by the second conference at The Hague. Still further, several distinct germs of the world executive department are already in active existence. Oldest and best of illustrations is that of the permanent secretary at Berne of the Universal Postal Union. This and other executive officers are not of a high grade, but they are truly executive. Their offices were established by world legislation, and they are genuine world executive officers. These developments show that the three necessary departments of all civilized governments — the legislative, the executive, and the judicial — are already actually existent or close at hand.

An excellent bird's-eye view of the official relations of nations to each other is gained by looking over the list of international documents put forth by the nations separately and collectively. One list, available for this writing, — the collection of G. F. de Martens, — opens the vista of the past back to the year 1494, when was made a treaty between Spain and Portugal concerning their discoveries in the ocean. All kinds of official relations between two nations, between one nation on one side and a group of two or more on the other, and between groups of nations, are here set forth in such variety and profusion as to furnish an embarrassment of riches to the historian seeking for illustrations. Here are documents — all of them of international importance and intent — relating to discoveries, territorial rights, boundaries, alliances, cessions, titles to thrones, rules for diplomatic officials, edicts, letters patent, conventions on a large variety of subjects, treaties of diverse nature by the hundred, agreements of peace, commerce, and amity, firmans, ultimatums, navigation regulations, passport arrangements, neutrality stipulations, extradition understandings, subsidies, decrees, embargoes, monetary privileges, indemnities, capitulations, arbitrations, hospital guaranties, mediations, combinations of various sorts, antislavery action, protection of subjects, immigration, naturalization, dismemberment of nations, reciprocity bargains, demolition of fortresses, manifestoes, papal bulls on political matters when the papacy was a political power, and so on in infinite variety.

As we look back upon these activities of many hundred years and, at one glance, sweep over this constant recurrence every year, and, in most instances, many times in the year, in some years amounting to about two hundred documents, having to do with official relations between the nations; and as we realize still further that the official communications were not a thousandth part of the interrelations which were really in progress between the peoples of the earth from one end to the other in way of trade and travel, of friendship and hostility, of learning and pleasure, it is so clear that further proof is needless that here is in actual operation a genuine unity of all mankind, and that it is only by unpardonable pride and folly that the truth is persistently denied officially.

After all that is said about the many forms of the movements which have promoted the unity of mankind, it remains most pertinent of all that the one great force which has made political unity possible is the inherent and fundamental unity of the race, energizing to its natural, legitimate, and inevitable consummation. Political unity trails along behind the real unity. The latter has been for hundreds and thousands of years asserting itself, but never more forcibly or in more ways than to-day, by travel from continent to continent, by official relations between the fragments of the race, and by a thousand various ways whereby the common bond has asserted itself supreme over the divisive forces of space, of religion, of commercial contests, of national hostility, of suspicion, of language, and of natural inability to sympathize with different types of mental action and different standards of personal morals. Unity created in men as men, not developed by men as creators, has been stimulating them for many centuries, and to-day it is the dynamic which runs international railroad and steamship lines and carries men and women into all nooks and corners of foreign countries, to see new peoples, to learn new languages, to read new literature, to study new histories, and to develop that new world spirit and race enthusiasm which is thrilling all nations to-day as they look forward to the mutual friendship, peace, and prosperity which is their natural right and destiny, and which they are now about to achieve. Unconsciously the masses of the nations are illustrating the unity of the human race. Their statesmen are just beginning to realize the truth and to act upon it. Now that the stage of self-consciousness of the race has come, it is reasonable to predict that there will be intelligent shaping of means to the end, and that henceforth there will be more rapid progress toward the realization of the ideal. Thus far the movement has been by men blindfolded and with no clear mental perception of the goal. To-day the eyes see, the mind is conscious of itself and of the goal before it. Henceforth progress must be to the movement of the past as the locomotive to the man on foot.

CHAPTER II

THE FIRST BOOK OF WORLD LAW

It is no longer a question whether the whole human race shall be one organized political body. Events of the last few years, with their prophetic voices, have proclaimed the truth so that hearers have no doubt. What was foretold by scientific men and by political and humanitarian world conferences of official delegates of the nations in the latter part of the nineteenth century, what was still more distinctly asserted by the first peace conference at The Hague, but was even then not noticed by every one, was at length, by the second peace conference, declared so clearly that doubt was forever removed. Henceforth it is only a question of time how soon the political organization shall be completed and the nations acknowledge the supremacy of world sovereignty through a formal statement of world law.

Speaking politically, world law is the will of the world expressed officially. It can be shown beyond doubt that official expression has been made of the will of the world in repeated instances by so many nations acting together regarding particular matters that their will may reasonably be taken as the will of all the world. These expressions of world will which are now recognized as true world law, of a class different from international law and higher than that law, are here gathered into one volume. They form the First Book of World Law. Their development, though it knits together threads which extend back into the past for hundreds and perhaps, in some cases, thousands of years, has been rapid in recent years only. Here is a formative era of vast historical importance in the development of the human race from the collisions of warring tribes to the official and sympathetic action of nations with some degree of civilization.

This collection of world law is made at a time when the self-consciousness of the nations as a political unit has barely come to the surface through the recommendation of the second peace conference that a third be called, with the evident understanding that the third will be followed by a fourth, and then by others indefinitely until the fully developed political organism of the world shall carry on the activities of the body of mankind as its needs impel, as its intelligence directs, and as its will acts.

Of necessity, in the nature of the case, the First Book of World Law must gather up the unconscious acts of world sovereignty and bring them into continuous and harmonious relation. It must lay the foundation so clearly that even those whose study is superficial can no longer doubt its true nature, nor deny intelligently that on such foundation, as certainly as that mankind has a future and that in that future progress will be made, will be reared the magnificent temple of world law, — the will of mankind, acting with the intelligence of mankind in perceiving the unwritten laws imposed upon mankind by the Supreme Intelligence and Power, and adapting itself to the forces amid which it exists. Such must be the First Book of World Law.

But already the contents of the Second Book of World Law are evident. Out of the era when the contents of the First Book were enacted, out of the stage of civilization in which were developed the principles of international law, based on no authority higher than the unofficial mandates of human reason commanding the assent of all reasonable nations to the common sentiments of humanity and justice which asserted their imperative claims even amid the carnage of the battlefield and the horrors of the siege, — out of this and out of the achievements of the Hague conferences has come a recognition of the need that these unofficially formulated mandates be given formal statement and be sealed by official ratification.

On the basis of international law must rise world law as a higher expression of the agreement of the will of the nations. It must be endowed with binding force upon every nation. The nations will submit to it voluntarily. The minority of the nations will not be coerced by the mighty armies of the majority into submission. Each nation, for there will eventually be no majority and no minority, will yield because it is right so to do, and to refuse further to submit would not be right and would be so recognized. International law must be codified by world statesmen into world law. That codification will be the Second Book of World Law. Its preparation may be predicted confidently because already the movement to that end has begun and the distinct proposition has been made in high circles. It is not too bold a forecast of the work of the Third Hague Conference to say that a part of its action, at least, will relate to a codification of international law to the end that the formal statement may be ratified by the nations and so be raised to the higher status of world law.

But the First Book of World Law and the Second Book of World Law have their clear limitations. They include and bring to date the developments of the past. But the human race advances. Not only that; it is advancing faster than ever, and its progress is always with accelerating rapidity. At the third conference new principles will be formulated. Very likely these will be incorporated in the Second Book. Just in what order the details will be worked out will depend upon forces operative at the time; but soon, perhaps by the fourth conference, will be such further formulation of principles to be ratified that the Third Book of World Law will be brought into being, as a session of the Congress of the United States makes possible a new book of laws, and as each session of each legislature of the several states of the United States results in a new volume. By that time the nature of the peace conference as the true germ of the world legislature will have long been generally recognized; and from that time on, the Fourth, the Fifth, and the succeeding books of World Law will take their place in the series, until a new codification is made and the numbering begins again.

CHAPTER III

ANTECEDENTS OF THE WORLD LEGISLATURE

Plausible reason can be given for predicting that the Hague conferences will prove to have been in the historic line of development of a true legislative body for all mankind. But the political unity of the world can come about only by the overthrow of some theories which are held very stoutly by the statesmen of the nations to-day. Men in politics to-day have a different attitude toward political truth from men's attitude in other fields of progress. In physics new truth is welcomed gladly; it is not received with resentment or hostility, if it is demonstrated reasonably to be truth; it is welcomed and obeyed, for it is known that penalty follows its violation. But with religion and world politics it is different. In the relations of men to each other the most fundamental truth is that mankind is one, and that already it is one organic body. Absolute national sovereignty is a theory which the foremost statesmen of the great nations have strenuously insisted upon; but the demonstration is very simple that the absoluteness does not prevail even within the boundaries of the nation itself which claims to have absolute sovereignty, for it is a well-settled principle of international law that treaties are the supreme law of the land for any nation; that is, a people's obligations to other people of whom they claim to be independent are supreme over their relations to each other, and the obligation which grows out of the fact that the nation is a part of mankind is supreme over all claims of independence. Therefore the claim of any nation and the claims of all nations to absolute sovereignty are mere idle words, contradicted by the supreme obligations of every nation during every hour of its existence.

Sovereignty is an attribute of mankind as a whole. It is not an attribute of any of the parts of mankind. Below the status of sovereignty the relations of the parts to the central authority — whether much or little absolute control of national and local affairs shall be left to national and local authority — is purely a question of expediency as to the best system of maintaining national, local, and personal rights. Those rights are sacred, and to be guarded by law as sacredly in case of nations as in case of persons; but the nations have no sovereignty over against world sovereignty, any more than persons have sovereignty over against their national government. Sovereignty is one thing; rights are another. Sovereignty, in the true sense, inheres in nothing less than the whole of mankind. That sovereignty must maintain national and local rights.

The first practical step in getting the nations into their true world relations is thus to have them admit the truth that they are parts of a world whole, and that any contradictory doctrine cannot stand for a moment. Still further, every insistence upon the false doctrine carries a penalty with it, just as violation of physical law carries a penalty.

One of the fascinating features in the history of the nations is their constant illustration of the unity of the human race and their tendency toward world centralization, in spite of all the facts and the follies which split up mankind into mutually destructive fragments. Take, for instance, the list of international documents which has been mentioned, the collection which bears the name of G. F. de Martens, and which finds its modern counterpart in the valuable tables of international events and documents which are published in several nations, — in the United States in the *American Journal of International Law*. In thousands of cases there are recorded negotiations of two nations with each other, taking form in treaties and in a large variety of communications of less rank, all of which are based on and illustrate the unity of all and the impossibility of any one nation existing in either peace or war without complicated relations with almost every other nation on earth. But all of these may be passed over in order to reach the more significant and more fertile class, that in which three or more nations act in concert for the strengthening of bonds between them, for their mutual advantage in opposing conditions dangerous to both, and for the breaking down of obstacles to a closer union between them, whereby the masses of their people may tend to become assimilated and amalgamated either by trade or travel or intermarriage, or by all combined.

Alliances or leagues of independent political powers go back to the dim past, and there is no certainty when the most remote will be discovered. But every reader who has a Bible will find in the fourteenth chapter of Genesis, at a date which is given as about 1913 B.C., a combination of four kings in war against five; and the fact that their kingdoms were doubtless small does not weaken the illustration. Again, at a date given as 1451 B.C., the kings in the land of Canaan combined to resist the invading Israelites. The Ætolian League, from 320 to 189 B.C., and the Achæan League, from 280 to 146 B.C., in Greece, are later illustrations. In Europe in the Middle Ages we read of the Hanseatic league of 1140 A.D., of various combinations of the Grisons of Switzerland in 1396, and of their union in 1471. The dukes of Calabria, Brittany, and Bourbon made their "League for the Public Good" in 1464 against Louis XI of France, and from that time on occasionally in Europe there were combinations of more than two Powers for limited periods, while international relations between the nations in groups of twos showed increasing frequency. The world was moving all the time and was getting together, notwithstanding the frightfully destructive wars which annihilated large portions of the population.

In the early part of the eighteenth century some multiple combinations of nations are to be noticed. In 1703 Great Britain, the Netherlands, and Portugal made an alliance at Lisbon. In 1718 there was a quadruple alliance of Great Britain, France, Austria, and Spain, to which Sardinia was admitted in 1720. But the illustrations are few till we cross into the nineteenth century and in 1806 note the formation of the Confederation of the Rhine, which in 1807 had come to include thirty-four independent states. In 1815 came the Congress of Vienna, following the Napoleonic wars, attended by eight Powers, which established the so-called Concert of Europe and was attended by an alliance of Great Britain, Prussia, Austria, and Russia, which France was invited to join through a note sent by the four Powers to the Duc de Richelieu, November 4, 1818. The theory of the balance of power in Europe was first recognized in the peace conferences of Münster and Osnabrück in 1648. In 1821 ten states joined in establishing the free navigation of the Elbe. In 1830 Great Britain, Austria, France, Prussia, and Russia joined in decreeing the separation of Belgium from Holland. In 1854 Great Britain, France, Austria, and Russia took joint action regarding Turkey.

But after the Crimean War, with its horrors, after the liberation of

Italy, after the Civil War in the United States, when all civilization must have had its fill of blood, came the rush of the nations into their modern world relations. The word "rush" is used in retrospect. At the time it did not seem to be a rush. Certainly the principal participants in the events did not realize their vital historic relations, but as we look back we see things in a clearer light than that in which the actors saw them, and the years seem nearer together as they recede in perspective.

In 1864 came the convention of Geneva, a humanitarian movement which grew out of the sufferings of the sick and the wounded in the Crimean War, in the main. It resulted in the establishment of the Red Cross Society, now a world institution; and the Geneva convention has become world legislation, to be given its due standing in history.

In 1863 was held an international conference in Paris to consider the subject of a postal union, and it was the lineal predecessor of the famous meeting at Berne in 1874 which resulted in the establishment of the Universal Postal Union, of which every nation on earth is now a member if it is sufficiently organized to have a government by which it can be represented.

From that date of 1874 onward, international conferences and congresses, held by official delegates of more or fewer nations, have met in large number and for various purposes in the advancement of the welfare of mankind. Many of these conferences formulated propositions which were ratified by the home governments and thus became official statements of so many nations that they are now the formal will of the world, or world law, the expressed will of mankind taken as an organized whole.

The climax was reached in the second peace conference at The Hague in 1907, when practically all the nations were participants, and when the self-consciousness of all mankind, as a single organic body, came into being and found expression in the adoption of the recommendation that a third conference be held, — that recommendation growing out of a proposition that the Hague conference be made a permanent body, with regular sittings, from which it was expected that a true world legislature would develop in due time.

In the *American Journal of International Law* for January, 1908 (p. 27), Professor James Brown Scott, who was officially listed among the delegates from the United States to the second peace conference as "solicitor of the department of state, technical delegate," says: "The friends of peace and arbitration had wished to make the conference at The Hague a permanent institution, meeting at regular and stated intervals, known in advance. The American delegation had the honor to urge the adoption of such a resolution or recommendation and succeeded in substance, although the language is not so clear and crisp as one would like to see it." Then follows the official recommendation for a third conference; and there can be no doubt that a series of official world gatherings of delegates for the expression of the will of the world has begun. It promises to lead to a true world legislature. When this shall have come, then world law will enter upon a new stage of development.

Attention is called to the imperative form of the language, with full imperative meaning, which occurs repeatedly in the world legislation; and the mandate is only veiled in many other cases where it is not positively expressed. Consider a few citations: "Each government shall"; "the governments shall only apply"; "the government of each country is obliged"; "the government shall make known"; "each signatory Power shall select"; "a Power desiring to adhere shall make its intention known"; "the contracting Powers shall furnish." Authority is here put upon each and every nation. It matters not whether the Power to obey is Germany with its mighty army, or Great Britain with its formidable navy, or the United States with its aggressive confidence of ability to overcome any earthly opposition, or Russia spreading itself over a vast area of the habitable globe, — each and all, equally with puny Panama and tiny Montenegro, is in that position where a supreme authority commands it: "Thou shalt"; and "Thou shalt not."

This authority, fearless before a mighty army, indifferent to a formidable navy, serene in the presence of aggressive confidence, unwearied by thousands of miles of distance, impartial between mighty empires and tiny republics, in striking contrast to the material forces which it dominates, is the imperial power of truth and justice, revealed to and expressed by the united mind of the human race as a political unit. Mankind commands; great and small Powers equally obey.

By the status of to-day each and every Power, by its own will, makes itself a part of the whole which puts compulsion upon itself.

In a sense the obedience is self-imposed, for any Power remaining outside of the new formal world relation would not be compelled to come in. Still further, being in, it is not to be presumed that military compulsion would be put upon it by the other Powers if it were to refuse to render the required obedience. Agreement of the judgment and conscience of each Power with the judgment and conscience of the whole is relied upon by each and every Power to make every Power, singly, obedient to the will of the whole. If disobedience shall occur, doubtless it will be left to time and to the influence of the judgment and conscience of the other Powers to enlighten the judgment and conscience of the disobedient Power so that it will renounce its disobedience.

It will not escape the notice of the observer that in the case of world legislation there is a correspondence to the relation of an individual will to the forces amid which it lives. That will can refuse obedience, but the forces are supreme over his outward conduct just the same. He is free to choose the right or the wrong; but if he chooses the wrong, he must bear the full penalty without mitigation. He is free when he obeys; but his obedience, being a result of recognition of the right and justice in the forces which demand obedience, brings with it a prosperity and blessing in total contrast to the loss and suffering from disobedience. Law has its perfect work in each alternative.

So the will of the Powers as a united, organized whole, embodying their judgment and conscience, is rightly a law for each individual Power. True world legislation is realized by the formal expression of the united will of the Powers, and all mankind is brought into conscious harmony of action as never before. With the beginning of world legislation, therefore, comes the beginning of an era of peace and prosperity far in excess of anything ever yet enjoyed by the human race.

World sovereignty, be it further noticed, is claimed and formally exercised in world legislation already accomplished. Not merely the doctrine, but the fact, is put forward by the Powers acting together in their legislation, which is a matter of record, although, in contradiction, no nominally sovereign Power yet formally acknowledges that there is even the doctrine of world sovereignty, still less the fact. Here, again, the truth in the development of the political unity of mankind has outrun the appreciation of those who have been participants in its expression.

In addition to the commands put upon the Powers themselves by the organized Powers of the world, there are in all the following conventions taken together many instances where the single organized world Power puts its commands upon the several international bureaus which have been established by some of the conventions. These bureaus are true executive departments of the single world Power; and so we have the perfect function of the world legislature imposing its will upon the true world executive, its servant.

To open the eyes to what is already an accomplished fact is the urgent need of the times in the education of the nations. World sovereignty is here. It is in active operation to-day. It only remains for the nations to admit the truth and to incorporate it more practically and intelligently into their relations with each other.

Be it further observed that, though the nations are nominally free to enter into the new world relations or not, yet, like the individual will amid the forces which are supreme over its outward action, they are really in the world relations whether or not they formally acknowledge the truth. This world sovereignty, therefore, is not in any real sense a result of any federation, and never can be dependent upon any idea of federation, but is absolutely supreme over any possible agreement or coming together by the nations upon any understanding which implies that they can come in or stay out as they please. World sovereignty, as already proclaimed by the "Thou shalt" and the "Thou shalt not" of world legislation already in full operation, springs from and is a worthy expression of the genuine unity of mankind, beyond the power of any and all nations to change by an atom; and its clear recognition by all the Powers will hasten their harmonious unity as an organized political whole, which they are now in the process of realizing. World sovereignty must be obeyed for the welfare of each and every part, and each and every Power will promote its own welfare and the welfare of all in proportion as it promptly recognizes and obeys this rightful, supreme authority.

CHAPTER IV

THE UNIVERSAL POSTAL UNION

Among the precedents which we find in the action of the near or the remote past which bear directly upon the organization of the nations into a political unit are those relating to postal service, to alliances or confederations, to arbitration, to mediation, and to reciprocity. Certainly nothing seems to have been further from the thought of the actors in these historic movements than the truth that they were contributing to evolution in a direct line toward the political unity of the world. It is a fascinating study to trace back to the past the roots of these present flourishing growths.

In the Universal Postal Union we find the first great illustration of the united action of the nations, the first act of world legislation which includes all of the world. That union was formed in 1874. If we follow the years back, we find that the union was preceded by postal conventions between nations, and that there was a natural evolution from the less to the greater. Postal conventions presupposed postal developments within separate countries; and so the taproot of the formal unity of the nations runs back to a stage when it could not be predicted by contemporaries, but only by the man of faith and prophetic vision, what the development would be.

Back to the time of Cyrus, 550 B.C., we go, and find him credited with first establishing a system of postriders. He built posthouses and had regular lines of couriers. There was the true germ of the Universal Postal Union, unless an older claimant to the honor can prove his case. In the year 31 B.C. Augustus established posts in the Roman Empire. We read that in 800 A.D. Charlemagne had them. In England, says the record, the beginning was in 1481, when riders on post horses, a relay of twenty men, were charged with the service of carrying to King Edward IV the news regarding his war with the stubborn Scots. Under date of 1543, says the record, there was a similar arrangement. Queen Elizabeth, in 1581, appointed the first chief postmaster of England. In 1632 the line of postriders to the north was made international by extending it to Edinburgh. By 1635 there had come to be a regular postal service between London and most of England, Scotland, and Ireland. Other countries were having their own developments in the meantime.

Now for the international developments. Under date of September 12, 1817, a postal convention was made between the Netherlands and France, which seems to be the first international postal arrangement by treaty. Out of this precedent came, in due time, the Universal Postal Union. The document is short and provides that the people of France and the Netherlands respectively shall be free to send letters, packages, merchandise, and printed matter from one realm to the other without regard to the boundary line between the countries. Suitable postal regulations were made, and the precedent was fully and clearly established.

But it was not followed as soon as we should now expect. On April 16, 1831, — this interval of nearly fourteen years shows how slowly the idea gained ground, — a postal convention was signed between Austria and France. To this an addition was made on May 18, 1843. On August 9, 1838, France and the Holy See at Rome concluded a postal convention of twenty-six articles for the direct transmission of mail matter between them by sea. On August 27, 1838, at Paris, was concluded a postal convention in thirty-three articles between France and Sardinia. In 1843, February 11, was concluded a postal convention between Austria and Russia. So the benefits of being friendly and accommodating toward each other were realized in practice; and the wonder is that the people were not bright enough to see the universal principle underlying this mutually profitable and peace-promoting arrangement and to extend its application to many other phases of their official interrelations. But their furious jealousies, their revengeful and piratical hostilities, their apprehensions from the armed hosts of each other, and their desire to guard their future by crippling the enemy of the present, blinded them to the presence of the angel of peace and prosperity, whose wings might have been seen through the wrappings of their postal packages sent from one country to another. But still there was progress. Further preparation for the great consummation is seen in the postal convention of May 1, 1843, between France and Great Britain. In 1846, October 1, record is made of a similar convention between Great Britain and Prussia. In 1849, July 2, Austria and Switzerland entered into a postal arrangement, and the next day saw one between Parma and Modena.

So the idea spread till in 1874, at Berne, Switzerland, on October 9, was concluded the treaty between twenty nations for the establishment of a general postal union, the ratifications of which made it effective May 3, 1875. The nations were these: Germany, Austria-Hungary, Belgium, Denmark, Egypt, Spain, the United States, France, Great Britain, Greece, Italy, Luxemburg, the Netherlands, Portugal, Roumania, Russia, Servia, Sweden and Norway, Switzerland, and Turkey. Since then, by subsequent conventions, the union has been enlarged till to-day it includes every nation on earth which has sufficient organization to be capable of making an official agreement with other nations. As the postal convention stands to-day, signed at Rome, May 26, 1906, it includes the following nations and dependencies, given in the order in which they stand in the official document of the United States which contains the convention: Germany and German protectorates, the United States of America and the island possessions of the United States of America, Argentine Republic, Austria, Belgium, Bolivia, Bosnia-Herzegovina, Brazil, Bulgaria, Chile, Chinese Empire, republic of Colombia, Kongo Free State, empire of Korea, republic of Costa Rica, Crete, republic of Cuba, Denmark and Danish colonies, Dominican republic, Egypt, Ecuador, Spain and Spanish colonies, Ethiopian empire, France, Algeria, French colonies and protectorates of Indo-China, the whole of the other French colonies, Great Britain and various British colonies, British India, the Commonwealth of Australia, Canada, New Zealand, British colonies of South Africa, Greece, Guatemala, republic of Hayti, republic of Honduras, Hungary, Italy and the Italian colonies, Japan, republic of Liberia, Luxemburg, Mexico, Montenegro, Nicaragua, Norway, republic of Panama, Paraguay, the Netherlands, the Dutch colonies, Peru, Persia, Portugal and Portuguese colonies, Roumania, Russia, Salvador, Servia, kingdom of Siam, Sweden, Switzerland, Tunis, Turkey, Uruguay, and United States of Venezuela.

The revision undertaken by the plenipotentiaries of the above-named countries was, in virtue of Article 25 of the universal postal convention, concluded at Washington on June 15, 1897, which convention, in its turn, was the outgrowth of conventions before it. This revised convention of 1906 must stand, therefore, as probably the best of all illustrations of the development of world law. After the opening in due form, it proceeds as follows:

ARTICLE 1. DEFINITION OF THE POSTAL UNION

The countries between which the present convention is concluded, as well as those which may adhere to it hereafter, form, under the title of Universal Postal Union, a single postal territory for the reciprocal exchange of correspondence between their post offices.

ARTICLE 2. ARTICLES TO WHICH THE CONVENTION APPLIES

The stipulations of this convention extend to letters, post cards, both single and with reply paid, printed papers of every kind, commercial papers, and samples of merchandise originating in one of the countries of the union and intended for another of those countries. They also apply to the exchange by mail of the articles above mentioned between the countries of the union and countries foreign to the union, whenever the services of two of the contracting parties at least are used for that exchange.

ARTICLE 3. CONVEYANCE OF MAILS BETWEEN CONTIGUOUS COUNTRIES; THIRD SERVICES

(1) The postal administrations of contiguous countries, or countries able to correspond directly with each other without availing themselves of the services of a third administration, determine, by common consent, the conditions of the conveyance of the mails which they exchange across the frontier or from one frontier to the other.

(2) In the absence of any contrary arrangement, the direct sea conveyance between two countries by means of packets or vessels depending upon one of them is considered as a third service; and this conveyance, as well as any performed between two offices of the same country, by the medium of sea or territorial services maintained by another country, is regulated by the stipulations of the following article.

ARTICLE 4. TRANSIT RATES

(1) The right of transit is guaranteed throughout the entire territory of the union.

(2) Consequently the several postal administrations of the union may send reciprocally, through the medium of one or of several of them, either closed mails or articles in open mail, according to the needs of the traffic and the convenience of the postal service.

(3) Articles exchanged in closed mails between two administrations of the union, by means of the services of one or of several other administrations of the union,

are subject to the following transit charges to be paid to each of the countries traversed or whose services participate in the conveyance, viz.:

1st. For territorial transits:

a. 1 franc 50 centimes per kilogram of letters and post cards and 20 centimes per kilogram of other articles, if the distance traversed does not exceed 3000 kilometers;

b. 3 francs per kilogram of letters and post cards and 40 centimes per kilogram of other articles, if the distance traversed exceeds 3000 kilometers but does not exceed 6000 kilometers;

c. 4 francs 50 centimes per kilogram of letters and post cards and 60 centimes per kilogram of other articles, if the distance traversed exceeds 6000 kilometers but does not exceed 9000 kilometers;

d. 6 francs per kilogram of letters and post cards and 80 centimes per kilogram of other articles, if the distance traversed exceeds 9000 kilometers.

2d. For sea transits:

a. 1 franc 50 centimes per kilogram of letters and post cards and 20 centimes per kilogram of other articles, if the distance traversed does not exceed 300 nautical miles. Sea conveyance over a distance not exceeding 300 nautical miles is, however, gratuitous if the administration concerned already receives, on account of the mails conveyed, the remuneration applicable to territorial transit;

b. 4 francs per kilogram of letters and post cards and 50 centimes per kilogram of other articles, exchanged over a distance exceeding 300 nautical miles between European countries, between Europe and ports of Africa and Asia on the Mediterranean and the Black Sea, or between one of these ports and another, and between Europe and North America. The same rates are applicable to conveyance, by services open to the whole union, between two ports of a single state, as well as between the ports of two states served by the same line of packets when the sea transit involved does not exceed 1500 nautical miles;

c. 8 francs per kilogram of letters and post cards and 1 franc per kilogram of other articles, for all transits not included in the categories given above in paragraphs *a* and *b.*

In the case of sea conveyance effected by two or more administrations, the charges paid for the entire transit cannot exceed 8 francs per kilogram of letters and post cards and 1 franc per kilogram of other articles; these charges are, when occasion arises, shared between the administrations participating in the service, in proportion to the distances traversed, without prejudice to any other arrangement which may be made between the parties interested.

(4) Correspondence exchanged in open mail between two administrations of the union are subject to the following transit charges per article, and irrespective of weight or destination, namely: letters, 6 centimes each; post cards, 2½ centimes each; other articles, 2½ centimes each.

(5) The transit rates specified in the present article do not apply to conveyance within the union by means of extraordinary services specially established or maintained by one administration at the request of one or several other administrations. The conditions of this category of conveyance are regulated by mutual consent between the administrations concerned.

Moreover, in all cases where the transit, either by land or by sea, is at present gratuitous or subject to more advantageous conditions, such state of things is maintained.

Nevertheless, territorial transit services exceeding 3000 kilometers may profit by the provisions of paragraph (3) of the present article.

(6) The expenses of transit are borne by the administration of the country of origin.

(7) The general accounting for those expenses takes place on the basis of statements prepared once in every six years, during a period of twenty-eight days to be determined in the detailed regulations provided for in Article 20 hereafter.

For the period between the date on which the convention of Rome comes into force and the date on which the transit statistics mentioned in the detailed regulations provided for in Article 20 become operative, transit rates will be paid in accordance with the stipulations of the convention of Washington.

(8) The articles mentioned in paragraphs (3) and (4) of Article 11 hereafter, the reply halves of double post cards returned to the country of origin, articles redirected or missent, undelivered articles, advices of delivery, post-office money orders, and all other documents relative to the postal service are exempt from all charges for territorial or sea transit.

(9) When the annual balance of the transit accounts between two administrations does not exceed 1000 francs, the debtor administration is relieved of all payment on that account.

ARTICLE 5. RATES OF POSTAGE AND GENERAL CONDITIONS

(1) The rates of postage for the conveyance of postal articles throughout the entire extent of the union, including their delivery at the residence of the addressees in the countries of the union where a delivery is or shall be organized, are fixed as follows:

1st. For letters, 25 centimes in case of prepayment, and double that amount in the contrary case, for each letter not exceeding 20 grams in weight; and 15 centimes in case of prepayment, and double that amount in the contrary case, for every weight of 20 grams or fraction of 20 grams above the initial weight of 20 grams;

2d. For post cards, in case of prepayment, 10 centimes for single cards or for each of the two halves of reply post cards, and double that amount in the contrary case;

3d. For printed papers of every kind, commercial papers, and samples of merchandise, 5 centimes for each article or packet bearing a particular address and for every weight of 50 grams or fraction of 50 grams, provided that such article or packet does not contain any letter or manuscript note having the character of actual and personal correspondence, and that it be made up in such a manner as to admit of its being easily examined.

The charge on commercial papers cannot be less than 25 centimes per packet, and the charge on samples cannot be less than 10 centimes per packet.

(2) In addition to the rates fixed by the preceding paragraph there may be levied:

1st. For every article subject to the sea-transit charges prescribed in paragraph (3), 2d, *c*, of Article 4, and in all the relations to which these transit rates are applicable, a uniform surtax which may not exceed 25 centimes per single rate for letters, 5 centimes per post card, and 5 centimes per 50 grams or fraction of 50 grams for other articles;

2d. For every article conveyed by means of services maintained by administrations foreign to the union, or of extraordinary services in the union giving rise to special expenses, a surcharge in proportion to those expenses.

When the rate of prepayment for the single post card comprises one or other of the surcharges authorized in the two preceding paragraphs, the same rate is applicable to each half of the reply-paid post card.

(3) In case of insufficient prepayment, correspondence of every kind is liable to a charge equal to double the amount of the deficiency, to be paid by the addressees; but that charge may not exceed that which is levied in the country of destination on unpaid correspondence of the same nature, weight, and origin.

(4) Articles other than letters and post cards must be prepaid at least partly.

(5) Packets of samples of merchandise may not contain any article having a salable value; they must not exceed 350 grams in weight, or measure more than 30 centimeters in length, 20 centimeters in breadth, and 10 centimeters in depth, or, if they are in the form of a roll, 30 centimeters in length and 15 centimeters in diameter.

(6) Packets of commercial papers and printed papers may not exceed 2 kilograms in weight, or measure more than 45 centimeters in any direction. Packets in the form of a roll may, however, be allowed to pass through the post so long as they do not exceed 10 centimeters in diameter and 75 centimeters in length.

(7) Stamps or forms of prepayment obliterated or not, as well as all printed papers constituting the sign of a monetary value, save the exceptions authorized by the detailed regulations provided for in Article 20 of the present convention, are excluded from transmission at the reduced rate.

ARTICLE 6. REGISTERED ARTICLES; RETURN RECEIPTS; REQUESTS FOR INFORMATION

(1) The articles specified in Article 5 may be registered.

The reply halves of reply-paid post cards cannot, however, be registered by the original senders of such cards.

(2) Every registered article is liable, at the charge of the sender:

1st. To the ordinary prepaid rate of postage on the article, according to its nature.

2d. To a fixed registration fee of 25 centimes at most, including a receipt given to the sender.

(3) The sender of a registered article may obtain an advice of the delivery of such article, by paying, at the time when he asks for such an advice, a fixed fee

of 25 centimes at most. The same fee may be charged for inquiries concerning registered articles, if the sender has not already paid the special fee for an advice of delivery.

ARTICLE 7. ARTICLES MARKED WITH TRADE CHARGES

(1) Registered articles may be sent marked with trade charges to be collected on delivery between countries of which the administrations agree to provide this service.

These articles are subject to the same regulations and rates as registered articles.

The maximum trade charge which may be collected on any one registered article is fixed at 1000 francs or at the equivalent of that sum.

(2) In the absence of any contrary arrangement between the administrations of the countries concerned, the amount collected from the addressee is to be transmitted to the sender by means of a money order, after deducting a commission of 10 centimes for the service of collection, and the ordinary rate chargeable for money orders calculated on the amount of the balance.

The amount of an undeliverable money order of this kind remains at the disposal of the administration of the country in which the article marked with a trade charge originated.

(3) For the loss of a registered article marked with a trade charge the responsibility of the postal service is fixed under the conditions laid down in Article 8 hereafter for registered articles not marked with trade charges.

After the delivery of the article the administration of the country of destination is responsible for the amount of the trade charge, unless it can prove that the conditions prescribed for such articles by the detailed regulations contemplated in Article 20 of the present convention have not been fulfilled. Nevertheless the omission from the letter bill of the entry "Remb." and of the amount of the trade charge does not affect the responsibility of the administration of the country of destination for failing to collect the amount.

ARTICLE 8. RESPONSIBILITY FOR REGISTERED ARTICLES

(1) In case of the loss of a registered article, and except in cases beyond control, the sender, or, at the request of the sender, the addressee, is entitled to an indemnity of 50 francs.

(2) Countries prepared to undertake risks arising from causes beyond control are authorized to collect from the sender on this account a supplementary rate of not more than 25 centimes for each registered article.

(3) The obligation of paying the indemnity rests with the administration to which the dispatching office is subordinate. To that administration is reserved a remedy against the administration responsible, that is to say, against the administration on the territory or in the service of which the loss took place.

In case of the loss, under circumstances beyond control, on the territory or in the service of a country undertaking the risks mentioned in the preceding paragraph, of a registered article sent from another country, the country where the loss occurred is responsible for it to the dispatching office, if the latter undertakes risks in cases beyond control in dealing with its own public.

(4) Until the contrary be proved, the responsibility rests with the administration which, having received the article without making any observation, cannot establish the delivery to the addressee or the regular transfer to the following administration, as the case may be. For articles addressed "Poste Restante," or held at the disposition of the addressees, the responsibility ceases on delivery to a person who has proved his identity according to the rules in force in the country of destination, and whose name and description correspond to those indicated in the address.

(5) The payment of the indemnity by the dispatching office ought to take place as soon as possible, and at the latest within a year of the date of the application. The responsible office is bound to refund to the dispatching office, without delay, the amount of the indemnity paid by the latter.

The office of origin is authorized to make payment to the sender on account of the office, whether intermediate or of destination, which, after application has been made in due course, has let a year pass without settling the matter. Moreover, in cases where an office whose responsibility is duly established has at the outset declined to pay the indemnity, such office must take upon itself, in addition to the indemnity, the subsidiary expenses resulting from the unwarranted delay in payment.

(6) It is understood that the application for an indemnity is only entertained if made within a year of the posting of the registered article; after this term the applicant has no right to any indemnity.

(7) If the loss has occurred in course of conveyance without its being possible to ascertain on the territory or in the service of what country the loss took place, the administrations concerned bear the loss in equal shares.

(8) Administrations cease to be responsible for registered articles for which the owners have given a receipt and accepted delivery.

ARTICLE 9. WITHDRAWAL OF ARTICLES, CORRECTION OF ADDRESS, ETC.

(1) The sender of a letter or other article can have it withdrawn from the post or have its address altered, so long as such article has not been delivered to the addressee.

(2) The request for such withdrawal is sent by mail or by telegraph at the expense of the sender, who must pay as follows:

1st. For every request by mail, the amount payable for a registered single letter;

2d. For every request by telegraph, the charge for a telegram according to the ordinary tariff.

(3) The sender of a registered article marked with a trade charge can, under the conditions laid down for requests for alteration of address, demand the total or partial canceling of the amount of the trade charge.

(4) The stipulations of this article are not obligatory for countries of which the legislation does not permit the sender to dispose of an article in its course through the post.

ARTICLE 10. FIXING OF RATES IN MONEY OTHER THAN THE FRANC

Those countries of the union which have not the franc for their monetary unit fix their charges at the equivalents, in their respective currencies, of the rates determined by the various articles of the present convention. Such countries have the option of rounding fractions in conformity with the table inserted in the detailed regulations mentioned in Article 20 of the present convention.

The administrations which maintain post offices forming part of the union in nonunion countries fix their rates in the local currency, in the same manner. When two or several administrations maintain such offices in the same nonunion country, the local equivalents to be adopted by all such offices are fixed by mutual arrangement between the administrations concerned.

ARTICLE 11. PREPAYMENT; REPLY COUPONS; EXEMPTIONS FROM POSTAGE

(1) Prepayment of postage on every description of article can be effected only by means of postage stamps valid in the country of origin for the correspondence of private individuals. It is not, however, permitted to make use, in the international service, of postage stamps produced with an object special and peculiar to the country of issue, such as the so-called commemorative postage stamps of temporary validity.

Reply post cards bearing postage stamps of the country in which these cards were issued are considered as duly prepaid, as also are newspapers or packets of newspapers without postage stamps but with the superscription "Abonnements-poste" (subscription by mail), which are sent in virtue of the special arrangement for newspaper subscriptions, provided for in Article 19 of the present convention.

(2) Reply coupons can be exchanged between the countries of which the administrations have agreed to participate in such exchange. The minimum selling price of a reply coupon is 28 centimes, or the equivalent of this sum in the money of the country which sells it.

This coupon is exchangeable in all countries parties to the arrangement for a postage stamp of 25 centimes or the equivalent of that sum in the money of the country where the exchange is requested. The detailed regulations contemplated in Article 20 of the convention determine the other conditions of this exchange, and in particular the intervention of the international bureau in manufacturing, supplying, and accounting for the coupons.

(3) Official correspondence relative to the postal service exchanged between postal administrations, between these administrations and the international bureau, and between post offices in union countries, is exempt from prepayment by means of ordinary postage stamps, and is free from liability to charge.

(4) The same privilege is accorded to correspondence concerning prisoners of war, dispatched or received, either directly or, as intermediary, by the special information offices established on behalf of such persons, in belligerent countries or in neutral countries which have received belligerents on their territories.

Correspondence intended for prisoners of war or dispatched by them is likewise exempt from postal charges, not only in the countries of origin and destination, but in intermediary countries.

Belligerents received and held in a neutral country are assimilated to prisoners of war, properly so called, in so far as the application of the above-mentioned stipulations is concerned.

(5) Articles posted on the high seas in the letter box on board a vessel or placed in the hands of postal agents on board or of the commanders of ships may be prepaid by means of the postage stamps, and according to the tariff of the country to which the said vessel belongs or by which it is maintained. If the mailing on board takes place during the stay at one of the two terminal points of the voyage or at any intermediate port of call, prepayment can only be effected by means of the postage stamps and according to the tariff of the country in the waters of which the vessel happens to be.

ARTICLE 12. POSTAGE KEPT BY COLLECTING COUNTRY

(1) Each administration keeps the whole of the sums which it collects by virtue of the foregoing Articles 5, 6, 7, 10, and 11, exceptions being made in the case of the credit due for the money orders referred to in paragraph (2) of Article 7, and also in regard to reply coupons (Article 11).

(2) Consequently there is no necessity under this head for any accounts between the several administrations of the union, subject always to the reservations made in paragraph (1) of the present article.

(3) Letters and other postal articles cannot be subjected, either in the country of origin or in that of destination, to any postal tax or postal fee at the expense of the senders or addressees other than those contemplated by the articles above mentioned.

ARTICLE 13. SPECIAL-DELIVERY ARTICLES

(1) At the request of the senders, all classes of articles are delivered at the addresses by a special messenger immediately on arrival, in those countries of the union which consent to undertake this service in their reciprocal relations.

(2) Such articles, which are marked "express," are subject to a special charge for delivery; this charge is fixed at 30 centimes, and must be fully paid in advance by the sender, in addition to the ordinary postage. It belongs to the administration of the country of origin.

(3) When an article is destined for a place where there is no post office authorized to deliver correspondence by express messenger, the postal administration of the country of destination can levy an additional charge up to the amount of the fee fixed for express delivery in its inland service, less the fixed charge paid by the sender, or its equivalent in the money of the country which levies this additional charge.

The additional charge provided for above is recoverable in case of redirection or nondelivery, and is retained by the administration which has raised it.

(4) " Express " articles upon which the total amount of the charges payable in advance has not been prepaid are delivered by the ordinary means, unless they have been treated as expressed by the office of origin.

ARTICLE 14. REFORWARDING: UNDELIVERED ARTICLES

(1) No additional postage is charged for the reforwarding of postal articles within the union.

(2) Undelivered articles do not, when returned, give rise to the restitution of the transit charges due to intermediate administrations for the previous conveyance of such correspondence.

(3) Unpaid letters and post cards and insufficiently paid articles of every description, which are returned to the country of origin as redirected or as undeliverable, are liable, at the expense of the addressees or senders, to the same rates as similar articles addressed directly from the country of the first destination to the country of origin.

ARTICLE 15. MAILS EXCHANGED WITH WARSHIPS

(1) Closed mails may be exchanged between the post offices of any one of the contracting countries and the commanding officers of naval divisions or ships of war of the same country stationed abroad, or between the commanding officer of one of those naval divisions or ships of war and the commanding officer of another division or ship of the same country, through the medium of the sea or land services maintained by other countries.

(2) Articles of every description inclosed in these mails must consist exclusively of such as are addressed to or sent by the officers and crews of the ships to or from which the mails are forwarded; the rates and conditions of dispatch applicable to them are determined, according to its internal regulations, by the postal administration of the country to which the ships belong.

(3) In the absence of any arrangement to the contrary between the offices concerned, the post office which dispatches or receives the mails in question is accountable to the intermediate offices for transit charges calculated in accordance with the stipulations of Article 4.

ARTICLE 16. PROHIBITIONS

(1) Commercial papers, samples, and printed papers which do not fulfill the conditions laid down for articles of these categories in Article 5 of the present convention and in the regulations contemplated in Article 20 are not to be forwarded.

(2) If occasion arise, these articles are sent back to the post office of origin and returned, if possible, to the sender, save where, in the case of articles prepaid at least partially, the administration of the country of destination is authorized by its laws or by its internal regulations to deliver them.

(3) It is forbidden:

1st. To send by post:

a. Samples and other articles which, from their nature, may expose the postal officials to danger or soil or damage the correspondence;

b. Explosive, inflammable, or dangerous substances; animals and insects, living or dead, except in the cases provided for in the regulations contemplated in Article 20 of the convention;

2d. To insert in ordinary or registered correspondence, consigned to the post:

a. Coin;

b. Articles liable to customs duty;

c. Articles of gold and silver, precious stones, jewelry and other precious articles, but only where their insertion or transmission is forbidden by the legislation of the countries concerned;

d. Any articles whatsoever of which the importation or circulation is prohibited in the country of destination.

(4) Packets falling under the prohibitions of the foregoing paragraph (3), which have been erroneously admitted to transmission, should be returned to the post office of origin, except in cases where the administration of the country of destination is authorized by its laws or by its internal regulations to dispose of them otherwise.

Explosive, inflammable, or dangerous substances, however, are not returned to the country of origin; they are destroyed on the spot under the direction of the administration which has detected their presence.

(5) The right is, moreover, reserved to the government of every country of the union to refuse to convey over its territory, or to deliver, articles passing at reduced rates in regard to which the laws, ordinances, or decrees which regulate the conditions of their publication or circulation in that country have not been complied with, or correspondence of any kind bearing ostensibly inscriptions, designs, etc., forbidden by the legal enactments or regulations in force in the same country.

ARTICLE 17. RELATIONS WITH COUNTRIES OUTSIDE THE UNION

(1) Offices of the union which have relations with countries situate outside the union are to lend their assistance to all the other offices of the union:

1st. For the transmission, by their services, either in open mail or in closed mails, if this method of transmission is admitted by mutual agreement between the offices of origin and destination of the mails, of articles addressed to or originating in countries outside the union;

2d. For the exchange of articles either in open mail or in closed mails across the territories or by means of services maintained by the said countries outside the union;

3d. That the articles conveyed may be subject outside the union, as within the union, to the transit rates determined by Article 4.

(2) The charges for the total sea transit, within and without the union, may not exceed 15 francs per kilogram of letters and post cards and 1 franc per kilogram of other articles. If occasion arise, these charges are divided, in the ratio of distances, between the offices taking part in the sea conveyance.

(3) The charges for transit, by land or sea, without as well as within the limits of the union, on the articles to which the present article applies, are established in the same manner as the transit charges relating to articles exchanged between union countries by means of the services of other countries of the union.

(4) The transit charges on articles for countries outside the postal union are payable by the office of the country of origin, which fixes the postage rates in its services for the said articles, but these rates may not be lower than the normal union tariff.

(5) The transit charges on articles originating in countries outside the union are not payable by the office of the country of destination. That office delivers without charge articles transmitted to it as fully prepaid; it charges unpaid articles double the prepaid rate applicable in its own service to similar articles addressed to the country where the said articles originate, and insufficiently prepaid articles double the deficiency; but the charge may not exceed that which is levied on unpaid articles of the same nature, weight, and origin.

(6) With regard to responsibility in the matter of registered articles, the articles are treated:

For transmission within the limits of the union in accordance with the stipulations of the present convention;

For transmission without the limits of the union in accordance with the conditions notified by the office of the union which serves as the intermediate office.

ARTICLE 18. COUNTERFEIT POSTAGE STAMPS

The high contracting parties undertake to adopt, or to propose to their respective legislatures, the necessary measures for punishing the fraudulent use of counterfeit postage stamps or stamps already used for the prepayment of correspondence. They also undertake to adopt, or to propose to their respective legislatures, the necessary measures for prohibiting and repressing the fraudulent manufacture, sale, offering for sale, or distribution of embossed and adhesive stamps in use in the postal service, forged or imitated in such a manner as to be mistakable for the embossed and adhesive stamps issued by the administration of any one of the contracting countries.

ARTICLE 19. SPECIAL ARRANGEMENTS FOR PARTICULAR SERVICES

The services concerning letters and boxes of declared value, postal money orders, postal parcels, collection of bills and drafts, certificates of identity, subscriptions to newspapers, etc., form the subject of special arrangements between the various countries or groups of countries composing the union.

ARTICLE 20. REGULATIONS OF EXECUTION; SPECIAL AGREEMENT BETWEEN ADMINISTRATIONS

(1) The postal administrations of the various countries composing the union are competent to draw up, by common consent, in the form of regulations of execution, all the measures of order and detail which are judged necessary.

(2) The several administrations may, moreover, make amongst themselves the necessary arrangements on the subject of questions which do not concern the union generally, provided that those arrangements do not derogate from the present convention.

(3) The administrations concerned are, however, permitted to come to mutual arrangements for the adoption of lower rates of postage within a radius of 30 kilometers.

ARTICLE 21. INTERNAL LAWS; RESTRICTED UNIONS

(1) The present convention does not involve alteration in the legislation of any country as regards anything which is not provided for by the stipulations contained in this convention.

(2) It does not restrict the right of the contracting parties to maintain and to conclude treaties, as well as to maintain and establish more restricted unions, with a view to the reduction of postage rates or to any other improvement of postal relations.

ARTICLE 22. INTERNATIONAL BUREAU

(1) Under the name of the International Bureau of the Universal Postal Union a central office is maintained which is conducted under the supervision of the Swiss postal administration, and of which the expenses are borne by all the administrations of the union.

(2) This bureau is charged with the duty of collecting, collating, publishing, and distributing information of every kind which concerns the international postal service; of giving, at the request of the parties concerned, an opinion upon questions in dispute; of making known proposals for modifying the acts of the congress; of notifying alterations adopted; and, in general, of taking up such studies and labors as may be confided to it in the interest of the postal union.

ARTICLE 23. DISPUTES TO BE SETTLED BY ARBITRATION

(1) In case of disagreement between two or more members of the union as to the interpretation of the present convention, or as to the responsibility resting on an administration by the application of the said convention, the question in dispute is decided by arbitration. To that end each of the administrations concerned chooses another member of the union not directly interested in the matter.

(2) The decision of the arbitrators is given by an absolute majority of votes.

(3) In case of an equality of votes the arbitrators choose, with the view of settling the difference, another administration equally uninterested in the question in dispute.

(4) The stipulations of the present article apply equally to all the agreements concluded by virtue of the foregoing Article 19.

ARTICLE 24. ADHESIONS TO THE CONVENTION

(1) Countries which have not taken part in the present convention are admitted to adhere to it upon their demand.

(2) This adhesion is notified through the diplomatic channel to the government of the Swiss Confederation, and by that government to all the countries of the union.

(3) It implies, as a right, accession to all the clauses and admission to all the advantages for which the present convention stipulates.

(4) It devolves upon the government of the Swiss Confederation to determine, by common consent with the government of the country concerned, the share to be contributed by the administration of this latter country toward the expenses of the international bureau, and, if necessary, the rates to be levied by that administration in conformity with the foregoing Article 10.

ARTICLE 25. CONGRESSES AND CONFERENCES

(1) Congresses of plenipotentiaries of the contracting countries, or simple administrative conferences, according to the importance of the questions to be solved, are held, when a demand for them is made or approved by two thirds, at least, of the governments or administrations, as the case may be.

(2) A congress shall, in any case, be held not later than five years after the date of the entry into force of the acts concluded at the last congress.

(3) Each country may be represented either by one or several delegates, or by the delegation of another country. But it is understood that the delegate or delegates of one country can be charged with the representation of two countries only, including the country they represent.

(4) In the deliberations each has one vote only.

(5) Each congress settles the place of meeting of the next congress.

(6) For conferences, the administrations settle the places of meeting on the proposal of the international bureau.

ARTICLE 26. PROPOSALS MADE BETWEEN CONGRESSES

(1) In the interval which elapses between the meetings, any postal administration of a country of the union has the right to address to the other administrations belonging to it, through the medium of the international bureau, proposals concerning the *régime* of the union.

In order to be considered, every proposal must be supported by at least two administrations, without counting that from which the proposal emanates. When the international bureau does not receive, at the same time as the proposal, the necessary number of declarations of support, the proposal falls.

(2) Every proposal is subject to the following procedure:

A period of six months is allowed to the administrations of the union to examine the proposals and to communicate their observations, if any, to the international bureau. Amendments are not admitted. The answers are tabulated by the international bureau, and communicated to the administrations, with an invitation to declare themselves for or against. Those who have not furnished their vote within a period of six months, counting from the date of the second circular of the international bureau notifying to them the observations which have been received, are considered as abstaining.

(3) In order to become binding, the proposals must obtain:

1st. Unanimity of votes if they involve the addition of new stipulations or any modification of the stipulations of the present article or of Articles 2, 3, 4, 5, 6, 7, 8, 9, 12, 13, 15, 18, 27, 28, and 29;

2d. Two thirds of the votes if they involve a modification of the stipulations of the convention other than those of Articles 2, 3, 4, 5, 6, 7, 8, 9, 12, 13, 15, 18, 26, 27, 28, and 29;

3d. Simply an absolute majority, if they affect the interpretation of the stipulations of the convention, except in the case of dispute contemplated by the foregoing Article 23.

(4) Resolutions duly adopted are sanctioned, in the first two cases, by a diplomatic declaration, which the government of the Swiss Confederation is charged with the duty of preparing and transmitting to all the governments of the contracting countries; and in the third case by a simple notification from the international bureau to all the administrations of the union.

(5) No modification or resolution adopted is binding until at least three months after its notification.

ARTICLE 27. PROTECTORATES AND COLONIES INCLUDED IN THE UNION

For the application of the foregoing Articles 22, 25, and 26, the following are considered as forming a single country or administration, as the case may be:

1st. The German protectorates of Africa;

2d. The German protectorates of Asia and Australasia;

3d. The Empire of British India;

4th. The Dominion of Canada;

5th. The Commonwealth of Australia with British New Guinea;

6th. The whole of the British colonies and protectorates of South Africa;

7th. The whole of all the other British colonies;

8th. The whole of the island possessions of the United States of America, comprising at present the islands of Hawaii, the Philippine islands, and the islands of Porto Rico and of Guam;

9th. The whole of the Danish colonies;

10th. The whole of the Spanish colonies;

11th. Algeria;

12th. The French colonies and protectorates in Indo-China;

13th. The whole of the other French colonies;

14th. The whole of the Italian colonies;

15th. The whole of the Dutch colonies;

16th. The Portuguese colonies of Africa;

17th. The whole of the other Portuguese colonies.

ARTICLE 28. DURATION OF THE CONVENTION

The present convention shall come into operation on the 1st of October, 1907, and shall remain in force for an indefinite period; but each contracting party has the right of withdrawing from the union, by means of a notice given one year in advance by its government to the government of the Swiss Confederation.

ARTICLE 29. ABROGATION OF PREVIOUS CONVENTIONS; RATIFICATION

(1) From the date on which the present convention comes into effect, all the stipulations of the treaties, conventions, agreements, or other acts previously concluded between the various countries or administrations, in so far as those stipulations are not in accordance with the terms of the present convention, are abrogated, without prejudice to the rights reserved by the foregoing Article 21.

(2) The present convention shall be ratified as soon as possible. The acts of ratification shall be exchanged at Rome.

(3) In faith of which the plenipotentiaries of the above-named countries have signed the present convention at Rome on the twenty-sixth of May, one thousand nine hundred and six.

[Signatures]

FINAL PROTOCOL

At the moment of proceeding to sign the conventions settled by the universal postal congress of Rome, the undersigned plenipotentiaries have agreed as follows:

I. Note is taken of the declaration made by the British delegates in the name of their government to the effect that it has assigned to New Zealand, with the Cook Islands and other island dependencies, the vote which Article 27, 7th, of the convention attributes to "the whole of the other British colonies."

II. In modification of Article 27 of the convention, a second vote is accorded to the Netherlands colonies, in favor of the Netherlands East Indies.

III. In modification of the stipulations of paragraph (1) of Article 5, it is agreed that, as a temporary measure, postal administrations, which in consequence of the organization of their internal service, or for other causes, cannot adopt the principle of the increase of the unit of weight for letters from 15 to 20 grams, and that of the reduction of the charge above the first unit of weight to 15 centimes for each supplementary rate instead of 25 centimes, are authorized to postpone the application of these two stipulations or of one or other of them, so far as regards letters originating in their service, until the day when they are in a position to apply them, and to conform in the meantime to the measures prescribed on this subject by the Congress of Washington.

IV. In modification of Article 6 of the convention, which fixes at 25 centimes the maximum charge for registration, it is agreed that countries out of Europe are authorized to maintain this maximum at 50 centimes, inclusive of the delivery of a registry receipt to the sender.

V. By way of exception to the provisions of paragraph (3) of Article 12 of the convention, Persia has the right of collecting from the addressees of printed papers of all kinds received from foreign countries a tax of 5 centimes per article distributed. This right is accorded to it provisionally.

The same right is accorded to China in the event of its adhering to the principal conventions.

VI. By way of exception to the provisions of Article 4 of the convention and to the corresponding paragraphs of the regulations relative thereto, it is agreed as follows in regard to the transit rates to be paid to the Russian administration on account of correspondence exchanged by way of the Siberian railway:

1st. The accounting for transit charges in respect of the articles mentioned above shall be based, from the date of the opening of the aforesaid railway, on special returns taken every three years during the first twenty-eight days of the month of May or of the month of November (alternately) of the second year of each triennial period, such returns to take effect retrospectively from the first year.

2d. The statistics of May, 1908, shall regulate the payments to be made from the date of the commencement of the traffic in question until the end of the year 1909. The statistics of November, 1911, shall apply to the years 1910, 1911, and 1912, and so on.

3d. If a country of the union commences the dispatch of its articles by way of the Siberian railway during the period covered by the above-mentioned statistics, Russia has the right to demand the taking of separate statistics relating exclusively to such articles.

4th. The payment of transit charges due to Russia for the first and, if necessary, for the second year of each triennial period, is to be made provisionally at the end of the year on the basis of the preceding statistics, subject to a subsequent settlement of accounts in accordance with the results of the new statistics.

5th. Transit in open mail is not admitted by the aforesaid railway.

Japan has the right to apply the stipulations of each paragraph of the present article in regard to the settlement of transit rates due to Japan for the land or sea transit of articles exchanged by way of the Japanese railway in China (Manchuria), and so far as concerns the inadmissibility of transit in open mail.

VII. Salvador, which forms part of the postal union, not having been represented at the congress, the protocol remains open to it in order that it may adhere to the conventions which have been concluded there or only to one or other of them.

It remains open with the same object:

a. To Nicaragua and to Peru, whose delegates at the congress were not furnished with full powers;

b. To the Dominican republic, whose delegate was obliged to be absent when the acts were signed.

The protocol likewise remains open to the Chinese empire and the empire of Ethiopia, whose delegates to the congress have announced the intention of those countries to enter the Universal Postal Union on a date to be fixed hereafter.

VIII. The protocol remains open to those countries whose representatives have to-day signed only the principal convention, or only a certain number of the conventions settled by the congress, in order to admit of their adherence to the other conventions signed this day, or to one or other of them.

IX. The adhesions contemplated in the foregoing Article VII must be notified to the government of Italy by the respective governments in diplomatic form. The term accorded to them for that notification will expire on the 1st of July, 1907.

X. In the event of one or more of the contracting parties to the postal conventions signed to-day at Rome not ratifying one or other of those conventions, this convention shall be none the less valid for the states which shall have ratified it.

In faith of which the undermentioned plenipotentiaries have drawn up the present final protocol, which shall have the same force and validity as if its provisions were inserted in the text itself of the conventions to which it relates, and they have signed it on a single copy, which shall remain in the archives of the government of Italy, and of which a copy shall be delivered to each party.

Done at Rome, the 26th of May, 1906.

[Signatures]

DETAILED REGULATIONS FOR THE EXECUTION OF THE CONVENTION

The undersigned, having regard to Article 20 of the universal postal convention concluded at Rome on the 26th of May, 1906, have, in the name of their respective administrations, settled by common consent the following measures for insuring the execution of the said convention.

I. FORWARDING OF THE MAILS

(1) Each administration is bound to forward, by the most rapid routes at its disposal for its own mails, the closed mails and the articles in open mail which are delivered to it by another administration.

In the event of an administration finding itself obliged, by exceptional circumstances, to suspend temporarily the dispatch of closed mails and articles in open mail which are delivered to it by another administration, it is bound at once to notify the fact, if necessary by telegraph, to the administration or administrations concerned.

(2) Administrations which avail themselves of the option to levy supplementary charges, as representing the extraordinary expenses pertaining to certain routes, are free not to forward by those routes, when other means of communication exist, any insufficiently paid articles for which the employment of the said routes has not been expressly prescribed by the senders.

II. EXCHANGE IN CLOSED MAILS

(1) The exchange of articles in closed mails between the administrations of the union is regulated by common consent between the administrations concerned, and according to the necessities of the service.

(2) If an exchange is to take place through the medium of one or more countries, timely notice must be given to the administrations of those countries.

(3) It is, moreover, obligatory, in this latter case, to make up closed mails whenever a request to that effect is made by one of the intermediate administrations on the ground that the number of articles sent in open mail is such as to hinder its work.

(4) In case of alteration in a service of closed mails established between two administrations through the medium of one or several other countries, the administration which has originated the alteration gives notice thereof to the administrations of the countries through the medium of which this exchange is effected.

III. EXTRAORDINARY SERVICES

The extraordinary services of the union giving rise to special charges, the fixing of which is reserved by Article 4 of the convention for arrangement between the administrations concerned, are exclusively:

1st. Those which are maintained for the accelerated conveyance by land of the Indian mail;

2d. That which is established for the conveyance of mails by railway between Colon and Panama.

IV. FIXING OF THE RATES OF POSTAGE

(1) In execution of Article 10 of the convention, the administrations of the countries of the union which have not the franc for their monetary unit, or which maintain postal agencies outside the union, levy their rates of postage according to the following equivalents:

Countries of the union	25 centimes	15 centimes	10 centimes	5 centimes
Germany	20 pfennig		10 pfennig	5 pfennig
German protectorates:				
German East Africa (territory of ——)	15 heller		7½ heller	4 heller
German Southwest Africa (territory of ——)	20 pfennig		10 pfennig	5 pfennig
Cameroons	20 pfennig		10 pfennig	5 pfennig
Carolines and Palaos (Islands)	20 pfennig		10 pfennig	5 pfennig
Kiautschou	10 cents		4 cents	2 cents
Marianne (Islands), excluding the island of Guam	20 pfennig		10 pfennig	5 pfennig
Marshall Islands	20 pfennig		10 pfennig	5 pfennig
German New Guinea	20 pfennig		10 pfennig	5 pfennig
Samoa	20 pfennig		10 pfennig	5 pfennig
Territory of Togo	20 pfennig		10 pfennig	5 pfennig
United States of America	5 cents		2 cents	1 cent
Island possessions of the United States of America				
Island of Guam	5 centavos		2 centavos	1 centavo
Philippine Islands	5 centavos		2 centavos	1 centavo
Porto Rico	5 centavos		2 centavos	1 centavo
Argentine Republic	12 centavos		6 centavos	3 centavos
Austria	25 deniers de couronne		10 deniers de couronne	5 deniers de couronne
Bolivia	10 centavos		4 centavos	2 centavos
Bosnia-Herzegovina	25 deniers de couronne		10 deniers de couronne	5 deniers de couronne
Brazil	200 reis		100 reis	50 reis
Chile	5 centavos		2 centavos	1 centavo
Colombia	5 centavos (gold)	3 centavos (gold)	2 centavos (gold)	1 centavo (gold)
Corea	10 sen	6 sen	4 sen	2 sen
Costa Rica	10 centimos de colon	7 centimos de colon	4 centimos de colon	2 centimos de colon

Countries of the union	25 centimes	15 centimes	10 centimes	5 centimes
Cuba	5 centavos	. . . . . .	2 centavos	1 centavo
Denmark	20 öre	. . . . . .	10 öre	5 öre
Danish colony				
Greenland	20 öre	. . . . . .	10 öre	5 öre
Dominican republic	5 centavos	. . . . . .	2 centavos	1 centavo
Egypt	10 millièmes de livre	6 millièmes de livre	4 millièmes de livre	2 millièmes de livre
Ecuador	5 centavos	3 centavos	2 centavos	1 centavo
Spanish settlements in the Gulf of Guinea	5 centavos	. . . . . .	2 centavos	1 centavo
Great Britain	2½ pence	1½ pence	1 penny	½ penny
British colonies and possessions				
South Africa				
Bechuanaland (protectorate), Cape of Good Hope, Natal and Zululand, Orange River Colony, Southern Rhodesia, Transvaal	2½ pence	1½ pence	1 penny	½ penny
Australia (with British Guinea)	2½ pence	1½ pence	1 penny	½ penny
Canada	5 cents	3 cents	2 cents	1 cent
British India	2½ annas	1½ annas	1 anna	½ anna
New Zealand (with the Cook Islands)	2½ pence	1½ pence	1 penny	½ penny
Other British colonies and possessions				
East Africa and Uganda	2½ annas	1½ annas	1 anna	½ anna
Antigua	2½ pence	1½ pence	1 penny	½ penny
Ascension	2½ pence	1½ pence	1 penny	½ penny
Bahama Islands	2½ pence	1½ pence	1 penny	½ penny
Barbados	2½ pence	1½ pence	1 penny	½ penny
Bermudas	2½ pence	1½ pence	1 penny	½ penny
British North Borneo	10 cents de dollar	6 cents de dollar	4 cents de dollar	2 cents de dollar
Cayman Islands	2½ pence	1½ pence	1 penny	½ penny
Ceylon	15 centièmes de roupie	9 centièmes de roupie	6 centièmes de roupie	3 centièmes de roupie
Cyprus	2 piastres ou 80 paras	1½ piastres ou 60 paras	1 piastre ou 40 paras	½ piastre ou 20 paras
Gold Coast	2½ pence	1½ pence	1 penny	½ penny
Dominica	2½ pence	1½ pence	1 penny	½ penny
Falkland Islands	2½ pence	1½ pence	1 penny	½ penny
Fiji Islands	2½ pence	1½ pence	1 penny	½ penny
Gambia	2½ pence	1½ pence	1 penny	½ penny
Gibraltar	2½ pence	1½ pence	1 penny	½ penny
Grenada and the Grenadines	2½ pence	1½ pence	1 penny	½ penny
British Guiana	5 cents	3 cents	2 cents	1 cent
British Honduras	5 cents	3 cents	2 cents	1 cent
Hongkong	10 cents de dollar	6 cents de dollar	4 cents de dollar	2 cents de dollar
Jamaica	2½ pence	1½ pence	1 penny	½ penny
Labuan	10 cents de dollar	6 cents de dollar	4 cents de dollar	2 cents de dollar
Malta	2½ pence	1½ pence	1 penny	½ penny
Mauritius and dependencies	15 centièmes de roupie	9 centièmes de roupie	6 centièmes de roupie	3 centièmes de roupie
Montserrat	2½ pence	1½ pence	1 penny	½ penny
Nevis	2½ pence	1½ pence	1 penny	½ penny
St. Christopher	2½ pence	1½ pence	1 penny	½ penny
St. Helena	2½ pence	1½ pence	1 penny	½ penny
St. Lucia	2½ pence	1½ pence	1 penny	½ penny
St. Vincent	2½ pence	1½ pence	1 penny	½ penny
Southern Nigeria	2½ pence	1½ pence	1 penny	½ penny
Sarawak	10 cents de dollar	6 cents de dollar	4 cents de dollar	2 cents de dollar
Sierra Leone	2½ pence	1½ pence	1 penny	½ penny
Somaliland	2½ annas	1½ annas	1 anna	½ anna
Straits Settlements	8 cents de dollar	. . . . . .	3 cents de dollar	1 cent de dollar
Tobago	2½ pence	1½ pence	1 penny	½ penny
Newfoundland	5 cents	3 cents	2 cents	1 cent
Trinidad	2½ pence	1½ pence	1 penny	½ penny
Turks Islands	2½ pence	1½ pence	1 penny	½ penny
Virgin Islands	2½ pence	1½ pence	1 penny	½ penny
Zanzibar	2½ annas	1½ annas	1 anna	½ anna
Guatemala	25 centavos	. . . . . .	10 centavos	5 centavos
Hayti	5 centavos de piastre	. . . . . .	2 centavos de piastre	1 centavo de piastre
Republic of Honduras	10 centavos	. . . . . .	4 centavos	2 centavos
Hungary	25 deniers de couronne	15 deniers de couronne	10 deniers de couronne	5 deniers de couronne

Countries of the union	25 centimes	15 centimes	10 centimes	5 centimes
Italian colony				
Benadir	2½ annas		1 anna	2 besas
Japan	10 sen	6 sen	4 sen	2 sen
Liberia	5 cents		2 cents	1 cent
Mexico	10 centavos	6 centavos	4 centavos	2 centavos
Montenegro	25 deniers de couronne		10 deniers de couronne	5 deniers de couronne
Nicaragua	25 centavos		10 centavos	5 centavos
Norway	20 öre		10 öre	5 öre
Panama	10 centavos (silver)		4 centavos (silver)	2 centavos (silver)
Paraguay	45 centavos de peso		18 centavos de peso	9 centavos de peso
Netherlands	12½ cents	7½ cents	5 cents	2½ cents
Dutch colonies				
Dutch Antilles	12½ cents	7½ cents	5 cents	2½ cents
Dutch Guiana	12½ cents	7½ cents	5 cents	2½ cents
Dutch Indies	12½ cents	7½ cents	5 cents	2½ cents
Peru	10 centavos		4 centavos	2 centavos
Persia	13 chahis		6 chahis	3 chahis
Portugal (including Azores and Madeira)	50 reis	30 reis	20 reis	10 reis
Portuguese colonies				
Portuguese African colonies	50 reis	30 reis	20 reis	10 reis
Portuguese India	2 tangas	15 reis	10 reis	5 reis
Portuguese Macao and Timor	10 avos	6 avos	4 avos	2 avos
Russia	10 kopeks		4 kopeks	2 kopeks
Salvador	5 centavos		2 centavos	1 centavo
Siam	12 atts	8 atts	5 atts	3 atts
Sweden	20 öre		10 öre	5 öre
Turkey	40 paras		20 paras	10 paras
Uruguay	5 centésimos de peso	3 centésimos de peso	2 centésimos de peso	1 centésimo de peso

NOTE. The order of the names of countries and the spelling of foreign names and of monetary terms stand as in the official publications of the United States.

(2) In case of alteration in the monetary system of any one of the countries above mentioned, or of an important modification in the value of its money, the administration of that country must come to an understanding with the Swiss postal administration in order to modify the above equivalents; it devolves upon this latter administration to notify the change to all the other offices of the union through the medium of the international bureau.

(3) The monetary fractions resulting either from the complement of the charge applicable to insufficiently paid articles, or from the fixing of the charges for articles exchanged with countries foreign to the union, or from the combination of the union charges with the surcharges contemplated by Article 5 of the convention, may be rounded by the administrations which levy the payments. But the sum to be added on this account must in no case exceed the value of one twentieth of a franc (five centimes).

V. EXCEPTIONS IN THE MATTER OF WEIGHT

As an exceptional measure it is agreed that states which, by reason of their internal regulations, are unable to adopt the decimal metrical system of weight, have the option of substituting for it the ounce avoirdupois (28.3465 grams), assimilating one ounce to 20 grams for letters, and two ounces to 50 grams for other articles; and of raising, if needful, the limit of the single rate of postage of newspapers to four ounces, but under the express condition that, in the latter case, the postage on newspapers be not less than 10 centimes, and that an entire rate of postage be charged for each copy of the newspaper, even though several newspapers be included in the same packet.

VI. POSTAGE STAMPS

(1) The postage stamps representing the typical rates of the union or their equivalent in the currency of each country are manufactured in the following colors:

Stamps of the value of 25 centimes in dark blue;

Stamps of the value of 10 centimes in red;

Stamps of the value of 5 centimes in green.

(2) Postage stamps must be inscribed on their face with the value which they represent for the prepayment of articles in accordance with the table of equivalents inserted in the preceding Article IV.

The indication of the number of monetary units or fraction of the unit used to express this value is made in Arabic figures.

(3) Postage stamps may be specially perforated by means of a punch (with initials or otherwise), subject to the conditions prescribed by the administration issuing them.

(4) It is recommended that the postage stamps be affixed in the upper right-hand corner of the address side. It is not forbidden, however, to affix the stamps in some other part either of the address side or on the back.

VII. REPLY COUPONS

(1) The reply coupons, of which optional use is provided for by Article 11 of the convention, are in conformity with the Form *A* annexed to the present regulations and printed under the supervision of the international bureau on paper bearing in watermark the words:

25 c. . . . . 25 c.
Union postale universelle

(2) The international bureau furnishes the coupons at the cost of printing, etc., to the administrations which apply for them.

(3) Each administration sells the coupons at a price fixed by itself, but this price may not be lower than the minimum of 28 centimes (gold) fixed by Article 11 of the convention.

(4) Coupons tendered by the public are exchanged for a postage stamp or stamps of a nominal value of 25 centimes in the countries which adopt this service.

(5) The coupons so exchanged are sent quarterly or annually to the international bureau, after classification according to the countries of origin; they are accompanied by a list showing the number for each of those countries.

(6) At the end of the year the international bureau sends to each administration concerned an account in duplicate showing:

a. On the debit side, the value in francs and centimes of the coupons issued by that administration and exchanged for postage stamps of other administrations in the course of the year. The coupons are attached as vouchers;

b. On the credit side, the value in francs and centimes of the coupons issued by other offices and exchanged for postage stamps by the administration in question during the same period;

c. The credit or debit balance.

For purposes of preparing this account the value of the coupon is calculated at 28 centimes per unit.

(7) After examination one copy of the account is returned, duly accepted, to the international bureau. All accounts not returned to the bureau by the time appointed for the settlement are regarded as regular.

(8) Six months after the dispatch of the accounts the international bureau effects the settlement in such a manner as to reduce as far as possible the number of payments to be made.

VIII. CORRESPONDENCE WITH COUNTRIES FOREIGN TO THE UNION

Offices of the union which have relations with countries foreign to the union furnish to the other offices of the union a list of those countries, indicating:

1st. Rates for sea or land transit applicable to conveyance outside the limits of the union;

2d. The kind of articles admitted;

3d. Whether prepayment is obligatory or optional;

4th. The limit, for each category of articles, of validity of postage prepaid (to destination, to port of disembarkation, etc.);

5th. Extent of pecuniary responsibility as regards registered articles;

6th. Whether advices of delivery are obtainable or not; and

7th. As far as possible, the rates of postage from the country outside the union to the countries of the union.

IX. APPLICATION OF STAMPS

(1) Articles dispatched from countries of the union are impressed with a stamp indicating as far as possible in Roman characters the place of origin and the date of posting.

Moreover, all the valid postage stamps should be obliterated.

(2) On arrival, the office of destination impresses its date stamp on the back of the letters and on the front of post cards.

The first office of destination can, moreover, impress its date stamp on the front of the second half of reply-paid post cards.

(3) Missent articles must be date-stamped by the office to which they are sent in error. This obligation is imposed not only on stationary offices but also on traveling post offices as far as possible.

(4) The stamping of articles deposited on board vessels in the movable boxes, or in the hands of the postal agents on board, or of the commanders, devolves, in the cases contemplated by paragraph (5) of Article 11 of the convention, upon the postal agent on board, or, if there be none, on the post office to which the articles are handed over for disposal. In the latter case this office marks the articles with its ordinary date stamp, and with the word *Paquebot* either in manuscript or by means of an autograph stamp or an ordinary stamp.

(5) Articles originating in countries foreign to the union are marked, by the office of the union which first received them, with a stamp indicating the place and date of entry into the service of that office.

(6) Unpaid or insufficiently paid articles are, in addition, impressed with the stamp T (tax to be paid), the application of which devolves upon the office of the country of origin in the case of articles originating in the union, and upon the office of the country of entry in the case of articles originating in countries foreign to the union.

(7) Articles to be delivered by special delivery are impressed with a stamp bearing in large letters the word "Express." Administrations are, however, authorized to substitute for that stamp a printed label or a written inscription underlined with a colored pencil.

Articles which have been marked "Express" by the office of origin are delivered by special messenger, even when prepayment has been omitted or is insufficient. In such cases the office of exchange of the country of destination is bound to report the irregularity by verification note to the central administration to which the office of origin is subordinate. This verification note must state very precisely the origin and date of mailing of the article.

(8) Every article which does not bear the stamp T is considered to be paid and treated accordingly, unless there be an obvious error.

(9) Postage stamps not canceled in consequence of error or omission on the part of the office of origin must be canceled in the usual way by the office which detects the irregularity.

X. INDICATION OF THE NUMBER OF RATES

When a letter or other article of correspondence, unpaid or insufficiently prepaid, is liable, by reason of its weight, to more than a single rate of postage, the office of origin, or of entry into the union, as the case may be, indicates in the upper left-hand corner of the address, in ordinary figures, the number of rates.

XI. INSUFFICIENT PREPAYMENT

(1) When an article is insufficiently prepaid by means of postage stamps, the dispatching office indicates by means of a stamp or other process, in easily read figures placed by the side of the postage stamps, double the amount of the deficiency, expressing it in francs and centimes.

An exception is made, however, in the case of articles which have become insufficiently prepaid in consequence of redirection, and to which the stipulations of Article XXVII of the present regulations are applicable.

(2) According to this indication, the office of exchange of the country of the destination taxes the article with the amount marked, in conformity with the provisions of paragraph (3) of Article 5 of the convention.

(3) If postage stamps not available for prepayment have been employed, no account is taken of them. This circumstance is indicated by the figure naught (0) placed by the side of the postage stamps.

XII. CONDITIONS APPLICABLE TO REGISTERED ARTICLES

(1) Articles addressed to initials or in pencil are not admitted to registration.

(2) No special conditions as to form or fastening are prescribed for registered articles. Each office has the right to apply to such articles the regulations in force in its inland service.

(3) Registered articles should bear in the upper left-hand corner of the address labels in conformity with or analogous to the Form *B* annexed to the present regulations, indicating in Roman characters the name of the office of origin and the number under which the article is entered in the records of that office.

Nevertheless, administrations whose inland regulations do not at present admit the use of labels may postpone the introduction of this arrangement and continue the use of stamps to distinguish registered articles.

It is, however, compulsory for offices which have not adopted the label Form *B* to designate each registered article by a number. This number must be written in the upper left-hand corner of the address. It is obligatory for forwarding offices to designate the article by the original number.

(4) Unpaid or insufficiently paid registered articles are forwarded to the addressees without charge, but the office which receives an article in these conditions is bound to report the case by bulletin of verification to the administration to which the office of origin is subordinate. The bulletin must make precise mention of the origin, the date of mailing, the weight, the nature, and the number of the article, as well as the value of the postage stamps affixed to the registered article in the case of insufficient prepayment.

This rule does not apply to registered articles which, in consequence of redirection, became liable to higher postage. Such articles are treated in conformity with the provisions of (2) of Article XXVII of the present regulations.

XIII. INDEMNITY FOR THE LOSS OF A REGISTERED ARTICLE

When the indemnity due for the loss of a registered article has been paid by one administration, on behalf of another administration which is responsible for the loss, the latter is bound to repay the amount within three months after receiving notice of the payment. This repayment is effected either by means of a postal money order or a draft, or in specie current in the country to which payment is due. When the repayment of the indemnity involves expenses, they are always borne by the indebted office.

XIV. RETURN RECEIPTS FOR REGISTERED ARTICLES

(1) Articles for which the sender requests a return receipt must be marked very clearly with the inscription, *Avis de réception*, or be stamped with the letters A. R.

(2) They are accompanied by a form in accordance with or analogous to the Form *C* annexed; this form is made out by the office of origin or by any other office which the dispatching office may appoint, and is attached by string tied crosswise to the article to which it relates. If it does not reach the office of destination, the latter makes one out for itself.

Return receipts must be drawn up in French or must bear a sublineary translation in that language.

(3) The office of destination, after having duly filled up Form *C*, returns it under cover to the office of origin.

(4) When the sender requests a return receipt for a registered article after the article has been posted, the office of origin enters in a Form *C*, after affixing to it a postage stamp representing the fee for an advice of delivery, an exact description of the registered article (its nature, office of origin, date of posting, number, complete address of the addressee).

This form is attached to a Form *H* and treated according to the provisions of Article XXX of the present regulations, with the exception that, in case of the regular delivery of the article to which the advice of delivery relates, the office of destination withdraws the Form *H* and returns Form *C*, duly completed, to the office of origin in the manner prescribed by the preceding paragraph (3).

Each administration has the option, if it desires to combine Form *C* and Form *H* in one form.

(5) If a return receipt duly applied for by the sender at the time of posting is not received back after a proper interval in the office of origin, inquiry for the missing return receipt is instituted in accordance with the procedure prescribed by the foregoing (4). In this case, however, instead of affixing a postage stamp to Form *C*, the office of origin inscribes it with the heading " Duplicate of return receipt, etc."

(6) The special arrangements adopted by administrations in pursuance of paragraph (5) of Article XXX of the present regulations for the transmission of inquiries respecting registered articles are applicable to requests for advices of delivery made after the article has been posted.

XV. REGISTERED ARTICLES MARKED WITH TRADE CHARGES

(1) Registered articles marked with trade charges must bear on the address side the heading *Remboursement*, written or printed in a prominent manner, and followed by the indication of the amount of the trade charge in the money of the country of destination, unless there are arrangements to the contrary between the administrations interested. This amount is expressed in Roman characters, in words, and in figures, without erasure or correction, even if certified. The sender must indicate on the front or on the back his name and address, likewise in Roman characters.

(2) Registered articles marked with trade charges must bear on the address side an orange-colored label similar to Form *D* annexed to the present regulations.

(3) If the addressee does not pay the amount of the trade charges within an interval of seven days, in relations between European countries, and within an interval of fifteen days in relations between countries of Europe and countries outside of Europe, or between these last-mentioned countries themselves, reckoning from the day after that of arrival at the office of destination, the article is sent back to the office of origin.

(4) In the absence of any other arrangement, the sum recovered, after deduction of the commission provided for in Article 7, (2), of the convention and of the ordinary money-order rate, is converted into a money order with the heading "Remb." on the face, and made out for the amount of the surplus in accordance with the detailed regulations for the execution of the money-order agreement. On the coupon of the order the name and address of the addressee of the article marked with a trade charge must be entered, as well as the date and place of posting of the article.

(5) In the absence of any arrangement to the contrary, articles marked with trade charges may be reforwarded from one of the countries participating in this service to another of those countries. In case of redirection, the sender's marking of the trade charge is preserved intact. Upon the office of final destination alone devolves the conversion into its currency of the amount of the trade charges, in accordance with the rate of exchange in force for money orders, in cases where its monetary system is not that in which the trade charges are expressed; it also devolves upon that office to draw a money order for the amount of the trade charges on the country of origin.

XVI. POST CARDS

(1) Post cards must bear on the face the heading *Carte postale* in French, or the equivalent of this heading in another language. This heading is, however, not obligatory for single post cards emanating from private industry.

The dimensions of the cards may not exceed 14 centimeters in length and 9 centimeters in width, nor be less than 10 centimeters in length and 7 centimeters in width. Post cards must be sent uninclosed, that is to say, without wrapper or envelope.

Post cards must be manufactured of cardboard or of paper of such consistency as not to hinder manipulation.

(2) The postage stamps must, as far as possible, be affixed to the upper right-hand corner of the face. The address of the recipient, as well as indications relating to the postal service (registered, advice of delivery, etc.), must likewise appear on the face, of which the right-hand half at least is reserved for these indications. The sender may dispose of the back and of the left-hand half of the face, subject to the stipulations of the following paragraph.

(3) With the exception of stamps for prepayment, the public is forbidden to join or attach to post cards any objects whatever. Nevertheless, the name and address of the recipient, as well as the name and address of the sender, may appear on gummed labels not exceeding 2 centimeters by 5. It is likewise permitted to affix on the back and on the left-hand half of the face illustrations or photographs on very thin paper, provided that they adhere completely to the card.

(4) Post cards with reply paid must display on the face in French, as heading on the first half, *Carte postale avec réponse payée;* on the second half, *Carte postale-réponse.* Each of the two halves must, moreover, fulfill the other conditions laid down for single post cards; one half is doubled over the other, and they must not be closed in any manner whatsoever.

The sender of a post card with reply paid may indicate his name and address on the face of the "Reply" half, either in writing or by affixing a label.

The prepayment of the "Reply" half by means of the postage stamp of the country which has issued the card is valid only if the two halves of the reply-paid post card were attached to one another when received from the country of origin, and if the "Reply" half is dispatched from the country where it has been received by post to the said country of origin. If these conditions are not fulfilled, it is treated as an unpaid post card.

(5) Post cards not fulfilling, so far as regards the prescribed indications, dimensions, external form, etc., the conditions laid down by the present article for this class of articles, are treated as letters.

XVII. COMMERCIAL PAPERS

(1) The following are considered as commercial papers, and allowed to pass as such at the reduced postage specified in Article 5 of the convention: All papers and all documents, whether writings or drawings, produced wholly or partly by hand, not having the character of an actual and personal correspondence, such as open letters and post cards of ancient date which have already fulfilled their original purpose, papers of legal procedure, deeds of all kinds drawn up by public functionaries, way bills or bills of lading, invoices, the various documents of insurance companies, copies of or extracts from acts under private signature, written on stamped or unstamped paper, musical scores, or sheets of music in manuscript, the manuscripts of works or of newspapers forwarded separately, pupils' exercises in original or with corrections, but without any comment on the work, etc.

(2) Commercial papers are subject, so far as regards form and conditions of transmission, to the regulations prescribed for printed papers (Article XIX following).

XVIII. SAMPLES.

(1) Samples of merchandise are only allowed to pass at the reduced postage which is fixed for them by Article 5 of the convention under the following conditions:

They must be placed in bags, boxes, or removable envelopes, in such a manner as to admit of easy inspection.

They must possess no salable value, nor bear any writing, except the name or the commercial style of the sender, the address of the person for whom they are intended, a manufacturer's or trade mark, numbers, prices, and indications relative to weight or measurement and dimensions, or to the quantity to be disposed of, or such as are necessary to determine the origin and the nature of the goods.

(2) Articles of glass, packets containing liquids, oils, fatty substances, dry powders, whether dyes or not, as well as packets of live bees, may be admitted to transmission as samples of merchandise, provided that they be packed in the following manner:

1st. Articles of glass must be securely packed (boxes of metal or of wood) in a way to prevent all danger to the correspondence and postal officers.

2d. Liquids, oils, and substances easily liquefied must be inclosed in glass bottles hermetically sealed. Each bottle must be placed in a wooden box furnished with sawdust, cotton, or spongy material in sufficient quantity to absorb the liquid in the event of the bottle becoming broken. Finally, the box itself must be inclosed in a case of metal, of wood with a screw top, or of strong and thick leather.

When perforated wooden blocks are used, having a thickness of at least 2½ millimeters in the thinnest part, sufficiently provided inside with absorbent material and supplied with a lid, it is not necessary that the blocks shall be inclosed in a second case.

3d. Fatty substances which are not easily liquefied, such as ointments, soft soap, resin, etc., the transmission of which offers less inconvenience, must be inclosed in an inner cover (box, bag of linen or parchment, etc.), which must itself be placed in a second box of wood, metal, or strong and thick leather.

4th. Dry coloring powders must be placed in bags of leather, rubber-dressed linen, or oiled paper of stout substance; and dry powders, not dyes, in boxes of metal, wood, or cardboard. These bags or boxes are themselves inclosed in a bag of linen or parchment.

5th. Live bees must be inclosed in boxes so constructed as to avoid all danger and to allow the contents to be ascertained.

(3) Transmission at the sample rate is likewise accorded to keys sent singly, fresh cut flowers, articles of natural history (dried or preserved animals and plants, geological specimens, etc.), tubes of serum, and pathological objects rendered innocuous by their mode of preparation and packing. These articles must not be sent for a commercial purpose, and the packing must be in accordance with the general regulations concerning samples of merchandise.

XIX. PRINTED PAPERS OF EVERY KIND

(1) The following are considered as printed papers, and allowed to pass as such at the reduced postage sanctioned by Article 5 of the convention: Newspapers and periodical works, books, stitched or bound, pamphlets, sheets of music, visiting cards, address cards, proofs of printing with or without the manuscripts relating thereto, papers impressed with points or with characters in relief for the use of the blind, engravings, photographs and albums containing photographs, pictures, drawings, plans, maps, catalogues, prospectuses, announcements and notices of various kinds, printed, engraved, lithographed or autographed, and, in general, all impressions or copies obtained upon paper, parchment, or cardboard, by means of printing, engraving, lithography, autography, or any other mechanical process easy to recognize except the copying press and the typewriter.

To printed papers are assimilated reproductions of a manuscript or typewritten original when they are obtained by a mechanical process of polygraphy (chromography, etc.); but, in order to pass at the reduced postage, these reproductions must be brought to the post-office counter to the number of at least 20 copies, precisely identical.

(2) Printed papers which bear any marks whatever capable of constituting a conventional language, or, save the exceptions specifically authorized by the present article, those of which the text has been modified after printing, cannot be sent at the reduced rate applicable to printed matter.

(3) It is allowed:

(*a*) To indicate on the outside of the missive the name, commercial style, the profession, and the address of the sender;

(*b*) To add in manuscript, on printed visiting cards and also on Christmas and New Year cards, the address of the sender, his title, as well as good wishes, congratulations, thanks, condolences, or other formulas of courtesy, expressed in five words at most or by means of conventional initials (p. f., etc.);

(*c*) To indicate or alter in a printed paper, in manuscript or by a mechanical process, the date of dispatch, the signature, or the commercial style, and the profession, as well as the address of the sender and of the addressee;

(*d*) To inclose the "copy" with corrected proofs, and to make in those proofs alterations and additions which relate to accuracy, form, and printing. In case of want of space these additions may be made on separate sheets;

(*e*) To correct also errors in printing in printed documents other than proofs;

(*f*) To erase certain parts of a printed text;

(*g*) To make prominent by means of marks and to underline words or passages of the text to which it is desired to draw attention;

(*h*) To insert or correct in manuscript or by a mechanical process figures in prices current, tenders for advertisements, stock and share lists, trade circulars and prospectuses, as well as the traveler's name and the date and place of his intended visit, in travelers' announcements;

(*i*) To indicate in manuscript, in advices of the departures and arrivals of ships, the dates of those departures and arrivals, as well as the names of the ships;

(*j*) To indicate in manuscript in advices of the dispatch of goods, the date of those dispatches;

(*k*) To indicate in cards of invitation and notices of meetings the name of the person invited, the date, the object, and the place of the gathering;

(*l*) To add a dedication on books, sheets of music, newspapers, photographs, and engravings, as well as to inclose the relative invoice;

(*m*) In forms of order or subscription for library works, books, newspapers, engravings, pieces of music, to indicate in manuscript the works required or offered, and to erase or underline the whole or part of the printed communications;

(*n*) To paint fashion plates, maps, etc.;

(*o*) To add, in manuscript or by a mechanical process, to cuttings from newspapers and periodical publications the title, date, number, and address of the publication from which the article is extracted.

(4) Printed papers must be either placed in wrappers, upon rollers, between boards, in cases open at both sides or at both ends, or in unclosed envelopes, or be simply folded in such a manner as not to conceal the nature of the packet, or, lastly, tied with a string easy to unfasten.

(5) Address cards and all printed matter of the form and substance of an unfolded card may be forwarded without wrapper, envelope, fastening, or fold.

(6) Cards bearing the inscription "Post Card" or the equivalent of this inscription in any language are allowed to pass at the rate for printed matter, provided that they conform to the general conditions prescribed in the present article for this category of articles. Those which do not fulfill these conditions are regarded as post cards and treated accordingly, subject always to the application of the provisions of paragraph (5) of Article XVI of the present regulations.

XX. ARTICLES GROUPED TOGETHER

It is permitted to inclose in one and the same packet samples of merchandise, printed matter, and commercial papers, but subject to the following conditions:

1st. That each article taken singly does not exceed the limits which are applicable to it as regards weight and size;

2d. That the total weight does not exceed 2 kilograms per packet;

3d. That the minimum charge be 25 centimes if the packet contains commercial papers, and 10 centimes if it consists of printed matter and samples.

XXI. LETTER BILLS

(1) The letter bills which accompany the mails exchanged between two administrations of the union are in conformity with the Form *E* appended to the present regulations. They are placed in colored envelopes marked distinctly *Feuille d'avis* ("Letter Bill").

(2) If occasion arises, the number of separate bags or packets composing the mail to which the letter bill relates is indicated in the upper right-hand corner.

If there be no arrangement to the contrary, in cases of exchanges by sea the dispatching offices must number the letter bills in the upper left-hand corner, in an annual series for each office of origin and for each office of destination, mentioning as far as possible, above the number, the name of the steamer or vessel which carries the mail.

(3) At the head of the letter bill there is to be an entry of the total number of registered articles, of the packets or bags containing those articles, and, by means of a stamp, of a label, or of a manuscript note, of the presence of articles intended for express delivery.

(4) The registered articles are entered individually in Table No. 1 of the letter bill with the following details: the name of the office of origin and the number given to the article at that office and the place of destination; or the name of the office of origin, the name of the addressee, and the place of destination.

In the column headed "Observations" the letters A. R. are inscribed against the entry of registered articles for which an advice of delivery is required. In the same column the note *Remb.*, followed by the indication in figures of the amount of the trade charge, is added against the entry of articles marked with trade charges.

(5) When the number of registered articles habitually sent from one office of exchange to another requires it, use must be made of one or more special and separate lists to take the place of Table No. 1 of the letter bill.

When use is made of several lists, the number of registered articles which can be entered on one and the same list is limited to 30.

The number of registered articles inscribed on the lists, the number of lists, and the number of packets or sacks containing those articles must be entered on the letter bill.

(6) In Table No. 2 are to be entered, with such details as the table requires, the closed mails contained in the direct mail to which the letter bill relates.

(7) Under the heading *Recommandations d'office* ("Official Registrations") are entered open letters on official business, the various communications or registered articles sent by the office of dispatch in connection with the service, as well as the number of returned empty sacks.

(8) When it is deemed necessary, for certain exchanges, to make new tables or headings in the letter bill, such a measure may be adopted by common consent between the administrations concerned.

(9) When an office of exchange has no letters, etc., to forward to a corresponding office, it must, nevertheless, make up in the usual form a mail consisting simply of a blank letter bill.

(10) When closed mails are sent by one administration to another, to be conveyed by means of private ships, the number or weight of the letters and other articles must be indicated in the letter bill and on the address of the mails if the office of embarkation requires it.

XXII. TRANSMISSION OF REGISTERED ARTICLES

(1) Registered articles, and, if there be any, the special lists contemplated in § 5 of Article XXI are collected in one or more separate packets or sacks, which are to be suitably made up or closed and sealed so as to preserve the contents. The registered articles are arranged in each packet in the order of their entry in the list. When several separate lists are used, each of them is tied up with the registered articles to which it relates.

In no case must the registered articles be mixed with ordinary correspondence.

(2) To the outside of the packet of registered articles the special envelope containing the letter bill is attached by a string tied crosswise; when the registered articles are inclosed in a sack, the envelope in question is attached to the neck of the bag.

If there is more than one packet or sack of registered articles, each of the additional packets or sacks is supplied with a label, indicating the nature of the contents.

The packets or sacks of registered articles are placed in the center of the mail in such a manner as to attract the attention of the officer who opens it.

(3) The mode of packing and forwarding registered articles, prescribed above, applies only to ordinary exchanges. For important exchanges it is for the offices

concerned to prescribe by common consent special arrangements, subject in the one case as in the other to exceptional measures to be taken by the heads of the offices of exchange, when they have to insure the transmission of registered articles which, from their nature, form, or size, would not be capable of being inclosed in the principal mail.

XXIII. TRANSMISSION OF SPECIAL-DELIVERY ARTICLES

(1) Ordinary articles intended for special delivery are combined in a special bundle and inserted, by the offices of exchange, in the envelope containing the letter bill which accompanies the mail.

When the case arises, a label placed in this bundle indicates the presence in the mail of correspondence of this nature, which by reason of its form or size cannot be placed with the letter bill.

(2) Registered articles intended for special delivery are arranged in order among the other registered articles, and the entry "Express" is made in the column headed "Observations" of the letter bill in respect of each article.

XXIV. MAKING UP THE MAILS

(1) As a general rule, the articles of which the mails consist must be classified and tied up in bundles according to the nature of the articles, the prepaid articles being separated from the unpaid and insufficiently prepaid.

Letters bearing traces of violation or damage must have the fact noted on them and be marked with the stamp of the office making the note.

Money orders sent in open mail are made up in a separate packet after subdivision, if necessary, into as many bundles as there are countries of destination. This packet is inserted, whenever practicable, by the offices of exchange in the envelope containing the letter bill which accompanies the mail.

(2) In territorial exchanges every mail, after having been tied with string, is wrapped in strong paper sufficient in quantity to prevent damage to the contents, then tied again with string on the outside, and sealed with wax by means of the official seal. The mail is furnished with a printed address bearing, in small characters, the name of the dispatching office, and in larger characters the name of the office of destination: "From —— for ——."

Mails sent by sea are inclosed in sacks properly closed, sealed with wax or with lead, and labeled. The same rule applies in the case of mails sent by land when their size requires it.

(3) The labels used for mails sent in sacks must be of linen, leather, or parchment, or of paper affixed to blocks. The label should indicate in a legible manner the office of origin and that of destination.

(4) When the number or bulk of the mails necessitates the use of more than one sack, separate sacks must as far as possible be utilized:

a. For letters and post cards;

b. For other articles.

Each sack must bear the indication of its contents.

The packet or sack of registered articles is placed in one of the sacks of letters. This sack is distinguished by the letter F marked plainly on the label.

(5) No sack must exceed 40 kilograms in weight.

(6) The sacks must be returned empty to the country of origin by the next mail, in the absence of other arrangements between the corresponding offices.

The return of empty sacks must be effected by such offices of exchange of the corresponding countries as are respectively appointed for the purpose by the administrations interested, after previous understanding.

The empty sacks must be rolled up and tied together in suitable bundles; the label blocks, if any, being placed in the inside of the sacks. The bundles must be supplied with a label showing the name of the office of exchange whence the sacks have been received on every occasion when they are returned through another office of exchange.

If the sacks to be returned are not too numerous, they may be placed in the sacks containing correspondence. In the contrary case, they must be placed separately in sealed sacks, labeled with the name of the respective offices of exchange. The labels must be marked *Sacs vides* ("empty sacks").

XXV. VERIFICATION OF THE MAILS

(1) The office of exchange which receives a mail ascertains whether the entries in the letter bill and in the registered-letter list, if there be one, are correct.

The mails must be delivered in good condition. Nevertheless, the receipt of a mail cannot be refused on account of its bad condition. In the case of a mail for an office other than that which has received it, it must be packed up afresh, but the original packing should be preserved as far as possible. The repacking is preceded by a verification of the contents, if there is reason to suppose that they are not intact.

(2) When the office of exchange detects errors or omissions, it immediately makes the necessary corrections on the letter bills or lists, taking care to erase by a stroke of the pen the erroneous entries in such a manner as to leave the original entries legible.

(3) These corrections are made by two officers. Except in the case of an obvious error, they are accepted in preference to the original statement.

(4) A bulletin of verification, in conformity with the Form *F* annexed to the present regulations, is prepared by the receiving office, and sent without delay, officially registered, to the dispatching office.

In the case contemplated in paragraph (1) of the present article, a copy of the bulletin of verification is inserted in the repacked mail.

(5) The dispatching office, after examination, returns the bulletin with any observations to which it may give rise.

(6) In case of the failure of a mail, of one or more registered articles, of the letter bill, or of the special list, the fact is immediately verified in the prescribed manner by two officers of the exchange office of destination, and notified to the dispatching office by means of a bulletin of verification officially registered. Nevertheless, when the absence of a mail is the result of a failure of connections the

verification note is not sent registered. If circumstances require, the dispatching office of exchange may also be advised by telegram, at the expense of the office which sends the telegram. At the same time a duplicate of the bulletin of verification is sent by the office of destination, in the same conditions as the original, to the administration to which the dispatching office is subordinate; and when it is a case of the nonreceipt of one or more registered articles, of the letter bill, or of the special list of registered articles, this duplicate must be accompanied by the sack or envelope, and by the seal of the packet of the articles in question, or of the sack, and by the string, the label, and the seal of the mail, if the packet itself has not been found.

As soon as a mail which had been reported to the office of origin or an intermediate office as missing comes to hand, a second bulletin of verification is to be addressed to such office announcing the receipt of the mail.

When the failure of a mail is duly explained on the waybill, and if this mail reaches the office of destination by the next opportunity, the preparation of a bulletin of verification is not necessary.

(7) In the event of the loss of a closed mail, intermediate offices become responsible for the registered articles contained in the mail, within the limits of Article 8 of the convention, provided that the nonreceipt of such mail shall have been notified to them as soon as possible.

(8) Where the office of destination has not forwarded to the dispatching office by the first mail after verification a bulletin reporting errors or irregularities of any kind, the absence of that document is to be regarded as evidence of the due receipt of the mail and its contents, until the contrary be proved.

XXVI. MAILS EXCHANGED WITH SHIPS OF WAR

(1) The establishment of an exchange of closed mails between a post office of the union and naval divisions or ships of war of the same nationality, or between one naval division or ship of war and another of the same nationality, must be notified, as far as possible in advance, to the intermediate offices.

(2) The address of such mails should be in the following form:

From the post office of . . . .

For {the (nationality) naval division of (name of the division) at . . . . .
the (nationality) ship (name of the ship) at . . . .}

(Country)

or

From the (nationality) naval division of (name of the division) at . . . .
From the (nationality) ship (name of the ship) at . . . .
For the post office of . . . .

(Country)

or

From the (nationality) naval division (name of the division) at . . . . .
From the (nationality) ship (name of the ship) at . . . .

For {the (nationality) naval division (name of the division) at . . . . . .
the (nationality) ship (name of the ship) at . . . .}

(Country)

(3) Mails addressed to or sent from naval divisions or ships of war are forwarded, unless specially addressed as to route, by the most rapid routes, and in the same conditions as mails exchanged between post offices.

When mails for a naval division or ship of war are sent uninclosed, the captain of the steamer conveying them holds them at the disposal of the commanding officer of the naval division or ship addressed, in case the latter should require delivery of the mails while the steamer is on her way.

(4) If the ships are not at the place of destination when mails addressed to them arrive there, the mails are kept at the post office until taken away by the addressee or forwarded to another place. Reforwarding may be demanded, either by the post office of origin, or by the commanding officer of the naval division or the ship addressed, or, lastly, by a consul of the same nationality.

(5) Such of the mails in question as bear the inscription "To the care of the consul at —— " are delivered at the consulate of the country of origin. At the request of the consul they may afterwards be received back into the postal service and reforwarded to the place of origin or to another address.

(6) Mails addressed to a ship of war are regarded as being in transit up to the time of their delivery to the commanding officer of that ship of war, even when they shall have been originally addressed to the care of a post office or to a consul intrusted with the duty of acting as forwarding agent; they are not, therefore, regarded as having arrived at their address so long as they shall not have been delivered to the ship of war concerned.

XXVII. REFORWARDED ARTICLES

(1) In execution of Article 14 of the convention, and subject to the exceptions specified in paragraph (2) following, articles of every kind circulating in the union, addressed to persons who have changed their residence, are treated by the delivering office as if they had been addressed directly from the place of origin to the place of the new destination.

(2) With regard to articles in the domestic service of one country of the union, which enter, in consequence of reforwarding, into the service of another country of the union, or to articles exchanged between two countries of the union which have adopted in their reciprocal relations a lower rate than the ordinary union postage, but entering, in consequence of reforwarding, into the service of a third country of the union as regards which the rate is the ordinary union postage, or, lastly, to letters or packets exchanged, so far as their first transmission is concerned, between places in two neighboring countries of the union within a radius for which there exists a reduced rate, but redirected to other places in these countries or to another country of the union, the following rules are observed:

1st. Articles unpaid or insufficiently paid for their first transmission are subjected by the delivering office to the charge applicable to articles of the same nature addressed directly from the place of origin to that of the new destination.

2d. Articles regularly prepaid for their first transmission, on which the complementary postage pertaining to the further transmission has not been paid before their second dispatch, are subjected, according to their nature, by the delivering office to a charge equal to the difference between the amount of postage already prepaid and that which would have been chargeable if the articles had been dispatched in the first instance to the new destination. The amount of this difference must be expressed in francs and centimes, by the side of the postage stamps, by the reforwarding office.

In both cases the charges provided for above are leviable from the addressees, even if, owing to successive redirections, the articles should return to the country of origin.

(3) When articles originally addressed from one part to another of a country of the union, and prepaid in money, are reforwarded to another country, the reforwarding office must indicate on each article the amount, expressed in francs and centimes, of the difference between the amount paid and the international rate.

(4) Missent articles of all kinds are reforwarded without delay, by the quickest route, to destination.

(5) Articles of all kinds, ordinary or registered, which, being wrongly or insufficiently addressed, are returned to the senders in order that they may rectify or complete the address, are not, when posted with the direction rectified or completed, regarded as reforwarded articles, but as being really fresh articles; and they are consequently liable to fresh postage.

XXVIII. UNDELIVERED ARTICLES

(1) Articles of all kinds which are not delivered, from whatever cause, must be returned, as soon as possible after the period for keeping them required by the regulations of the country of destination, and at latest at the expiration of six months in relations with countries beyond sea, and of two months in other relations, through the medium of the respective offices of exchange, and in a special bundle labeled "Rebuts" and bearing indication of the country where the articles originated. The periods of two months and six months are reckoned from the end of the month in which the articles have reached the office of destination.

(2) Nevertheless, undelivered registered articles are returned to the office of exchange of the country of origin, as if they were registered correspondence addressed to that country, except that opposite the detailed advice in Table No. 1 of the letter bill, or in the separate list, the word "Rebuts" is entered in the column of observations by the returning office.

(3) As an exception, two corresponding offices may, by mutual consent, adopt a different mode of returning undelivered articles. They may also come to an understanding to dispense with the reciprocal return of certain printed papers considered as destitute of value, as well as insufficiently prepaid "chain letters" (known as snowball letters) which have been refused by the addressee, when the office of destination has ascertained, after consultation with the addressee, that the letters in question are actually "chain letters."

(4) Before returning to the office of origin articles which for any reason have not been delivered, the office of destination must indicate in a clear and concise

manner in the French language, on each article, the cause of the nondelivery in the following form: "not known," "refused," "traveling," "gone away," "not claimed," "deceased," etc. This indication is made by the application of a stamp or by affixing a label. Each office has the option of adding a translation, in its own language, of the cause of nondelivery, and any other useful particulars.

(5) If articles mailed in one country of the union to an address within that country are sent by persons resident in another country, and have, in consequence of nondelivery, to be returned to the senders abroad, they enter into the international system. In such a case the redirecting office and the delivering office apply to the said articles the provisions of (2) and (3) of the preceding Article XXVII.

(6) Articles for seamen and others addressed to the care of a consul, and returned by him to the local post office as unclaimed, are to be treated in the manner prescribed by (1) or (2) as the case may be, for returned articles in general. The amount of the charges paid by the consul on these articles is at the same time to be refunded to him by the local post office.

XXIX. APPLICATIONS FOR ORDINARY ARTICLES NOT RECEIVED

(1) Every application respecting an ordinary article which has failed to reach its destination gives rise to the following procedure:

1st. A form in conformity with the Form *G* annexed hereto is handed to the applicant, who is requested to fill up as exactly as possible the portion which concerns him.

2d. The office at which the application originates transmits the form directly to the corresponding office. It is transmitted officially without any written communication.

3d. The corresponding office causes the form to be handed to the addressee or sender, as the case may be, with the request that particulars on the subject may be furnished.

4th. With these particulars added, the form is sent back officially to the office which prepared it.

5th. When the application proves to be well founded, it is transmitted to the central administration in order to serve as a basis for further investigations.

6th. In the absence of any understanding to the contrary, the form is drawn up in French or bears a French translation.

(2) Any administration can demand, by notification addressed to the international bureau, that applications which concern its service shall be transmitted to its central administration or to an office specially designated by it.

XXX. APPLICATION FOR REGISTERED ARTICLES

(1) For applications for registered articles a form is used in conformity with or similar to the Form *H* annexed to the present regulations. The office of the country of origin, after having entered the dates of dispatch of the articles in question to the next service, transmits this form directly to the office of destination.

(2) Nevertheless, in relations with countries beyond sea and of those countries between each other, the application is sent from office to office, following the same route as the article under inquiry.

(3) In the case contemplated in (1) above, when the office of destination is in a position to furnish information as to the ultimate fate of the article under inquiry, it returns the form, filled in with the proper information, to the office of origin.

When the fate of an article which has passed in open mail through several services cannot be immediately ascertained in the service of the country of destination, the office of destination sends the form to the first intermediate office, which, after having entered the particulars of the transmissions of the article to the next service, forwards the application to the next office, and so on, until the ultimate fate of the article under inquiry is ascertained. The office which has effected delivery to the addressee, or which, should it so happen, is unable to furnish proof either of delivery or of regular transmission to another administration, records the fact on the form and returns it to the office of origin.

(4) In the case contemplated in (2) above, the inquiries are prosecuted from the office of origin to the office of destination. Each office enters on the form the particulars of the transmission to the next office, and sends it forward to that office. The office which has effected delivery to the addressee, or which, should it so happen, is unable to furnish proof either of the delivery or of regular transmission to another administration, records the fact on the form and returns it to the office of origin.

(5) The Forms *H* are drawn up in French, or bear a sublineary translation in that language. They must indicate the full address of the addressee and be accompanied, as far as possible, by a facsimile of the envelope or of the address of the article. They are transmitted without covering letter in a closed envelope. Each administration is free to require, by notification addressed to the international bureau, that applications concerning its service shall be transmitted either to its central administration, or to an office specially designated, or, lastly, directly to the office of destination, or, if the administration in question is only concerned as an intermediary, to the office of exchange to which the article was sent.

(6) The foregoing provisions do not apply to cases of violation of mails, loss of mails, etc., which require a fuller correspondence between administrations.

XXXI. WITHDRAWAL OF ARTICLES AND CORRECTION OF ADDRESSES

(1) For requests to have articles returned or reforwarded, as well as for requests to have addresses corrected, the sender must use a form in accordance with the Form *I* annexed to the present regulations. In handing this application to the post office, the sender must establish his identity and produce the certificate of posting, if there be one. The administration of the country of origin assumes the responsibility in regard to identity, and, after its establishment, the course is as follows:

1st. If the request is meant to be sent by post, the form, together with a perfect facsimile of the envelope or address of the missive, is dispatched in a registered cover directly to the office of destination.

2d. If the request is to be made by telegraph, the form is handed over to the telegraph service, charged with the transmission of its terms to the office of destination.

(2) On receipt of the Form *I* or of the telegram taking its place, the office of destination searches for the articles in question and takes such steps as may be necessary.

If, however, the case be one of an alteration of address requested by telegraph, the office of destination only retains the letter and awaits the arrival of the necessary facsimile before complying with the request.

If the search is fruitless, or if the article has already been delivered to the addressee, or if the request by telegraph is not sufficiently explicit to admit of the identification of the article in question with certainty, the fact is at once communicated to the office of origin, which informs the applicant accordingly.

(3) In the absence of any understanding to the contrary, Form *I* is drawn up in French, or bears a sublineary translation in that language, and, in cases where the telegraph is resorted to, the telegram is sent in French.

(4) A simple correction of address (without modification of the name or description of the addressee) can also be claimed directly from the delivering office, that is to say, without fulfilling the formalities prescribed for the alteration of address properly so called.

(5) Any administration can require, by notification addressed to the international bureau, that the exchange of applications, so far as such administration is concerned, shall be effected through the medium of its central administration or of an office specially designated.

In cases where the exchange of applications is effected through the medium of the central administrations, requests sent directly by the offices of origin to the offices of destination must be taken into account to the extent that the articles concerned shall be withheld from delivery until the arrival of the application from the central administration.

Administrations which avail themselves of the option accorded by the first paragraph of the present clause bear the charges involved by the transmission, in their inland service, by post or by telegraph, of the communications to be exchanged with the delivering office.

Recourse must be had to the telegraph when the sender has himself used it, and the office of destination cannot be advised in time by post.

XXXII. USE OF POSTAGE STAMPS PRESUMED TO BE FRAUDULENT

(1) Subject to the regulations laid down by the laws of each country, even in cases where the provisions of the present article do not expressly stipulate for this reservation, the undermentioned procedure is followed for reporting the use of fraudulent postage stamps for the prepayment of postage:

a. When the presence of a fraudulent postage stamp (counterfeit or already used), on any article whatever, is detected at the time of dispatch by the post office of a country whose law does not require the immediate seizure of the article, the stamp is not altered in any way, and the article, inclosed in an envelope addressed to the delivering office, is forwarded officially registered.

b. This formality is notified without delay to the administrations of the countries of origin and destination, by means of an advice in conformity with Form *K* annexed to the present regulations. A copy of that advice is, moreover, transmitted to the delivering office in the envelope which incloses the article bearing the supposed fraudulent postage stamp.

c. The addressee is summoned in order to establish the offense.

The delivery of the article takes place only if the addressee or his representative pays the charge due and consents to make known the name and address of the sender, and to place at the disposal of the post office, after having taken cognizance of the contents, the entire article, if it is inseparable from the offense itself, or else the part of the article (envelope, wrapper, portion of letter, etc.) which contains the address and the stamp stated to be fraudulent.

d. The result of the investigation is set forth in a formal report in conformity with the Form *L* annexed to the present regulations, in which report are recorded the incidents that have happened, such as failure to appear, refusal to receive the article or to open it, or to make known the sender, etc. This document is signed by the postal official and by the addressee of the article or his representative; if the latter refuses to sign, the refusal is recorded in place of the signature.

The formal report is transmitted, with the relative vouchers, to the postal administration of the country of origin, which, with the aid of those documents, takes proceedings, if necessary, to repress the infringement according to its internal laws.

XXXIII. TRANSIT STATISTICS

(1) The statistics to be taken in execution of Articles 4 and 17 of the convention for the settlement of transit charges within and outside the limits of the union, are prepared once in every six years according to the stipulations of the following articles, during the first 28 days of the month of November or of May alternately.

The statistics of November, 1907, will apply to the years 1908 to 1913 inclusive; the statistics of May, 1913, will apply to the years 1914 to 1919 inclusive, and so on.

(2) In the event of the adhesion to the union of a country having important relations, countries of the union which might, by reason of that circumstance, find their position modified as regards the payment of transit charges, have the right of demanding special statistics relating exclusively to the country which has lately entered.

(3) When an important modification takes place in the movement of correspondence, and, provided that such modification affects a period or periods amounting to a total of 12 months at least, the offices concerned come to an

understanding for settling among themselves — if necessary, by means of new statistics — the division of the transit charges in proportion to the part taken by the said offices in the conveyance of the correspondence to which these charges relate.

XXXIV. CLOSED MAILS

(1) Articles exchanged in closed mails between two offices of the union, or between an office of the union and an office foreign to the union, across the territory or by means of the services of one or several other offices, form the subject of a statement in conformity with the Form *M* attached to the present regulations, which is filled up in accordance with the following stipulations:

During each statistical period separate sacks or packets must be made up of "letters and post cards" and "other articles." These bags or packets must be provided with a label "L. C." and "A. O." respectively.

By way of exception to the stipulations of Article XXIV of the present regulations, each administration has the option, during the statistical period, of inclosing registered articles other than letters or post cards in one of the sacks or packets intended for other articles, mentioning this fact on the letter bill; but if, in conformity with the said Article XXIV, these registered articles are inclosed in a sack or packet of letters, they are treated, so far as the weight statistics are concerned, as forming part of the letter correspondence.

(2) As regards mails from one union country for another union country, the dispatching office of exchange enters, on the letter bill for the exchange office of destination, the gross weight of the letters and post cards and that of the other articles, without distinction of the origin or destination of the correspondence. The gross weight includes the weight of the packing, but not that of empty sacks packed in separate sacks. These entries are checked by the office of destination, which immediately informs the office of origin, by means of a bulletin of verification, of any error in the statement of that office, amounting to a difference in weight of more than 50 grams.

(3) As soon as possible after the conclusion of the statistical operations the offices of destination prepare the statements (Form *M*), making out as many copies as there are offices concerned, including that of the place of dispatch. These statements are forwarded by the offices of exchange which have prepared them to the offices of exchange of the debtor office for acceptance by signature. These offices, after having accepted the statements, forward them to the central administration to which they are subordinate, for distribution among the offices concerned.

(4) As regards closed mails exchanged between a union country and a country outside the union, through the medium of one or several union offices, the offices of exchange of the union country prepare, in respect of the mails sent or received, a statement (Form *M*) which they forward to the office of exit or entry, and that office prepares, at the end of the statistical period, a general statement in as many copies as there are offices concerned, including itself and the debtor union office. A copy of this statement is forwarded to the debtor office, as well as to each of the offices which have taken part in the conveyance of the mails.

(5) After each statistical period the administrations which have dispatched mails in transit send the list of such mails to the different administrations whose services they have made use of.

(6) The mere warehousing at a port of closed mails brought by one vessel and intended to go on by another does not give rise to the payment of territorial transit charges to the post office of the place where the mails are warehoused.

(7) It is incumbent on the administrations of countries to which ships of war belong, to prepare statements (Form *M*) relative to the mails sent or received by such ships. These mails must, during the statistical period, bear on the labels the following indications:

a. The nature of the contents, and the gross weight, according to the stipulations of (1) of the present article;

b. The route followed or to be followed.

In the event of a mail addressed to a ship of war being reforwarded during the statistical period, the reforwarding office notifies the fact to the office of the country to which the ship belongs.

XXXV. ARTICLES IN OPEN MAIL

(1) Ordinary and registered articles as well as insured letters forwarded in open mail during a statistical period form the subject of an entry on the letter bill, by the dispatching office of exchange in the following manner:

Articles in Open Mail	Number
Letters	
Post cards	
Other articles	

Articles exempt from all transit charges in accordance with the stipulations of (8) of Article 4 of the convention are not included in these figures.

(2) The corresponding office of exchange, after verification of the entry on the letter bill, takes over the articles for dispatch to destination among its own correspondence.

(3) Every error in the statement of the dispatching office of exchange is reported immediately to that office by means of a verification note.

(4) When no article is sent in open mail, the dispatching office enters at the head of the letter bill, the remark:

Pas de correspondances à découvert ("No articles in open mail").

XXXVI. ACCOUNT OF TRANSIT EXPENSES

(1) The number of articles forwarded in open mail and the weight of the closed mails, both multiplied by 13, serve as the basis of special accounts determining in francs and centimes the yearly transit payments due to each office. In cases where this multiplier does not correspond to the periodicity of the service, or

when it is a question of extraordinary dispatches made during the statistical period, the administrations concerned come to an agreement for the adoption of another multiplier. The duty of preparing the accounts devolves on the creditor office, which forwards them to the debtor office. The multiplier agreed on holds good in each case for the six years of the same statistical period.

(2) In order to take into account the weight of the sacks and packing and of the classes of articles exempt from all transit charges in conformity with the stipulations of (8) of Article 4 of the convention, the total amount of the account for closed mails is reduced by 10 per cent.

(3) The detailed accounts are prepared, in duplicate, as nearly as possible in conformity with Forms *N*, *O*, and *P* attached to the present regulations.

(4) The preparation and dispatch of the detailed accounts should be effected with as little delay as possible, and, at the latest, before the expiration of the year following the statistical year.

In any case, if the office which has sent the account has received no notice of amendments within an interval of six months, reckoning from the date of dispatch, the account is regarded as fully accepted.

(5) In the absence of any understanding to the contrary between the administrations concerned, the general account, including the territorial and sea transit charges, is prepared by the international bureau.

(6) With this object, as soon as the reciprocal detailed accounts between two administrations have been prepared, a statement (Form *Q*) showing the total amounts of these accounts is prepared by each of the two administrations and forwarded by them without delay, and at the latest before the expiration of the second year following the statistical year, to the international bureau.

In the event of one of the administrations not having furnished items in the time fixed above, the items of the other administrations hold good.

In the event of two administrations having agreed between themselves to effect a special settlement, the statement shall bear the inscription *Compte réglé à part — à titre d'information* ("Account settled separately — for purposes of information") and shall not be included in the general account.

In case of difference between the corresponding items of two administrations, the international bureau invites them to come to an agreement and to communicate to it the sums definitely fixed. In the case provided for in (4), paragraph 2, of the present article, the statements should bear the indication: *Aucune observation de l'office débiteur n'est parvenue dans le délai règlementaire* ("No comment has been received from the debtor office within the prescribed period").

(7) The international bureau effects the suppressions provided for in Article 4, (9), of the principal convention, and notifies the same to the offices concerned.

(8) At the end of the first quarter of the year 1909, and of each following year, the international bureau combines in an annual account of transit charges the statements which have reached it up to that time. This account shows:

a. The total debit and credit of each administration;

b. The debit balance or the credit balance of each administration, representing the difference between the total of the debit and the total of the credit;

c. The sums to be paid by the debtor administrations;

d. The sums to be received by the creditor administrations.

The totals of the two classes of balances under the letters *a* to *d* must necessarily be equal.

The international bureau shall arrange for the number of payments to be made by the debtor administrations to be reduced so far as practicable.

(9) The annual accounts are to be forwarded by the international bureau to the administrations of the union as early as possible.

XXXVII. SETTLEMENT OF TRANSIT CHARGES

(1) The annual balance resulting from the account of the international bureau is paid by the debtor office to the creditor office by means of drafts. If the creditor office has the franc for its monetary unit, the drafts are drawn in effective francs on a place in the creditor country at the option of the debtor office. If the creditor office has not the franc for its monetary unit, the drafts are drawn at the option of the debtor office either in hard cash (francs) on Paris or on a place in the creditor country, or else in the money of the creditor country and on a place in that country; in the latter case the offices interested agree upon the course to be followed and, if necessary, on the rate of conversion of the balance due into the metallic currency of the creditor country. The costs of payment are borne by the debtor office.

(2) The payment of the annual balance must be made with as little delay as possible and at latest before the expiration of a period of three months after the receipt of the liquidation account in the case of countries in Europe, and of four months in the case of other countries. If this period is exceeded, the sums due by one office to another office are chargeable with interest, at the rate of 5 per cent per annum, from the date of the expiration of the period of grace mentioned.

XXXVIII. DIVISION OF THE EXPENSES OF THE INTERNATIONAL BUREAU

(1) The ordinary expenses of the international bureau must not exceed the sum of 125,000 francs annually, irrespective of the special expenses to which the meeting of a congress or of a conference gives rise.

(2) The Swiss postal administration supervises the expenses of the international bureau, makes the necessary advances, and prepares the annual account, which is communicated to all the other administrations.

(3) For the apportionment of the expenses the countries of the union are divided into seven classes, each contributing in the proportion of a certain number of units, viz.:

1st class	25 units
2d class	20 units
3d class	15 units

4th class	10 units
5th class	5 units
6th class	3 units
7th class	1 unit

(4) These coefficients are multiplied by the number of countries of each class, and the total of the products thus obtained furnishes the number of units by which the whole expense is to be divided. The quotient gives the amount of the unit of expense.

(5) The countries of the union are classified as follows, in view of the division of expenses:

1st class. Germany, Austria, United States of America, France, Great Britain, Hungary, British India, Commonwealth of Australia, Canada, the British colonies and protectorates of South Africa, the whole of the other British colonies and protectorates, Italy, Japan, Russia, Turkey;

2d class. Spain;

3d class. Belgium, Brazil, Egypt, Netherlands, Roumania, Sweden, Switzerland, Algeria, French colonies and protectorates in Indo-China, the whole of the other French colonies, the whole of the insular possessions of the United States of America, Dutch East Indies;

4th class. Denmark, Norway, Portugal, Portuguese colonies in Africa, the whole of the other Portuguese colonies;

5th class. Argentine Republic, Bosnia-Herzegovina, Bulgaria, Chile, Colombia, Greece, Mexico, Peru, Servia, Tunis;

6th class. Bolivia, Costa Rica, Cuba, Dominican republic, Ecuador, Guatemala, Haiti, republic of Honduras, Luxemburg, republic of Nicaragua, republic of Panama, Paraguay, Persia, republic of Salvador, kingdom of Siam, Uruguay, Venezuela, German protectorates in Africa, German protectorates in Asia and Australasia, Danish colonies, colony of Curaçao (or Dutch West Indies), colony of Surinam (or Dutch Guiana);

7th class. Kongo Free State, Korea, Crete, Spanish establishments in the Gulf of Guinea, the whole of the Italian colonies, Liberia, Montenegro.

XXXIX. COMMUNICATIONS TO BE ADDRESSED TO THE INTERNATIONAL BUREAU

(1) The international bureau serves as the medium for regular notifications of a general kind concerning international relations.

(2) The administrations belonging to the union must communicate to each other specially through the medium of the international bureau:

1st. The particulars of the surcharges which, by virtue of Article 5 of the convention, they levy in addition to the union rate, whether for sea postage or for expenses of extraordinary conveyance, as well as a list of the countries in relation to which these surcharges are levied, and, if needful, the designation of the routes giving rise to the surcharges;

2d. Three complete sets of their postage stamps, with an indication, when the case arises, of the date on which postage stamps of previous issues cease to be valid;

3d. Notice whether they mean to use the option left to administrations to apply or not to apply certain general stipulations of the convention and of the present regulations;

4th. The reduced rates which they have adopted, either in virtue of special arrangements concluded under Article 21 of the convention, or in execution of Article 20 of the convention, and a statement of the relations in which these reduced rates are applicable;

5th. The list of articles prohibited from importation or from transit, and of those which are admitted conditionally to conveyance in their respective services. This list must show separately the articles in question according to the mode of conveyance, namely:

a. By "letter post" (letters, printed papers, samples);

b. By "parcel post" (in relations between participating or nonparticipating countries); and

c. Optionally under another form (by the medium of postal administrations or of other carrying agencies).

(3) Every modification subsequently introduced, in regard to one or other of the five points above mentioned, must be notified without delay in the same manner.

(4) The international bureau receives besides from all the administrations of the union two copies of all the documents which they publish, whether relating to the inland service or to the international service.

XL. GENERAL STATISTICS

(1) Every administration sends to the international bureau, at the end of the month of July in each year, as complete a series as possible of statistical returns relating to the preceding year, arranged in tables in conformity with or analogous to the Forms *R* and *S* annexed.

(2) Those services in which each transaction is recorded are dealt with in periodical statements based upon the entries made.

(3) With regard to all other transactions, every year a count is made in bulk of correspondence of all kinds without distinction between letters, post cards, printed papers, commercial papers, and samples of merchandise, and every three years, at latest, a count of the different classes of correspondence.

The statistics are taken for daily exchanges during one week, from the second Thursday of October, and for exchanges not daily during four weeks from the first of the same month.

In the interval which elapses between the special statistics the estimate of the different classes is made on the basis of the proportionate figures derived from the preceding special statistics.

(4) To the international bureau is intrusted the duty of printing and distributing the statistical forms to be filled up by each administration, and of furnishing to any administrations on application all necessary information as to the rules to be followed, in order to insure, as far as possible, uniformity of practice in taking the statistics.

XLI. DUTIES OF THE INTERNATIONAL BUREAU

(1) The international bureau prepares general statistics for each year.

(2) It publishes, by the aid of the documents which are put at its disposal, a special journal in the German, English, and French languages.

(3) The international bureau publishes, in accordance with information furnished in virtue of the stipulations of the foregoing Article XXXIX, an official summary of all the notifications of general interest concerning the execution of the convention and the present regulations in each country of the union. Subsequent modifications are made known by means of half-yearly supplements. In urgent cases, however, when an administration expressly demands the immediate publication of a change brought about in its service, the international bureau makes it the subject of a special circular.

Similar summaries concerning the execution of the special arrangements of the union may be published by the international bureau at the request of the administrations participating in those arrangements.

(4) All the documents published by the international bureau are distributed to the administrations of the union, in the proportion of the number of contributing units assigned to each by the foregoing Article XXXVIII.

(5) Any additional copies and documents which may be applied for by these administrations are paid for separately at prime cost.

(6) The international bureau must, moreover, hold itself always at the disposal of members of the union for the purpose of furnishing them with any special information they may require upon questions relating to the international postal service.

(7) The international bureau makes known demands for the modification or interpretation of the stipulations which regulate the union. It notifies the results of each application, and no modification or resolution adopted is binding until three months at least after its notification.

(8) The international bureau effects the balance and liquidation of accounts of every description between the administrations of the union which declare their wish to use that bureau as a medium under the conditions laid down by Article XLII of the following.

(9) The international bureau prepares the business to be submitted to congresses or conferences. It undertakes the necessary copying and printing, the editing and distribution of amendments, minutes of proceedings, and other information.

(10) The director of the international bureau attends the sittings of the congresses or conferences and takes part in the discussions, but without the power of voting.

(11) On the subject of his proceedings he makes an annual report, which is communicated to all the administrations of the union.

(12) The official language of the international bureau is the French language.

(13) It is the duty of the international bureau to publish an alphabetical dictionary of all the post offices of the world, with special indication of such of those offices as undertake services which have not yet become general. That dictionary is kept up to date by means of supplements or in any other manner which the international bureau shall consider suitable. The dictionary mentioned in the present paragraph is issued at prime cost to the administrations which apply for it.

(14) It is the duty of the international bureau to arrange for the manufacture and supply of the reply coupons provided for in Article 11 of the principal convention, as well as to prepare and liquidate the accounts connected with this service specified in Article VII of the present regulations.

XLII. CENTRAL OFFICE OF SETTLEMENT AND LIQUIDATION OF ACCOUNTS BETWEEN THE ADMINISTRATIONS OF THE UNION

(1) It is the duty of the international bureau of the Universal Postal Union to effect the balance and liquidation of accounts of every description relative to the international postal service between administrations of countries of the union which have the franc for their monetary unit, or which are agreed on the rate of conversion of their money into francs and centimes (specie).

The administrations which intend to claim for this service of liquidation the assistance of the international bureau, arrange accordingly with each other and with the bureau.

Notwithstanding its adhesion, each administration retains the right of preparing at will special accounts for different branches of the service, and of effecting the settlement of them at its own convenience with the corresponding administrations, without employing the medium of the international bureau, to which, according to the tenor of the preceding paragraph, it merely indicates for what branches of the service and in respect of what countries it applies for the help of the bureau.

At the request of the administrations concerned, telegraph accounts can also be notified to the international bureau to be included in the setting off of balances.

Administrations which have used the medium of the international bureau for the balancing and liquidation of accounts may cease to use that medium three months after giving notice to the said bureau to that effect.

(2) After the detailed accounts have been checked and agreed upon, the debtor administrations transmit to the creditor administrations, for each class of operations, an acknowledgment made out in francs and centimes, of the amount of the balance of the two detailed accounts, indicating the object of the credit and the period to which it relates.

As regards money-order business, however, the acknowledgment must be transmitted by the debtor office as soon as it has prepared its own detailed account, and has received the detailed account of the corresponding office, without waiting for verification of details. The discrepancies subsequently brought to light are adjusted in the first account which offers.

In the absence of any understanding to the contrary, an administration desiring for its own accounting purposes to have general accounts, has to prepare them itself and to submit them to the corresponding administration for acceptance.

Administrations may come to an understanding for the adoption of another system in their relations.

(3) Each administration addresses monthly or quarterly, if special circumstances render it desirable, to the international bureau a table showing the total credit due to it on the individual accounts, as well as the total of the sums which are due to it from each of the contracting administrations; each credit appearing in this table must be substantiated by an acknowledgment from the indebted office.

This table should reach the international bureau not later than the 19th of each month or of the first month of each quarter, otherwise its liquidation is liable to be deferred until the month or the quarter following.

(4) The international bureau ascertains, by comparing the acknowledgments, if the tables are correct. Every correction that is necessary is notified to the offices concerned.

The debit of each administration to another is carried forward into a summary; and in order to arrive at the total amount owing by each administration, it suffices to add up the different columns of this summary.

(5) The international bureau combines the tables and the summaries in one general balance sheet showing:

a. The total of the debit and of the credit of each administration;

b. The balance against or in favor of each administration, representing the difference between the total of the debit and the total of the credit;

c. The sums to be paid by some of the members of the union to a single administration, or, reciprocally, the sums to be paid by the latter to the former.

The totals of the two categories of balances under *a* and *b* must of necessity be equal.

It shall be arranged, as far as possible, that each administration, in order to liquidate its debts, shall have to make only one or two distinct payments.

Nevertheless, an administration which habitually finds a sum exceeding 50,000 francs due to it from another administration has the right to claim remittances on account.

These remittances on account are entered both by the creditor administration and by the debtor administration, at the foot of the tables to be forwarded to the international bureau (see § 3).

(6) The acknowledgments (see § 3) transmitted to the international bureau with the tables are classified according to the different administrations.

They serve as the basis for settling the accounts of each of the administrations concerned. In this settlement there should appear:

a. The sums relating to the special accounts concerning the different exchanges;

b. The total of the sums resulting from all the special accounts with respect to each of the administrations concerned;

c. The totals of the sums due to all the creditor administrations on account of each branch of the service, as well as their general total.

This total should be equal to the total of the debit which appears in the summary.

At the foot of the account the balance is prepared between the total of the debit and the total of the credit resulting from the tables forwarded by the administrations to the international bureau (see § 3). The net amount of the debit or of the credit should be equal to the debit balance or to the credit balance carried into the general balance sheet. Moreover, the account determines the manner of settlement, that is to say, it indicates the administrations to which payment must be made by the administration indebted.

The accounts must be transmitted to the administrations interested by the international bureau not later than the 22d of each month.

(7) Payment of the sums due, in virtue of an account from one administration to another, must be effected as soon as possible and at the latest a fortnight after receipt of the account by the debtor administration. As regards other conditions of payment the stipulations of § 1 of the preceding Article XXXVII hold good. The stipulations of § 2 of the said article are, if the case arise, applicable in case of nonpayment of the balance within the fixed period.

Debit or credit balances not exceeding 500 francs can be carried forward to the settlement of the following month, provided, however, that the administrations concerned are in monthly communication with the international bureau. The amount brought forward is entered in the summaries and in the accounts for the creditor and debtor administrations. The debtor administration furnishes, in such case, to the creditor administration an acknowledgment of the sum due, to be carried into the next table.

XLIII. LANGUAGE

(1) The letter bills, tables, statements, and other forms used by the administrations of the union in their reciprocal relations must be drawn up in the French language, with or without an interlineary translation in another language, unless the administrations concerned arrange otherwise by direct agreement.

(2) As regards official correspondence, the present state of things is maintained, unless any other arrangement should subsequently be arrived at by common consent between the administrations concerned.

XLIV. JURISDICTION OF THE UNION

(1) The following are considered as belonging to the Universal Postal Union:

1st. The German post offices established in China and in Morocco, as subordinate to the postal administration of Germany;

2d. The Principality of Lichtenstein, as subordinate to the postal administration of Austria;

3d. Iceland and the Faröe Islands, as forming part of Denmark;

4th. The Spanish possessions on the north coast of Africa, as forming part of Spain; the republic of Andorra, and the postal establishments of Spain in Morocco, as subordinate to the postal administration of Spain;

5th. The principality of Monaco and the French post offices established in Morocco and in China, as subordinate to the postal administration of France;

6th. The post offices which the administration of the French colonies and protectorates of Indo-China maintains in China, as subordinate to that administration;

7th. The postal agencies which the postal administration of Gibraltar maintains in Morocco;

8th. The post offices which the administration of the British colony of Hongkong maintains in China;

9th. The Indian postal establishments of Aden, Muscat, the Persian Gulf, and Guadur, as subordinate to the postal administration of British India;

10th. The republic of San Marino and the Italian post office at Tripoli in Barbary, as subordinate to the postal administration of Italy;

11th. The post offices which the Japanese administration has established in China;

12th. The grand duchy of Finland, as forming an integral part of the empire of Russia, the Russian post offices established in China, as subordinate to the Russian postal administration;

13th. Basutoland, as subordinate to the postal administration of the Colony of the Cape of Good Hope;

14th. Walfisch Bay, as forming part of the Colony of the Cape of Good Hope;

15th. The Norwegian post office established at Advent Bay on the west of Spitzbergen, as subordinate to the administration of posts of Norway.

(2) In the interval which elapses between the meetings, the administrations of union countries opening in countries foreign to the union post offices which are to be regarded as belonging to the union, communicate the fact to the administrations of all the other union countries, through the medium of the international bureau.

XLV. PROPOSALS MADE IN THE INTERVAL BETWEEN MEETINGS

(1) In the interval which elapses between the meetings, the postal administration of every country of the union has the right of addressing to the other participating administrations, through the medium of the international bureau, proposals concerning the present regulations.

(2) Every proposal is subject to the following procedure:

A period of six months is allowed to administrations to examine the proposals and communicate their observations, if any, to the international bureau. Amendments are not admitted. The answers are tabulated by the international bureau and communicated to the administrations with an invitation to express themselves for or against. The administrations which have not declared their votes within a period of six months, counting from the date of the second circular of the international bureau notifying to them the observations made, are regarded as abstaining.

(3) In order to become binding the proposals must obtain:

1st. Unanimity of votes, if they relate to the addition of new stipulations or to the modification of the stipulations of the present article and of Articles III, IV, VIII, XIII, XXXI, XXXII, XXXIII, XXXVII, and XLVI;

2d. Two thirds of the votes, if they relate to the modification of the stipulations of Articles I, II, V, VI, XI, XII, XIV, XV, XVI, XVII, XVIII, XIX, XX, XXII, XXV, XXVI, XXVII, XXXVI, XL, XLII, XLIII, and XLIV;

3d. Simply an absolute majority, if they relate to the modification of stipulations other than those indicated above, or to the interpretation of the various provisions of the regulations, except in the case of litigation contemplated by Article 23 of the convention.

(4) Resolutions adopted in due form are made binding by a simple notification from the international bureau to all the administrations of the union.

(5) No modification or resolution adopted is binding until at least three months after its notification.

XLVI. DURATION OF THE REGULATIONS

The present regulations shall be put into execution on the day on which the convention of the 26th of May, 1906, comes into force. They shall have the same duration as that convention, unless they be renewed by common consent between the parties concerned.

Done at Rome, the 26th of May, 1906.

[Signatures]

NOTE. Not all the official translations and texts are consistent with each other in system of indicating subdivisions.

CHAPTER V

WORLD LAW IN ARBITRATION

During recent years the efforts of the nations for peace have been largely directed toward establishing some form of arbitration for the settlement of international differences. Most sublime in conception and most successful in execution of all efforts has been the Hague court of arbitration, established by the Hague peace conference of 1899.

In a book review in the American *Journal of International Law*, April, 1907, page 544, W. L. Penfield says: "There are abundant evidences in the remains of ancient Greek and Roman literature that the resort to arbitration was practiced not only for the settlement of disputes between private parties, but also between states. . . . There are numerous instances of the resort to arbitration during the Middle Ages for the settlement of such (political) differences, but they were mostly between petty princes and states and of a minor character. In the following ages the recourse to arbitration became less frequent. Francis the First and the Swiss cantons, in the sixteenth century, set the first example in modern times of a permanent treaty of arbitration." Cromwell "made a treaty with the states of the Netherlands, which provided for a fair and friendly arbitration of differences between those states and the Commonwealth."

Arbitration on a large scale is a modern practice. In the long array of official international documents, begun by G. F. de Martens, the earliest record we find of arbitration is that of June 21, 1714, relative to the sovereignties of Monaco and Savoy. According to the record, the prince of Monaco was in a recalcitrant attitude toward the king of Sicily in his capacity of duke of Savoy, and by the treaty of Utrecht of April 11, 1713, provision was made for arbitration of the amount of territory and of the loyalty due from the prince to the duke. Commissioners were appointed, according to the ninth article of the treaty, by the kings of France and Great Britain respectively to settle the trouble, and the decision was against the prince. As far as the record shows, here was a clear, official, and successful instance of arbitration, just the sort to make an encouraging precedent for the future.

But the future did not appreciate the quality or the value of the precedent. Armed conflict, with woe to the vanquished, was the universal practice of the European nations for many years following, just as if no such thing as arbitration had been tried. Not for more than one hundred years do we find in this record another instance of arbitration of the differences of political sovereigns.

But in the meantime we do find several instances of mediation which may properly be mentioned here as at least partially in line with the historic movement which was leading up to the memorable consummation in the world court of arbitration.

The record of May 13, 1779, telling of the belligerent relations of her Majesty the Empress of all the Russias, and the king of Prussia, mentions the appointment of plenipotentiaries of the empress and of the king of France as mediators for the work of pacification, and the success of the effort is spread upon the page of history, credit being given formally to the mediation.

It was a fruitful precedent, for on March 12, 1783, there follows a record of like success attending the mediation of the plenipotentiaries of Catherine II, empress of all the Russias, and of Joseph II, emperor of Rome and king of Hungary and Bohemia, in establishing peace between the belligerent powers of France and Great Britain.

In the same class, perhaps, though it was apparently a somewhat different case, seems to come the mediation of Napoleon, as the First Consul of the republic of France, between the parties which divided Switzerland. Under date of February 19, 1803, as an act of mediation, he established, as the record puts it, because of affection, interest, and the demand of the senate, after investigation by persons appointed for the purpose, new constitutions for many of the cantons of Switzerland, and put their people upon a new political basis.

In 1816, March 26, was pronounced a decision of arbitration by a commission appointed according to an agreement of February 25, 1803, to pass upon the claims of princes and states respectively regarding the octroi duties along the Rhine. Here appears to have been a genuine case of arbitration, making another precedent in a small way for the greater events to follow at long intervals afterwards.

The same year, July 1, another arbitration is recorded. According to the ninth article of the last act of the Congress of Vienna, June 9, 1815, referring to arbitration the question of the right of succession in the duchy of Bouillon, the commission of arbitrators having assembled at Leipzig, their decision was duly announced and another illustration was added to the growing list.

Still again, the third instance in 1816, the record says that on August 15 was signed at Zurich by David von Wyss, burgomaster of Zurich, Vincenz von Ruthmann, schultheiss of the republic of Lucerne, and B. Pfister, burgomaster of Schaffhausen, an arbitral decision relative to the differences between the cantons of Uri and Tessin regarding Levantine tolls.

Fourth in this year 1816, so fruitful for this kind of official action, on October 16 we find the record of an arbitration reached by a commission on the arrears of interest on the debt of Holland. It shows that in the June previous a commission of seven members had been named by the governments of France and the Netherlands upon this subject. The commission was thus constituted: two members were named by the French government; two by the king of the Netherlands; then two neutrals were named, one each by France and the Netherlands; then, to make sure that everything was as evenly balanced as possible, the two neutrals chose the seventh member. With this abundance of precaution a characteristic arbitral decision of four to three was reached. But it seems to have held and to have settled the matter.

In the following year, 1817, on July 27, we find a record that a convention on three different subjects was concluded between Prussia and Saxony by the mediation of Austria.

In 1822, on April 22, the record mentions an arbitral decision rendered by the emperor Alexander upon the first article of the treaty of Ghent between the United States of America and Great Britain; and on July 12 of the same year is recorded a convention between his Majesty the Emperor of Russia, and the United States for carrying into effect his imperial Majesty's award on the first article of the treaty of Ghent. The record mentions the preliminaries of the arbitration as follows:

"His Majesty the King of the United Kingdom of Great Britain and Ireland, and the President of the United States of America having agreed, in pursuance of the fifth article of the convention concluded at London on the twentieth day of October, 1818, to refer the difference which had arisen between the two governments upon the true construction and meaning of the first article of the treaty of peace and amity concluded at Ghent on the twenty-fourth day of December, 1814, to the friendly arbitration of his Majesty the Emperor of all the Russias, mutually engaging to consider his decision final and conclusive, and his said imperial Majesty having, after due consideration, given his decision upon these differences, in the following terms, to wit," — then follows the decision that the United States has a just claim for indemnification.

But diplomatic matters moved very slowly regarding the issue, and on November 13, 1826, the United States and Great Britain concluded another convention for the execution of the convention of July 22, 1822, and the arbitral decision of the emperor of Russia.

Further difficulty arose over the interpretation of the treaty of Ghent, for we find that on September 27, 1827, a convention was concluded to submit to arbitration the points disputed between the United States and Great Britain concerning the fifth article of that treaty, from which we quote:

"Whereas, it is provided by the fifth article of the treaty of Ghent that in case the commissioners appointed under that article for the settlement of the boundary line therein described should not be able to agree upon such boundary line, the report or reports of those commissioners, stating the points on which they had differed, should be submitted to some friendly sovereign or state, and that the decision given by such sovereign or state on such points of difference should be considered by the contracting parties as final and conclusive; that case having now arisen, . . . ," they go on to arrange for the arbitration.

But other difficulty arose, and the record bears witness with its entry of January 10, 1831, to an arbitral decision by the king of the Netherlands upon the disputed point of the fifth article of the treaty of Ghent concluded in 1814 between the United States and Great Britain. This arbitral decision was against the United States, and on January 12 is recorded the protest of the minister of the United States against it. But there seems to have been no further obstacle to its enforcement, and arbitration scored another victory.

So the practice became familiar, and from these beginnings grew up that faith in the method which had a conspicuous illustration in the Geneva award of damages in the case of the *Alabama* claims of the United States against Great Britain in 1871. In 1899 came the memorable consummation in the act of the Hague peace conference for the establishment of the world court of arbitration. That expression of the will of the ratifying nations comes so nearly to being the will of the world that it is reasonable to regard it as true world legislation, and to give it its due and honorable place in world law which has been formally enacted.

The participating nations, with their numbers of delegates respectively, were as follows: Germany, five; the United States, six; Austria-Hungary, six; Belgium, three; Bulgaria, two; China, three; Denmark, two; Spain, four; France, six; Great Britain, five; Greece, one; Italy, five; Japan, five; Luxemburg, two; Mexico, two; the Netherlands, five; Persia, two; Portugal, five; Roumania, three; Russia, eight; Servia, three; Siam, four; Sweden and Norway, five; Switzerland, three; Turkey, four, — making ninety-nine in all.

This conference at The Hague in 1899, though called officially a "peace conference," really had a large function in the development of the legislative body of the world; and it is to be ranked as a political conference rather than a peace conference, and is to be given the exalted place in the political history of mankind which it deserves. There is given below the introduction with which it was published to the world, as follows:

FINAL ACT OF THE INTERNATIONAL PEACE CONFERENCE

The international peace conference, convoked in the best interests of humanity by his Majesty the Emperor of all the Russias, assembled on the invitation of the government of her Majesty the Queen of the Netherlands in the Royal House in the Wood at The Hague, on the 18th May, 1899. The Powers enumerated in the following list took part in the conference, to which they appointed the delegates named below:

[Names]

In a series of meetings, between the 18th May and the 29th July, 1899, in which the constant desire of the delegates above mentioned has been to realize, in the fullest manner possible, the generous views of the august initiator of the conference and the intentions of their governments, the conference has agreed, for submission for signature by the plenipotentiaries, on the text of the conventions and declarations enumerated below and annexed to the present act:

I. Convention for the peaceful adjustment of international differences.

II. Convention regarding the laws and customs of war by land.

III. Convention for the adaptation to maritime warfare of the principles of the Geneva convention of the 22d August, 1864.

IV. Three declarations:

1. To prohibit the launching of projectiles and explosives from balloons or by other similar new methods;

2. To prohibit the use of projectiles, the only object of which is the diffusion of asphyxiating or deleterious gases;

3. To prohibit the use of bullets which expand or flatten easily in the human body, such as bullets with a hard envelope, of which the envelope does not entirely cover the core, or is pierced with incisions.

These conventions and declarations shall form so many separate acts. These acts shall be dated this day, and may be signed up to the 31st December, 1899, by the plenipotentiaries of the Powers represented at the international peace conference at The Hague.

Guided by the same sentiments, the conference has adopted unanimously the following resolution:

"The conference is of the opinion that the restriction of military charges, which are at present a heavy burden on the world, is extremely desirable for the increase of the material and moral welfare of mankind."

It has, besides, formulated the following wishes:

1. The conference, taking into consideration the preliminary step taken by the Swiss federal government for the revision of the Geneva convention, expresses the wish that steps may be shortly taken for the assembly of a special conference having for its object the revision of that convention.

This wish was voted unanimously.

2. The conference expresses the wish that the questions of the rights and duties of neutrals may be inserted in the program of a conference in the near future.

3. The conference expresses the wish that the questions with regard to rifles and naval guns, as considered by it, may be studied by the governments with the object of coming to an agreement respecting the employment of new types and calibers.

4. The conference expresses the wish that the governments, taking into consideration the proposals made at the conference, may examine the possibility of an agreement as to the limitation of armed forces by land and sea, and of war budgets.

5. The conference expresses the wish that the proposal which contemplates the declaration of the inviolability of private property in naval warfare may be referred to a subsequent conference for consideration.

6. The conference expresses the wish that the proposal to settle the question of the bombardment of ports, towns, and villages by a naval force may be referred to a subsequent conference for consideration.

The last five wishes were voted unanimously, saving some abstentions.

In faith of which, the plenipotentiaries have signed the present act and have affixed their seals thereto.

Done at The Hague, 29th July, 1899, in one copy only, which shall be deposited in the ministry for foreign affairs, and of which copies, duly certified, shall be delivered to all the Powers represented at the conference.

[Signatures]

CONVENTION FOR THE PEACEFUL ADJUSTMENT OF INTERNATIONAL DIFFERENCES

His Majesty the Emperor of Germany, King of Prussia; his Majesty the Emperor of Austria, King of Bohemia, etc., and Apostolic King of Hungary; his Majesty the King of Belgians; his Majesty the Emperor of China; his Majesty the King of Denmark; his Majesty the King of Spain and in his name her Majesty the Queen Regent of the kingdom; the President of the United States of America; the President of the United Mexican States; the President of the French republic; her Majesty the Queen of the United Kingdom of Great Britain and Ireland, Empress of India; his Majesty the King of the Hellenes; his Majesty the King of Italy; his Majesty the Emperor of Japan; his Royal Highness the Grand Duke of Luxemburg, Duke of Nassau; his Highness the Prince of Montenegro; her Majesty the Queen of the Netherlands; his imperial Majesty the Shah of Persia; his Majesty the King of Portugal and of the Algarves, etc.; his Majesty the King of Roumania; his Majesty the Emperor of all the Russias; his Majesty the King of Servia; his Majesty the King of Siam; his Majesty the King of Sweden and Norway; the Swiss Federal Council; his Majesty the Emperor of the Ottomans; and his Royal Highness the Prince of Bulgaria,

Animated by a strong desire to concert for the maintenance of the general peace;

Resolved to second by their best efforts the friendly settlement of international disputes;

Recognizing the solidarity which unites the members of the society of civilized nations;

Desirous of extending the empire of law, and of strengthening the appreciation of international justice;

Convinced that the permanent institution of a court of arbitration, accessible to all, in the midst of the independent Powers, will contribute effectively to this result;

Having regard to the advantages attending the general and regular organization of arbitral procedure;

Sharing the opinion of the august initiator of the international peace conference that it is expedient to record in an international agreement the principles of equity and right on which are based the security of states and the welfare of peoples;

Being desirous of concluding a convention to this effect, have appointed as their plenipotentiaries, to wit:

[Names]

Who, after communication of their full powers, found in good and due form, have agreed on the following provisions: [What follows is superseded by the convention of 1907, relating to arbitration, given afterward. The convention with respect to the laws and customs of war on land is also superseded by the convention of 1907, given afterward. The convention for the adaptation to maritime warfare of the principles of the Geneva convention of August 22, 1864, is also superseded by the convention of 1907, given afterward, as are the above-named conventions also, in their proper place in the conventions of 1907.]

The Second Peace Conference

It was at the second peace conference, held at The Hague in 1907, that the self-consciousness of the race came to the surface sufficiently to look forward to a third conference as the next step in a series which might be indefinite in number and would mark the opening of a new era in the history of the human race. In some distinguished circles that conference was pronounced, just at its close, to be a failure and a fiasco; but it already stands in the light of history as a conspicuous success.

Below is a list of the nations which participated in the second peace conference at The Hague, with the number of delegates sent by each: Germany, seven; the United States, nine; the Argentine Republic, five; Austria-Hungary, eight; Belgium, three; Bolivia, two; Brazil, four; Bulgaria, three; Chile, three; China, six; Colombia, three; Cuba, three; Denmark, three; the Dominican republic, two; Ecuador, two; Spain, five; France, nine; Great Britain, eleven; Greece, three; Guatemala, two; Haiti, three; Italy, five; Japan, five; Luxemburg, two; Mexico, three; Montenegro, three; Nicaragua, one; Norway, three; Panama, one; Paraguay, one; the Netherlands, nine; Peru, two; Persia, three; Portugal, five; Roumania, three; Russia, eight; Salvador, two; Servia, three; Siam, three; Sweden, four; Switzerland, three; Turkey, five; Uruguay, three; Venezuela, one; making one hundred seventy-four in all.

Under date of October 18, 1907, the completed work of the conference was given to the world, and the translation into English from the official French is as follows:

TEXT OF THE FINAL ACT

The second international peace conference, proposed in the first instance by the President of the United States of America, having been convoked on the invitation of his Majesty the Emperor of all the Russias, by her Majesty the Queen of the Netherlands, assembled on the 15th June, 1907, at The Hague, in the Hall of the Knights, for the purpose of giving a fresh development to the humanitarian principles which served as a basis for the work of the first conference of 1899.

The following Powers took part in the conference and appointed the delegates named below. [Here follow the names.]

At a series of meetings, held from the 15th June to the 18th October, 1907, in which the above delegates were throughout animated by the desire to realize, in the fullest possible measure, the generous views of the august initiator of the conference and the intentions of their governments, the conference drew up for submission for signature by the plenipotentiaries, the text of the conventions and of the declaration enumerated below and annexed to the present act:

I. Convention for the pacific settlement of international disputes.

II. Convention respecting the limitation of the employment of force for the recovery of contract debts.

III. Convention relative to the opening of hostilities.

IV. Convention respecting the laws and customs of war on land.

V. Convention respecting the rights and duties of neutral powers and persons in case of war on land.

VI. Convention relative to the status of enemy merchant ships at the outbreak of hostilities.

VII. Convention relative to the conversion of merchant ships into warships.

VIII. Convention relative to the laying of automatic submarine contact mines.

IX. Convention respecting bombardment by naval forces in time of war.

X. Convention for the adaptation to naval war of the principles of the Geneva convention.

XI. Convention relative to certain restrictions with regard to the exercise of the right of capture in naval war.

XII. Convention relative to the creation of an international prize court.

XIII. Convention concerning the rights and duties of neutral powers in naval war.

XIV. Declaration prohibiting the discharge of projectiles and explosives from balloons.

These conventions and declaration shall form so many separate acts. These acts shall be dated this day, and may be signed up to the 30th June, 1908, at The Hague, by the plenipotentiaries of the Powers represented at the second peace conference.

The conference, actuated by the spirit of mutual agreement and concession characterizing its deliberations, has agreed upon the following declaration, which, while reserving to each of the Powers represented full liberty of action as regards voting, enables them to affirm the principles which they regard as unanimously admitted.

It is unanimous:

1. In admitting the principle of compulsory arbitration;

2. In declaring that certain disputes, in particular those relating to the interpretation and application of the provisions of international agreements, may be submitted to compulsory arbitration without any restriction.

Finally, it is unanimous in proclaiming that although it has not yet been found feasible to conclude a convention in this sense, nevertheless the divergencies of opinion which have come to light have not exceeded the bounds of judicial controversy, and that by working together here during the past four months the collected Powers not only have learned to understand one another and to draw closer together, but have succeeded in the course of this long collaboration in evolving a very lofty conception of the common welfare of humanity.

The conference has further unanimously adopted the following resolution:

The second peace conference confirms the resolution adopted by the conference of 1899 in regard to the limitation of military expenditure; and inasmuch as military expenditure has considerably increased in almost every country since that time, the conference declares that it is eminently desirable that the governments should resume the serious examination of this question.

It has besides expressed the following opinions:

1. The conference calls the attention of the signatory Powers to the advisability of adopting the annexed draft convention for the creation of a judicial arbitration court, and of bringing it into force as soon as an agreement has been reached respecting the selection of the judges and the constitution of the court.

2. The conference expresses the opinion that in case of war the responsible authorities, civil as well as military, should make it their special duty to insure and safeguard the maintenance of pacific relations, more especially of the commercial and industrial relations between the inhabitants of the belligerent states and neutral countries.

3. The conference expresses the opinion that the Powers should regulate, by special treaties, the position, as regards military charges, of foreigners residing within their territories.

4. The conference expresses the opinion that the preparation of regulations relative to the laws and customs of naval war should figure in the program of the next conference, and that in any case the Powers may apply, as far as possible, to war by sea the principles of the convention relative to the laws and customs of war on land.

Finally, the conference recommends to the Powers the assembly of a third peace conference, which might be held within a period corresponding to that which has elapsed since the preceding conference, at a date to be fixed by common agreement between the Powers, and it calls their attention to the necessity of preparing the program of this third conference a sufficient time in advance to insure its deliberations being conducted with the necessary authority and expedition.

In order to attain this object the conference considers that it would be very desirable that, some two years before the probable date of the meeting, a preparatory committee should be charged by the governments with the task of collecting the various proposals to be submitted to the conference, of ascertaining what subjects are ripe for embodiment in an international regulation, and of preparing a program which the governments should decide upon in sufficient time to enable it to be carefully examined by the countries interested. This committee should further be intrusted with the task of proposing a system of organization and procedure for the conference itself.

In faith whereof the plenipotentiaries have signed the present act and have affixed their seals thereto.

Done at The Hague, the 18th October, 1907, in a single copy, which shall remain deposited in the archives of the Netherland government, and duly certified copies of which shall be sent to all the Powers represented at the conference.

ANNEX TO THE FIRST OPINION EXPRESSED BY THE SECOND PEACE CONFERENCE

DRAFT CONVENTION RELATIVE TO THE CREATION OF A JUDICIAL ARBITRATION COURT

PART I. CONSTITUTION OF THE JUDICIAL ARBITRATION COURT

ART. 1. With a view to promoting the cause of arbitration, the contracting Powers agree to constitute, without altering the status of the Permanent Court of Arbitration, a judicial arbitration court, of free and easy access, composed of judges representing the various juridical systems of the world, and capable of insuring continuity in jurisprudence of arbitration.

ART. 2. The judicial arbitration court is composed of judges and deputy judges chosen from persons of the highest moral reputation, and all fulfilling conditions qualifying them, in their respective countries, to occupy high legal posts or be jurists of recognized competence in matters of international law.

The judges and deputy judges of the court are appointed, as far as possible, from the members of the Permanent Court of Arbitration. The appointment shall be made within the six months following the ratification of the present convention.

ART. 3. The judges and deputy judges are appointed for a period of twelve years, counting from the date on which the appointment is notified to the administrative council created by the convention for the pacific settlement of international disputes. Their appointments can be renewed.

Should a judge or deputy judge die or retire, the vacancy is filled in the manner in which his appointment was made. In this case the appointment is made for a fresh period of twelve years.

ART. 4. The judges of the judicial arbitration court are equal and rank according to the date on which their appointment was notified. The judge who is senior in point of age takes precedence when the date of notification is the same.

The deputy judges are assimilated, in the exercise of their functions, with the judges. They rank, however, below the latter.

ART. 5. The judges enjoy diplomatic privileges and immunities in the exercise of their functions, outside their own country.

Before taking their seats the judges and deputy judges must swear, before the administrative council, or make a solemn affirmation, to exercise their functions impartially and conscientiously.

ART. 6. The court annually nominates three judges to form a special delegation and three more to replace them should the necessity arise. They may be reelected. They are balloted for. The persons who secure the largest number of votes are considered elected. The delegation itself elects its president, who, in default of a majority, is appointed by lot.

A member of the delegation cannot exercise his duties when the Power which appointed him, or of which he is a national, is one of the parties.

The members of the delegation are to conclude all matters submitted to them, even if the period for which they have been appointed judges has expired.

ART. 7. A judge may not exercise his judicial functions in any case in which he has, in any way whatever, taken part in the decision of a national tribunal, of a tribunal of arbitration, or of a commission of inquiry, or has figured in the suit as counsel or advocate for one of the parties.

A judge cannot act as agent or advocate before the judicial arbitration court or the Permanent Court of Arbitration, before a special tribunal of arbitration or a commission of inquiry, nor act for one of the parties in any capacity whatsoever so long as his appointment lasts.

ART. 8. The court elects its president and vice president by an absolute majority of the votes cast. After two ballots the election is made by a bare majority and, in case the votes are even, by lot.

ART. 9. The judges of the judicial arbitration court receive an annual salary of 6000 Netherland florins. This salary is paid at the end of each half year, reckoned from the date on which the court meets for the first time.

In the exercise of their duties during the sessions or in the special cases covered by the present convention, they receive the sum of 100 florins per diem. They are further entitled to receive a traveling allowance fixed in accordance with regulations existing in their own country. The provisions of the present paragraph are applicable also to a deputy judge when acting for a judge.

These emoluments are included in the general expenses of the court dealt with in Article 31, and are paid through the international bureau created by the convention for the pacific settlement of international disputes.

ART. 10. The judges may not accept from their own government or from that of any other Power any remuneration for services connected with their duties in their capacity of members of the court.

ART. 11. The seat of the judicial court of arbitration is at The Hague, and cannot be transferred, unless absolutely obliged by circumstances, elsewhere.

The delegation may choose, with the assent of the parties concerned, another site for its meetings, if special circumstances render such a step necessary.

ART. 12. The administrative council fulfills with regard to the judicial court of arbitration the same functions as to the Permanent Court of Arbitration.

ART. 13. The international bureau acts as registry to the judicial court of arbitration, and must place its offices and staff at the disposal of the court. It has charge of the archives and carries out the administrative work.

The secretary general of the bureau discharges the functions of registrar.

The necessary secretaries to assist the registrar, translators, and shorthand writers are appointed and sworn in by the court.

ART. 14. The court meets in session once a year. The session opens the third Wednesday in June and lasts until all the business on the agenda has been transacted.

The court does not meet in session if the delegation considers that such meeting is unnecessary. However, when a Power is party in a case actually pending before the court, the pleadings in which are closed or about to be closed, it may insist that the session should be held.

When necessary, the delegation may summon the court in extraordinary session.

ART. 15. A report of the doings of the court shall be drawn up every year by the delegation. This report shall be forwarded to the contracting Powers through the international bureau. It shall also be communicated to the judges and deputy judges of the court.

ART. 16. The judges and deputy judges, members of the judicial arbitration court, can also exercise the functions of judge and deputy judge in the international prize court.

PART II. COMPETENCY AND PROCEDURE

ART. 17. The judicial court of arbitration is competent to deal with all cases submitted to it, in virtue either of a general undertaking to have recourse to arbitration or of a special agreement.

ART. 18. The delegation is competent:

1. To decide the arbitrations referred to in the preceding article, if the parties concerned are agreed that the summary procedure laid down in Part IV, chapter 4, of the convention for the pacific settlement of international disputes is to be applied;

2. To hold an inquiry under and in accordance with Part III of the said convention, in so far as the delegation is intrusted with such inquiry by the parties acting in common agreement. With the assent of the parties concerned, and as an exception to Article 7, paragraph 1, the members of the delegation who have taken part in the inquiry may sit as judges, if the case in dispute is submitted to the arbitration of the court or of the delegation itself.

ART. 19. The delegation is also competent to settle the *compromis* referred to in Article 52 of the convention for the pacific settlement of international disputes if the parties are agreed to leave it to the court.

It is equally competent to do so, even when the request is only made by one of the parties concerned, if all attempts have failed to reach an understanding through the diplomatic channel, in the case of:

1. A dispute covered by a general treaty of arbitration concluded or renewed after the present convention has come into force, providing for a *compromis* in all disputes, and not either explicitly or implicitly excluding the settlement of the *compromis* from the competence of the delegation. Recourse cannot, however, be had to the court if the other party declares that in its opinion the dispute does not belong to the category of questions to be submitted to compulsory arbitration, unless the treaty of arbitration confers upon the arbitration tribunal the power of deciding this preliminary question.

2. A dispute arising from contract debts claimed from one Power by another Power as due to its nationals, and for the settlement of which the offer of arbitration has been accepted. This arrangement is not applicable if acceptance is subject to the condition that the *compromis* should be settled in some other way.

ART. 20. Each of the parties concerned may nominate a judge of the court to take part, with power to vote, in the examination of the case submitted to the delegation.

If the delegation acts as a commission of inquiry, this task may be intrusted to persons other than the judges of the court. The traveling expenses and remuneration to be given to the said persons are fixed and borne by the Powers appointing them.

ART. 21. The contracting powers only may have access to the judicial arbitration court set up by the present convention.

ART. 22. The judicial court of arbitration follows the rules of procedure laid down in the convention for the pacific settlement of international disputes, except in so far as the procedure is laid down in the present convention.

ART. 23. The court determines what language it will itself use and what languages may be used before it.

ART. 24. The international bureau serves as channel for all communications to be made to the judges during the interchange of pleadings provided for in Article 63, paragraph 2, of the convention for the pacific settlement of international disputes.

ART. 25. For all notices to be served, in particular on the parties, witnesses, or experts, the court may apply direct to the government of the state on whose territory the service is to be carried out. The same rule applies in the case of steps being taken to procure evidence.

The requests addressed for this purpose can only be rejected when the Power applied to considers them likely to impair its sovereign rights or its safety. If the request is complied with, the fees charged must only comprise the expenses actually incurred.

The court is equally entitled to act through the Power on whose territory it sits.

Notices to be given to parties in the place where the court sits may be served through the international bureau.

ART. 26. The discussions are under the control of the president or vice president, or, in case they are absent or cannot act, of the senior judge present.

The judge appointed by one of the parties cannot preside.

ART. 27. The court considers its decisions in private, and the proceedings are secret.

All decisions are arrived at by a majority of the judges present. If the number of judges is even and equally divided, the vote of the junior judge, in the order of precedence laid down in Article 4, paragraph 1, is not counted.

ART. 28. The judgment of the court must give the reasons on which it is based. It contains the names of the judges taking part in it; it is signed by the president and registrar.

ART. 29. Each party pays its own costs and an equal share of the costs of the trial.

ART. 30. The provisions of Articles 21 to 29 are applicable by analogy to the procedure before the delegation.

When the right of attaching a member to the delegation has been exercised by one of the parties only, the vote of the member attached is not recorded if the votes are evenly divided.

ART. 31. The general expenses of the court are borne by the contracting Powers.

The administrative council applies to the Powers to obtain the funds requisite for the working of the court.

ART. 32. The court itself draws up its own rules of procedure, which must be communicated to the contracting Powers.

After the ratification of the present convention the court shall meet as early as possible in order to elaborate these rules, elect the president and vice president, and appoint the members of the delegation.

ART. 33. The court may propose modifications in the provisions of the present convention concerning procedure. These proposals are communicated through the Netherland government to the contracting Powers, which will consider together as to the measures to be taken.

PART III. FINAL PROVISIONS

ART. 34. The present convention shall be ratified as soon as possible.

The ratifications shall be deposited at The Hague.

A *procès-verbal* of the deposit of each ratification shall be drawn up, of which a duly certified copy shall be sent through the diplomatic channel to all the signatory Powers.

ART. 35. The convention shall come into force six months after its ratification.

It shall remain in force for twelve years, and shall be tacitly renewed for periods of twelve years, unless denounced.

The denunciation must be notified, at least two years before the expiration of each period, to the Netherland government, which will inform the other Powers.

The denunciation shall only have effect in regard to the notifying Power. The convention shall continue in force as far as the other Powers are concerned.

CONVENTION FOR THE PACIFIC SETTLEMENT OF INTERNATIONAL DISPUTES

His Majesty the German Emperor, King of Prussia; etc.:

Animated by the sincere desire to work for the maintenance of general peace;

Resolved to promote by all the efforts in their power the friendly settlement of international disputes;

Recognizing the solidarity uniting the members of the society of civilized nations;

Desirous of extending the empire of law and of strengthening the appreciation of international justice;

Convinced that the permanent institution of a tribunal of arbitration accessible to all, in the midst of independent Powers, will contribute effectively to this result;

Having regard to the advantages attending the general and regular organization of the procedure of arbitration;

Sharing the opinion of the august initiator of the international peace conference that it is expedient to record in an international agreement the principles of equity and right on which are based the security of states and the welfare of peoples;

Being desirous, with this object, of insuring the better working in practice of commissions of inquiry and tribunals of arbitration, and of facilitating recourse to arbitration in cases which allow of a summary procedure;

Have deemed it necessary to revise in certain particulars and to complete the work of the first peace conference for the pacific settlement of international disputes;

The high contracting parties have resolved to conclude a new convention for this purpose, and have appointed the following as their plenipotentiaries:

[Names of plenipotentiaries]

Who, after having deposited their full powers, found in good and due form, have agreed upon the following:

Part I. The Maintenance of General Peace

Art. 1. With a view to obviating as far as possible recourse to force in the relations between states, the contracting Powers agree to use their best efforts to insure the pacific settlement of international differences.

Part II. Good Offices and Mediation

Art. 2. In case of serious disagreement or dispute, before an appeal to arms, the contracting Powers agree to have recourse, as far as circumstances allow, to the good offices or mediation of one or more friendly Powers.

Art. 3. Independently of this recourse, the contracting Powers deem it expedient and desirable that one or more Powers, strangers to the dispute, should, on their own initiative and as far as circumstances may allow, offer their good offices or mediation to the states at variance.

Powers strangers to the dispute have the right to offer good offices or mediation even during the course of hostilities.

The exercise of this right can never be regarded by either of the parties in dispute as an unfriendly act.

Art. 4. The part of the mediator consists in reconciling the opposing claims and appeasing the feelings of resentment which may have arisen between the states at variance.

Art. 5. The functions of the mediator are at an end when once it is declared, either by one of the parties to the dispute or by the mediator himself, that the means of reconciliation proposed by him are not accepted.

Art. 6. Good offices and mediation undertaken either at the request of the parties in dispute or on the initiative of Powers strangers to the dispute have exclusively the character of advice, and never have binding force.

Art. 7. The acceptance of mediation cannot, unless there be an agreement to the contrary, have the effect of interrupting, delaying, or hindering mobilization or other measures of preparation for war.

If it takes place after the commencement of hostilities, the military operations in progress are not interrupted in the absence of an agreement to the contrary.

Art. 8. The contracting Powers are agreed in recommending the application, when circumstances allow, of special mediation in the following form:

In case of a serious difference endangering peace, the states at variance choose respectively a Power, to which they intrust the mission of entering into direct communication with the Power chosen on the other side, with the object of preventing the rupture of pacific relations.

For the period of this mandate, the term of which, unless otherwise stipulated, cannot exceed thirty days, the states in dispute cease from all direct communication on the subject of the dispute, which is regarded as referred exclusively to the mediating Powers, which must use their best efforts to settle it.

In case of a definite rupture of pacific relations, these Powers are charged with the joint task of taking advantage of any opportunity to restore peace.

Part III. International Commissions of Inquiry

Art. 9. In disputes of an international nature involving neither honor nor vital interests, and arising from a difference of opinion on points of fact, the contracting Powers deem it expedient and desirable that the parties who have not been able to come to an agreement by means of diplomacy, should, as far as circumstances allow, institute an international commission of inquiry, to facilitate a solution of these disputes by elucidating the facts by means of an impartial and conscientious investigation.

Art. 10. International commissions of inquiry are constituted by special agreement between the parties in dispute.

The inquiry convention defines the facts to be examined; it determines the mode and time in which the commission is to be formed and the extent of the powers of the commissioners.

It also determines, if there is need, where the commission is to sit and whether it may remove to another place, the language the commission shall use and the languages the use of which shall be authorized before it, as well as the date on which each party must deposit its statement of facts, and, generally speaking, all the conditions upon which the parties have agreed.

If the parties consider it necessary to appoint assessors, the convention of inquiry shall determine the mode of their selection and the extent of their powers.

Art. 11. If the inquiry convention has not determined where the commission is to sit, it will sit at The Hague.

The place of meeting, once fixed, cannot be altered by the commission except with the assent of the parties.

If the inquiry convention has not determined what languages are to be employed, the question shall be decided by the commission.

Art. 12. Unless an undertaking is made to the contrary, commissions of inquiry shall be formed in the manner determined by Articles 45 and 57 of the present convention.

Art. 13. Should one of the commissioners or one of the assessors, should there be any, either die, or resign, or be unable for any reason whatever to discharge his functions, the same procedure is followed for filling the vacancy as was followed for appointing him.

ART. 14. The parties are entitled to appoint special agents to attend the commission of inquiry, whose duty it is to represent them and to act as intermediaries between them and the commission.

They are further authorized to engage counsel or advocates, appointed by themselves, to state their case and uphold their interests before the commission.

ART. 15. The international bureau of the Permanent Court of Arbitration acts as registry for the commission which sit at The Hague, and it shall place its offices and staff at the disposal of the contracting Powers for the use of the commission of inquiry.

ART. 16. If the commission meets elsewhere than at The Hague, it appoints a secretary general, whose office serves as registry.

It is the function of the registry, under the control of the president, to make the necessary arrangements for the sittings of the commission, the preparation of the minutes, and, while the inquiry lasts, for the charge of the archives, which shall subsequently be transferred to the international bureau at The Hague.

ART. 17. In order to facilitate the constitution and working of commissions of inquiry, the contracting Powers recommend the following rules, which shall be applicable to the inquiry procedure in so far as the parties do not adopt other rules.

ART. 18. The commission shall settle the details of the procedure not covered by the special inquiry convention or the present convention, and shall arrange all the formalities required for dealing with the evidence.

ART. 19. On the inquiry both sides must be heard.

At the dates fixed, each party communicates to the commission and to the other party the statements of facts, if any, and, in all cases, the instruments, papers, and documents which it considers useful for ascertaining the truth, as well as the list of witnesses and experts whose evidence it wishes to be heard.

ART. 20. The commission is entitled, with the assent of the Powers, to move temporarily to any place where it considers it may be useful to have recourse to this means of inquiry, or to send one or more of its members. Permission must be obtained from the state on whose territory it is proposed to hold the inquiry.

ART. 21. Every investigation, and every examination of a locality, must be made in the presence of the agents and counsel of the parties or after they have been duly summoned.

ART. 22. The commission is entitled to ask from either party for such explanations and information as it considers necessary.

ART. 23. The parties undertake to supply the commission of inquiry, as fully as they may think possible, with all means and facilities necessary to enable it to become completely acquainted with, and to accurately understand, the facts in question.

They undertake to make use of the means at their disposal, under their municipal law, to insure the appearance of the witnesses or experts who are in their territory and have been summoned before the commission.

If the witnesses or experts are unable to appear before the commission, the parties will arrange for their evidence to be taken before the qualified officials of their own country.

ART. 24. For all notices to be served by the commission in the territory of a third contracting Power, the commission shall apply direct to the government of the said Power. The same rule applies in the case of steps being taken on the spot to procure evidence.

The requests for this purpose are to be executed so far as the means at the disposal of the Power applied to under its municipal law allow. They cannot be rejected unless the Power in question considers they are calculated to impair its sovereign rights or its safety.

The commission will equally be always entitled to act through the Power on whose territory it sits.

ART. 25. The witnesses and experts are summoned on the request of the parties or by the commission of its own motion, and, in every case, through the government of the state in whose territory they are.

The witnesses are heard in succession and separately, in the presence of the agents and counsel, and in the order fixed by the commission.

ART. 26. The examination of witnesses is conducted by the president.

The members of the commission may, however, put to each witness questions which they consider likely to throw light on and complete his evidence, or get information on any point concerning the witness within the limits of what is necessary in order to get at the truth.

The agents and counsel of the parties may not interrupt the witness when he is making his statement, nor put any direct question to him, but they may ask the president to put such additional questions to the witness as they think expedient.

ART. 27. The witness must give his evidence without being allowed to read any written draft. He may, however, be permitted by the president to consult notes or documents if the nature of the facts referred to necessitates their employment.

ART. 28. A minute of the evidence of the witness is drawn up forthwith and read to the witness. The latter may make such alterations and additions as he thinks necessary, which will be recorded at the end of his statement.

When the whole of his statement has been read to the witness, he is asked to sign it.

ART. 29. The agents are authorized, in the course of or at the close of the inquiry, to present in writing to the commission and to the other party such statements, requisitions, or summaries of the facts as they consider useful for ascertaining the truth.

ART. 30. The commission considers its decisions in private and the proceedings are secret.

All questions are decided by a majority of the members of the commission.

If a member declines to vote, the fact must be recorded in the minutes.

ART. 31. The sittings of the commission are not public, nor the minutes and documents connected with the inquiry published except in virtue of a decision of the commission taken with the consent of the parties.

ART. 32. After the parties have presented all the explanations and evidence, and the witnesses have all been heard, the president declares the inquiry terminated, and the commission adjourns to deliberate and to draw up its report.

ART. 33. The report is signed by all the members of the commission.

If one of the members refuses to sign, the fact is mentioned; but the validity of the report is not affected.

ART. 34. The report of the commission is read at a public sitting, the agents and counsel of the parties being present or duly summoned.

A copy of the report is given to each party.

ART. 35. The report of the commission is limited to a statement of facts, and has in no way the character of an award. It leaves to the parties entire freedom as to the effect to be given to the statement.

ART. 36. Each party pays its own expenses and an equal share of the expenses incurred by the commission.

PART IV. INTERNATIONAL ARBITRATION

Chapter I. The System of Arbitration

ART. 37. International arbitration has for its object the settlement of disputes between states by judges of their own choice, and on the basis of respect for law.

Recourse to arbitration implies an engagement to submit in good faith to the award.

ART. 38. In questions of a legal nature, and especially in the interpretation or application of international conventions, arbitration is recognized by the contracting Powers as the most effective and at the same time the most equitable means of settling disputes which diplomacy has failed to settle.

Consequently it would be desirable that, in disputes about the above-mentioned questions, the contracting Powers should, if the case arose, have recourse to arbitration, in so far as circumstances permit.

ART. 39. The arbitration convention is concluded for questions already existing or for questions which may arise eventually.

It may embrace any dispute or only disputes of a certain category.

ART. 40. Independently of general or private treaties expressly stipulating recourse to arbitration as obligatory on the contracting Powers, the said Powers reserve to themselves the right of concluding new agreements, general or particular, with a view to extending compulsory arbitration to all cases which they may consider it possible to submit to it.

Chapter II. The Permanent Court of Arbitration

ART. 41. With the object of facilitating an immediate recourse to arbitration for international differences, which it has not been possible to settle by diplomacy, the contracting Powers undertake to maintain the Permanent Court of Arbitration, as established by the first peace conference, accessible at all times, and operating, unless otherwise stipulated by the parties, in accordance with the rules of procedure inserted in the present convention.

ART. 42. The permanent court is competent for all arbitration cases, unless the parties agree to institute a special tribunal.

ART. 43. The permanent court sits at The Hague.

An international bureau serves as registry for the court. It is the channel for communications relative to the meetings of the court; it has charge of the archives and conducts all the administrative business.

The contracting Powers undertake to communicate to the bureau, as soon as possible, a certified copy of any conditions of arbitration arrived at between them, and of any award concerning them delivered by a special tribunal.

They likewise undertake to communicate to the bureau the laws, regulations, and documents eventually showing the execution of the awards given by the court.

ART. 44. Each contracting Power selects four persons at the most, of known competency in questions of international law, of the highest moral reputation, and disposed to accept the duties of arbitrator.

The persons thus selected are inscribed, as members of the court, in a list which shall be notified to all the contracting Powers by the bureau.

Any alteration in the list of arbitrators is brought by the bureau to the knowledge of the contracting Powers.

Two or more Powers may agree on the selection in common of one or more members.

The same person can be selected by different Powers.

The members of the court are appointed for a term of six years. These appointments are renewable.

Should a member of the court die or resign, the same procedure is followed for filling the vacancy as was followed for appointing him. In this case the appointment is made for a fresh period of six years.

ART. 45. When the contracting Powers wish to have recourse to the permanent court for the settlement of a difference which has arisen between them, the arbitrators called upon to form the tribunal with jurisdiction to decide this difference must be chosen from the general list of members of the court.

Failing the direct agreement of the parties on the composition of the arbitration tribunal, the following course shall be pursued:

Each party appoints two arbitrators, of whom one only can be its national, or chosen from among the persons who have been selected by it as members of the permanent court. These arbitrators together choose an umpire.

If the votes are equally divided, the choice of the umpire is intrusted to a third Power, selected by the parties by common accord.

If an agreement is not arrived at on this subject, each party selects a different Power, and the choice of the umpire is made in concert by the Powers thus selected.

If, within two months' time, these two Powers cannot come to an agreement, each of them presents two candidates taken from the list of members of the permanent court, exclusive of the members selected by the parties and not being nationals of either of them. Drawing lots determines which of the candidates thus presented shall be umpire.

ART. 46. The tribunal being thus composed, the parties notify to the bureau their determination to have recourse to the court, the text of their *compromis*, and the names of the arbitrators.

The bureau communicates without delay to each arbitrator the *compromis* and the names of the other members of the tribunal.

The tribunal assembles at the date fixed by the parties. The bureau makes the necessary arrangements for the meeting.

The members of the tribunal, in the exercise of their duties and out of their own country, enjoy diplomatic privileges and immunities.

ART. 47. The bureau is authorized to place its offices and staff at the disposal of the contracting Powers for the use of any special board of arbitration.

The jurisdiction of the permanent court may, within the conditions laid down in the regulations, be extended to disputes between noncontracting Powers, or between contracting Powers and noncontracting Powers, if the parties are agreed on recourse to this tribunal.

ART. 48. The contracting Powers consider it their duty, if a serious dispute threatens to break out between two or more of them, to remind these latter that the permanent court is open to them.

Consequently they declare that the fact of reminding the parties at variance of the provisions of the present convention, and the advice given to them, in the highest interests of peace, to have recourse to the permanent court, can only be regarded as friendly actions.

In case of dispute between two Powers, one of them can always address to the international bureau a note containing a declaration that it would be ready to submit the dispute to arbitration.

The bureau must at once inform the other Power of the declaration.

ART. 49. The permanent administrative council, composed of the diplomatic representatives of the contracting Powers accredited to The Hague and of the Netherland minister for foreign affairs, who will act as president, is charged with the direction and control of the international bureau.

The council settles its rules of procedure and all other necessary regulations.

It decides all questions of administration which may arise with regard to the operations of the court.

It has entire control over the appointment, suspension, or dismissal of the officials and employees of the bureau.

It fixes the payments and salaries and controls the general expenditure.

At meetings duly summoned the presence of nine members is sufficient to render valid the discussions of the council. The decisions are taken by a majority of votes.

The council communicates to the contracting Powers without delay the regulations adopted by it. It furnishes them with an annual report on the labors of the court, the working of the administration, and the expenditure. The report likewise contains a résumé of what is important in the documents communicated to the bureau by the Powers in virtue of Article 43, paragraphs 3 and 4.

ART. 50. The expenses of the bureau shall be borne by the contracting Powers in the proportion fixed for the international bureau of the Universal Postal Union.

The expenses to be charged to the adhering Powers shall be reckoned from the date on which their adhesion comes into force.

Chapter III. Arbitration Procedure

ART. 51. With a view to encouraging the development of arbitration, the contracting Powers have agreed on the following rules, which are applicable to arbitration procedure, unless other rules have been agreed on by the parties.

ART. 52. The Powers which have recourse to arbitration sign a *compromis*, in which the subject of the dispute is clearly defined, the time allowed for appointing arbitrators, the form, order, and time in which the communication referred to in Article 63 must be made, and the amount of the sum which each party must deposit in advance to defray the expenses.

The *compromis* likewise defines, if there is occasion, the manner of appointing arbitrators, any special powers which may eventually belong to the tribunal, where it shall meet, the language it shall use, and the languages the employment of which shall be authorized before it, and, generally speaking, all the conditions on which the parties are agreed.

ART. 53. The permanent court is competent to settle the *compromis*, if the parties are agreed to have recourse to it for the purpose.

It is similarly competent, even if the request is only made by one of the parties, when all attempts to reach an understanding through the diplomatic channel have failed, in the case of:

1. A dispute covered by a general treaty of arbitration concluded or renewed after the present convention has come into force, and providing for a *compromis* in all disputes and not either explicitly or implicitly excluding the settlement of the *compromis* from the competence of the court. Recourse cannot, however, be had to the court if the other party declares that in its opinion the dispute does not belong to the category of disputes which can be submitted to compulsory arbitration, unless the treaty of arbitration confers upon the arbitration tribunal the power of deciding this preliminary question.

2. A dispute arising from contract debts claimed from one Power by another Power as due to its nationals, and for the settlement of which the offer of arbitration has been accepted. This arrangement is not applicable if acceptance is subject to the condition that the *compromis* should be settled in some other way.

ART. 54. In the cases contemplated in the preceding article, the *compromis* shall be settled by a commission consisting of five members selected in the manner arranged for in Article 45, paragraphs 3 to 6.

The fifth member is president of the commission ex officio.

ART. 55. The duties of arbitrator may be conferred on one arbitrator alone or on several arbitrators selected by the parties as they please, or chosen by them from the members of the Permanent Court of Arbitration established by the present convention.

Failing the constitution of the tribunal by direct agreement between the parties, the course referred to in Article 45, paragraphs 3 to 6, is followed.

ART. 56. When a sovereign or the chief of a state is chosen as arbitrator, the arbitration procedure is settled by him.

ART. 57. The umpire is president of the tribunal ex officio.

When the tribunal does not include an umpire, it appoints its own president.

ART. 58. When the *compromis* is settled by a commission, as contemplated in Article 54, and in the absence of an agreement to the contrary, the commission itself shall form the arbitration tribunal.

ART. 59. Should one of the arbitrators either die, retire, or be unable for any reason whatever to discharge his functions, the same procedure is followed for filling the vacancy as was followed for appointing him.

ART. 60. The tribunal sits at The Hague, unless some other place is selected by the parties.

The tribunal can only sit in the territory of a third Power with the latter's consent.

The place of meeting once fixed cannot be altered by the tribunal, except with the consent of the parties.

ART. 61. If the question as to what languages are to be used has not been settled by the *compromis*, it shall be decided by the tribunal.

ART. 62. The parties are entitled to appoint special agents to attend the tribunal to act as intermediaries between themselves and the tribunal.

They are further authorized to retain for the defense of their rights and interests before the tribunal counsel or advocates appointed by themselves for this purpose.

The members of the permanent court may not act as agents, counsel, or advocates except on behalf of the Power which appointed them members of the court.

ART. 63. As a general rule, arbitration procedure comprises two distinct phases, — pleadings and oral discussions.

The pleadings consist in the communication by the respective agents to the members of the tribunal and the opposite party of cases, counter-cases, and, if necessary, of replies; the parties annex thereto all papers and documents called for in the case. This communication shall be made either directly or through the intermediary of the international bureau, in the order and within the time fixed by the *compromis*.

The time fixed by the *compromis* may be extended by mutual agreement by the parties, or by the tribunal when the latter considers it necessary for the purpose of reaching a just decision.

The discussions consist in the oral development before the tribunal of the arguments of the parties.

ART. 64. A certified copy of every document produced by one party must be communicated to the other party.

ART. 65. Unless special circumstances arise, the tribunal does not meet until the pleadings are closed.

ART. 66. The discussions are under the control of the president.

They are only public if it be so decided by the tribunal, with the assent of the parties.

They are recorded in minutes drawn up by the secretaries appointed by the president. These minutes are signed by the president and by one of the secretaries and alone have an authentic character.

ART. 67. After the close of the pleadings the tribunal is entitled to refuse discussion of all new papers or documents which one of the parties may wish to submit to it without the consent of the other party.

ART. 68. The tribunal is free to take into consideration new papers or documents to which its attention may be drawn by the agents or counsel of the parties.

In this case the tribunal has the right to require the production of these papers or documents, but is obliged to make them known to the opposite party.

ART. 69. The tribunal can, besides, require from the agents of the parties the production of all papers, and can demand all necessary explanations. In case of refusal the tribunal takes note of it.

ART. 70. The agents and the counsel of the parties are authorized to present orally to the tribunal all the arguments they may consider expedient in defense of their case.

ART. 71. They are entitled to raise objections and points. The decisions of the tribunal on these points are final and cannot form the subject of any subsequent discussion.

ART. 72. The members of the tribunal are entitled to put questions to the agents and counsel of the parties, and to ask them for explanations on doubtful points.

Neither the questions put nor the remarks made by members of the tribunal in the course of the discussions can be regarded as an expression of opinion by the tribunal in general or by its members in particular.

ART. 73. The tribunal is authorized to declare its competence in interpreting the *compromis*, as well as the other acts and documents which may be invoked, and in applying the principles of law.

ART. 74. The tribunal is entitled to issue rules of procedure for the conduct of the case, to decide the forms, order, and time in which each party must conclude its arguments, and to arrange all the formalities required for dealing with the evidence.

ART. 75. The parties undertake to supply the tribunal, as fully as they consider possible, with all the information required for deciding the case.

ART. 76. For all notices which the tribunal has to serve in the territory of a third contracting Power, the tribunal shall apply direct to the government of that Power. The same rule applies in the case of steps being taken to procure evidence on the spot.

The requests for this purpose are to be executed as far as the means at the disposal of the Power applied to under its municipal law allow. They cannot be rejected unless the Power in question considers them calculated to impair its own sovereign rights or its safety.

The court will equally be always entitled to act through the Power on whose territory it sits.

ART. 77. When the agents and counsel of the parties have submitted all the explanations and evidence in support of their case the president shall declare the discussion closed.

ART. 78. The tribunal considers its decisions in private and the proceedings remain secret.

All questions are decided by a majority of the members of the tribunal.

ART. 79. The award must give the reasons on which it is based. It contains the names of the arbitrators; it is signed by the president and registrar or by the secretary acting as registrar.

ART. 80. The award is read out in public sitting, the agents and counsel of the parties being present or duly summoned to attend.

ART. 81. The award, duly pronounced and notified to the agents of the parties, settles the dispute definitively and without appeal.

ART. 82. Any dispute arising between the parties as to the interpretation and execution of the award shall, in the absence of an agreement to the contrary, be submitted to the tribunal which pronounced it.

ART. 83. The parties can reserve in the *compromis* the right to demand the revision of the award.

In this case, and unless there be an agreement to the contrary, the demand must be addressed to the tribunal which pronounced the award. It can only be made on the ground of the discovery of some new fact calculated to exercise a decisive influence upon the award, and which was unknown to the tribunal and to the party which demanded the revision at the time the discussion was closed.

Proceedings for revision can only be instituted by a decision of the tribunal expressly recording the existence of the new fact, recognizing in it the character described in the preceding paragraph, and declaring the demand admissible on this ground.

The *compromis* fixes the period within which the demand for revision must be made.

ART. 84. The award is not binding except on the parties in dispute.

When it concerns the interpretation of a convention to which Powers other than those in dispute are parties, they shall inform all the signatory Powers in good time. Each of these Powers is entitled to intervene in the case. If one or more avail themselves of this right, the interpretation contained in the award is equally binding on them.

ART. 85. Each party pays its own expenses and an equal share of the expenses of the tribunal.

Chapter IV. Arbitration by Summary Procedure

ART. 86. With a view to facilitating the working of the system of arbitration in disputes admitting of a summary procedure, the contracting Powers adopt the following rules, which shall be observed in the absence of other arrangements and subject to the reservation that the provisions of Chapter III apply so far as may be.

ART. 87. Each of the parties in dispute appoints an arbitrator. The two arbitrators thus selected choose an umpire. If they do not agree on this point, each of them proposes two candidates taken from the general list of the members of the permanent court exclusive of the members appointed by either of the parties and not being nationals of either of them; which of the candidates thus proposed shall be the umpire is determined by lot.

The umpire presides over the tribunal, which gives its decisions by a majority of votes.

ART. 88. In the absence of any previous agreement the tribunal, as soon as it is formed, settles the time within which the two parties must submit their respective cases to it.

ART. 89. Each party is represented before the tribunal by an agent, who serves as intermediary between the tribunal and the government who appointed him.

ART. 90. The proceedings are conducted exclusively in writing. Each party, however, is entitled to ask that witnesses and experts should be called. The tribunal has, for its part, the right to demand oral explanations from the agents of the two parties, as well as from the experts and witnesses whose appearance in court it may consider useful.

PART V. FINAL PROVISIONS

ART. 91. The present convention, duly ratified, shall replace, as between the contracting Powers, the convention for the pacific settlement of international disputes of the 29th July, 1899.

ART. 92. The present convention shall be ratified as soon as possible.

The ratifications shall be deposited at The Hague.

The first deposit of ratifications shall be recorded in a *procès-verbal* signed by the representatives of the Powers which take part therein, and by the Netherland minister for foreign affairs.

The subsequent deposits of ratifications shall be made by means of a written notification, addressed to the Netherland government and accompanied by the instrument of ratification.

A duly certified copy of the *procès-verbal* relative to the first deposit of ratifications, of the notifications mentioned in the preceding paragraph, and of the instruments of ratification, shall be immediately sent by the Netherland government, through the diplomatic channel, to the Powers invited to the second peace conference, as well as to those Powers which have adhered to the convention. In the cases contemplated in the preceding paragraph the said government shall at the same time inform the Powers of the date on which it received the notification.

ART. 93. Nonsignatory Powers which have been invited to the second peace conference may adhere to the present convention.

The Power which desires to adhere notifies its intention in writing to the Netherland government, forwarding to it the act of adhesion, which shall be deposited in the archives of the said government.

This government shall immediately forward to all the other Powers invited to the second peace conference a duly certified copy of the notification as well as of the act of adhesion, mentioning the date on which it received the notification.

ART. 94. The conditions on which the Powers which have not been invited to the second peace conference may adhere to the present convention shall form the subject of a subsequent agreement between the contracting Powers.

ART. 95. The present convention shall take effect, in the case of the Powers which were not a party to the first deposit of ratifications, sixty days after the date of the *procès-verbal* of this deposit, and, in the case of the Powers which ratify subsequently or which adhere, sixty days after the notification of their ratification or of their adhesion has been received by the Netherland government.

ART. 96. In the event of one of the contracting parties wishing to denounce the present convention, the denunciation shall be notified in writing to the Netherland government, which shall immediately communicate a duly certified copy of the notification to all the other Powers, informing them of the date on which it was received.

The denunciation shall only have effect in regard to the notifying Power, and one year after the notification has reached the Netherland government.

ART. 97. A register kept by the Netherland minister for foreign affairs shall give the date of the deposit of ratifications effected in virtue of Article 92, paragraphs 3 and 4, as well as the date on which the notifications of adhesion (Article 93, paragraph 2) or of denunciation (Article 96, paragraph 1) have been received.

Each contracting Power is entitled to have access to this register and to be supplied with duly certified extracts from it.

In faith whereof the plenipotentiaries have appended their signatures to the present convention.

Done at The Hague, the 18th October, 1907, in a single copy, which shall remain deposited in the archives of the Netherland government, and duly certified copies of which shall be sent, through the diplomatic channel, to the contracting Powers.

CONVENTION RESPECTING THE LIMITATION OF THE EMPLOYMENT OF FORCE FOR THE RECOVERY OF CONTRACT DEBTS

His Majesty the German Emperor, King of Prussia; etc.:

Being desirous of avoiding between nations armed conflicts of a pecuniary origin arising from contract debts which are claimed from the government of one country by the government of another country as due to its nationals,

Have resolved to conclude a convention to this effect, and have appointed the following as their plenipotentiaries:

[Names of plenipotentiaries]

Who, after depositing their full powers, found in good and due form, have agreed upon the following provisions:

ART. 1. The contracting Powers agree not to have recourse to armed force for the recovery of contract debts claimed from the government of one country by the government of another country as being due to its nationals.

This undertaking is, however, not applicable when the debtor state refuses or neglects to reply to an offer of arbitration; or, after accepting the offer, prevents any *compromis* from being agreed on; or, after the arbitration, fails to submit to the award.

ART. 2. It is further agreed that the arbitration mentioned in paragraph 2 of the foregoing article shall be subject to the procedure laid down in Part IV, Chapter III, of the Hague convention for the pacific settlement of international disputes. The award shall determine, except where otherwise agreed between the parties, the validity of the claim, the amount of the debt, and the time and mode of payment.

ART. 3. The present convention shall be ratified as soon as possible.

The ratifications shall be deposited at The Hague.

The first deposit of ratifications shall be recorded in a *procès-verbal* signed by the representatives of the Powers taking part therein, and by the Netherland minister for foreign affairs.

The subsequent deposits of ratifications shall be made by means of a written notification addressed to the Netherland government and accompanied by the instrument of ratification.

A duly certified copy of the *procès-verbal* relative to the first deposit of ratifications, of the notifications mentioned in the preceding paragraph, as well as of the instruments of ratification, shall be sent immediately by the Netherland government, through the diplomatic channel, to the Powers invited to the second peace conference, as well as to the other Powers which have adhered to the convention. In the cases contemplated in the preceding paragraph the said government shall inform them at the same time of the date on which it received the notification.

ART. 4. Nonsignatory Powers may adhere to the present convention.

The Power which desires to adhere notifies its intention in writing to the Netherland government, forwarding to it the act of adhesion, which shall be deposited in the archives of the said government.

The said government shall forward immediately to all the other Powers invited to the second peace conference a duly certified copy of the notification, as well as of the act of adhesion, mentioning the date on which it received the notification.

ART. 5. The present convention shall come into force, in the case of the Powers which were a party to the first deposit of ratifications, sixty days after the date of the *procès-verbal* of this deposit; in the case of the Powers which ratify subsequently or which adhere, sixty days after the notification of their ratification or of their adhesion has been received by the Netherland government.

ART. 6. In the event of one of the contracting Powers wishing to denounce the present convention, the denunciation shall be notified in writing to the Netherland government, which shall immediately communicate a duly certified copy of the notification to all the other Powers, informing them at the same time of the date on which it was received.

The denunciation shall only have effect in regard to the notifying Power, and one year after the notification has reached the Netherland government.

ART. 7. A register kept by the Netherland ministry for foreign affairs shall give the date of the deposit of ratifications made in virtue of Article 3, paragraphs 3 and 4, as well as the date on which the notifications of adhesion (Article 4, paragraph 2) or of denunciation (Article 6, paragraph 1) were received.

Each contracting Power is entitled to have access to this register and to be supplied with duly certified extracts from it.

In faith whereof the plenipotentiaries have appended their signatures to the present convention.

Done at The Hague, the 18th October, 1907, in a single copy, which shall remain deposited in the archives of the Netherland government, and duly certified copies of which shall be sent to the contracting Powers through the diplomatic channel.

CONVENTION RELATIVE TO THE OPENING OF HOSTILITIES

His Majesty the German Emperor, King of Prussia; etc.:

Considering that it is important, in order to insure the maintenance of pacific relations, that hostilities should not commence without previous warning;

That it is equally important that the existence of a state of war should be notified without delay to neutral Powers;

Being desirous of concluding a convention to this effect, have appointed the following as their plenipotentiaries:

[Names of plenipotentiaries]

Who, after depositing their full powers, found in good and due form, have agreed upon the following provisions:

ART. 1. The contracting Powers recognize that hostilities between themselves must not commence without previous and explicit warning, in the form either of a reasoned declaration of war or of an ultimatum with conditional declaration of war.

ART. 2. The existence of a state of war must be notified to the neutral Powers without delay, and shall not take effect in regard to them until after the receipt of a notification, which may, however, be given by telegraph. Neutral Powers, nevertheless, cannot rely on the absence of notification if it is clearly established that they were in fact aware of the existence of a state of war.

ART. 3. Article 1 of the present convention shall take effect in case of war between two or more of the contracting Powers.

Article 2 is binding as between a belligerent power which is a party to the convention and neutral Powers which are also parties to the convention.

ART. 4. The present convention shall be ratified as soon as possible.

The ratifications shall be deposited at The Hague.

The first deposit of ratifications shall be recorded in a *procès-verbal* signed by the representatives of the Powers which take part therein, and by the Netherland minister for foreign affairs.

The subsequent deposits of ratifications shall be made by means of a written notification addressed to the Netherland government and accompanied by the instrument of ratification.

A duly certified copy of the *procès-verbal* relative to the first deposit of ratifications, of the notifications mentioned in the preceding paragraph, as well as of the instruments of ratification, shall be at once sent by the Netherland government, through the diplomatic channel, to the Powers invited to the second peace conference, as well as to the other Powers which have adhered to the convention. In the cases contemplated in the preceding paragraph the said government shall at the same time inform them of the date on which it received the notification.

ART. 5. Nonsignatory Powers may adhere to the present convention.

The Power which wishes to adhere notifies in writing its intention to the Netherland government, forwarding to it the act of adhesion, which shall be deposited in the archives of the said government.

The said government shall at once forward to all the other Powers a duly certified copy of the notification as well as of the act of adhesion, stating the date on which it received the notification.

ART. 6. The present convention shall come into force, in the case of the Powers which were a party to the first deposit of ratifications, sixty days after the date of the *procès-verbal* of that deposit, and, in the case of the Powers which ratify subsequently or which adhere, sixty days after the notification of their ratification or of their adhesion has been received by the Netherland government.

ART. 7. In the event of one of the high contracting parties wishing to denounce the present convention, the denunciation shall be notified in writing to the Netherland government, which shall at once communicate a duly certified copy of the notification to all the other Powers, informing them of the date on which it was received.

The denunciation shall only have effect in regard to the notifying Power, and one year after the notification has reached the Netherland government.

ART. 8. A register kept by the Netherland ministry for foreign affairs shall give the date of the deposit of ratifications made in virtue of Article 4, paragraphs 3 and 4, as well as the date on which the notifications of adhesion (Article 5, paragraph 2) or of denunciation (Article 7, paragraph 1) have been received.

Each contracting Power is entitled to have access to this register and to be supplied with duly certified extracts from it.

In faith whereof the plenipotentiaries have appended their signatures to the present convention.

Done at The Hague, the 18th October, 1907, in a single copy, which shall remain deposited in the archives of the Netherland government, and duly certified copies of which shall be sent, through the diplomatic channel, to the Powers which have been invited to the second peace conference.

CONVENTION RESPECTING THE LAWS AND CUSTOMS OF WAR ON LAND

His Majesty the German Emperor, King of Prussia; etc.:

Seeing that, while seeking means to preserve peace and prevent armed conflicts between nations, it is likewise necessary to bear in mind the case where the appeal to arms has been brought about by events which their care was unable to avert;

Animated by the desire to serve, even in this extreme case, the interests of humanity and the ever-progressive needs of civilization;

Thinking it important, with this object, to revise the general laws and customs of war, either with a view to defining them with greater precision or to confining them within such limits as would mitigate their severity as far as possible;

Have deemed it necessary to complete and explain in certain particulars the work of the first peace conference, which, following on the Brussels Conference of 1874, and inspired by the ideas dictated by a wise and generous forethought, adopted provisions intended to define and govern the usages of war on land.

According to the views of the high contracting parties, these provisions, the wording of which has been inspired by the desire to diminish the evils of war, as far as military requirements permit, are intended to serve as a general rule of conduct for the belligerents in their mutual relations and in their relations with the inhabitants.

It has not, however, been found possible at present to concert regulations covering all the circumstances which arise in practice;

On the other hand, the high contracting parties clearly do not intend that unforeseen cases should, in the absence of a written undertaking, be left to the arbitrary judgment of military commanders.

Until a more complete code of the laws of war has been issued, the high contracting parties deem it expedient to declare that, in cases not included in the regulations adopted by them, the inhabitants and the belligerents remain under the protection and the rule of the principles of the law of nations, as they result from the usages established among civilized peoples, from the laws of humanity, and the dictates of the public conscience.

They declare that it is in this sense especially that Articles 1 and 2 of the regulations adopted must be understood.

The high contracting parties, wishing to conclude a fresh convention to this effect, have appointed the following as their plenipotentiaries:

[Names of plenipotentiaries]

Who, after having deposited their full powers, found in good and due form, have agreed upon the following:

ART. 1. The contracting Powers shall issue instructions to their armed land forces which shall be in conformity with the regulations respecting the laws and customs of war on land, annexed to the present convention.

ART. 2. The provisions contained in the regulations referred to in Article 1, as well as in the present convention, do not apply except between contracting Powers, and then only if all the belligerents are parties to the convention.

ART. 3. A belligerent party which violates the provisions of the said regulations shall, if the case demands, be liable to pay compensation. It shall be responsible for all acts committed by persons forming part of its armed forces.

ART. 4. The present convention, duly ratified, shall, as between the contracting Powers, be substituted for the convention of the 29th July, 1899, respecting the laws and customs of war on land.

The convention of 1899 remains in force as between the Powers which signed it, and which do not also ratify the present convention.

ART. 5. The present convention shall be ratified as soon as possible.

The ratifications shall be deposited at The Hague.

The first deposit of ratifications shall be recorded in a *procès-verbal* signed by the representatives of the Powers which take part therein, and by the Netherland minister for foreign affairs.

The subsequent deposits of ratifications shall be made by means of a written notification, addressed to the Netherland government and accompanied by the instrument of ratification.

A duly certified copy of the *procès-verbal* relative to the first deposit of ratifications, of the notifications mentioned in the preceding paragraph, as well as of the instruments of ratification, shall be immediately sent by the Netherland government, through the diplomatic channel, to the Powers invited to the second peace conference, as well as to the other Powers which have adhered to the convention. In the cases contemplated in the preceding paragraph the said government shall at the same time inform them of the date on which it received the notification.

ART. 6. Nonsignatory Powers may adhere to the present convention.

The Power which desires to adhere notifies in writing its intention to the Netherland government, forwarding to it the act of adhesion, which shall be deposited in the archives of the said government.

This government shall at once transmit to all the other Powers a duly certified copy of the notification as well as of the act of adhesion, mentioning the date on which it received the notification.

ART. 7. The present convention shall come into force, in the case of the Powers which were a party to the first deposit of ratifications, sixty days after the date of the *procès-verbal* of this deposit; and, in the case of the Powers which ratify subsequently or which adhere, sixty days after the notification of their ratification or of their adhesion has been received by the Netherland government.

ART. 8. In the event of one of the contracting Powers wishing to denounce the present convention, the denunciation shall be notified in writing to the Netherland government, which shall at once communicate a duly certified copy of the notification to all the other Powers, informing them of the date on which it was received.

The denunciation shall only have effect in regard to the notifying Power, and one year after the notification has reached the Netherland government.

ART. 9. A register kept by the Netherland ministry for foreign affairs shall give the date of the deposit of ratifications made in virtue of Article 5, paragraphs 3 and 4, as well as the date on which the notifications of adhesion (Article 6, paragraph 2) or of denunciation (Article 8, paragraph 1) were received.

Each contracting Power is entitled to have access to this register and to be supplied with duly certified extracts.

In faith whereof the plenipotentiaries have appended their signatures to the present convention.

Done at The Hague, the 18th October, 1907, in a single copy, which shall remain deposited in the archives of the Netherland government, and duly certified copies of which shall be sent, through the diplomatic channel, to the Powers which have been invited to the second peace conference.

ANNEX TO THE CONVENTION

REGULATIONS RESPECTING THE LAWS AND CUSTOMS OF WAR ON LAND

SECTION I. ON BELLIGERENTS

Chapter I. The Qualifications of Belligerents

ART. 1. The laws, rights, and duties of war apply not only to armies, but also to militia and volunteer corps fulfilling the following conditions:

1. To be commanded by a person responsible for his subordinates;
2. To have a fixed distinctive emblem recognizable at a distance;
3. To carry arms openly; and
4. To conduct their operations in accordance with the laws and customs of war.

In countries where militia or volunteer corps constitute the army, or form part of it, they are included under the denomination "army."

ART. 2. The inhabitants of a territory which has not been occupied, who, on the approach of the enemy, spontaneously take up arms to resist the invading troops without having had time to organize themselves in accordance with Article 1, shall be regarded as belligerents if they carry arms openly and if they respect the laws and customs of war.

ART. 3. The armed forces of the belligerent parties may consist of combatants and noncombatants. In the case of capture by the enemy, both have a right to be treated as prisoners of war.

Chapter II. Prisoners of War

ART. 4. Prisoners of war are in the power of the hostile government, but not of the individuals or corps who capture them.

They must be humanely treated.

All their personal belongings, except arms, horses, and military papers, remain their property.

ART. 5. Prisoners of war may be interned in a town, fortress, camp, or other place, and bound not to go beyond certain fixed limits; but they cannot be confined except as an indispensable measure of safety and only while the circumstances which necessitate the measure continue to exist.

ART. 6. The state may utilize the labor of prisoners of war according to their rank and aptitude, officers excepted. The tasks shall not be excessive and shall have no connection with the operations of the war.

Prisoners may be authorized to work for the public service, for private persons, or on their own account.

Work done for the state is paid at the rates in force for work of a similar kind done by soldiers of the national army, or, if there are none in force, at a rate according to the work executed.

When the work is for other branches of the public service or for private persons, the conditions are settled in agreement with the military authorities.

The wages of the prisoners shall go toward improving their position, and the balance shall be paid them on their release, after deducting the cost of their maintenance.

ART. 7. The government into whose hands prisoners of war have fallen is charged with their maintenance.

In the absence of a special agreement between the belligerents, prisoners of war shall be treated as regards board, lodging, and clothing on the same footing as the troops of the government who captured them.

ART. 8. Prisoners of war shall be subject to the laws, regulations, and orders in force in the army of the state in whose power they are. Any act of insubordination justifies the adoption toward them of such measures of severity as may be considered necessary.

Escaped prisoners who are retaken before being able to rejoin their own army or before leaving the territory occupied by the army which captured them are liable to disciplinary punishment.

Prisoners who, after succeeding in escaping, are again taken prisoners, are not liable to any punishment on account of the previous flight.

ART. 9. Every prisoner of war is bound to give, if he is questioned on the subject, his true name and rank, and if he infringes this rule, he is liable to have the advantages given to prisoners of his class curtailed.

ART. 10. Prisoners of war may be set at liberty on parole if the laws of their country allow, and in such cases they are bound, on their personal honor, scrupulously to fulfill, both toward their own government and the government by whom they were made prisoners, the engagements they have contracted.

In such cases their own government is bound neither to require of nor accept from them any service incompatible with the parole given.

ART. 11. A prisoner of war cannot be compelled to accept his liberty on parole; similarly, the hostile government is not obliged to accede to the request of the prisoner to be set at liberty on parole.

ART. 12. Prisoners of war liberated on parole and recaptured bearing arms against the government to whom they had pledged their honor, or against the allies of that government, forfeit their right to be treated as prisoners of war, and can be brought before the courts.

ART. 13. Individuals who follow an army without directly belonging to it, such as newspaper correspondents and reporters, sutlers and contractors, who fall into the enemy's hands and whom the latter thinks expedient to detain, are entitled to be treated as prisoners of war, provided they are in possession of a certificate from the military authorities of the army which they were accompanying.

ART. 14. An inquiry office for prisoners of war is instituted on the commencement of hostilities in each of the belligerent states, and, when necessary, in neutral countries which have received belligerents in their territory. It is the function of this office to reply to all inquiries about the prisoners. It receives from the various services concerned full information respecting internments and transfers, releases on parole, exchanges, escapes, admissions into hospital, deaths, as well as other information necessary to enable it to make out and keep up to date an individual return for each prisoner of war. The office must state in this return the regimental number, name and surname, age, place of origin, rank, unit, wounds, date and place of capture, internment, wounding, and death, as well as any observations of a special character. The individual return shall be sent to the government of the other belligerent after the conclusion of peace.

It is likewise the function of the inquiry office to receive and collect all objects of personal use, valuables, letters, etc., found on the field of battle or left by prisoners who have been released on parole, or exchanged, or who have escaped, or died in hospitals or ambulances, and to forward them to those concerned.

ART. 15. Relief societies for prisoners of war, which are properly constituted in accordance with the laws of their country and with the object of serving as the channel for charitable effort, shall receive from the belligerents, for themselves and their duly accredited agents, every facility for the efficient performance of their humane task within the bounds imposed by military necessities and administrative regulations. Agents of these societies may be admitted to the places of internment for the purpose of distributing relief, as also to the halting places of repatriated prisoners, if furnished with a personal permit by the military authorities, and on giving an undertaking in writing to comply with all measures of order and police which the latter may issue.

ART. 16. Inquiry offices enjoy the privilege of free postage. Letters, money orders, and valuables, as well as parcels by post, intended for prisoners of war, or dispatched by them, shall be exempt from all postal duties in the countries of origin and destination, as well as in the countries they pass through.

Presents and relief in kind for prisoners of war shall be admitted free of all import or other duties, as well as of payments for carriage by the state railways.

ART. 17. Officers taken prisoners shall receive the same rate of pay as officers of corresponding rank in the country where they are detained, the amount to be ultimately refunded by their own government.

ART. 18. Prisoners of war shall enjoy complete liberty in the exercise of their religion, including attendance at the services of whatever church they may belong to, on the sole condition that they comply with the measures of order and police issued by the military authorities.

ART. 19. The wills of prisoners of war are received or drawn up in the same way as for soldiers of the national army.

The same rules shall be observed regarding death certificates as well as for the burial of prisoners of war, due regard being paid to their grade and rank.

ART. 20. After the conclusion of peace the repatriation of prisoners of war shall be carried out as quickly as possible.

Chapter III. The Sick and Wounded

ART. 21. The obligations of belligerents with regard to the sick and wounded are governed by the Geneva convention.

SECTION II. HOSTILITIES

Chapter I. Means of Injuring the Enemy, Sieges, and Bombardments

ART. 22. The right of belligerents to adopt means of injuring the enemy is not unlimited.

ART. 23. In addition to the prohibitions provided by special conventions, it is especially forbidden:

a. To employ poison or poisoned weapons;

b. To kill or wound treacherously individuals belonging to the hostile nation or army;

c. To kill or wound an enemy who, having laid down his arms, or having no longer means of defense, has surrendered at discretion;

d. To declare that no quarter will be given;

e. To employ arms, projectiles, or material calculated to cause unnecessary suffering;

f. To make improper use of a flag of truce, of the national flag, or of the military insignia and uniform of the enemy, as well as the distinctive badges of the Geneva convention;

g. To destroy or seize the enemy's property, unless such destruction or seizure be imperatively demanded by the necessities of war;

h. To declare abolished, suspended, or inadmissible in a court of law the rights and actions of the nationals of the hostile party.

A belligerent is likewise forbidden to compel the nationals of the hostile party to take part in the operations of war directed against their own country, even if they were in the belligerent's service before the commencement of the war.

ART. 24. Ruses of war and the employment of measures necessary for obtaining information about the enemy and the country are considered permissible.

ART. 25. The attack or bombardment, by whatever means, of towns, villages, dwellings, or buildings which are undefended is prohibited.

ART. 26. The officer in command of an attacking force must, before commencing a bombardment, except in cases of assault, do all in his power to warn the authorities.

ART. 27. In sieges and bombardments all necessary steps must be taken to spare, as far as possible, buildings dedicated to religion, art, science, or charitable purposes, historic monuments, hospitals, and places where the sick and wounded are collected, provided they are not being used at the time for military purposes.

It is the duty of the besieged to indicate the presence of such buildings or places by distinctive and visible signs, which shall be notified to the enemy beforehand.

ART. 28. The pillage of a town or place, even when taken by assault, is prohibited.

Chapter II. Spies

ART. 29. A person can only be considered a spy when, acting clandestinely or on false pretenses, he obtains or endeavors to obtain information in the zone of operations of a belligerent, with the intention of communicating it to the hostile party.

Thus soldiers not wearing a disguise who have penetrated into the zone of operations of the hostile army, for the purpose of obtaining information, are not considered spies. Similarly, the following are not considered spies: soldiers and civilians, carrying out their mission openly, intrusted with the delivery of dispatches intended either for their own army or for the enemy's army. To this class belong likewise persons sent in balloons for the purpose of carrying dispatches and, generally, of maintaining communications between the different parts of an army or a territory.

ART. 30. A spy taken in the act shall not be punished without previous trial.

ART. 31. A spy who, after rejoining the army to which he belongs, is subsequently captured by the enemy, is treated as a prisoner of war, and incurs no responsibility for his previous acts of espionage.

Chapter III. Flags of Truce

ART. 32. A person is regarded as bearing a flag of truce who has been authorized by one of the belligerents to enter into communication with the other, and who advances bearing a white flag. He has a right to inviolability, as well as the trumpeter, bugler, or drummer, the flag bearer, and interpreter who may accompany him.

ART. 33. The commander to whom a flag of truce is sent is not in all cases obliged to receive it.

He may take all the necessary steps to prevent the envoy taking advantage of his mission to obtain information.

In case of abuse he has the right to detain the envoy temporarily.

ART. 34. The envoy loses his rights of inviolability if it is proved in a clear and incontestable manner that he has taken advantage of his privileged position to provoke or commit an act of treachery.

Chapter IV. Capitulations

ART. 35. Capitulations agreed upon between the contracting parties must take into account the rules of military honor.

Once settled, they must be scrupulously observed by both parties.

Chapter V. Armistices

ART. 36. An armistice suspends military operations by mutual agreement between the belligerent parties. If its duration is not defined, the belligerent parties may resume operations at any time, provided always that the enemy is warned within the time agreed upon, in accordance with the terms of the armistice.

ART. 37. An armistice may be general or local. The first suspends the military operations of the belligerent states everywhere; the second only between certain fractions of the belligerent armies and within a fixed radius.

ART. 38. An armistice must be notified officially and in good time to the competent authorities and to the troops. Hostilities are suspended immediately after the notification, or on the date fixed.

ART. 39. It rests with the contracting parties to settle, in the terms of the armistice, what communications may be held in the theater of war with the inhabitants, and between the inhabitants of one belligerent state and those of the other.

ART. 40. Any serious violation of the armistice by one of the parties gives the other party the right of denouncing it, and even, in cases of urgency, of recommencing hostilities immediately.

ART. 41. A violation of the terms of the armistice by private persons acting on their own initiative only entitles the injured party to demand the punishment of the offenders or, if necessary, compensation for the losses sustained.

SECTION III. MILITARY AUTHORITY OVER THE TERRITORY OF THE HOSTILE STATE

ART. 42. Territory is considered occupied when it is actually placed under the authority of the hostile army.

The occupation extends only to the territory where such authority has been established and can be exercised.

ART. 43. The authority of the legitimate Power having in fact passed into the hands of the occupant, the latter shall take all the measures in his power to restore, and insure, as far as possible, public order and safety, while respecting, unless absolutely prevented, the laws in force in the country.

ART. 44. A belligerent is forbidden to force the inhabitants of territory occupied by it to furnish information about the army of the other belligerent, or about its means of defense.

ART. 45. It is forbidden to compel the inhabitants of occupied territory to swear allegiance to the hostile Power.

ART. 46. Family honor and rights, the lives of persons, and private property, as well as religious convictions and practice, must be respected.

Private property cannot be confiscated.

ART. 47. Pillage is formally forbidden.

ART. 48. If, in the territory occupied, the occupant collects the taxes, dues, and tolls imposed for the benefit of the state, he shall do so, as far as is possible, in accordance with the rules of assessment and incidence in force, and shall in consequence be bound to defray the expenses of the administration of the occupied territory to the same extent as the legitimate government was so bound.

ART. 49. If, in addition to the taxes mentioned in the above article, the occupant levies other money contributions in the occupied territory, this shall only be for the needs of the army or of the administration of the territory in question.

ART. 50. No general penalty, pecuniary or otherwise, shall be inflicted upon the population on account of the acts of individuals for which they cannot be regarded as jointly and severally responsible.

ART. 51. No contribution shall be collected except under a written order, and on the responsibility of a commander in chief.

The collection of the said contribution shall only be effected as far as possible in accordance with the rules of assessment and incidence of the taxes in force.

For every contribution a receipt shall be given to the contributors.

ART. 52. Requisitions in kind and services shall not be demanded from municipalities or inhabitants except for the needs of the army of occupation. They shall be in proportion to the resources of the country, and of such a nature as not to involve the inhabitants in the obligation of taking part in military operations against their own country.

Such requisitions and services shall only be demanded on the authority of the commander in the locality occupied.

Contributions in kind shall as far as possible be paid for in cash; if not, a receipt shall be given and the payment of the amount due shall be made as soon as possible.

ART. 53. An army of occupation can only take possession of cash, funds, and realizable securities which are strictly the property of the state, depots of arms, means of transport, stores and supplies, and, generally, all movable property belonging to the state which may be used for military operations.

All appliances, whether on land, at sea, or in the air, adapted for the transmission of news, or for the transport of persons or things, exclusive of cases governed by naval law, depots of arms, and, generally, all kinds of ammunition of war, may be seized, even if they belong to private individuals, but must be restored and compensation fixed when peace is made.

ART. 54. Submarine cables connecting an occupied territory with a neutral territory shall not be seized or destroyed except in the case of absolute necessity. They must likewise be restored and compensation fixed when peace is made.

ART. 55. The occupying state shall be regarded only as administrator and usufructuary of public buildings, real estate, forests, and agricultural estates belonging to the hostile state, and situated in the occupied country. It must safeguard the capital of these properties, and administer them in accordance with the rules of usufruct.

ART. 56. The property of municipalities, that of institutions dedicated to religion, charity and education, the arts and sciences, even when state property, shall be treated as private property.

All seizure of, destruction, or willful damage done to institutions of this character, historic monuments, works of art and science, is forbidden, and should be made the subject of legal proceedings.

CONVENTION RESPECTING THE RIGHTS AND DUTIES OF NEUTRAL POWERS AND PERSONS IN CASE OF WAR ON LAND

His Majesty the German Emperor, King of Prussia; etc.:

With a view to laying down more clearly the rights and duties of neutral Powers in case of war on land and regulating the position of the belligerents who have taken refuge in neutral territory;

Being likewise desirous of defining the meaning of the term "neutral," pending the possibility of settling, in its entirety, the position of neutral individuals in their relations with the belligerents;

Have resolved to conclude a convention to this effect, and have, in consequence, appointed the following as their plenipotentiaries:

[Names of plenipotentiaries]

Who, after having deposited their full powers, found in good and due form, have agreed upon the following provisions:

Chapter I. The Rights and Duties of Neutral Powers

ART. 1. The territory of neutral Powers is inviolable.

ART. 2. Belligerents are forbidden to move troops or convoys of either munitions of war or supplies across the territory of a neutral Power.

ART. 3. Belligerents are likewise forbidden to:

a. Erect on the territory of a neutral Power a wireless telegraphy station or other apparatus for the purpose of communicating with belligerent forces on land or sea;

b. Use any installation of this kind established by them before the war on the territory of a neutral Power for purely military purposes, and which has not been opened for the service of public messages.

ART. 4. Corps of combatants cannot be formed nor recruiting agencies opened on the territory of a neutral Power to assist the belligerents.

ART. 5. A neutral Power must not allow any of the acts referred to in Articles 2 to 4 to occur on its territory.

It is not called upon to punish acts in violation of its neutrality unless the said acts have been committed on its own territory.

ART. 6. The responsibility of a neutral Power is not engaged by the fact of persons crossing the frontier separately to offer their services to one of the belligerents.

ART. 7. A neutral Power is not called upon to prevent the export or transport, on behalf of one or other of the belligerents, of arms, munitions of war, or, in general, of anything which can be of use to an army or a fleet.

ART. 8. A neutral Power is not called upon to forbid or restrict the use, on behalf of the belligerents, of telegraph or telephone cables or of wireless telegraphy apparatus belonging to it or to companies or private individuals.

ART. 9. Every measure of restriction or prohibition taken by a neutral Power in regard to the matters referred to in Articles 7 and 8 must be impartially applied by it to both belligerents.

A neutral Power must see to the same obligation being observed by companies or private individuals owning telegraph or telephone cables or wireless-telegraphy apparatus.

ART. 10. The fact of a neutral Power resisting, even by force, attempts to violate its neutrality cannot be regarded as a hostile act.

Chapter II. Belligerents Interned and Wounded tended in Neutral Territory

ART. 11. A neutral Power which receives on its territory troops belonging to the belligerent armies shall intern them, as far as possible, at a distance from the theater of war.

It may keep them in camps and even confine them in fortresses or in places set apart for this purpose.

It shall decide whether officers can be left at liberty on giving their parole not to leave the neutral territory without permission.

ART. 12. In the absence of a special convention to the contrary, the neutral Power shall supply the interned with the food, clothing, and relief required by humanity.

At the conclusion of peace the expenses caused by the internment shall be made good.

ART. 13. A neutral Power which receives escaped prisoners of war shall leave them at liberty. If it allows them to remain in its territory it may assign them a place of residence.

The same rule applies to prisoners of war brought by troops taking refuge in the territory of a neutral Power.

ART. 14. A neutral Power may authorize the passage into its territory of the sick and wounded belonging to the belligerent armies, on condition that the trains bringing them shall carry neither personnel or war material. In such a case the neutral Power is bound to take whatever measures of safety and control are necessary for the purpose.

The sick or wounded brought under these conditions into neutral territory by one of the belligerents, and belonging to the hostile party, must be guarded by the neutral Power so as to insure their not taking part again in the military operations. The same duty shall devolve on the neutral state with regard to wounded or sick of the other army who may be committed to its care.

ART. 15. The Geneva convention applies to sick and wounded interned in neutral territory.

Chapter III. Neutral Persons

ART. 16. The nationals of a state which is not taking part in the war are considered as neutrals.

ART. 17. A neutral cannot avail himself of his neutrality:

a. If he commits hostile acts against a belligerent;

b. If he commits acts in favor of a belligerent, particularly if he voluntarily enlists in the ranks of the armed force of one of the parties.

In such a case the neutral shall not be more severely treated by the belligerent as against whom he has abandoned his neutrality than a national of the other belligerent state could be for the same act.

ART. 18. The following acts shall not be considered as committed in favor of one belligerent in the sense of Article 17, letter *b*:

a. Supplies furnished or loans made to one of the belligerents, provided that the person who furnishes the supplies or who makes the loans lives neither in the territory of the other party nor in the territory occupied by him, and that the supplies do not come from these territories;

b. Services rendered in matters of police or civil administration.

Chapter IV. Railway Material

ART. 19. Railway material coming from the territory of neutral Powers, whether it be the property of the said Powers or of companies or private persons, and recognizable as such, shall not be requisitioned or utilized by a belligerent except where and to the extent that it is absolutely necessary. It shall be sent back as soon as possible to the country of origin.

A neutral Power may likewise, in case of necessity, retain and utilize to an equal extent material coming from the territory of the belligerent Power.

Compensation shall be paid by one party or the other in proportion to the material used, and to the period of usage.

Chapter V. Final Provisions

ART. 20. The provisions of the present convention do not apply except between contracting Powers, and then only if all the belligerents are parties to the convention.

ART. 21. The present convention shall be ratified as soon as possible.

The ratifications shall be deposited at The Hague.

The first deposit of ratifications shall be recorded in a *procès-verbal* signed by the representatives of the Powers which take part therein and by the Netherland minister for foreign affairs.

The subsequent deposits of ratifications shall be made by means of a written notification, addressed to the Netherland government and accompanied by the instrument of ratification.

A duly certified copy of the *procès-verbal* relative to the first deposit of ratifications, of the notifications mentioned in the preceding paragraph, and of the instruments of ratification shall be immediately sent by the Netherland government, through the diplomatic channel, to the Powers invited to the second peace conference as well as to the other Powers which have adhered to the convention. In the cases contemplated in the preceding paragraph the said government shall at the same time inform them of the date on which it received the notification.

ART. 22. Nonsignatory Powers may adhere to the present convention.

The Power which desires to adhere notifies its intention in writing to the Netherland government, forwarding to it the act of adhesion, which shall be deposited in the archives of the said government.

This government shall immediately forward to all the other Powers a duly certified copy of the notification as well as of the act of adhesion, mentioning the date on which it received the notification.

ART. 23. The present convention shall come into force, in the case of the Powers which were a party to the first deposit of ratifications, sixty days after the date of the *procès-verbal* of this deposit; and, in the case of the Powers which ratify subsequently or which adhere, sixty days after the notification of their ratification or of their adhesion has been received by the Netherland government.

ART. 24. In the event of one of the contracting Powers wishing to denounce the present convention, the denunciation shall be notified in writing to the Netherland government, which shall immediately communicate a duly certified copy of the notification to all the other Powers, informing them at the same time of the date on which it was received.

The denunciation shall only have effect in regard to the notifying Power, and one year after the notification has reached the Netherland government.

ART. 25. A register kept by the Netherland ministry of foreign affairs shall give the date of the deposit of ratifications made in virtue of Article 21, paragraphs 3 and 4, as well as the date on which the notifications of adhesion (Article 22, paragraph 2) or of denunciation (Article 24, paragraph 1) have been received.

Each contracting Power is entitled to have access to this register and to be supplied with duly certified extracts from it.

In faith whereof the plenipotentiaries have appended their signatures to the present convention.

Done at The Hague, the 18th October, 1907, in a single copy, which shall remain deposited in the archives of the Netherland government, and duly certified copies of which shall be sent, through the diplomatic channel, to the Powers which have been invited to the second peace conference.

CONVENTION RELATIVE TO THE STATUS OF ENEMY MERCHANT SHIPS AT THE OUTBREAK OF HOSTILITIES

His Majesty the German Emperor, King of Prussia; etc.:

Anxious to insure the security of international commerce against the surprises of war, and wishing, in accordance with modern practice, to protect as far as possible operations undertaken in good faith and in process of being carried out before the outbreak of hostilities,

Have resolved to conclude a convention to this effect, and have appointed the following persons as their plenipotentiaries:

[Names of plenipotentiaries]

Who, after having deposited their full powers, found in good and due form, have agreed upon the following provisions:

ART. 1. When a merchant ship belonging to one of the belligerent Powers is at the commencement of hostilities in an enemy port, it is desirable that it should be allowed to depart freely, either immediately or after a reasonable number of days of grace, and to proceed, after being furnished with a pass, direct to its port of destination or any other port indicated.

The same rule should apply in the case of a ship which has left its last port of departure before the commencement of the war and entered a port belonging to the enemy while still ignorant that hostilities had broken out.

ART. 2. A merchant ship unable, owing to circumstances of *force majeure*, to leave the enemy port within the period contemplated in the above article, or which was not allowed to leave, cannot be confiscated.

The belligerent may only detain it, without payment of compensation, but subject to the obligation of restoring it after the war, or requisition it on payment of compensation.

ART. 3. Enemy merchant ships which left their last port of departure before the commencement of the war, and are encountered on the high seas while still ignorant of the outbreak of hostilities cannot be confiscated. They are only liable to detention on the understanding that they shall be restored after the war without compensation, or to be requisitioned, or even destroyed, on payment of compensation, but in such case provision must be made for the safety of the persons on board as well as the security of the ship's papers.

After touching at a port in their own country or at a neutral port, these ships are subject to the laws and customs of maritime war.

ART. 4. Enemy cargo on board the vessels referred to in Articles 1 and 2 is likewise liable to be detained and restored after the termination of the war without payment of compensation, or to be requisitioned on payment of compensation, with or without the ship.

The same rule applies in the case of cargo on board the vessels referred to in Article 3.

ART. 5. The present convention does not affect merchant ships whose build shows that they are intended for conversion into warships.

ART. 6. The provisions of the present convention do not apply except between contracting Powers, and then only if all the belligerents are parties to the convention.

ART. 7. The present convention shall be ratified as soon as possible.

The ratifications shall be deposited at The Hague.

The first deposit of ratifications shall be recorded in a *procès-verbal* signed by the representatives of the Powers which take part therein and by the Netherland minister for foreign affairs.

The subsequent deposits of ratifications shall be made by means of a written notification addressed to the Netherland government and accompanied by the instrument of ratification.

A duly certified copy of the *procès-verbal* relative to the first deposit of ratifications, of the notifications mentioned in the preceding paragraph, as well as of the instruments of ratification, shall be at once sent by the Netherland government, through the diplomatic channel, to the Powers invited to the second peace conference, as well as to the other Powers which have adhered to the convention. In the cases contemplated in the preceding paragraph the said government shall at the same time inform them of the date on which it received the notification.

ART. 8. Nonsignatory Powers may adhere to the present convention.

The Power which desires to adhere notifies in writing its intention to the Netherland government, forwarding to it the act of adhesion, which shall be deposited in the archives of the said government.

The said government shall at once transmit to all the other Powers a duly certified copy of the notification as well as of the act of adhesion, stating the date on which it received the notification.

ART. 9. The present convention shall come into force, in the case of the Powers which were a party to the first deposit of ratifications, sixty days after the date of the *procès-verbal* of that deposit; and, in the case of the Powers which ratify subsequently or which adhere, sixty days after the notification of their ratification or of their adhesion has been received by the Netherland government.

ART. 10. In the event of one of the contracting Powers wishing to denounce the present convention, the denunciation shall be notified in writing to the Netherland government, which shall at once communicate a certified copy of the notification to all the other Powers, informing them of the date on which it was received.

The denunciation shall only have effect in regard to the notifying Power, and one year after the notification has reached the Netherland government.

ART. 11. A register kept by the ministry for foreign affairs shall give the date of the deposit of ratifications made in virtue of Article 7, paragraphs 3 and 4, as well as the date on which the notifications of adhesion (Article 8, paragraph 2) or of denunciation (Article 10, paragraph 1) have been received.

Each contracting Power is entitled to have access to this register and to be supplied with certified extracts from it.

In faith whereof the plenipotentiaries have appended to the present convention their signatures.

Done at The Hague, the 18th October, 1907, in a single copy, which shall remain deposited in the archives of the Netherland government, and duly certified copies of which shall be sent, through the diplomatic channel, to the Powers which have been invited to the second peace conference.

CONVENTION RELATIVE TO THE CONVERSION OF MERCHANT SHIPS INTO WARSHIPS

His majesty the German Emperor, King of Prussia; etc.:

Whereas it is desirable, in view of the incorporation in time of war of merchant ships in the fighting fleet, to define the conditions subject to which this operation may be effected;

Whereas, however, the contracting Powers have been unable to come to an agreement on the question whether the conversion of a merchant ship into a warship may take place upon the high seas, it is understood that the question of the place where such conversion is effected remains outside the scope of this agreement and is in no way affected by the following rules;

Being desirous of concluding a convention to this effect, have appointed the following as their plenipotentiaries:

[Names of plenipotentiaries]

Who, after having deposited their full powers, found in good and due form, have agreed upon the following provisions:

ART. 1. A merchant ship converted into a warship cannot have the rights and duties accruing to such vessels unless it is placed under the direct authority, immediate control, and responsibility of the Power whose flag it flies.

ART. 2. Merchant ships converted into warships must bear the external marks which distinguish the warships of their nationality.

ART. 3. The commander must be in the service of the state and duly commissioned by the competent authorities. His name must figure on the list of the officers of the fighting fleet.

ART. 4. The crew must be subject to military discipline.

ART. 5. Every merchant ship converted into a warship must observe in its operations the laws and customs of war.

ART. 6. A belligerent who converts a merchant ship into a warship must, as soon as possible, announce such conversion in the list of warships.

ART. 7. The provisions of the present convention do not apply except between contracting Powers, and then only if all the belligerents are parties to the convention.

ART. 8. The present convention shall be ratified as soon as possible.

The ratifications shall be deposited at The Hague.

The first deposit of ratifications shall be recorded in a *procès-verbal* signed by the representatives of the Powers who take part therein, and by the Netherland minister for foreign affairs.

The subsequent deposits of ratifications shall be made by means of a written notification, addressed to the Netherland government and accompanied by the instrument of ratification.

A duly certified copy of the *procès-verbal* relative to the first deposit of ratifications, of the notifications mentioned in the preceding paragraph, as well as of the instruments of ratification, shall be at once sent by the Netherland government, through the diplomatic channel, to the Powers invited to the second peace conference, as well as to the other Powers which have adhered to the convention. In the cases contemplated in the preceding paragraph the said government shall at the same time inform them of the date on which it received the notification.

ART. 9. Nonsignatory Powers may adhere to the present convention.

The Power which desires to adhere notifies its intention in writing to the Netherland government, forwarding to it the act of adhesion, which shall be deposited in the archives of the said government.

That government shall at once transmit to all the other Powers a duly certified copy of the notification as well as of the act of adhesion, stating the date on which it received the notification.

ART. 10. The present convention shall come into force, in the case of the Powers which were a party to the first deposit of ratifications, sixty days after the date of the *procès-verbal* of this deposit; and, in the case of the Powers which ratify subsequently or which adhere, sixty days after the notification of their ratification or of their adhesion has been received by the Netherland government.

ART. 11. In the event of one of the contracting Powers wishing to denounce the present convention, the denunciation shall be notified in writing to the Netherland government, which shall at once communicate a duly certified copy of the notification to all the other Powers, informing them of the date on which it was received.

The denunciation shall only have effect in regard to the notifying Power, and one year after the notification has reached the Netherland government.

ART. 12. A register kept by the Netherland ministry for foreign affairs shall give the date of the deposit of ratifications made in virtue of Article 8, paragraphs 3 and 4, as well as the date on which the notifications of adhesion (Article 9, paragraph 2) or of denunciation (Article 11, paragraph 1) have been received.

Each contracting Power is entitled to have access to this register and to be supplied with duly certified extracts from it.

In faith whereof the plenipotentiaries have appended their signatures to the present convention.

Done at The Hague, the 18th October, 1907, in a single copy, which shall remain deposited in the archives of the Netherland government, and duly certified copies of which shall be sent, through the diplomatic channel, to the Powers which have been invited to the second peace conference.

CONVENTION RELATIVE TO THE LAYING OF AUTOMATIC SUBMARINE CONTACT MINES

His Majesty the German Emperor, King of Prussia; etc.:

Inspired by the principle of the freedom of sea routes, the common highways of all nations;

Seeing that, although the existing position of affairs makes it impossible to forbid the employment of automatic submarine contact mines, it is nevertheless desirable to restrict and regulate their employment in order to mitigate the severity of war and to insure, as far as possible, to peaceful navigation the security to which it is entitled despite the existence of war;

Until such time as it is found possible to formulate rules on the subject which shall insure to the interests involved all the guarantees desirable;

Have resolved to conclude a convention for this purpose, and have appointed the following as their plenipotentiaries:

[Names of plenipotentiaries]

Who, after having deposited their full powers, found in good and due form, have agreed upon the following provisions:

ART. 1. It is forbidden:

(1) To lay unanchored automatic contact mines, except when they are so constructed as to become harmless one hour at most after the person who laid them ceases to control them;

(2) To lay anchored automatic contact mines which do not become harmless as soon as they have broken loose from their moorings;

(3) To use torpedoes which do not become harmless when they have missed their mark.

ART. 2. It is forbidden to lay automatic contact mines off the coast and ports of the enemy, with the sole object of intercepting commercial shipping.

ART. 3. When anchored automatic contact mines are employed, every possible precaution must be taken for the security of peaceful shipping.

The belligerents undertake to do their utmost to render these mines harmless within a limited time, and, should they cease to be under surveillance, to notify the danger zones as soon as military exigencies permit, by a notice addressed to shipowners, which must also be communicated to the governments through the diplomatic channel.

ART. 4. Neutral Powers which lay automatic contact mines off their coasts must observe the same rules and take the same precautions as are imposed on belligerents.

The neutral Power must inform shipowners, by a notice issued in advance, where automatic contact mines have been laid. This notice must be communicated at once to the governments through the diplomatic channel.

ART. 5. At the close of the war the contracting Powers undertake to do their utmost to remove the mines which they had laid, each Power removing its own mines.

As regards anchored automatic contact mines laid by one of the belligerents off the coast of the other, their position must be notified to the other party by the Power which laid them, and each Power must proceed with the least possible delay to remove the mines in its own waters.

ART. 6. The contracting Powers which do not at present own perfected mines of the pattern contemplated in the present convention, and which, consequently, could not at present carry out the rules laid down in Articles 1 and 3, undertake to convert the *matériel* of their mines as soon as possible, so as to bring it into conformity with the foregoing requirements.

ART. 7. The provisions of the present convention do not apply except between contracting Powers, and then only if all the belligerents are parties to the convention.

ART. 8. The present convention shall be ratified as soon as possible.

The ratifications shall be deposited at The Hague.

The first deposit of ratifications shall be recorded in a *procès-verbal* signed by the representatives of the Powers which take part therein, and by the Netherland minister for foreign affairs.

The subsequent deposits of ratifications shall be made by means of a written notification addressed to the Netherland government and accompanied by the instrument of ratification.

A duly certified copy of the *procès-verbal* relative to the first deposit of ratifications, of the notifications mentioned in the preceding paragraph, as well as of the instruments of ratification, shall be at once sent by the Netherland government, through the diplomatic channel, to the Powers invited to the second peace conference, as well as to the other Powers which have adhered to the convention. In the cases contemplated in the preceding paragraph the said government shall inform them at the same time of the date on which it has received the notification.

ART. 9. Nonsignatory Powers may adhere to the present convention.

The Power which desires to adhere notifies in writing its intention to the Netherland government, transmitting to it the act of adhesion, which shall be deposited in the archives of the said government.

This government shall at once transmit to all the other Powers a duly certified copy of the notification as well as of the act of adhesion, stating the date on which it received the notification.

ART. 10. The present convention shall come into force, in the case of the Powers which were a party to the first deposit of ratifications, sixty days after the date of the *procès-verbal* of this deposit; and, in the case of the Powers which ratify subsequently or adhere, sixty days after the notification of their ratification or of their adhesion has been received by the Netherland government.

ART. 11. The present convention shall remain in force for seven years, dating from the sixtieth day after the date of the first deposit of ratifications.

Unless denounced, it shall continue in force after the expiration of this period.

The denunciation shall be notified in writing to the Netherland government, which shall at once communicate a duly certified copy of the notification to all the Powers, informing them of the date on which it was received.

The denunciation shall only have effect in regard to the notifying Power, and six months after the notification has reached the Netherland government.

ART. 12. The contracting Powers undertake to reopen the question of the employment of automatic contact mines six months before the expiration of the period contemplated in the first paragraph of the preceding article, in the event of the question not having been already reopened and settled by the third peace conference.

If the contracting Powers conclude a fresh convention relative to the employment of mines, the present convention shall cease to be applicable from the moment it comes into force.

ART. 13. A register kept by the Netherland ministry for foreign affairs shall give the date of the deposit of ratifications made in virtue of Article 8, paragraphs 3 and 4, as well as the date on which the notifications of adhesion (Article 9, paragraph 2) or of denunciation (Article 11, paragraph 3) have been received.

Each contracting Power is entitled to have access to this register and to be supplied with duly certified extracts from it.

In faith whereof the plenipotentiaries have appended their signatures to the present convention.

Done at The Hague, the 18th October, 1907, in a single copy, which shall remain deposited in the archives of the Netherland government, and duly certified copies of which shall be sent, through the diplomatic channel, to the Powers which have been invited to the second peace conference.

CONVENTION RESPECTING BOMBARDMENT BY NAVAL FORCES IN TIME OF WAR

His Majesty the German Emperor, King of Prussia; etc.:

Animated by the desire to realize the wish expressed by the first peace conference respecting the bombardment by naval forces of undefended ports, towns, and villages;

Whereas it is expedient that bombardments by naval forces should be subject to rules of general application which would safeguard the rights of the inhabitants and assure the preservation of the more important buildings, by applying as far as possible to this operation of war the principles of the regulation of 1899 respecting the laws and customs of land war;

Actuated, accordingly, by the desire to serve the interests of humanity and to diminish the severity and disasters of war;

Have resolved to conclude a convention to this effect, and have, for this purpose, appointed the following as their plenipotentiaries:

[Names of plenipotentiaries]

Who, after depositing their full powers, found in good and due form, have agreed upon the following provisions:

Chapter I. The Bombardment of Undefended Ports, Towns, Villages, Dwellings, or Buildings

ART. 1. The bombardment by naval forces of undefended ports, towns, villages, dwellings, or buildings is forbidden.

A place cannot be bombarded solely because automatic submarine contact mines are anchored off the harbor.

ART. 2. Military works, military or naval establishments, depots of arms or war *matériel*, workshops or plant which could be utilized for the needs of the hostile fleet or army, and the ships of war in the harbor, are not, however, included in this prohibition. The commander of a naval force may destroy them with artillery, after a summons followed by a reasonable time of waiting, if all other means are impossible, and when the local authorities have not themselves destroyed them within the time fixed.

He incurs no responsibility for any unavoidable damage which may be caused by a bombardment under such circumstances.

If for military reasons immediate action is necessary, and no delay can be allowed the enemy, it is understood that the prohibition to bombard the undefended town holds good, as in the case given in paragraph 1, and that the commander shall take all due measures in order that the town may suffer as little harm as possible.

ART. 3. After due notice has been given, the bombardment of undefended ports, towns, villages, dwellings, or buildings may be commenced, if the local authorities, after a formal summons has been made to them, decline to comply with requisitions for provisions or supplies necessary for the immediate use of the naval force before the place in question.

These requisitions shall be in proportion to the resources of the place. They shall only be demanded in the name of the commander of the said naval force, and they shall, as far as possible, be paid for in cash; if not, they shall be evidenced by receipts.

ART. 4. Undefended ports, towns, villages, dwellings, or buildings may not be bombarded on account of failure to pay money contributions.

Chapter II. General Provisions

ART. 5. In bombardment by naval forces all the necessary measures must be taken by the commander to spare as far as possible sacred edifices, buildings used for artistic, scientific, or charitable purposes, historic monuments, hospitals, and places where the sick or wounded are collected, on the understanding that they are not used at the same time for military purposes.

It is the duty of the inhabitants to indicate such monuments, edifices, or places by visible signs, which shall consist of large stiff rectangular panels divided diagonally into two colored triangular portions, the upper portion black, the lower portion white.

ART. 6. If the military situation permits, the commander of the attacking naval force, before commencing the bombardment, must do his utmost to warn the authorities.

ART. 7. A town or place, even when taken by storm, may not be pillaged.

Chapter III. Final Provisions

ART. 8. The provisions of the present convention do not apply except between contracting Powers, and then only if all the belligerents are parties to the convention.

ART. 9. The present convention shall be ratified as soon as possible.

The ratifications shall be deposited at The Hague.

The first deposit of ratifications shall be recorded in a *procès-verbal* signed by the representatives of the Powers which take part therein, and by the Netherland minister of foreign affairs.

The subsequent deposits of ratifications shall be made by means of a written notification addressed to the Netherland government and accompanied by the instrument of ratification.

A duly certified copy of the *procès-verbal* relative to the first deposit of ratifications, of the notifications mentioned in the preceding paragraph, as well as of the instruments of ratification, shall be at once sent by the Netherland government, through the diplomatic channel, to the Powers invited to the second peace conference, as well as to the other Powers which have adhered to the convention. In the cases contemplated in the preceding paragraph the said government shall inform them at the same time of the date on which it received the notification.

ART. 10. Nonsignatory Powers may adhere to the present convention.

The Power which desires to adhere shall notify its intention to the Netherland government, forwarding to it the act of adhesion, which shall be deposited in the archives of the said government.

This government shall immediately forward to all the other Powers a duly certified copy of the notification, as well as of the act of adhesion, mentioning the date on which it received the notification.

ART. 11. The present convention shall come into force, in the case of the Powers which were a party to the first deposit of ratifications, sixty days after the date of the *procès-verbal* of that deposit; and, in the case of the Powers which ratify subsequently or which adhere, sixty days after the notification of their ratification or of their adhesion has been received by the Netherland government.

ART. 12. In the event of one of the contracting Powers wishing to denounce the present convention, the denunciation shall be notified in writing to the Netherland government, which shall at once communicate a duly certified copy of the notification to all the other Powers, informing them of the date on which it was received.

The denunciation shall only have effect in regard to the notifying Power, and one year after the notification has reached the Netherland government.

ART. 13. A register kept by the Netherland minister for foreign affairs shall give the date of the deposit of ratifications made in virtue of Article 9, paragraphs 3 and 4, as well as the date on which the notifications of adhesion (Article 10, paragraph 2) or of denunciation (Article 12, paragraph 1) have been received.

Each contracting Power is entitled to have access to this register and to be supplied with duly certified extracts from it.

In faith whereof the plenipotentiaries have appended their signatures to the present convention.

Done at The Hague, the 18th October, 1907, in a single copy, which shall remain deposited in the archives of the Netherland government, and duly certified copies of which shall be sent, through the diplomatic channel, to the Powers which have been invited to the second peace conference.

CONVENTION FOR THE ADAPTATION TO NAVAL WAR OF THE PRINCIPLES OF THE GENEVA CONVENTION

His Majesty the German Emperor, King of Prussia; etc.:

Animated alike by the desire to diminish, as far as depends on them, the inevitable evils of war;

And wishing with this object to adapt to maritime warfare the principles of the Geneva convention of the 6th July, 1906;

Have resolved to conclude a convention for the purpose of revising the convention of the 29th July, 1899, relative to this question, and have appointed the following as their plenipotentiaries:

[Names of plenipotentiaries]

Who, after having deposited their full powers, found in good and due form, have agreed upon the following provisions:

ART. 1. Military hospital ships, that is to say, ships constructed or assigned by states specially and solely with a view to assisting the wounded, sick, and shipwrecked, the names of which have been communicated to the belligerent Powers at the commencement or during the course of hostilities, and in any case before they are employed, shall be respected and cannot be captured while hostilities last.

These ships, moreover, are not on the same footing as warships as regards their stay in a neutral port.

ART. 2. Hospital ships, equipped wholly or in part at the expense of private individuals or officially recognized relief societies, shall be likewise respected and exempt from capture, if the belligerent Power to whom they belong has given them an official commission and has notified their names to the hostile Power at the commencement of or during hostilities, and in any case before they are employed.

These ships must be provided with a certificate from the competent authorities declaring that the vessels have been under their control while fitting out and on final departure.

ART. 3. Hospital ships, equipped wholly or in part at the expense of private individuals or officially recognized societies of neutral countries, shall be respected and exempt from capture, on condition that they are placed under the control of one of the belligerents, with the previous consent of their own government and with the authorization of the belligerent himself, and that the latter has notified their name to his adversary at the commencement of or during hostilities, and in any case before they are employed.

ART. 4. The ships mentioned in Articles 1, 2, and 3 shall afford relief and assistance to the wounded, sick, and shipwrecked of the belligerents without distinction of nationality.

The governments undertake not to use these ships for any military purpose.

These vessels must in no wise hamper the movements of the combatants.

During and after an engagement they will act at their own risk and peril.

The belligerents shall have the right to control and search them; they can refuse to help them, order them off, make them take a certain course, and put a commissioner on board; they can even detain them, if important circumstances require it.

As far as possible, the belligerents shall enter in the log of the hospital ships the orders which they give them.

ART. 5. Military hospital ships shall be distinguished by being painted white outside, with a horizontal band of green about a meter and a half in breadth.

The ships mentioned in Articles 2 and 3 shall be distinguished by being painted white outside, with a horizontal band of red about a meter and a half in breadth.

The boats of the ships above mentioned, as also small craft which may be used for hospital work, shall be distinguished by similar painting.

All hospital ships shall make themselves known by hoisting, with their national flag, the white flag with a red cross provided by the Geneva convention; and further, if they belong to a neutral state, by flying at the mainmast the national flag of the belligerent under whose control they are placed.

Hospital ships which, in the terms of Article 4, are detained by the enemy, must haul down the national flag of the belligerent to whom they belong.

The ships and boats above mentioned which wish to insure by night the freedom from interference to which they are entitled, must, subject to the assent of the belligerent they are accompanying, take the necessary measures to render their special painting sufficiently plain.

ART. 6. The distinguishing signs referred to in Article 5 can only be used, whether in time of peace or war, for protecting or indicating the ships therein mentioned.

ART. 7. In the case of a fight on board a warship, the sick wards shall be respected and spared as far as possible.

The said sick wards and the *matériel* belonging to them remain subject to the laws of war; they cannot, however, be used for any purpose other than that for which they were originally intended, so long as they are required for the sick and wounded.

The commander, however, into whose power they have fallen may apply them to other purposes, if the military situation requires it, after seeing that the sick and wounded on board are properly provided for.

ART. 8. Hospital ships and sick wards of vessels are no longer entitled to protection if they are employed for the purpose of injuring the enemy.

The fact of the staff of the said ships and sick wards being armed for maintaining order and for defending the sick and wounded, and the presence of wireless-telegraphy apparatus on board, is not a sufficient reason for withdrawing protection.

ART. 9. Belligerents may appeal to the charity of the commanders of neutral merchant ships, yachts, or boats to take on board and tend the sick and wounded.

Vessels responding to this appeal, and also vessels which have of their own accord rescued sick, wounded, or shipwrecked men, shall enjoy special protection and certain immunities. In no case can they be captured for having such persons on board, but, apart from special undertakings that have been made to them, they remain liable to capture for any violations of neutrality they may have committed.

ART. 10. The religious, medical, and hospital staff of any captured ship is inviolable, and its members cannot be made prisoners of war. On leaving the ship they take away with them the objects and surgical instruments which are their own private property.

This staff shall continue to discharge its duties while necessary, and can afterwards leave, when the commander in chief considers it possible.

The belligerents must guarantee to the said staff, when it has fallen into their hands, the same allowances and pay which are given to the staff of corresponding rank in their own navy.

ART. 11. Sailors and soldiers on board, when sick or wounded, as well as other persons officially attached to fleets or armies, whatever their nationality, shall be respected and tended by the captors.

ART. 12. Any warship belonging to a belligerent may demand that sick, wounded, or shipwrecked men on board military hospital ships, hospital ships belonging to relief societies or to private individuals, merchant ships, yachts, or boats, whatever the nationality of these vessels, should be handed over.

ART. 13. If sick, wounded, or shipwrecked persons are taken on board a neutral warship, every possible precaution must be taken that they do not again take part in the operations of the war.

ART. 14. The shipwrecked, wounded, or sick of one of the belligerents who fall into the power of the other belligerent are prisoners of war. The captor must decide, according to circumstances, whether to keep them, send them to a port of his own country, to a neutral port, or even to an enemy port. In this last case prisoners thus repatriated cannot serve again while the war lasts.

ART. 15. The shipwrecked, sick, or wounded, who are landed at a neutral port with the consent of the local authorities, must, unless an arrangement is made to the contrary between the neutral state and the belligerent states, be guarded by the neutral state so as to prevent them again taking part in the operations of the war.

The expenses of tending them in hospitals and interning them shall be borne by the state to which the shipwrecked, sick, or wounded persons belong.

ART. 16. After every engagement the two belligerents, so far as military interests permit, shall take steps to look for the shipwrecked, sick, and wounded, and to protect them, as well as the dead, against pillage and ill treatment.

They shall see that the burial, whether by land or sea, or cremation of the dead, shall be preceded by a careful examination of the corpse.

ART. 17. Each belligerent shall send, as early as possible, to the authorities of his country, navy, or army the military marks or documents of identity found on the dead and the description of the sick and wounded picked up by him.

The belligerents shall keep each other informed as to internments and transfers, as well as to the admissions into hospital and deaths, which have occurred among the sick and wounded in their hands. They shall collect all the objects of personal use, valuables, letters, etc., which are found in the captured ships, or which have been left by the sick or wounded who died in hospital, in order to have them forwarded to the persons concerned by the authorities of their own country.

ART. 18. The provisions of the present convention do not apply except between contracting Powers, and then only if all the belligerents are parties to the convention.

ART. 19. The commanders in chief of the belligerent fleets must see that the above articles are properly carried out; they will have also to see to cases not covered thereby, in accordance with the instructions of their respective governments and in conformity with the general principles of the present convention.

ART. 20. The signatory Powers shall take the necessary measures for bringing the provisions of the present convention to the knowledge of their naval forces, and especially of the members entitled thereunder to immunity, and for making them known to the public.

ART. 21. The signatory Powers likewise undertake to enact or to propose to their legislatures, if their criminal laws are inadequate, the measures necessary for checking in time of war individual acts of pillage and ill treatment in respect to the sick and wounded in the fleet, as well as for punishing, as an unjustifiable adoption of naval or military marks, the unauthorized use of the distinctive marks mentioned in Article 5 by vessels not protected by the present convention.

They will communicate to each other, through the Netherland government, the enactments for preventing such acts at the latest within five years of the ratification of the present convention.

ART. 22. In the case of operations of war between the land and sea forces of belligerents, the provisions of the present convention do not apply except between the forces actually on board ship.

ART. 23. The present convention shall be ratified as soon as possible.

The ratifications shall be deposited at The Hague.

The first deposit of ratifications shall be recorded in a *procès-verbal* signed by the representatives of the Powers taking part therein, and by the Netherland minister for foreign affairs.

Subsequent deposits of ratifications shall be made by means of a written notification addressed to the Netherland government and accompanied by the instrument of ratification.

A certified copy of the *procès-verbal* relative to the first deposit of ratifications, of the notifications mentioned in the preceding paragraph, as well as of the instruments of ratification, shall be at once sent by the Netherland government, through the diplomatic channel, to the Powers invited to the second peace conference, as well as to the other Powers which have adhered to the convention. In the cases contemplated in the preceding paragraph the said government shall inform them at the same time of the date on which it received the notification.

ART. 24. Nonsignatory Powers which have accepted the Geneva convention of the 6th July, 1906, may adhere to the present convention.

The Power which desires to adhere notifies its intention to the Netherland government in writing, forwarding to it the act of adhesion, which shall be deposited in the archives of the said government.

The said government shall at once transmit to all the other Powers a duly certified copy of the notification as well as of the act of adhesion, mentioning the date on which it received the notification.

ART. 25. The present convention, duly ratified, shall replace as between contracting Powers the convention of the 29th July, 1899, for the adaptation to maritime warfare of the principles of the Geneva convention.

The convention of 1899 remains in force as between the Powers which signed it, but which do not also ratify the present convention.

ART. 26. The present convention shall come into force, in the case of the Powers which were a party to the first deposit of ratifications, sixty days after the date of the *procès-verbal* of this deposit, and, in the case of the Powers which ratify subsequently or which adhere, sixty days after the notification of their ratification or of their adhesion has been received by the Netherland government.

ART. 27. In the event of one of the contracting Powers wishing to denounce the present convention, the denunciation shall be notified in writing to the Netherland government, which shall at once communicate a duly certified copy of the notification to all the other Powers, informing them at the same time of the date on which it was received.

The denunciation shall only have effect in regard to the notifying Power, and one year after the notification has reached the Netherland government.

ART. 28. A register kept by the Netherland ministry for foreign affairs shall give the date of the deposit of ratifications made in virtue of Article 23, paragraphs 3 and 4, as well as the date on which the notifications of adhesion (Article 24, paragraph 2) or of denunciation (Article 27, paragraph 1) have been received.

Each contracting Power is entitled to have access to this register and to be supplied with duly certified extracts from it.

In faith whereof the plenipotentiaries have appended their signatures to the present convention.

Done at The Hague, the 18th October, 1907, in a single copy, which shall remain deposited in the archives of the Netherland government, and duly certified copies of which shall be sent, through the diplomatic channel, to the Powers which have been invited to the second peace conference.

CONVENTION RELATIVE TO CERTAIN RESTRICTIONS WITH REGARD TO THE EXERCISE OF THE RIGHT OF CAPTURE IN NAVAL WAR

His Majesty the German Emperor, King of Prussia; etc.:

Recognizing the necessity of more effectively insuring than hitherto the equitable application of law to the international relations of maritime Powers in time of war;

Considering that, for this purpose, it is expedient, in giving up or, if necessary, in harmonizing for the common interest certain conflicting practices of long standing, to commence codifying in regulations of general application the guaranties due to peaceful commerce and legitimate business, as well as the conduct of hostilities by sea; that it is expedient to lay down in written mutual engagements the principles which have hitherto remained in the uncertain domain of controversy or have been left to the discretion of governments;

That, from henceforth, a certain number of rules may be made, without affecting the common law now in force with regard to the matters which that law has left unsettled;

Have appointed the following as their plenipotentiaries:

[Names of plenipotentiaries]

Who, after having deposited their full Powers, found in good and due form, have agreed upon the following provisions:

Chapter I. Postal Correspondence

ART. 1. The postal correspondence of neutrals or belligerents, whatever its official or private character may be, found on the high seas on board a neutral or enemy ship, is inviolable. If the ship is detained, the correspondence is forwarded by the captor with the least possible delay.

The provisions of the preceding paragraph do not apply, in case of violation of blockade, to correspondence destined for or proceeding from a blockaded port.

ART. 2. The inviolability of postal correspondence does not exempt a neutral mail ship from the laws and customs of maritime war as to neutral merchant ships in general. The ship, however, may not be searched except when absolutely necessary, and then only with as much consideration and expedition as possible.

Chapter II. The Exemption from Capture of Certain Vessels

ART. 3. Vessels used exclusively for fishing along the coast or small boats employed in local trade are exempt from capture, as well as their appliances, rigging, tackle, and cargo.

They cease to be exempt as soon as they take any part whatever in hostilities.

The contracting Powers agree not to take advantage of the harmless character of the said vessels in order to use them for military purposes while preserving their peaceful appearance.

ART. 4. Vessels charged with religious, scientific, or philanthropic missions are likewise exempt from capture.

Chapter III. Regulations regarding the Crews of Enemy Merchant Ships captured by a Belligerent

ART. 5. When an enemy merchant ship is captured by a belligerent, such of its crew as are nationals of a neutral state are not made prisoners of war.

The same rule applies in the case of the captain and officers likewise nationals of a neutral state, if they promise formally in writing not to serve on an enemy ship while the war lasts.

ART. 6. The captain, officers, and members of the crew, when nationals of the enemy state, are not made prisoners of war, on condition that they make a formal promise in writing not to undertake, while hostilities last, any service connected with the operations of the war.

ART. 7. The names of the persons retaining their liberty under the conditions laid down in Article 5, paragraph 2, and in Article 6, are notified by the belligerent captor to the other belligerent. The latter is forbidden knowingly to employ the said persons.

ART. 8. The provisions of the three preceding articles do not apply to ships taking part in the hostilities.

Chapter IV. Final Provisions

ART. 9. The provisions of the present convention do not apply except between contracting Powers, and then only if all the belligerents are parties to the convention.

ART. 10. The present convention shall be ratified as soon as possible.

The ratifications shall be deposited at The Hague.

The first deposit of ratifications shall be recorded in a *procès-verbal* signed by the representatives of the Powers taking part therein, and by the Netherland minister for foreign affairs.

Subsequent deposits of ratifications shall be made by means of a written notification addressed to the Netherland government and accompanied by the instrument of ratification.

A duly certified copy of the *procès-verbal* relative to the first deposit of ratifications, of the notifications mentioned in the preceding paragraph, as well as of the instruments of ratification, shall be at once sent by the Netherland government, through the diplomatic channel, to the Powers invited to the second peace conference, as well as to the other Powers which have adhered to the convention. In the cases contemplated in the preceding paragraph the said government shall inform them at the same time of the date on which it received the notification.

ART. 11. Nonsignatory Powers may adhere to the present convention.

The Power which desires to adhere notifies its intention in writing to the Netherland government, forwarding to it the act of adhesion, which shall be deposited in the archives of the said government.

This government shall at once transmit to all the other Powers a duly certified copy of the notification as well as of the act of adhesion, mentioning the date on which it received the notification.

ART. 12. The present convention shall come into force, in the case of the Powers which were a party to the first deposit of ratifications, sixty days after the *procès-verbal* of that deposit, and, in the case of the Powers which ratify subsequently or which adhere, sixty days after the notification of their ratification or of their adhesion has been received by the Netherland government.

ART. 13. In the event of one of the contracting Powers wishing to denounce the present convention, the denunciation shall be notified in writing to the Netherland government, which shall at once communicate a duly certified copy of the notification to all the other Powers, informing them of the date on which it was received.

The denunciation shall only have effect in regard to the notifying Power, and one year after the notification has reached the Netherland government.

ART. 14. A register kept by the Netherland ministry for foreign affairs shall give the date of the deposit of ratifications made in virtue of Article 10, paragraphs 3 and 4, as well as the date on which the notifications of adhesion (Article 11, paragraph 2) or of denunciation (Article 13, paragraph 1) have been received.

Each contracting Power is entitled to have access to this register and to be supplied with duly certified extracts from it.

In faith whereof the plenipotentiaries have appended their signatures to the present convention.

Done at The Hague, the 18th October, 1907, in a single copy, which shall remain deposited in the archives of the Netherland government, and duly certified copies of which shall be sent, through the diplomatic channel, to the Powers invited to the second peace conference.

CONVENTION RELATIVE TO THE CREATION OF AN INTERNATIONAL PRIZE COURT

His Majesty the German Emperor, King of Prussia; etc.:

Animated by the desire to settle in an equitable manner the differences which sometimes arise in the course of a naval war in connection with the decisions of national prize courts;

Considering that, if these courts are to continue to exercise their functions in the manner determined by national legislation, it is desirable that in certain cases an appeal should be provided, under conditions conciliating, as far as possible, the public and private interests involved in matters of prize;

Whereas, moreover, the institution of an international court, whose jurisdiction and procedure would be carefully defined, has seemed to be the best method of attaining this object;

Convinced, finally, that in this manner the hardships consequent on naval war would be mitigated; that, in particular, good relations will be more easily maintained between belligerents and neutrals and peace better assured;

Desirous of concluding a convention to this effect, have appointed the following as their plenipotentiaries: [Names of plenipotentiaries]

Who, after depositing their full powers, found in good and due form, have agreed upon the following provisions:

Part I. General Provisions

Art. 1. The validity of the capture of a merchant ship or its cargo is decided before a prize court in accordance with the present convention when neutral or enemy property is involved.

Art. 2. Jurisdiction in matters of prize is exercised in the first instance by the prize courts of the belligerent captor.

The judgments of these courts are pronounced in public or are officially notified to parties concerned who are neutrals or enemies.

Art. 3. The judgments of national prize courts may be brought before the international prize court:

1. When the judgment of the national prize courts affects the property of a neutral Power or individual;

2. When the judgment affects enemy property and relates to:

a. Cargo on board a neutral ship;

b. An enemy ship captured in the territorial waters of a neutral Power, when that Power has not made the capture the subject of a diplomatic claim;

c. A claim based upon the allegation that the seizure has been effected in violation either of the provisions of a convention in force between the belligerent Powers, or of an enactment issued by the belligerent captor.

The appeal against the judgment of the national court can be based on the ground that the judgment was wrong either in fact or in law.

Att. 4. An appeal may be brought:

1. By a neutral Power, if the judgment of the national tribunals injuriously affects its property or the property of its nationals (Article 3, 1), or if the capture of an enemy vessel is alleged to have taken place in the territorial waters of that Power (Article 3, 2, *b*);

2. By a neutral individual, if the judgment of the national court injuriously affects his property (Article 3, 1), subject, however, to the reservation that the Power to which he belongs may forbid him to bring the case before the court, or may itself undertake the proceedings in his place;

3. By an individual subject or citizen of an enemy Power, if the judgment of the national court injuriously affects his property in the cases referred to in Article 3, 2, except that mentioned in paragraph *b*.

Art. 5. An appeal may also be brought on the same conditions as in the preceding article by persons belonging either to neutral states or to the enemy, deriving their rights from and entitled to represent an individual qualified to appeal, and who have taken part in the proceedings before the national court. Persons so entitled may appeal separately to the extent of their interest.

The same rule applies in the case of persons belonging either to neutral states or to the enemy, who derive their rights from and are entitled to represent a neutral Power whose property was the subject of the decision.

Art. 6. When, in accordance with the above Article 3, the international court has jurisdiction, the national courts cannot deal with a case in more than two instances. The municipal law of the belligerent captor shall decide whether the case may be brought before the international court after judgment has been given in first instance or only after an appeal.

If the national courts fail to give final judgment within two years from the date of capture, the case may be carried direct to the international court.

ART. 7. If a question of law to be decided is covered by a treaty in force between the belligerent captor and a Power which is itself, or whose subject or citizen is, a party to the proceedings, the court is governed by the provisions of the said treaty.

In the absence of such provisions the court shall apply the rules of international law. If no generally recognized rule exists, the court shall give judgment in accordance with the general principles of justice and equity.

The above provisions apply equally to questions relating to the order and mode of proof.

If, in accordance with Article 3, 2, *c*, the ground of appeal is the violation of an enactment issued by the belligerent captor, the court will enforce the enactment.

The court may disregard failure to comply with the procedure laid down in the enactments of the belligerent captor, when it is of opinion that the consequences of complying therewith are unjust and inequitable.

ART. 8. If the court pronounces the capture of the vessel or cargo to be valid, they shall be disposed of in accordance with the laws of the belligerent captor.

If it pronounces the capture to be null, the court shall order restitution of the vessel or cargo, and shall fix, if there is occasion, the amount of the damages. If the vessel or cargo have been sold or destroyed, the court shall determine the compensation to be given to the owner on this account.

If the national court pronounced the capture to be null, the court can only be asked to decide as to the damages.

ART. 9. The contracting Powers undertake to submit in good faith to the decisions of the international prize court and to carry them out with the least possible delay.

PART II. CONSTITUTION OF THE INTERNATIONAL PRIZE COURT

ART. 10. The international prize court is composed of judges and deputy judges, who will be appointed by the contracting Powers, and must all be jurists of known proficiency in questions of international maritime law, and of the highest moral reputation.

The appointment of these judges and deputy judges shall be made within six months after the ratification of the present convention.

ART. 11. The judges and deputy judges are appointed for a period of six years, reckoned from the date on which the notification of their appointment is received by the administrative council established by the convention for the pacific settlement of international disputes of the 29th July, 1899. Their appointments can be renewed.

Should one of the judges or deputy judges die or resign, the same procedure is followed for filling the vacancy as was followed for appointing him. In this case the appointment is made for a fresh period of six years.

ART. 12. The judges of the international prize court are all equal in rank and have precedence according to the date on which the notification of their appointment was received (Article 11, paragraph 1), and if they sit by rota (Article 15, paragraph 2), according to the date on which they entered upon their duties. When the date is the same the senior in age takes precedence.

The deputy judges when acting are assimilated to the judges. They rank, however, after them.

ART. 13. The judges enjoy diplomatic privileges and immunities in the performance of their duties and when outside their own country.

Before taking their seat the judges must swear or make a solemn promise before the administrative council to discharge their duties impartially and conscientiously.

ART. 14. The court is composed of fifteen judges; nine judges constitute a quorum.

A judge who is absent or prevented from sitting is replaced by the deputy judge.

ART. 15. The judges appointed by the following contracting Powers: Germany, the United States of America, Austria-Hungary, France, Great Britain, Italy, Japan, and Russia, are always summoned to sit.

The judges and deputy judges appointed by the other contracting Powers sit by rota as shown in the table annexed to the present convention; their duties may be performed successively by the same person. The same judge may be appointed by several of the said Powers.

ART. 16. If a belligerent Power has, according to the rota, no judge sitting in the court, it may ask that the judge appointed by it should take part in the settlement of all cases arising from the war. Lots shall then be drawn as to which of the judges entitled to sit according to the rota shall withdraw. This arrangement does not affect the judge appointed by the other belligerent.

ART. 17. No judge can sit who has been a party, in any way whatever, to the sentence pronounced by the national courts, or has taken part in the case as counsel or advocate for one of the parties.

No judge or deputy judge can, during his tenure of office, appear as agent or advocate before the international prize court, nor act for one of the parties in any capacity whatever.

ART. 18. The belligerent captor is entitled to appoint a naval officer of high rank to sit as assessor, but with no voice in the decision. A neutral Power which is a party to the proceedings, or whose subject or citizen is a party, has the same right of appointment; if as the result of this last provision more than one Power is concerned, they must agree among themselves, if necessary by lot, on the officer to be appointed.

ART. 19. The court elects its president and vice president by an absolute majority of the votes cast. After two ballots the election is made by a bare majority, and, in case the votes are equal, by lot.

ART. 20. The judges on the international prize court are entitled to traveling allowances in accordance with the regulations in force in their own country, and in addition receive, while the court is sitting or while they are carrying out duties conferred upon them by the court, a sum of 100 Netherland florins per diem.

These payments are included in the general expenses of the court dealt with in Article 47, and are paid through the international bureau established by the convention of the 29th July, 1899.

The judges may not receive from their own government or from that of any other Power any remuneration in their capacity of members of the court.

ART. 21. The seat of the international prize court is at The Hague, and it cannot, except in the case of *force majeure*, be transferred elsewhere without the consent of the belligerents.

ART. 22. The administrative council fulfills, with regard to the international prize court, the same functions as to the Permanent Court of Arbitration, but only representatives of contracting Powers will be members of it.

ART. 23. The international bureau acts as registry to the international prize court and must place its offices and staff at the disposal of the court. It has charge of the archives and carries out the administrative work.

The secretary general of the international bureau acts as registrar.

The necessary secretaries to assist the registrar, translators, and shorthand writers are appointed and sworn in by the court.

ART. 24. The court determines which language it will itself use and what languages may be used before it.

In every case the official language of the national courts which have had cognizance of the case may be used before the court.

ART. 25. Powers which are concerned in a case may appoint special agents to act as intermediaries between themselves and the court. They may also engage counsel or advocates to defend their rights and interests.

ART. 26. A private person concerned in a case will be represented before the court by an attorney, who must be either an advocate qualified to plead before a court of appeal or a high court of one of the contracting states, or a lawyer practicing before a similar court, or, lastly, a professor of law at one of the higher teaching centers of those countries.

ART. 27. For all notices to be served, in particular on the parties, witnesses, or experts, the court may apply direct to the government of the state on whose territory the service is to be carried out. The same rule applies in the case of steps being taken to procure evidence.

The requests for this purpose are to be executed so far as the means at the disposal of the Power applied to under its municipal law allow. They cannot be rejected unless the Power in question considers them calculated to impair its sovereign rights or its safety. If the request is complied with, the fees charged must only comprise the expenses actually incurred.

The court is equally entitled to act through the Power on whose territory it sits.

Notices to be given to parties in the place where the court sits may be served through the international bureau.

Part III. Procedure in the International Prize Court

Art. 28. An appeal to the international prize court is entered by means of a written declaration made in the national court which has already dealt with the case, or addressed to the international bureau; in the latter case the appeal can be entered by telegram.

The period within which the appeal must be entered is fixed at 120 days, counting from the day the decision is delivered or notified (Article 2, paragraph 2).

Art. 29. If the notice of appeal is entered in the national court, this court, without considering the question whether the appeal was entered in due time, will transmit within seven days the record of the case to the international bureau.

If the notice of appeal is sent to the international bureau, the bureau will immediately inform the national court, when possible by telegraph. The latter will transmit the record as provided in the preceding paragraph.

When the appeal is brought by a neutral individual the international bureau at once informs by telegraph the individual's government, in order to enable it to enforce the rights it enjoys under Article 4, paragraph 2.

Art. 30. In the case provided for in Article 6, paragraph 2, the notice of appeal can be addressed to the international bureau only. It must be entered within thirty days of the expiration of the period of two years.

Art. 31. If the appellant does not enter his appeal within the period laid down in Articles 28 or 30, it shall be rejected without discussion.

Provided that he can show that he was prevented from so doing by *force majeure*, and that the appeal was entered within sixty days after the circumstances which prevented him entering it before had ceased to operate, the court can, after hearing the respondent, grant relief from the effect of the above provision.

Art. 32. If the appeal is entered in time, a certified copy of the notice of appeal is forthwith officially transmitted by the court to the respondent.

Art. 33. If, in addition to the parties who are before the court, there are other parties concerned who are entitled to appeal, or if, in the case referred to in Article 29, paragraph 3, the government who has received notice of an appeal has not announced its decision, the court will await, before dealing with the case, the expiration of the period laid down in Articles 28 or 30.

Art. 34. The procedure before the international court includes two distinct parts, — the written pleadings and oral discussions.

The written pleadings consist of the deposit and exchange of cases, counter-cases, and, if necessary, of replies, of which the order is fixed by the court, as also the periods within which they must be delivered. The parties annex thereto all papers and documents of which they intend to make use.

A certified copy of every document produced by one party must be communicated to the other party through the medium of the court.

Art. 35. After the close of the pleadings a public sitting is held on a day fixed by the court.

At this sitting the parties state their view of the case both as to the law and as to the facts.

The court may, at any stage of the proceedings, suspend speeches of counsel, either at the request of one of the parties or on their own initiative, in order that supplementary evidence may be obtained.

ART. 36. The international court may order the supplementary evidence to be taken either in the manner provided by Article 27, or before itself or one or more of the members of the court, provided that this can be done without resort to compulsion or the use of threats.

If steps are to be taken for the purpose of obtaining evidence by members of the court outside the territory where it is sitting, the consent of the foreign government must be obtained.

ART. 37. The parties are summoned to take part in all stages of the proceedings and receive certified copies of the minutes.

ART. 38. The discussions are under the control of the president or vice president, or, in case they are absent or cannot act, of the senior judge present.

The judge appointed by a belligerent party cannot preside.

ART. 39. The discussions take place in public, subject to the right of a government who is a party to the case to demand that they be held in private.

Minutes are taken of these discussions and signed by the president and registrar, and these minutes alone have an authentic character.

ART. 40. If a party does not appear despite the fact that he has been duly cited, or if a party fails to comply with some step within the period fixed by the court, the case proceeds without that party and the court gives judgment in accordance with the material at its disposal.

ART. 41. The court officially notifies to the parties decrees or decisions made in their absence.

ART. 42. The court takes into consideration in arriving at its decision all the facts, evidence, and oral statements.

ART. 43. The court considers its decision in private and the proceedings are secret.

All questions are decided by a majority of the judges present. If the number of judges is even and equally divided, the vote of the junior judge in the order of precedence laid down in Article 12, paragraph 1, is not counted.

ART. 44. The judgment of the court must give the reasons on which it is based. It contains the names of the judges taking part in it, and also of the assessors, if any; it is signed by the president and registrar.

ART. 45. The sentence is pronounced in public sitting, the parties concerned being present or duly summoned to attend; the sentence is officially communicated to the parties.

When this communication has been made, the court transmits to the national prize court the record of the case, together with copies of the various decisions arrived at and of the minutes of the proceedings.

ART. 46. Each party pays its own costs.

The party against whom the court decides bears, in addition, the costs of the trial, and also pays 1 per cent of the value of the subject matter of the case as a contribution to the general expenses of the international court. The amount of these payments is fixed in the judgment of the court.

If the appeal is brought by an individual, he will furnish the international bureau with security to an amount fixed by the court, for the purpose of guaranteeing eventual fulfillment of the two obligations mentioned in the preceding paragraph. The court is entitled to postpone the opening of the proceedings until the security has been furnished.

ART. 47. The general expenses of the international prize court are borne by the contracting Powers in proportion to their share in the composition of the court as laid down in Article 15 and in the annexed table. The appointment of deputy judges does not involve any contribution.

The administrative council applies to the Powers for the funds requisite for the working of the court.

ART. 48. When the court is not sitting, the duties conferred upon it by Article 32, Article 34, paragraphs 2 and 3, Article 35, paragraph 1, and Article 46, paragraph 3, are discharged by a delegation of three judges appointed by the court. This delegation decides by a majority of votes.

ART. 49. The court itself draws up its own rules of procedure, which must be communicated to the contracting Powers.

It will meet to elaborate these rules within a year of the ratification of the present convention.

ART. 50. The court may propose modifications in the provisions of the present convention concerning procedure. These proposals are communicated, through the medium of the Netherland government, to the contracting Powers, which will consider together as to the measures to be taken.

PART IV. FINAL PROVISIONS

ART. 51. The present convention does not apply as of right except when the belligerent Powers are all parties to the convention.

It is further fully understood that an appeal to the international prize court can only be brought by a contracting Power or the subject or citizen of a contracting Power.

In the cases mentioned in Article 5 the appeal is only admitted when both the owner and the person entitled to represent him are equally contracting Powers or the subjects or citizens of contracting Powers.

ART. 52. The present convention shall be ratified and the ratifications shall be deposited at The Hague as soon as all the Powers mentioned in Article 15 and in the table annexed are in a position to do so.

The deposit of the ratifications shall take place, in any case, on the 30th June, 1909, if the Powers which are ready to ratify furnish nine judges and nine deputy judges to the court, qualified to validly constitute a court. If not, the deposit shall be postponed until this condition is fulfilled.

A minute of the deposit of ratifications shall be drawn up, of which a certified copy shall be forwarded, through the diplomatic channel, to each of the Powers referred to in the first paragraph.

ART. 53. The Powers referred to in Article 15 and in the table annexed are entitled to sign the present convention up to the deposit of the ratifications contemplated in paragraph 2 of the preceding article.

After this deposit they can at any time adhere to it, purely and simply. A Power wishing to adhere notifies its intention in writing to the Netherland government, transmitting to it, at the same time, the act of adhesion, which shall be deposited in the archives of the said government. The latter shall send, through the diplomatic channel, a certified copy of the notification and of the act of adhesion to all the Powers referred to in the preceding paragraph, informing them of the date on which it has received the notification.

ART. 54. The present convention shall come into force six months from the deposit of the ratifications contemplated in Article 52, paragraphs 1 and 2.

The adhesions shall take effect sixty days after notification of such adhesion has been received by the Netherland government, or as soon as possible on the expiration of the period contemplated in the preceding paragraph.

The international court shall, however, have jurisdiction to deal with prize cases decided by the national courts at any time after the deposit of the ratifications or of the receipt of the notification of the adhesions. In such cases the period fixed in Article 28, paragraph 2, shall only be reckoned from the date when the convention comes into force as regards a Power which has ratified or adhered.

ART. 55. The present convention shall remain in force for twelve years from the time it comes into force, as determined by Article 54, paragraph 1, even in the case of Powers which adhere subsequently.

It shall be renewed tacitly from six years to six years unless denounced.

Denunciation must be notified in writing, at least one year before the expiration of each of the periods mentioned in the two preceding paragraphs, to the Netherland government, which will inform all the other contracting Powers.

Denunciation shall only take effect in regard to the Power which has notified it. The convention shall remain in force in the case of the other contracting Powers, provided that their participation in the appointment of judges is sufficient to allow of the composition of the court with nine judges and nine deputy judges.

ART. 56. In case the present convention is not in operation as regards all the Powers referred to in Article 15 and the annexed table, the administrative council shall draw up a list, on the lines of that article and table, of the judges and deputy judges through whom the contracting Powers will share in the composition of the court. The times allotted by the said table to judges who are summoned to sit in rota will be redistributed between the different years of the six-year period in such a way that, as far as possible, the number of the judges of the court in each year shall be the same. If the number of deputy judges is greater than that of the judges, the number of the latter can be completed by deputy judges chosen by lot among those Powers which do not nominate a judge.

The list drawn up in this way by the administrative council shall be notified to the contracting Powers. It shall be revised when the number of these Powers is modified as the result of adhesions or denunciations.

The change resulting from an adhesion is not made until the 1st January after the date on which the adhesion takes effect, unless the adhering Power is a belligerent Power, in which case it can ask to be at once represented in the court, the provision of Article 16 being, moreover, applicable if necessary.

When the total number of judges is less than eleven, seven judges form a quorum.

ART. 57. Two years before the expiration of each period referred to in paragraphs 1 and 2 of Article 55 any contracting Power can demand a modification of the provisions of Article 15 and of the annexed table, relative to its participation in the composition of the court. The demand shall be addressed to the administrative council, which will examine it and submit to all the Powers proposals as to the measures to be adopted. The Powers shall inform the administrative council of their decision with the least possible delay. The result shall be at once, and at least one year and thirty days before the expiration of the said period of two years, communicated to the Power which made the demand.

When necessary, the modifications adopted by the Powers shall come into force from the commencement of the new period.

In faith whereof the plenipotentiaries have appended their signatures to the present convention.

Done at The Hague, the 18th October, 1907, in a single copy, which shall remain deposited in the archives of the Netherland government, and duly certified copies of which shall be sent, through the diplomatic channel, to the Powers designated in Article 15 and in the table annexed.

ANNEX TO ARTICLE 15

DISTRIBUTION OF JUDGES AND DEPUTY JUDGES BY COUNTRIES FOR EACH YEAR OF THE PERIOD OF SIX YEARS

Judges	Deputy Judges	Judges	Deputy Judges
First Year		*Third Year*	
1. Argentina	Paraguay	1. Brazil	Santo Domingo
2. Colombia	Bolivia	2. China	Turkey
3. Spain	Spain	3. Spain	Portugal
4. Greece	Roumania	4. Netherlands	Switzerland
5. Norway	Sweden	5. Roumania	Greece
6. Netherlands	Belgium	6. Sweden	Denmark
7. Turkey	Persia	7. Venezuela	Haiti
Second Year		*Fourth Year*	
1. Argentina	Panama	1. Brazil	Guatemala
2. Spain	Spain	2. China	Turkey
3. Greece	Roumania	3. Spain	Portugal
4. Norway	Sweden	4. Peru	Honduras
5. Netherlands	Belgium	5. Roumania	Greece
6. Turkey	Luxemburg	6. Sweden	Denmark
7. Uruguay	Costa Rica	7. Switzerland	Netherlands

Judges	Deputy Judges	Judges	Deputy Judges
Fifth Year		*Sixth Year*	
1. Belgium	Netherlands	1. Belgium	Netherlands
2. Bulgaria	Montenegro	2. Chile	Salvador
3. Chile	Nicaragua	3. Denmark	Norway
4. Denmark	Norway	4. Mexico	Ecuador
5. Mexico	Cuba	5. Portugal	Spain
6. Persia	China	6. Servia	Bulgaria
7. Portugal	Spain	7. Siam	China

CONVENTION CONCERNING THE RIGHTS AND DUTIES OF NEUTRAL POWERS IN NAVAL WAR

His Majesty the German Emperor, King of Prussia; etc.:

With a view to harmonizing the divergent views which, in the event of naval war, are still held on the relations between neutral Powers and belligerent Powers, and to anticipating the difficulties to which such divergence of views might give rise;

Seeing that, even if it is not possible at present to concert measures applicable to all circumstances which may in practice occur, it is nevertheless undeniably advantageous to frame, as far as possible, rules of general application to meet the case where war has unfortunately broken out;

Seeing that, in cases not covered by the present convention, it is expedient to take into consideration the general principles of the law of nations;

Seeing that it is desirable that the Powers should issue detailed enactments to regulate the results of the attitude of neutrality when adopted by them;

Seeing that it is, for neutral Powers, an admitted duty to apply these rules impartially to the several belligerents;

Seeing that, in this category of ideas, these rules should not, in principle, be altered, in the course of the war, by a neutral Power, except in a case where experience has shown the necessity for such change for the protection of the rights of that Power;

Have agreed to observe the following common rules, which cannot, however, modify provisions laid down in existing general treaties, and have appointed as their plenipotentiaries, namely:

[Names of plenipotentiaries]

Who, after having deposited their full powers, found in good and due form, have agreed upon the following provisions:

Art. 1. Belligerents are bound to respect the sovereign rights of neutral Powers and to abstain, in neutral territory or neutral waters, from any act which would, if knowingly permitted by any Power, constitute a violation of neutrality.

Art. 2. Any act of hostility, including capture and the exercise of the right of search, committed by belligerent warships in the territorial waters of a neutral Power, constitutes a violation of neutrality and is strictly forbidden.

ART. 3. When a ship has been captured in the territorial waters of a neutral Power, this Power must employ, if the prize is still within its jurisdiction, the means at its disposal to release the prize with its officers and crew, and to intern the prize crew.

If the prize is not in the jurisdiction of the neutral Power, the captor government, or, the demand of that Power, must liberate the prize with its officers and crew.

ART. 4. A prize court cannot be set up by a belligerent on neutral territory or on a vessel in neutral waters.

ART. 5. Belligerents are forbidden to use neutral ports and waters as a base of naval operations against their adversaries, and in particular to erect wireless-telegraphy stations or any apparatus for the purpose of communicating with the belligerent forces on land or sea.

ART. 6. The supply, in any manner, directly or indirectly, by a neutral Power to a belligerent Power, of warships, ammunition, or war material of any kind whatever, is forbidden.

ART. 7. A neutral Power is not bound to prevent the export or transit, for the use of either belligerent, of arms, ammunitions, or, in general, of anything which could be of use to an army or fleet.

ART. 8. A neutral government is bound to employ the means at its disposal to prevent the fitting out or arming of any vessel within its jurisdiction which it has reason to believe is intended to cruise, or engage in hostile operations, against a Power with which that government is at peace. It is also bound to display the same vigilance to prevent the departure from its jurisdiction of any vessel intended to cruise or engage in hostile operations, which had been adapted entirely or partly within the said jurisdiction for use in war.

ART. 9. A neutral Power must apply impartially to the two belligerents the conditions, restrictions, or prohibitions made by it in regard to the admission into its ports, roadsteads, or territorial waters, of belligerent warships or of their prizes.

Nevertheless a neutral Power may forbid a belligerent vessel which has failed to conform to the orders and regulations made by it, or which has violated neutrality, to enter its ports or roadsteads.

ART. 10. The neutrality of a Power is not affected by the mere passage through its territorial waters of warships or prizes belonging to belligerents.

ART. 11. A neutral Power may allow belligerent warships to employ its licensed pilots.

ART. 12. In the absence of special provisions to the contrary in the legislation of a neutral Power, belligerent warships are not permitted to remain in the ports, roadsteads, or territorial waters of the said Power for more than twenty-four hours, except in the cases covered by the present convention.

ART. 13. If a Power which has been informed of the outbreak of hostilities learns that a belligerent warship is in one of its ports or roadsteads, or in its territorial waters, it must notify the said ship to depart within twenty-four hours or within the time prescribed by local regulations.

ART 14. A belligerent warship may not prolong its stay in a neutral port beyond the permissible time, except on account of damage or stress of weather. It must depart as soon as the cause of the delay is at an end.

The regulations as to the question of the length of time which these vessels may remain in neutral ports, roadsteads, or waters do not apply to warships devoted exclusively to religious, scientific, or philanthropic purposes.

ART. 15. In the absence of special provisions to the contrary in the legislation of a neutral Power, the maximum number of warships belonging to a belligerent which may be in one of the ports or roadsteads of that Power simultaneously shall be three.

ART. 16. When warships belonging to both belligerents are present simultaneously in a neutral port or roadstead, a period of not less than twenty-four hours must elapse between the departure of the ship belonging to one belligerent and the departure of the ship belonging to the other.

The order of departure is determined by the order of arrival, unless the ship which arrived first is so circumstanced that an extension of its stay is permissible.

A belligerent warship may not leave a neutral port or roadstead until twenty-four hours after the departure of a merchant ship flying the flag of its adversary.

ART. 17. In neutral ports and roadsteads belligerent warships may only carry out such repairs as are absolutely necessary to render them seaworthy, and may not add in any manner whatsoever to their fighting force. The local authorities of the neutral Power shall decide what repairs are necessary, and these must be carried out with the least possible delay.

ART. 18. Belligerent warships may not make use of neutral ports, roadsteads, and territorial waters, for replenishing or increasing their supplies of war material or their armament, or for completing their crews.

ART. 19. Belligerent warships may only revictual in neutral ports or roadsteads to bring up their supplies to the peace standard.

Similarly these vessels may only ship sufficient fuel to enable them to reach the nearest port in their own country. They may, on the other hand, fill up their bunkers built to carry fuel, when in neutral countries which have adopted this method of determining the amount of fuel to be supplied.

If, in accordance with the law of the neutral Power, the ships are not supplied with coal within twenty-four hours of their arrival, the permissible duration of their stay is extended by twenty-four hours.

ART. 20. Belligerent warships which have shipped fuel in a port belonging to a neutral Power may not within the succeeding three months replenish their supply in a port of the same Power.

ART. 21. A prize may only be brought into a neutral port on account of unseaworthiness, stress of weather, or want of fuel or provisions.

It must leave as soon as the circumstances which justified its entry are at an end. If it does not, the neutral Power must order it to leave at once; should it fail to obey, the neutral Power must employ the means at its disposal to release it with its officers and crew and to intern the prize crew.

ART. 22. A neutral Power must, similarly, release a prize brought into one of its ports under circumstances other than those referred to in Article 21.

ART. 23. A neutral Power may allow prizes to enter its ports and roadsteads, whether under convoy or not, when they are brought there to be sequestrated pending the decision of a prize court. It may have the prize taken to another of its ports.

If the prize is convoyed by a warship, the prize crew may go on board the convoying ship.

If the prize is not under convoy, the prize crew are left at liberty.

ART. 24. If, notwithstanding the notification of the neutral Power, a belligerent ship of war does not leave a port where it is not entitled to remain, the neutral Power is entitled to take such measures as it considers necessary to render the ship incapable of taking the sea during the war, and the commanding officer of the ship must facilitate the execution of such measures.

When a belligerent ship is detained by a neutral Power, the officers and crew are likewise detained.

The officers and crew thus detained may be left in the ship or kept either on another vessel or on land, and may be subjected to the measures of restriction which it may appear necessary to impose upon them. A sufficient number of men for looking after the vessel must, however, be always left on board.

The officers may be left at liberty on giving their word not to quit the neutral territory without permission.

ART. 25. A neutral Power is bound to exercise such surveillance as the means at its disposal allow, to prevent any violation of the provisions of the above articles occurring in its ports or roadsteads or in its waters.

ART. 26. The exercise by a neutral Power of the rights laid down in the present convention can under no circumstances be considered as an unfriendly act by one or other belligerent who has accepted the article relating thereto.

ART. 27. The contracting Powers shall communicate to each other in due course all laws, proclamations, and other enactments regulating in their respective countries the status of belligerent warships in their ports and waters, by means of a communication addressed to the government of the Netherlands and forwarded immediately by that government to the other contracting Powers.

ART. 28. The provisions of the present convention do not apply except to the contracting Powers, and then only if all the belligerents are parties to the convention.

ART. 29. The present convention shall be ratified as soon as possible.

The ratifications shall be deposited at The Hague.

The first deposit of ratifications shall be recorded in a *procès-verbal* signed by the representatives of the Powers which take part therein, and by the Netherland minister for foreign affairs.

The subsequent deposits of ratifications shall be made by means of a written notification addressed to the Netherland government and accompanied by the instrument of ratification.

A duly certified copy of the *procès-verbal* relative to the first deposit of ratifications, of the notifications mentioned in the preceding paragraph, as well as of the instruments of ratification, shall be at once sent by the Netherland government, through the diplomatic channel, to the Powers invited to the second peace conference, as well as to the other Powers which have adhered to the convention. In the cases contemplated in the preceding paragraph the said government shall inform them at the same time of the date on which it received the notification.

ART. 30. Nonsignatory Powers may adhere to the present convention.

The Power which desires to adhere notifies in writing its intention to the Netherland government, forwarding to it the act of adhesion, which shall be deposited in the archives of the said government.

That government shall at once transmit to all the other Powers a duly certified copy of the notification as well as of the act of adhesion, mentioning the date on which it received the notification.

ART. 31. The present convention shall come into force, in the case of the Powers which were a party to the first deposit of the ratifications, sixty days after the date of the *procès-verbal* of that deposit, and, in the case of the Powers who ratify subsequently or who adhere, sixty days after the notification of their ratification or of their adhesion has been received by the Netherland government.

ART. 32. In the event of one of the contracting Powers wishing to denounce the present convention, the denunciation shall be notified in writing to the Netherland government, who shall at once communicate a duly certified copy of the notification to all the other Powers, informing them of the date on which it was received.

The denunciation shall only have effect in regard to the notifying Power, and one year after the notification has been made to the Netherland government.

ART. 33. A register kept by the Netherland ministry for foreign affairs shall give the date of the deposit of ratifications made by virtue of Article 29, paragraphs 3 and 4, as well as the date on which the notifications of adhesion (Article 30, paragraph 2) or of denunciation (Article 32, paragraph 1) have been received.

Each contracting Power is entitled to have access to this register and to be supplied with duly certified extracts.

In faith whereof the plenipotentiaries have appended their signatures to the present convention.

Done at The Hague, the 18th October, 1907, in a single copy, which shall remain deposited in the archives of the Netherland government, and duly certified copies of which shall be sent, through the diplomatic channel, to the Powers which have been invited to the second peace conference.

DECLARATION PROHIBITING THE DISCHARGE OF PROJECTILES AND EXPLOSIVES FROM BALLOONS

The undersigned, plenipotentiaries of the Powers invited to the second international peace conference at The Hague, duly authorized to that effect by their governments,

Inspired by the sentiments which found expression in the Declaration of St. Petersburg of the 29th November (11th December), 1868, and being desirous of renewing the declaration of The Hague of the 29th July, 1899, which has now expired,

Declare:

The contracting Powers agree to prohibit, for a period extending to the close of the third peace conference, the discharge of projectiles and explosives from balloons or by other new methods of a similar nature.

The present declaration is only binding on the contracting Powers in case of war between two or more of them.

It shall cease to be binding from the time when, in a war between the contracting Powers, one of the belligerents is joined by a noncontracting Power.

The present declaration shall be ratified as soon as possible.

The ratifications shall be deposited at The Hague.

A *procès-verbal* shall be drawn up recording the receipt of the ratifications, of which a duly certified copy shall be sent, through the diplomatic channel, to all the contracting Powers.

Nonsignatory Powers may adhere to the present declaration. To do so, they must make known their adhesion to the contracting Powers by means of a written notification addressed to the Netherland government and communicated by it to all the other contracting Powers.

In the event of one of the high contracting parties denouncing the present declaration, such denunciation shall not take effect until a year after the notification made in writing to the Netherland government and forthwith communicated by it to all the other contracting Powers.

This denunciation shall only have effect in regard to the notifying Power.

In faith whereof the plenipotentiaries have appended their signatures to the present declaration.

Done at The Hague, the 18th October, 1907, in a single copy, which shall remain deposited in the archives of the Netherland government, and duly certified copies of which shall be sent, through the diplomatic channel, to the contracting Powers.

Prior to the germs of modern arbitration and not at all a cause of them, apparently, were certain instances of arbitration in Greece. The *American Journal of International Law* of April, 1911, p. 465, says:

"Instances of arbitration were comparatively frequent in ancient Greece, treaties of arbitration were concluded, and arbitral procedure outlined strikingly similar to the procedure of the present day. Even the tribunal of five judges was known to Greece, and a remarkable instance of arbitration is furnished in the settlement of a controversy between Prienè and Samos some two hundred and forty years before Christ."

Points of this case are given as taken from Newton's "Ancient Greek Inscriptions in the British Museum," edited by the Reverend E. L. Hicks.

CHAPTER VI

WORLD LAW CONCERNING NAVIGATION

An international marine conference was held in Washington, D.C., from October 16 to December 31, 1899, inclusive, upon the invitation of the United States of America. Twenty-eight nations participated. They were as follows, with the number of their representatives respectively: Austria-Hungary, two; Belgium, one; Brazil, two; Chile, two; China, three; Costa Rica, one; Denmark, two; France, five; Germany, five; Great Britain, nine; Guatemala, one; Hawaii, one; Honduras, one; Italy, one; Japan, two; Mexico, two; Netherlands, three; Nicaragua, one; Norway, two; Portugal, one; Russia, one; Siam, one; Spain, two; Sweden, one; Turkey, one; Uruguay, one; Venezuela, two; United States, eight; 64 in all.

The Final Act of the conference shows what action was taken upon each of the general divisions of subjects which were taken up for consideration. In some instances no action whatever was recommended. In other instances recommendations were made in much detail. Such of these as have been ratified by a sufficient number of nations are to be regarded as the will of the world upon the matter in question, and therefore the recommendations have come to have the status of world law. Summarizing the Final Act, it is noted that under the head of General Division 1, — "Marine signals or other means of plainly indicating the direction in which vessels are moving in fog, mist, falling snow, and thick weather, and at night," — the conference adopted a resolution whose opening words are these: "that in the opinion of the conference it is inexpedient to adopt course-indicating sound signals in foggy or thick weather."

Under the head of Regulations for Preventing Collisions at Sea, is given the following body of recommendation, which has become law by ratification by the nations; and it will be noticed that the word "shall" is used as if there were compulsory power behind the declaration.

Preliminary

These rules shall be followed by all vessels upon the high seas and in all waters connected therewith, navigable by seagoing vessels.

In the following rules every steam vessel which is under sail and not under steam is to be considered a sailing vessel, and every vessel under steam, whether under sail or not, is to be considered a steam vessel.

The word "steam-vessel" shall include any vessel propelled by machinery.

A vessel is "under way" within the meaning of these rules when she is not at anchor, or made fast to the shore, or aground.

Rules concerning Lights, etc.

The word "visible" in these rules, when applied to lights, shall mean visible on a dark night with a clear atmosphere.

ART. 1. The rules concerning lights shall be complied with in all weathers from sunset to sunrise, and during such time no other lights which may be mistaken for the prescribed lights shall be exhibited.

ART. 2. A steam vessel when under way shall carry:

(*a*) On or in front of the foremast, or, if a vessel without a foremast, then in the fore part of the vessel, at a height above the hull of not less than 20 feet, and if the breadth of the vessel exceeds 20 feet, then at a height above the hull not less than such breadth, so, however, that the light need not be carried at a greater height above the hull than 40 feet, a bright white light, so constructed as to show an unbroken light over an arc of the horizon of 20 points of the compass, so fixed as to throw the light 10 points on each side of the vessel, viz., from right ahead to two points abaft the beam on either side, and of such a character as to be visible at a distance of at least five miles.

(*b*) On the starboard side a green light so constructed as to show an unbroken light over an arc of the horizon of 10 points of the compass, so fixed as to throw the light from right ahead to two points abaft the beam on the starboard side, and of such a character as to be visible at a distance of at least two miles.

(*c*) On the port side a red light so constructed as to show an unbroken light over an arc of the horizon of 10 points of the compass, so fixed as to throw the light from right ahead to two points abaft the beam on the port side, and of such a character as to be visible at a distance of at least two miles.

(*d*) The said green and red side lights shall be fitted with inboard screens projecting at least three feet forward from the light, so as to prevent these lights from being seen across the bow.

(*e*) A steam vessel when under way may carry an additional white light similar in construction to the light mentioned in subdivision (*a*). These two lights shall be so placed in line with the keel that one shall be at least 15 feet higher than the other and in such a position with reference to the other that the lower light shall be forward of the upper one. The vertical distance between these lights shall be less than the horizontal distance.

ART. 3. A steam vessel when towing another vessel shall, in addition to her side lights, carry two bright white lights in a vertical line one over the other, not less than six feet apart, and when towing more than one vessel shall carry an additional bright white light six feet above or below such lights, if the length of the tow, measuring from the stern of the towing vessel to the stern of the last vessel towed, exceeds 600 feet. Each of these lights shall be of the same construction and character, and shall be carried in the same position as the white light mentioned in Article 2, (*a*), except the additional light, which may be carried at a height of not less than 14 feet above the hull.

Such steam vessel may carry a small white light abaft the funnel or after mast for the vessel towed to steer by, but such light shall not be visible forward of the beam.

ART. 4 (*a*). A vessel which from an accident is not under command shall carry at the same height as the white light mentioned in Article 2, (*a*), where they can best be seen, and if a steam vessel in lieu of that light, two red lights, in a vertical line one over the other, not less than six feet apart, and of such a character as to be visible all round the horizon at a distance of at least two miles; and shall by day carry in a vertical line one over the other, not less than six feet apart, where they can best be seen, two black balls or shapes, each two feet in diameter.

(*b*) A vessel employed in laying or in picking up a telegraph cable shall carry in the same position as the white light mentioned in Article 2, (*a*), and if a steam vessel in lieu of that light, three lights in a vertical line one over the other, not less than six feet apart. The highest and lowest of these lights shall be red, and the middle light shall be white, and they shall be of such a character as to be visible all round the horizon, at a distance of at least two miles. By day she shall carry in a vertical line one over the other, not less than six feet apart, where they can best be seen, three shapes not less than two feet in diameter, of which the highest and lowest shall be globular in shape and red in color, and the middle one diamond in shape and white.

(*c*) The vessels referred to in this article, when not making way through the water, shall not carry the side lights, but when making way shall carry them.

(*d*) The lights and shapes required to be shown by this article are to be taken by other vessels as signals that the vessel showing them is not under command and cannot therefore get out of the way.

These signals are not signals of vessels in distress and requiring assistance. Such signals are contained in Article 31.

ART. 5. A sailing vessel under way and any vessel being towed shall carry the same lights as are prescribed by Article 2 for a steam vessel under way, with the exception of the white lights mentioned therein, which they shall never carry.

ART. 6. Whenever, as in the case of small vessels under way during bad weather, the green and red side lights cannot be fixed, these lights shall be kept at hand, lighted and ready for use; and shall, on the approach of or to other vessels, be exhibited on their respective sides in sufficient time to prevent collision, in such manner as to make them most visible, and so that the green light shall not be seen on the port side nor the red light on the starboard side, nor, if practicable, more than two points abaft the beam on their respective sides.

To make the use of these portable lights more certain and easy, the lanterns containing them shall each be painted outside with the color of the light they respectively contain, and shall be provided with proper screens.

ART. 7. Steam vessels of less than 40, and vessels under oars or sails of less than 20, tons gross tonnage respectively, when under way shall not be obliged to carry the lights mentioned in Article 2, (*a*), (*b*), and (*c*), but if they do not carry them they shall be provided with the following lights:

1. Steam vessels of less than 40 tons shall carry:

(*a*) In the fore part of the vessel, on or in front of the funnel, where it can best be seen, and at a height above the gunwale of not less than nine feet, a bright white light constructed and fixed as prescribed in Article 2, (*a*), and of such a character as to be visible at a distance of at least two miles.

(*b*) Green and red side lights constructed and fixed as prescribed in Article 2, (*b*) and (*c*), and of such a character as to be visible at a distance of at least one mile, or a combined lantern showing a green light and a red light from right ahead to two points abaft the beam on their respective sides. Such lantern shall be carried not less than three feet below the white light.

2. Small steamboats, such as are carried by seagoing vessels, may carry the white light at a less height than nine feet above the gunwale, but it shall be carried above the combined lantern mentioned in subdivision 1, (*b*).

3. Vessels under oars or sails, of less than 20 tons, shall have ready at hand a lantern with a green glass on one side and a red glass on the other, which, on approach of or to other vessels, shall be exhibited in sufficient time to prevent collision, so that the green light shall not be seen on the port side nor the red light on the starboard side.

The vessels referred to in this article shall not be obliged to carry the lights prescribed by Article 4, (*a*), and Article 11, last paragraph.

ART. 8. Pilot vessels, when engaged on their station on pilotage duty, shall not show the lights required for other vessels, but shall carry a white light at the masthead, visible all round the horizon, and shall also exhibit a flare-up light or flare-up lights at short intervals, which shall never exceed 15 minutes.

On the near approach of or to other vessels they shall have their side lights lighted, ready for use, and shall flash or show them at short intervals, to indicate the direction in which they are heading, but the green light shall not be shown on the port side, nor the red light on the starboard side.

A pilot vessel of such a class as to be obliged to go alongside of a vessel to put a pilot on board, may show the white light instead of carrying it at the masthead, and may, instead of the colored lights above mentioned, have at hand ready for use a lantern with a green glass on the one side and a red glass on the other, to be used as prescribed above.

Pilot vessels, when not engaged on their station on pilotage duty, shall carry lights similar to those of other vessels of their tonnage.

ART. 9. Fishing vessels and fishing boats, when under way and when not required by this article to carry or show the lights therein named, shall carry or show the lights prescribed for vessels of their tonnage under way.

(*a*) Vessels and boats when fishing with drift nets shall exhibit two white lights from any part of the vessel where they can best be seen. Such lights shall be placed so that the vertical distance between them shall be not less than six feet and not more than 10 feet, and so that the horizontal distance between them, measured in a line with the keel, shall be not less than five feet and not more than 10 feet. The lower of these two lights shall be the more forward, and both of them shall be of such a character as to show all round the horizon, and to be visible at a distance of not less than three miles.

(*b*) Vessels when engaged in trawling, by which is meant the dragging of an apparatus along the bottom of the sea

1. If steam vessels, shall carry in the same position as the white light mentioned in Article 2, (*a*), a tricolored lantern so constructed and fixed as to show a white light from right ahead to two points on each bow, and a green light and a red light over an arc of the horizon from two points on either bow to two points abaft the beam on the starboard and port sides respectively; and not less than six nor more than 12 feet below the tricolored lantern, a white light in a lantern, so constructed as to show a clear and uniform and unbroken light all round the horizon.

2. If sailing vessels of seven tons gross tonnage and upwards, shall carry a white light in a lantern, so constructed as to show a clear, uniform, and unbroken light all round the horizon, and shall also be provided with a sufficient supply of red pyrotechnic lights, which shall each burn for at least 30 seconds, and shall be shown on the approach of or to other vessels in sufficient time to prevent collision.

In the Mediterranean Sea the vessels referred to in subdivision (*b*), 2, may use a flare-up light in lieu of a pyrotechnic light.

All lights mentioned in subdivision (*b*), 1 and 2, shall be visible at a distance of at least two miles.

3. If sailing vessels of less than seven tons gross tonnage, shall not be obliged to carry the white light mentioned in subdivision (*b*), 2, of this article, but if they do not carry such light, they shall have at hand, ready for use, a lantern showing a bright white light, which shall, on the approach of or to other vessels, be exhibited where it can best be seen, in sufficient time to prevent collision; and they shall also show a red pyrotechnic light, as prescribed in subdivision (*b*), 2, or in lieu thereof a flare-up light.

(*c*) Vessels and boats when line fishing with their lines out and attached to their lines, and when not at anchor or stationary, shall carry the same lights as vessels fishing with drift nets.

(*d*) Fishing vessels and fishing boats may at any time use a flare-up light in addition to the lights which they are by this article required to carry and show. All flare-up lights exhibited by a vessel when trawling or fishing with any kind of dragnet shall be shown at the after part of the vessel, excepting that, if the vessel is hanging by the stern to her fishing gear, they shall be exhibited from the bow.

(*e*) Every fishing vessel and every boat when at anchor shall exhibit a white light visible all round the horizon at a distance of at least one mile.

(*f*) If a vessel or boat when fishing becomes stationary in consequence of her gear getting fast to a rock or other obstruction, she shall show the light and make the fog signal prescribed for a vessel at anchor, respectively (see Article 15, (*d*), (*e*), and last paragraph).

(*g*) In fog, mist, falling snow, or heavy rainstorms, drift-net vessels attached to their nets, and vessels when trawling, dredging, or fishing with any kind of dragnet, and vessels line fishing with their lines out, shall, if of 20 tons gross tonnage or upwards respectively, at intervals of not more than one minute, make a blast; if steam vessels, with the whistle or siren, and if sailing vessels, with the foghorn, each blast to be followed by ringing the bell.

(*h*) Sailing vessels or boats fishing with nets or lines or trawls, when under way, shall in daytime indicate their occupation to an approaching vessel by displaying a basket or other efficient signal, where it can best be seen.

The vessels referred to in this article shall not be obliged to carry the lights prescribed by Article 4, (*a*), and Article 11, last paragraph.

ART. 10. A vessel which is being overtaken by another shall show from her stern to such last-mentioned vessel a white light or a flare-up light.

The white light required to be shown by this article may be fixed and carried in a lantern, but in such case the lantern shall be so constructed, fitted, and screened that it shall throw an unbroken light over an arc of the horizon of 12 points of the compass, viz., for six points from right aft on each side of the vessel, so as to be visible at a distance of at least one mile. Such light shall be carried as nearly as practicable on the same level as the side lights.

ART. 11. A vessel under 150 feet in length, when at anchor, shall carry forward, where it can best be seen, but at a height not exceeding 20 feet above the hull, a white light in a lantern so constructed as to show a clear, uniform, and unbroken light visible all round the horizon at a distance of at least one mile.

A vessel of 150 feet or upwards in length, when at anchor, shall carry in the forward part of the vessel, at a height of not less than 20 and not exceeding 40 feet above the hull, one such light, and at or near the stern of the vessel, and at such a height that it shall be not less than 15 feet lower than the forward light, another such light.

The length of a vessel shall be deemed to be the length appearing in her certificate of registry.

A vessel aground in or near a fairway shall carry the above light or lights and the two red lights prescribed by Article 4, (*a*).

ART. 12. Every vessel may, if necessary in order to attract attention, in addition to the lights which she is by these rules required to carry, show a flare-up light or use any detonating signal that cannot be mistaken for a distress signal.

ART. 13. Nothing in these rules shall interfere with the operation of any special rules made by the government of any nation with respect to additional station and signal lights for two or more ships of war or for vessels sailing under convoy, or with the exhibition of recognition signals adopted by shipowners, which have been authorized by their respective governments and duly registered and published.

ART. 14. A steam vessel proceeding under sail only, but having her funnel up, shall carry in daytime, forward, where it can best be seen, one black ball or shape two feet in diameter.

Sound Signals for Fog, etc.

ART. 15. All signals prescribed by this article for vessels under way shall be given:

1. By "steam vessels" on the whistle or siren.
2. By "sailing vessels and vessels towed" on the foghorn.

The words "prolonged blast" used in this article shall mean a blast of from four to six seconds' duration.

A steam vessel shall be provided with an efficient whistle or siren, sounded by steam or some substitute for steam, so placed that the sound may not be intercepted by any obstruction, and with an efficient foghorn, to be sounded by mechanical means, and also with an efficient bell. A sailing vessel of 20 tons gross tonnage or upwards shall be provided with a similar foghorn and bell.

In fog, mist, falling snow, or heavy rainstorms, whether by day or night, the signals described in this article shall be used as follows, viz.:

(*a*) A steam vessel having way upon her shall sound, at intervals of not more than two minutes, a prolonged blast.

(*b*) A steam vessel under way, but stopped and having no way upon her, shall sound, at intervals of not more than two minutes, two prolonged blasts, with an interval of about one second between them.

(*c*) A sailing vessel under way shall sound, at intervals of not more than one minute, when on the starboard tack one blast, when on the port tack two blasts in succession, and when with the wind abaft the beam, three blasts in succession.

(*d*) A vessel, when at anchor, shall, at intervals of not more than one minute, ring the bell rapidly for about five seconds.

(*e*) A vessel, at anchor at sea, when not in ordinary anchorage ground and when in such a position as to be an obstruction to vessels under way, shall sound, if a steam vessel, at intervals of not more than two minutes, two prolonged blasts with her whistle or siren, followed by ringing her bell; or, if a sailing vessel, at intervals of not more than one minute two blasts with her foghorn, followed by ringing her bell.

(*f*) A vessel, when towing, shall, instead of the signals prescribed in subdivisions (*a*) and (*c*) of this article, at intervals of not more than two minutes, sound three blasts in succession, viz., one prolonged blast followed by two short blasts. A vessel towed may give this signal, and she shall not give any other.

(*g*) A steam vessel wishing to indicate to another "the way is off my vessel, you may feel your way past me," may sound three blasts in succession, viz., short, long, short, with intervals of about one second between them.

(*h*) A vessel employed in laying or in picking up a telegraph cable shall, on hearing the fog signal of an approaching vessel, sound in answer three prolonged blasts in succession.

(*i*) A vessel under way, which is unable to get out of the way of an approaching vessel through being not under command or unable to maneuver as required by these rules, shall, on hearing the fog signal of an approaching vessel, sound in answer four short blasts in succession.

Sailing vessels and boats of less than 20 tons gross tonnage shall not be obliged to give the above-mentioned signals, but if they do not, they shall make some other efficient sound signal at intervals of not more than one minute.

NOTE. In all cases where the rules require a bell to be used, a drum may be substituted on board Turkish vessels, or a gong where such articles are used on board small seagoing vessels.

Speed of Ships to be Moderate in Fog, etc.

ART. 16. Every vessel shall, in a fog, mist, falling snow, or heavy rainstorms, go at a moderate speed, having careful regard to the existing circumstances and conditions.

A steam vessel hearing, apparently forward of her beam, the fog signal of a vessel the position of which is not ascertained, shall, so far as the circumstances of the case admit, stop her engines, and then navigate with caution until danger of collision is over.

STEERING AND SAILING RULES

PRELIMINARY — RISK OF COLLISION

Risk of collision can, when circumstances permit, be ascertained by carefully watching the compass bearing of an approaching vessel. If the bearing does not appreciably change, such risk should be deemed to exist.

ART. 17. When two sailing vessels are approaching one another, so as to involve risk of collision, one of them shall keep out of the way of the other as follows, viz.:

(*a*) A vessel which is running free shall keep out of the way of a vessel which is close-hauled.

(*b*) A vessel which is close-hauled on the port tack shall keep out of the way of a vessel which is close-hauled on the starboard tack.

(*c*) When both are running free, with the wind on different sides, the vessel which has the wind on the port side shall keep out of the way of the other.

(*d*) When both are running free, with the wind on the same side, the vessel which is to windward shall keep out of the way of the other vessel.

(*e*) A vessel which has the wind aft shall keep out of the way of the other vessel.

ART. 18. When two steam vessels are meeting end on, or nearly end on, so as to involve risk of collision, each shall alter her course to starboard, so that each may pass on the port side of the other.

This article applies only to cases where vessels are meeting end on, or nearly end on, in such a manner as to involve risk of collision, and does not apply to two vessels which must, if both keep on their respective courses, pass clear of each other.

The only cases to which it does apply are, when each of the two vessels is end on, or nearly end on, to the other; in other words, to cases in which, by day, each vessel sees the masts of the other in a line, or nearly in a line, with her own; and by night, to cases in which each vessel is in such a position as to see both the side lights of the other.

It does not apply, by day, to cases in which a vessel sees another ahead crossing her own course; or by night, to cases where the red light of one vessel is opposed to the red light of the other, or where the green light of one vessel is opposed to the green light of the other, or where a red light without a green light, or a green light without a red light, is seen ahead, or where both green and red lights are seen anywhere but ahead.

ART. 19. When two steam vessels are crossing, so as to involve risk of collision, the vessel which has the other on her own starboard side shall keep out of the way of the other.

ART. 20. When a steam vessel and a sailing vessel are proceeding in such directions as to involve risk of collision, the steam vessel shall keep out of the way of the sailing vessel.

ART. 21. Where by any of these rules one of two vessels is to keep out of the way, the other shall keep her course and speed.

ART. 22. Every vessel which is directed by these rules to keep out of the way of another vessel shall, if the circumstances of the case admit, avoid crossing ahead of the other.

ART. 23. Every steam vessel which is directed by these rules to keep out of the way of another vessel, shall, on approaching her, if necessary, slacken her speed, or stop, or reverse.

ART. 24. Notwithstanding anything contained in these rules, every vessel overtaking any other shall keep out of the way of the overtaken vessel.

Every vessel coming up with another vessel from any direction more than two points abaft her beam, i.e. in such a position, with reference to the vessel which she is overtaking, that at night she would be unable to see either of that vessel's side lights, shall be deemed to be an overtaking vessel; and no subsequent alteration of the bearing between the two vessels shall make the overtaking vessel a crossing vessel within the meaning of these rules, or relieve her of the duty of keeping clear of the overtaken vessel until she is finally past and clear.

As by day the overtaking vessel cannot always know with certainty whether she is forward of or abaft this direction from the other vessel, she should, if in doubt, assume that she is an overtaking vessel and keep out of the way.

ART. 25. In narrow channels every steam vessel shall, when it is safe and practicable, keep to that side of the fairway or mid-channel which lies on the starboard side of such vessel.

ART. 26. Sailing vessels under way shall keep out of the way of sailing vessels or boats fishing with nets, or lines, or trawls. This rule shall not give to any vessel or boat engaged in fishing the right of obstructing a fairway used by vessels other than fishing vessels or boats.

ART. 27. In obeying and constructing these rules due regard shall be had to all dangers of navigation and collision, and to any special circumstances which may render a departure from the above rules necessary in order to avoid immediate danger.

Sound Signals for Vessels in Sight of One Another

ART. 28. The words "short blast" used in this article shall mean a blast of about one second's duration.

When vessels are in sight of one another, a steam vessel under way, in taking any course authorized or required by these rules, shall indicate that course by the following signals on her whistle or siren, viz.:

One short blast to mean, "I am directing my course to starboard."

Two short blasts to mean, "I am directing my course to port."

Three short blasts to mean, "My engines are going full speed astern."

No Vessel, under any Circumstances, to neglect Proper Precautions

ART. 29. Nothing in these rules shall exonerate any vessel, or the owner, or master, or crew thereof, from the consequences of any neglect to carry lights or signals, or of any neglect to keep a proper lookout, or of the neglect of any precaution which may be required by the ordinary practice of seamen or by the special circumstances of the case.

Reservation of Rules for Harbors and Inland Navigation

ART. 30. Nothing in these rules shall interfere with the operation of a special rule, duly made by local authority, relative to the navigation of any harbor, river, or inland waters.

Distress Signals

ART. 31. When a vessel is in distress, and requires assistance from other vessels or from the shore, the following shall be the signals to be used or displayed by her, either together or separately, viz.:

In the daytime. (1) A gun fired at intervals of about a minute; (2) the International Code signal of distress indicated by N C; (3) the distant signal, consisting of a square flag, having either above or below it a ball or anything resembling a ball; (4) rockets or shells, as prescribed below, for use at night; (5) a continuous sounding with any fog-signal apparatus.

At night. (1) A gun fired at intervals of about a minute; (2) flames on the vessel (as from a burning tar barrel, oil barrel, etc.); (3) rockets or shells bursting in the air with a loud report and throwing stars of any color or description, fired one at a time at short intervals; (4) a continuous sounding with any fog-signal apparatus.

The following resolutions have been approved of by the conference, and are recommended to the attention of the Powers represented thereat, in an appendix to Rules of the Road:

1. The power of all lights should be expressed by referring them all to one standard, by which the light issuing from the lantern should be measured.

2. The minimum power only of each light should be definitely fixed, leaving it to the judgment of the parties responsible for fitting out the vessels with proper lanterns, to employ lamps of this or greater power.

3. The use of incandescent lamps should be permitted; the use of arc lights at present should be excluded for all purposes other than signaling and searching.

4. Each lantern should be so constructed that the minimum power of light can be found at every point where the light is to be visible, after the lamp has been fitted with proper screens.

5. The lanterns should be so constructed as to insure the light having at least the required minimum power in the ideal line connecting the lantern with the horizon, even though the vessel be heeled one way or the other 10 degrees.

6. The color of the glasses by which the coloring of the light is to be produced should be so chosen that, if possible, the red light shall have no admixture of green nor the green light of red rays, and that both colors can be readily and unmistakably distinguished.

7. No detailed description should be internationally adopted for the construction of the lamp or lantern, so that a fair chance may be given to inventors to produce serviceable articles.

8. The side lights should be so screened as to prevent the most convergent rays of the lights being seen across the bows more than half a point.

9. The side lights should be placed in steam vessels not forward of the mast-head light.

10. To meet the number of complaints as to the absence of proper lights on sailing vessels, the attention of the Powers is called to the better enforcement of the regulations in that behalf.

11. All steam whistles, sirens, foghorns, and bells should be thoroughly tested as to their efficiency, and should be capable of being heard at a stated minimum distance, and should be so regulated that the tones of whistles and sirens should be as distinct as possible from the sound of foghorns.

12. Steam vessels should be provided, if possible, with means of blowing off surplus steam when the engines are stopped, in such a manner as to occasion as little noise as possible.

13. In clear weather at sea no vessel should attempt to cross the bows of the leaders of any squadron of three or more ships of war in regular formation, nor unnecessarily to pass through the lines of such squadron.

14. In every case of collision between two vessels it should be the duty of the master or person in charge of each vessel, if and so far as he can do so without serious danger to his own vessel, crew, and passengers (if any), to stay by the other vessel until he has ascertained that she has no need of further assistance; and to render to the other vessel, her master, crew, and passengers (if any), such

assistance as may be practicable and as may be necessary in order to save them from any danger caused by the collision; and also to give to the master or person in charge of the other vessel the name of his own vessel and her port of registry, or the port or place to which she belongs, and also the name of the ports and places from which and to which she is bound.

GENERAL DIVISION 2

This Division relates to Regulations to determine the Seaworthiness of Vessels

The first sentence under the head says: "It is the opinion of the conference that, upon the subjects contained in the sections of this division, no international rule could be made which would secure beneficial results."

GENERAL DIVISION 3

Draft to which Vessels should be restricted when loaded. Uniform Maximum-Load Mark

The only utterance is this: "The conference are led to believe that notwithstanding the advantages which would be connected with the introduction of a uniform system of load marks, this matter is not ripe for consideration by this conference, and that it ought to be left to the negotiations to be carried on between the governments of the maritime nations."

GENERAL DIVISION 4

Uniform Regulations regarding the Designating and Marking of Vessels

(*a*) Position of name on vessel; (*b*) position of name of port of registry on vessel; (*c*) size of lettering; (*d*) uniform system of draft marks.

1. The name of every registered merchant vessel shall be marked upon each bow and upon the stern, and the port of registry of every such vessel shall be marked upon the stern. These names shall be marked in Roman letters in a light color on a dark ground, or in a dark color on a light ground, and be distinctly visible. The smallest letters used shall not be less than four inches high.

2. The draft of every registered vessel shall be marked upon the stem and sternpost in English feet or decimeters, in either Arabic or Roman numerals. The bottom of each numeral shall indicate the draft to that line.

GENERAL DIVISION 5

Saving Life and Property from Shipwreck

1. Saving of life and property from shipwreck at sea.

(*a*) Duties of vessels after collision.

(*b*) Apparatus for life saving to be carried on board ship (lifeboats, life preservers, life rafts, pumps, and fire-extinguishing apparatus).

(*c*) The use of oil and the necessary apparatus for its use.

(*d*) Uniform inspections as to (*b*) and (*c*).

2. Saving of life and property from shipwreck by operations from shore.

(*a*) Organization of, and methods employed by, life-saving institutions.

(*b*) The employment of drilled and disciplined crews at life-saving stations.

(*c*) The maintenance of a patrol upon dangerous coasts by night, and during thick weather by day, for warning off vessels standing into danger, and for the early discovery of wrecks.

(*d*) Uniform means of transmitting information between stranded vessels and the shore.

(*e*) Lifeboats, life-saving apparatus and appliances.

3. Official inquiries into causes and circumstances of shipwrecks and other casualties.

1. Resolved, In every case of collision between two vessels, it shall be the duty of the master or person in charge of each vessel, if and so far as he can do so without danger to his own vessel, crew, and passengers (if any), to stay by the other vessel until he has ascertained that she has no need of further assistance; and to render to the other vessel, her master, crew, and passengers (if any) such assistance as may be practicable and as may be necessary in order to save them from any danger caused by the collision; and also to give to the master or person in charge of the other vessel the name of his own vessel and of her port of registry, or of the port or place to which she belongs, and also the names of the ports and places from which and to which she is bound.

2. Resolved, That the conference approve of the principle of the "Rules made by the Board of Trade of Great Britain under the Merchant Shipping (Life-saving Appliances) Act, 1888," relating to boats and appliances to be carried on board ship for saving life; and recommend that the several governments adopt measures to secure compliance with this principle in regard to such boats and appliances for vessels of 150 tons and upwards gross tonnage.

It is also recommended that the principle of these rules be extended to all smaller craft as far as practicable; and that each vessel of this class should carry at least one life buoy of approved pattern and material, and for every person on board an efficient life belt or jacket.

3. Resolved, That the conference recommend that the several governments require all their seagoing vessels to carry a sufficient quantity of animal or vegetable oil for the purpose of calming the sea in rough weather, together with suitable means for applying it.

4. Resolved, That the conference recommend that all institutions for saving life from wrecked vessels prepare uniform instructions to mariners with reference to their coöperation with those attempting their rescue from the shore, and that said instructions include the following signals:

Upon the discovery of a wreck by night the life-saving force will burn a red pyrotechnic light or a red rocket to signify, "You are seen; assistance will be given as soon as possible."

A red flag waved on shore by day, or a red light, red rocket, or red Roman candle displayed by night, will signify, "Haul away."

A white flag waved on shore by day, or a white light slowly swung back and forth, or a white rocket or white Roman candle fired by night, will signify, "Slack away."

Two flags, a white and a red, waved at the same time on shore by day, or two lights, a white and a red, slowly swung at the same time, or a blue pyrotechnic light burned by night, will signify, "Do not attempt to land in your own boats. It is impossible."

A man on shore beckoning by day, or two torches burning near together by night, will signify, "This is the best place to land."

Any of these signals may be answered from the vessel as follows: In the daytime, by waving a flag, a handkerchief, a hat, or even the hand; at night, by firing a rocket, a blue light, or a gun, or by showing a light over the ship's gunwale for a short time and then concealing it.

And it is recommended that the several governments take measures to keep all their seagoing vessels supplied with copies of such instructions.

Resolved, That the conference recommend that the several nations provide by legislative enactments for official inquiry into the causes and circumstances of all shipwrecks and other serious casualties happening to their vessels.

GENERAL DIVISION 6

Necessary Qualifications for Officers and Seamen, including Tests for Sight and Color Blindness

(*a*) A uniform system of examination for the different grades.

(*b*) Uniform tests for visual power and color blindness.

(*c*) General knowledge of methods employed at life-saving stations.

(*d*) Uniform certificates of qualification.

1. Every man or boy going to sea as a seaman, or with the intention of becoming a seaman, should be examined for visual power and color blindness; and no man or boy should be permitted to serve on board any vessel in the capacity of seaman, or where he will have to stand lookout, whose visual power is below one half normal, or who is red and green color-blind.

2. Every man who shall qualify as an officer of a registered vessel or as a pilot after the adoption of these rules, except engineer officers, shall be required to have a certificate that he has the necessary visual power and that he is not red and green blind. He shall also have a certificate that he is familiar with the regulations for preventing collisions at sea and with the duties required of him in coöperating with a life-saving station in case his vessel is stranded.

3. It is recommended that each country provide means which will enable any boy or man intending to go to sea to have his eyes examined for visual power and color blindness, and to obtain a certificate of the result; also to enable the master of any vessel to have the eyes of any of his crew tested for the same purpose.

GENERAL DIVISION 7

Lanes for Steamers on Frequented Routes

(*a*) With regard to the avoidance of steamer collisions.

(*b*) With regard to the safety of fishermen.

(No international regulations were recommended.)

GENERAL DIVISION 8

Night Signals for communicating Information at Sea

(The only positive proposition was the following.)

The conference decided upon the following fog signals, to be allotted to pilots and to vessels seeking pilots:

For vessels requiring pilots, a prolonged blast followed by a short one.

For pilots wishing to offer their services, a short blast followed by a long blast.

And the conference recommend that they be inserted in the international code book under the pilot signals.

GENERAL DIVISION 9

Warnings of Approaching Storms

(*a*) The transmission of warnings.

(*b*) The uniformity of signals employed.

(No recommendations were made.)

[NOTE: Text omitted above is without force as world law.]

GENERAL DIVISION 10

Reporting, Marking, and Removing Dangerous Wrecks or Obstructions to Navigation

(*a*) A uniform method of reporting and marking dangerous wrecks and derelicts.

(*b*) The division of the labor, cost, and responsibility among the several maritime nations, either by geographical apportionment or otherwise:

Of the removal of dangerous derelicts;

And of searching for doubtful dangers with a view of removing them from the charts.

Resolutions submitted for the consideration of the Powers.

1. That it is advisable to make it the duty of any of the officers, or of the crew of a wreck or a derelict, to report as soon as possible after landing to the nearest harbor authority, if necessary through their consul, as follows:

(*a*) Name of the vessel abandoned.

(*b*) Her distinguishing number.

(*c*) Name of her home port, port from which she sailed, and place of destination.

(*d*) General description of the vessel and her rig.

(*e*) Place where abandoned (latitude and longitude as nearly as possible).

(*f*) Weather and current experienced before leaving the vessel, and, in case she was a derelict, the direction in which she would most likely drift.

(*g*) Whether or not it is intended to take any steps toward her recovery.

2. That a similar report should be made to the same authorities by the master of any vessel sighting a wreck or derelict, and a suitable entry made in the ship's log.

3. That such reports should be published in "Notices to Mariners," the daily press, and, if necessary, by giving telegraphic information to the ports which it most concerns.

4. That it is advisable to make it the duty of every commander or master of a vessel to report the fact that an iceberg or other dangerous field ice has been sighted, or a shoal, reef, or other obstruction has been discovered, to the harbor authorities or the hydrographic office of that country to which the port next reached belongs, giving a full description of the obstruction and all facts that may lead to the determination of its position; for instance, the time elapsed since the last reliable astronomical observation, and the rate of the chronometer. If the obstruction be a shoal or reef, the depth of water actually obtained by sounding on it should be given. Also when land is in sight the position of any off-lying shoal or reef should be determined by compass bearings of fixed objects in view, the error of the compass being stated, with information as to how and when that error was observed. Angles should also be taken between such objects, and a drawing of the coast and the position of the observer be added.

5. That whenever practicable it shall be the duty of the crew before abandoning a vessel (*a*) to hoist some distinctive signal, as B C F, "abandoned by the crew"; or C R T G, "Derelict"; or a ball, shape, or other similar mark, where it can best be seen, and where it should not be mistaken for any other authorized signal; (*b*) to let go the sheets and halyards of such sails as are not furled.

6. That the different maritime Powers interested in the navigation of that portion of the North Atlantic Ocean bordering the American coast and situated westward of a line drawn from the Bermuda Islands to Cape Race, Newfoundland, be invited to come to an agreement respecting the removal of derelicts in these waters under due official supervision.

7. That in countries which, by treaty, have acknowledged the exterritoriality of subjects of other Powers and their property, the consul or consuls concerned shall be instructed not to withhold his or their consent to the destruction of a wreck or parts thereof if it is shown that the wreck constitutes a danger to passing vessels, and if there is no apparent possibility that it will be removed within a reasonable time by the owners or the insurance companies interested.

GENERAL DIVISION 11

Notice of Dangers to Navigation

Notice of Changes in Lights, Buoys, and Other Day and Night Marks

(*a*) A uniform method of taking bearings, of designating them (whether true or magnetic), and of reporting them.

(*b*) A uniform method of reporting, indicating, and exchanging information by the several maritime nations, — to include the form of notices to mariners.

(*c*) A uniform method of distributing this information.

The conference invite the several maritime Powers to consider the following resolutions with a view to establishing uniformity in the subjects treated in "Notices to Mariners" and "Light Lists."

1. That all bearings should be given from seaward.

2. That the bearings of cuts of different-colored sectors of lights or bearings of lights defining a narrow channel should be expressed in degrees where practicable.

3. That all bearings expressed in degrees should count from north and south, from 0° to 90°, toward east and west.

4. That in designating bearings the letter E shall designate east, and the letter W shall designate west.

5. That whenever bearings are given the variation of the compass at the place should be stated.

6. That distances should be expressed in nautical miles and fractions thereof. The word "cable" should mean the tenth part of a nautical mile.

7. That whenever the longitude of a position is given it should be stated which prime meridian is adopted, and if other than that of Greenwich or Paris the difference of longitude should also be stated.

8. That in defining the visibility of a light it should be stated whether the distance is for "clear" or "mean" state of the weather.

9. That where the geographical range of a light is given it should be calculated as seen at high water from an observer 15 feet or five meters above the sea.

10. That a uniform classification of lights based on luminous intensity and on the character as seen by the mariner should be adopted.

11. That the central offices that issue "Notices to Mariners" or "Light Lists" should be permitted to correspond directly on such subjects.

12. That from countries where "Notices to Mariners" are published only in newspapers, copies of such papers should be sent to the various hydrographic offices.

GENERAL DIVISION 12

A Uniform System of Buoys and Beacons

(*a*) Uniformity in color of buoys.

(*b*) Uniformity in numbering of buoys.

On the principle of using four colors to mark the four sides of a shoal, the conference put forward the following scheme, based on the least change that would be necessary in altering the present systems to a uniform plan; and they bring it to the notice of the countries interested, as an example showing that uniformity is attainable if they will agree to consider the subject.

All shoals marked on the compass system to be marked:

On the north side by a single black or white color.

South side by red.

East side by half red and half white combined.

West side by half white and half black combined.

On rocks in fairway, with channels on either hand, to be marked black or red, with horizontal bands.

If such colors were adopted, then the following changes of color would be necessary. (Then follow statements of changes which would have to be made by certain countries named.)

The conference invite the various Powers interested to consider the following general principles, which they put forward as a basis on which to build up a uniform international buoyage system for districts other than those where the compass system is in use.

The term "starboard hand" shall denote that side of a navigable channel which is on the right hand of the mariner entering from seaward; the term "port hand" shall denote that side which is on the left hand under the same circumstances.

Color. Buoys defining the starboard hand shall be painted a single red color. Buoys defining the port hand shall be painted a single black color, or a parti-color. Buoys defining middle grounds shall be painted with horizontal bands.

Form. Wherever form is used as a distinctive character, buoys defining the starboard hand shall be conical, and those defining the port hand shall be can or spar.

Top marks. Countries where form is not used as a distinctive character for buoys may adopt as another distinctive feature for the buoys on either side of a channel, top marks resembling a cone to be used on the starboard side, or a cylinder on the port side of a channel.

Numbers and letters. Numbers, letters, and names may be painted on the buoys, but they must never be so large as to interfere with their distinctive coloring. Wherever numbers and letters are used they shall be in consecutive order, commencing from seaward.

Buoying and marking of wrecks. (*a*) All buoys and the topsides of vessels used for the marking of wrecks shall be painted green with a suitable white inscription.

(*b*) Where it is practicable, by day one ball shall be exhibited on the side of the vessel nearest the wreck and two placed vertically on the other side; three fixed white lights similarly arranged, but not the ordinary riding light, shall be shown from sunset to sunrise.

GENERAL DIVISION 13

The Establishment of a Permanent International Maritime Commission

(*a*) The composition of the commission.

(*b*) Its powers and authority.

Resolved, that for the present the establishment of a permanent international maritime commission is not considered expedient.

CHAPTER VII

DISARMAMENT

National disarmament plays but a small part in the development of the political unity of the world. Yet the thought is closely associated with measures which have played a large part in that development, so that it is fitting to give place to the subject in mention of the forces which have enacted world law and are promoting world unity. The more the attention of the world is turned to hopeful conditions, the sooner will the deep longings of the nations for peace and mutual good will result in actual and efficient world legislation. It is to be expected that there will be found in this field, too, a germ of true world law, for it is to be expected that the world-will, when it has adequate means of expression and action, will forbid nations to carry arms, just as state-will, in our country, forbids private citizens to carry arms.

Only twice is "disarmament" found in the de Martens list of many thousands of international communications. The first time it is in connection with a puny affair, and so ridiculous must it seem to a fighting statesman that he doubtless would omit reference to it altogether. But no beginning of disarmament is worthy of neglect, however humble it may be. So humble was this instance that probably the nations concerned have forgotten all about it, for they have not carried the idea further in their relations with each other, nor seemed to have learned from it. But under date of October 27, 1787, is an entry of a reciprocal declaration by France and Great Britain for a discontinuance of armaments. In the story following the entry it appears that there was an actual process of disarming. The documents in the case are as follows:

Reciprocal declarations of the courts of London and of Versailles to bring to an end the armaments made on account of the troubles in Holland.

DECLARATION

The events which have taken place in the Republic of the United Provinces not appearing to leave any subject of discussion and still less of contest between the two courts, the undersigned are authorized to demand if the intention of his most Christian Majesty is to give effect to the notification made the 16th of the month of last September by the minister plenipotentiary of his most Christian Majesty who, announcing that they would give aid in Holland, has occasioned the naval armaments on the part of his Majesty; which armaments have been reciprocated.

If the court of Versailles is disposed to explain itself regarding that matter and regarding its course adopted toward the republic in a manner in harmony with the desire shown on each side to preserve the good understanding between the two courts and always intended also, that there should not be any hostility on either side in consequence of what has transpired, his Majesty, always eager to concur with the friendly sentiments of his most Christian Majesty, will agree with him that the armaments and, in general, all preparations for war shall be discontinued on each side, and that the navies of the two nations shall be restored to a peace footing such as existed on January 1 of the present year.

At Versailles, October 27, 1787
DORSET, WILLIAM EDEN

COUNTER DECLARATION

The intention of his Majesty not being, and never having been, to interfere by force in the affairs of the Republic of the United Provinces, the communication made to the court of London the 16th of the last month by Mr. Barthélemy having had no other object than to announce to that court an intention, for which the motives no longer exist, especially since the king of Prussia has made part of his resolution, his Majesty has no difficulty in saying that he never wished to give any effect to the declaration above mentioned and that he cherishes no hostile intent relative to what has transpired in Holland. In consequence, his Majesty, desiring to concur with the sentiments of his Britannic Majesty for the preservation of the good feeling between the two courts, agrees with pleasure with his Britannic Majesty that the armaments and, in general, all preparations for war shall be discontinued on each side, and that the navies of the two nations shall be restored to a peace footing such as existed on January 1 of the present year.

At Versailles, October 27, 1787
LE COMTE DE MONTMORIN

In consequence of the declaration and the counter declaration exchanged this day, the undersigned, in the name of their respective sovereigns, agree that the armaments and, in general, all the preparations for war shall be discontinued on each side, and that the navies of the two nations shall be restored to a peace footing such as existed on January 1 of the present year.

At Versailles, October 27, 1787

DORSET, WILLIAM EDEN LE COMTE DE MONTMORIN

This precedent has marked historic value. It shows how disarmament can be agreed upon and actually accomplished. As a precedent it matters not that the occasion for arming had so dwindled in importance as not to be worth talking about, still less fighting over. Provided that the desire to disarm exists, — and it is only a recognition of the common sense of every nation that it would not arm unless it felt compelled to do so, — and it is also fully believed that national rights and honor will suffer no detriment by disarming, then here is a practical way of accomplishing the purpose, as far as any two nations are concerned. In this case each nation trusted the other and the trust was not abused. Each made practical surrender of itself to the honor of the other, not continuing the special preparations for fighting which it had made. Thus each nation in this case set a conspicuous example which shines by contrast with the policy of modern nations in persistently increasing their armaments, even though no war is in sight and though there is not a single one of all the nations on earth which it has reason to regard as Great Britain and France, at that time, had reason to regard each other, in consequence of the wars of their recent past and of the disposition and the preparation to fight which still remained. Yet, on this one particular matter, the desire to disarm being stronger than the desire to fight, in view of the worthlessness of the object of the contention, they courteously gave assurances of the entire absence of any hostile intent and laid aside the special arms which they had taken up. The desire and the act are the pertinent facts here, not the smallness of the subject of dispute.

But this case is a precedent of far greater value than for two nations alone. It points the way to a new enactment of world law which is possible even to-day, while the process of world legislation is no further advanced than the stages of the Hague conference. Instead of one nation's giving assurance to one other, if every one were to give the assurance to the whole world besides, as represented in the conference, that it had no intent of hostility and that it did not regard any subject of difference it had with any other nation as worth fighting over, then it would not go a step beyond the steps taken by Great Britain and France over a century ago. On that assurance each of those two nations took the other at its word and laid down the special arms which it had taken up. Upon the assurance, upon honor, by each nation, that it had no hostile intent upon any other, the way would be open for a laying down of arms to at least a partial degree. If the will of the nations should take form in a declaration for a mutual progressive diminution of armaments, and each should honorably live up to its obligations, it would go no further than Great Britain and France went. To that extent, at least, this puny precedent is of large historic value.

But the great precedent for disarmament is the agreement of 1817 between the United States and Great Britain not to arm on the Great Lakes. James Morton Callahan, writing in the Johns Hopkins series, says: "The first suggestion of the idea of making the Lake region neutral appears to have originated during the administration of President Washington, and with the President himself, as a means of preserving the peace at home." On May 6, 1794, John Randolph, secretary of state, wrote to John Jay, minister to Great Britain, that it would be well to consider whether in time of peace no troops should be kept within a limited distance of the Lakes. After the second war between the United States and Great Britain the record says that Lord Castlereagh wanted to prevent a contest for naval ascendancy. He proposed free commercial navigation of the Lakes, if the United States government would not preserve or construct any fortification within a limited distance of the shores, or maintain or construct any armed vessel in the course of the rivers emptying into them. The first definite proposal to disarm came from Albert Gallatin, September 6, 1814. For several years the proposition was pending. Each of the combatants in the war just closed was suspicious of the other, and it seemed at times as if the project were wholly chimerical. Yet each nation saw its self-interest, and on April 28, 1817, a final agreement was reached between Charles Bagot, the minister of Great Britain to the United States, and Richard Rush, the secretary of state of the United States. The agreement made by these two men was as follows:

1. The naval forces henceforth to be maintained upon the Great Lakes shall be confined to the following vessels on each side:

2. On Lake Ontario one vessel, not to exceed 100 tons burden, carrying not more than 20 men and one 18-pound cannon.

3. On the upper lakes two vessels of the same burden and armed in a like way.

4. On Lake Champlain one vessel of like size and armament.

5. All other armed vessels to be at once dismantled, and no other vessel of war shall be built or armed along the St. Lawrence River or the Great Lakes.

Each side kept this agreement in good faith and the dismantling of the war vessels followed promptly after the agreement was reached. Success may be attained in other cases if it could be in this. Here the two nations had just been at war with each other. Suspicion would have been plausible. Very naturally each side might have failed to carry out its agreement on the ground that the other could not be trusted. If the pessimistic view of the conduct of nations to each other under such circumstances is the sound one, then any disarmament is hopeless, no matter what agreements are reached. But the accomplished fact proved that nations will act honorably under such conditions and that it is safe to rely upon the national honor. If Great Britain and the United States could trust each other and disarm under those conditions, other nations, certainly, when they have not been at war for a long time, can follow the precedent. In 1812 the United States had forty-six forts along its Canadian frontier and Canada had about as many. Each nation had a considerable naval armament on the Lakes. The forts were destroyed, the ships were dismantled, and neither fort nor warship has ever been built since to vex the frontier on either side, and the peace has been kept absolutely. The rights of the two nations have been preserved. Neither has suffered the slightest encroachment upon its national honor, and an example has been set to all the world. It is a reasonable prediction that that example will yet be abundantly fruitful in the relations of the nations to each other.

CHAPTER VIII

THE WORLD'S PRIME MERIDIAN

Frederick Frelinghuysen, when Secretary of State of the United States, sent a circular letter under date of October 23, 1882, by direction of President Arthur, to the diplomatic representatives of the United States in foreign countries, to ascertain whether the governments of those countries would be likely to accept an invitation to "an international congress with the object of finally adopting a common meridian." In this letter he used these words:

> It may be well to state that, in the absence of a common and accepted standard for the computation of time for other than astronomical purposes, embarrassments are experienced in the ordinary affairs of modern commerce; that this embarrassment is especially felt since the extension of telegraphic and railway communications has joined states and continents possessing independent and widely separated meridional standards of time; that the subject of a common meridian has been for several years past discussed in this country and in Europe by commercial and scientific bodies, and the need of a general agreement upon a single standard recognized; and that, in recent European conferences especially, favor was shown to the suggestion that, as the United States possesses the greatest longitudinal extension of any country traversed by railway and telegraph lines, the initiatory measures for holding an international convention to consider so important a subject should be taken by this government.

Perhaps this statement is sufficient to show the reasons which led to world action. On the invitation of the United States, an international conference was held in Washington "for the purpose of fixing a prime meridian and a universal day." Its first session was on October 1, 1884, and it was dissolved on November 1 following. Twenty-five nations were represented by delegates as follows: Austria-Hungary, Brazil, Chile, Colombia, Costa Rica, France, Germany, Great Britain, Guatemala, Hawaii, Italy, Japan, Liberia, Mexico, the Netherlands, Paraguay, Russia, Salvador, San Domingo, Spain, Sweden, Switzerland, Turkey, the United States, and Venezuela. Each nation had one vote. The final act of the conference was as follows:

The President of the United States of America, in pursuance of a special provision of Congress, having extended to the governments of all nations in diplomatic relations with his own an invitation to send delegates to meet delegates from the United States in the city of Washington on the first of October, 1884, for the purpose of discussing and, if possible, fixing upon a meridian proper to be employed as a common zero of longitude and standard of time-reckoning throughout the whole world, this international meridian conference assembled at the time and place designated; and, after careful and patient discussion, has passed the following resolutions:

1. That it is the opinion of this congress that it is desirable to adopt a single prime meridian for all nations, in place of the multiplicity of initial meridians which now exist.

2. That the conference proposes to the governments here represented the adoption of the meridian passing through the center of the transit instrument at the observatory of Greenwich as the initial meridian for longitude.

3. That from this meridian longitude shall be counted in two directions up to 180 degrees, east longitude being plus and west longitude minus.

4. That the conference proposes the adoption of a universal day for all purposes for which it may be found convenient, and which shall not interfere with the use of local or other standard time where desirable.

5. That this universal day is to be a mean solar day; is to begin for all the world at the moment of mean midnight of the initial meridian, coinciding with the beginning of the civil day and date of that meridian; and is to be counted from zero up to twenty-four hours.

6. That the conference expresses the hope that, as soon as may be practicable, the astronomical and nautical days will be arranged everywhere to begin at mean midnight.

7. That the conference expresses the hope that the technical studies designed to regulate and extend the application of the decimal system to the division of angular space and of time shall be resumed, so as to permit the extension of this application to all cases in which it presents real advantages.

These seven resolutions were adopted by votes varying from unanimity in case of the first and sixth, or unanimity with two abstentions in case of the fourth, up to the vote of fourteen ayes, five noes, and six abstentions in case of the third, which was the strongest adverse vote. In due time, by sufficient ratification of the nations, the will of the world fixed the meridian of Greenwich as the standard, and thus the formal expression of that will has its rightful place in the body of world law.

CHAPTER IX

THE GENEVA CONVENTION FOR THE SEA

On December 21, 1904, there was signed at The Hague a convention for the exemption of hospital ships, in time of war, from the payment of all dues and taxes imposed for the benefit of the state. Nations were represented by plenipotentiaries as follows: Germany, Austria-Hungary, Belgium, China, Korea, Denmark, Spain, the United States, Mexico, France, Greece, Italy, Japan, Luxemburg, Montenegro, the Netherlands, Peru, Persia, Portugal, Roumania, Russia, Servia, Siam, and Switzerland. Each nation sent one delegate only (and sixteen of them were already the diplomatic representatives of their countries respectively at The Hague, while all of the others sent the diplomatic representative at some other European court, except Russia), save that the Netherlands government sent two. The conference agreed upon the following articles:

ART. 1. Hospital ships, concerning which the conditions set forth in Articles 1, 2, and 3 of the convention concluded at The Hague on July 29, 1899, for the adaptation to maritime warfare of the principles of the Geneva convention of August 22, 1864, are fulfilled, shall be exempted, in time of war, from all dues and taxes imposed on vessels for the benefit of the state, in the ports of the contracting parties.

ART. 2. The provision of the foregoing article does not prevent the application, by means of visitation or other formalities, of fiscal or other laws in force at said ports.

ART. 3. The rule laid down in Article 1 is binding only on the contracting Powers in case of war between two or more of them. The said rule shall cease to be binding from the time when a noncontracting Power shall join one of the belligerents in a war between contracting Powers.

ART. 4. The present convention, which, bearing the date of this day, may be signed until the first of October, 1905, by the Powers expressing their desire to do so, shall be ratified as soon as possible. The ratification shall be deposited at The Hague. A *procès-verbal* of the deposit of the ratifications shall be drawn up, and a copy thereof, duly certified, shall be delivered through the diplomatic channel to all the contracting Powers.

ART. 5. The nonsignatory Powers are permitted to adhere to the present convention after October 1, 1905. They shall, to that end, make their adhesion known to the contracting Powers by means of a written notification addressed to the government of the Netherlands and communicated by the latter to the other contracting Powers.

ART. 6. In the event of one of the high contracting Powers denouncing the present convention, such denunciation shall not take effect until one year after the notification made in writing to the government of the Netherlands and immediately communicated by the latter to all the other contracting Powers. This denunciation shall only affect the ratifying Power.

By ratification by the necessary number of Powers these articles became a part of the Geneva convention as a whole, and are thus a part of the body of world law.

CHAPTER X

INTERNATIONAL SANITATION

On May 14, 1880, there was approved by President Hayes a resolution adopted by both branches of the Congress of the United States, "that the President of the United States is hereby authorized to call an international sanitary conference to meet at Washington, District of Columbia, to which the several Powers having jurisdiction of ports likely to be infected with yellow fever or cholera shall be invited to send delegates, properly authorized, for the purpose of securing an international system of notification as to the actual sanitary condition of ports and places under the jurisdiction of such Powers, and of vessels sailing therefrom."

The conference began its sessions on January 5, 1881, and ended them on March 1, 1881. The following nations were represented: Argentine Republic, Austria-Hungary, Belgium, Bolivia, Brazil, Chile, Denmark, Germany, Spain, the United States, France, Great Britain, Hawaii, Haiti, Italy, Japan, Liberia, Mexico, the Netherlands, Portugal, Peru, Russia, Sweden and Norway, Turkey, and Venezuela. Each nation had one vote. The final act consisted of the following resolutions:

ART. 1. Each government shall have such an organized internal service as will enable it to be regularly informed of the state of the public health throughout the whole of its territory.

ART. 2. Each government shall publish a weekly bulletin of the statistics of mortality in its principal cities and ports, and shall give such bulletins the largest possible publicity.

ART. 3. In the interest of the public health the sanitary authorities of the countries represented in this conference are authorized to communicate directly with each other in order to keep themselves informed of all important facts which may come to their knowledge; but nothing herein contained shall relieve them from the duty of furnishing, at the same time, to the consuls in their respective jurisdictions the information they are required to give them.

ART. 4. A centralized international system of sanitary notification being deemed indispensable to the successful carrying out of measures for preventing the introduction of disease, it is advisable to create international organizations to be charged with the duty of collecting information in regard to the outbreak, spread, and disappearance of cholera, pest, yellow fever, etc., and of conveying such information to the parties interested.

A draft of a convention to carry out this object has been voted by the conference in the following manner. (Annex I.)

ART. 5. Bills of health shall be in the form hereto annexed (Annex II).

ART. 6. Bills of health shall be delivered at the port of departure by the responsible sanitary agent of the central government. The consul of the country of destination shall have the right to be present at the examination of ships made by the representatives of the territorial government under such rules as may be laid down by international agreement or treaty, and the authority to authenticate the bill of health and to add thereon such remarks as he may deem necessary.

ART. 7. Bills of health granted in compliance with international rules should be issued gratis.

ART. 8. A temporary and scientific sanitary commission shall be created by the nations most directly interested in protecting themselves against yellow fever, and by such others as may wish to take part in this arrangement, to be charged with the duty of studying all matters pertaining to the origin, development, and propagation of that disease. A draft of a convention to carry out this object has been voted by the conference in the following manner. (Annex III.)

ANNEX I

The draft of a convention mentioned in Article 4 above is as follows:

ART. 1. There shall be established in Vienna and Havana a permanent international sanitary agency of notification. The respective governments shall agree among themselves as to the formation of those agencies.

ART. 2. It will be the duty of the agency at Vienna to gather sanitary information from Europe, Asia, and Africa. The agency at Havana will extend its jurisdiction to the American continent and the islands belonging geographically thereto, — this system to be subject to such modifications as may be rendered necessary by the state of telegraphic communication.

ART. 3. The contracting governments shall have the right to establish, if necessary, a third agency in Asia.

ART. 4. The governments agreeing to this system of notification will send their sanitary reports to that agency in whose jurisdiction it is. Every agency shall send its notifications to those governments sending sanitary bulletins. The different agencies will exchange the information they receive among themselves, in order that it may be made known to the respective countries belonging to the jurisdiction of each.

ART. 5. There shall be no exceptions to this system, save in cases of extreme emergency. In such cases, however, a government may enter into communication with an agency to whose jurisdiction it does not belong.

ART. 6. In cases of doubt as to the correctness of the bulletins received, the agency is authorized to enter into communication with the respective governments, which will be obliged to furnish as soon as possible the information asked.

ART. 7. In those countries where international sanitary boards exist the agencies shall establish communication with them.

ART. 8. In those countries which have not a perfect sanitary organization, or which have not adopted the conclusions of this conference, the consuls of the contracting Powers shall meet in an international sanitary council, in order to give to the said agencies the information which cannot be obtained from the local authorities.

ART. 9. The governments of Spain and Austria-Hungary shall fix the annual budget of expenses, which they will submit to the participating governments.

ART. 10. The division of expenses between the different governments shall be as follows: Half of the expense will be divided in proportion to the number of population, and the other half in proportion to the amount of tonnage of the merchant marine combined with the commercial maritime value of every country.

ART. 11. The governments of Spain and Austria-Hungary shall submit at the end of every fiscal year the final accounts to every one of the interested governments.

ART. 12. The present convention is concluded for the space of ten years. Any government, however, is at liberty to renounce the convention after three years. The right is reserved to make such changes as any one of the governments taking part shall designate.

ANNEX II

[Annex II, the form of the international bill of health, consists of detailed description of the vessel, name of medical officer, number of passengers and crew, name of captain, place from and to, cargo, and like details, followed by mention of sanitary history of the vessel and condition of cargo, crew, passengers, and so on; then much detail about the sanitary condition of the port from which the vessel cleared.]

ANNEX III

The draft of a convention for a temporary scientific sanitary commission is as follows:

ART. 1. A temporary scientific sanitary commission will be established by the nations most deeply interested to protect themselves against yellow fever, and also by such nations as will adhere to these proposals.

ART. 2. The duties of this commission will be:

A. The study and ascertainment of the principal and permanent centers of the morbigene germs of the disease.

B. The conditions which favor its extension, and also the etiology and circumstances which aid its propagation in the respective centers and its diffusion to other countries.

C. The means to be employed to circumscribe more and more its effects, or to eradicate the disease entirely from the regions in which it originates, and from the countries lately attacked.

D. How to prevent transmission by vessels.

E. The best and most practical method of disinfection of ships, their cargoes and passengers.

F. Also everything relating to the prophylaxis and treatment of the disease.

ART. 3. The countries which desire to concur in the organization of this scientific commission will agree between themselves as to the instructions to be given to their delegates in order to facilitate their labors.

ART. 4. After having studied on the spot the different questions submitted to its investigations, this commission shall present a collective report indicating the most practical means to attain the end proposed.

No one of the resolutions was adopted unanimously. The most favorable vote was fourteen yeas and four abstentions on No. 8. The least favorable was eleven yeas to seven nays on No. 6.

On December 3, 1903, there was signed at Paris an international sanitary convention by the plenipotentiaries of the United States, Germany, Austria-Hungary, Belgium, Brazil, Spain, France, Great Britain, Greece, Italy, Luxemburg, Montenegro, the Netherlands, Persia, Portugal, Roumania, Russia, Servia, Switzerland, and Egypt. Officially, the reason for the convention was that these Powers "deemed it expedient to establish in a single arrangement the measures calculated to safeguard the public health against the invasion and propagation of plague and cholera." Further, "desiring to revise and supplement the international sanitary conventions at present in force," they agreed to the following provisions, which, from the number and rank of the Powers joining to establish them, must be accorded a place in world law.

TITLE I. GENERAL PROVISIONS

CHAPTER I. RULES TO BE OBSERVED BY THE COUNTRIES SIGNING THE CONVENTION, AS SOON AS PLAGUE OR CHOLERA APPEARS IN THEIR TERRITORY

Section I. Notification and Subsequent Communications to the Other Countries

ART. 1. Each government shall immediately notify the other governments of the first appearance in its territory of authentic cases of plague or cholera.

ART. 2. This notification shall be accompanied, or very promptly followed, by particulars regarding:

1. The neighborhood in which the disease has appeared.
2. The date of its appearance, its origin, and its form.
3. The number of established cases and the number of deaths.
4. In case of plague, the existence of plague or of an unusual mortality among rats and mice.
5. The measures immediately taken following this first appearance.

ART. 3. The notification and particulars contemplated in Articles 1 and 2 shall be sent to the diplomatic or consular offices in the capital of the infected country.

In the case of countries not represented there, they shall be transmitted directly by telegraph to the governments of such countries.

ART. 4. The notification and particulars contemplated in Articles 1 and 2 shall be followed by further communications sent regularly so as to keep the governments informed of the progress of the epidemic.

These communications, which shall be sent at least once a week and shall be as complete as possible, shall indicate more particularly the precautions taken to prevent the spread of the disease.

They shall specify: 1, The prophylactic measures applied with regard to sanitary or medical inspection, to isolation, and to disinfection; 2, the measures enforced upon the departure of vessels to prevent the exportation of the disease, and especially, in the case contemplated under No. 4 of Article 2 above, the measures taken against rats.

ART. 5. The prompt and faithful execution of the foregoing provisions is of prime importance.

The notifications are of no real value unless each government is itself opportunely informed of cases of plague and cholera and of doubtful cases occurring in its territory. It cannot therefore be too strongly recommended to the various governments that they make compulsory the announcement of cases of plague and cholera, and that they keep themselves informed of any unusual mortality among rats and mice, especially in ports.

ART. 6. It is understood that neighboring countries reserve the right to make special arrangements with a view to organizing a service of direct information among the heads of frontier departments.

Section II. Conditions which warrant the Consideration of a Territorial Area as being contaminated or as having again become Healthy

ART. 7. The notification of a single case of plague or cholera shall not involve the application, against the territorial area in which it has occurred, of the measures prescribed in Chapter II hereinbelow.

However, when several unimported cases of plague have appeared or when the cholera cases become localized, the area shall be declared contaminated.

ART. 8. In order to limit the measures to the stricken regions alone, the governments shall only apply them to arrivals from the contaminated areas.

By the word "area" is meant a portion of territory definitely specified in the particulars which accompany or follow the notification; for instance, a province, a government, a district, a department, a canton, an island, a commune, a city, a quarter of a city, a village, a port, a polder, a hamlet, etc., whatever be the area and population of these portions of territory.

However, this restriction to the contaminated area shall only be accepted upon the formal condition that the government of the contaminated country take the necessary measures, 1, to prevent the exportation of the articles enumerated under

Nos. 1 and 2 of Article 12 and coming from the contaminated area, unless they are previously disinfected; and, 2, to combat the spread of the epidemic.

When an area is contaminated, no restrictive measure shall be taken against arrivals from such area if such arrivals have left it at least five days before the beginning of the epidemic.

ART. 9. In order that an area may be considered as being no longer contaminated, it must be officially ascertained:

1. That there has been neither a death nor a new case of plague or cholera within five days after the isolation,[1] death, or cure of the last plague or cholera patient.

2. That all the measures of disinfection have been applied, and, in the case of plague, that the measures against rats have been executed.

CHAPTER II. MEASURES OF DEFENSE BY OTHER COUNTRIES AGAINST TERRITORIES DECLARED TO BE CONTAMINATED

Section I. Publication of the Prescribed Measures

ART. 10. The government of each country is obliged to publish immediately the measures which it believes necessary to prescribe with regard to arrivals from a contaminated country or territorial area.

It shall at once communicate this publication to the diplomatic or consular officer of the contaminated country residing in its capital, as well as to the international boards of health.

It shall likewise be obliged to make known through the same channels the revocation of these measures or any modifications which may be made therein.

In default of a diplomatic or consular office in the capital, the communications shall be made directly to the government of the country concerned.

Section II. Merchandise; Disinfection; Importation and Transit; Baggage

ART. 11. No merchandise is capable by itself of transmitting plague or cholera. It only becomes dangerous when contaminated by plague or cholera products.

ART. 12. Disinfection shall only be applied to merchandise and articles which the local health authority considers to be contaminated.

However, the merchandise or articles enumerated below may be subjected to disinfection or even prohibited entry independently of any proof that they are or are not contaminated:

1. Body linen, clothing worn (wearing apparel), and bedding which has been used.

When these articles are being transported as baggage or as a result of a change of residence (household goods), they shall not be prohibited and are subject to the provisions of Article 19.

[1] By "isolation" is meant the isolation of the patient and of the persons attending him permanently, and the prohibition of visits by any other person.

Packages left by soldiers and sailors and returned to their country after death are treated the same as the articles comprised in the first paragraph of No. 1.

2. Rags (including those for making paper), with the exception, as to cholera, of compressed rags transported as wholesale merchandise in hooped bales.

Fresh waste coming directly from spinning mills, weaving mills, manufactories, or bleacheries; artificial wools (shoddy) and fresh paper trimmings shall not be forbidden.

ART. 13. The transit of the merchandise and articles specified under Nos. 1 and 2 of the preceding article shall not be prohibited if they are so packed that they cannot be manipulated en route.

Likewise, when the merchandise or articles are transported in such a manner that it is impossible for them to have been in contact with contaminated articles en route, their transit across an infected territorial area shall not constitute an obstacle to their entry into the country of destination.

ART. 14. The merchandise and articles specified under Nos. 1 and 2 of Article 12 shall not be subject to the application of the measures prohibiting entry if it is proven to the authorities of the country of destination that they were shipped at least five days before the beginning of the epidemic.

ART. 15. The mode and place of disinfection, as well as the methods to be employed for the destruction of rats, shall be determined by the authorities of the country of destination. These operations should be performed in such a manner as to cause the least possible injury to the articles.

It shall devolve upon each nation to determine the question as to the possible payment of damages as a result of disinfection or of the destruction of rats.

If, on the occasion of the taking of measures for the destruction of rats on board vessels, the health authorities should levy a tax either directly or through a society or private individual, the rate of such tax must be fixed by a tariff published in advance and so calculated that no profit shall be derived by the nation or the health department from its application as a whole.

ART. 16. Letters and correspondence, printed matter, books, newspapers, business papers, etc. (parcels post not included), shall not be subjected to any restriction or disinfection.

ART. 17. Merchandise arriving by land or by sea shall not be detained at frontiers or in ports.

The only measures which it is permissible to prescribe with regard to them are specified in Article 12 hereinabove.

However, if merchandise arriving by sea in bulk or in defective bales has been contaminated during the passage by rats known to be stricken with plague, and if it cannot be disinfected, the destruction of the germs may be insured by storing it in a warehouse for a maximum period of two weeks.

It is understood that the application of this last measure shall not entail any delay upon the vessel or any extra expense as a result of the lack of warehouses in the ports.

ART. 18. When merchandise has been disinfected by applying the provisions of Article 12, or temporarily warehoused in accordance with the third paragraph of Article 17, the owner or his representative shall be entitled to demand from the health authority who has ordered the disinfection or storage, a certificate setting forth the measures taken.

ART. 19. *Baggage.* The disinfection of the soiled linen, wearing apparel, and articles of baggage or furniture (household goods) coming from a territorial area declared to be contaminated shall only take place in cases when the health authority considers them to be contaminated.

Section III. Measures in Ports and at Maritime Frontiers

ART. 20. *Classification of vessels.* A vessel is considered as *infected* which has plague or cholera on board, or which has presented one or more cases of plague or cholera within seven days.

A vessel is considered as *suspicious* on board of which there were cases of plague or cholera at the time of departure or have been during the voyage, but on which there have been no new cases within seven days.

A vessel is considered as *uninfected* which, although coming from an infected port, has had neither death nor any case of plague or cholera on board either before departure, during the voyage, or at the time of arrival.

ART. 21. Ships *infected with plague* shall be subjected to the following measures:

1. Medical inspection.

2. The patients shall be immediately landed and isolated.

3. The other persons shall also be landed, if possible, and subjected, from the date of their arrival, either to an observation[1] which shall not exceed five days and may be followed or not by a surveillance[2] of five days at most, or simply to a surveillance not to exceed ten days.

It is within the discretion of the health authority of the port to apply whichever of these measures appears preferable to him according to the date of the last case, the condition of the vessel, and the local possibilities.

4. The soiled linen, wearing apparel, and other articles of the crew[3] and passengers which are considered by the health authority as being contaminated shall be disinfected.

5. The parts of the vessel which have been occupied by persons stricken with plague, or which are considered by the health authority as being contaminated, shall be disinfected.

6. The destruction of the rats on the vessel shall take place before or after the discharge of the cargo as rapidly as possible, and at all events within a maximum period of forty-eight hours, avoiding injury to the cargo, the plating, and the engines.

[1] By "observation" is meant the isolation of the passengers, either on board a vessel or at a sanitary station, before they are granted pratique.

[2] By "surveillance" is meant that the passengers are not isolated and that they immediately obtain pratique, but that the attention of the authorities is called to them wherever they go, and that they are subjected to a medical examination to ascertain the state of their health.

[3] The term "crew" is applied to all persons who form or have formed part of the crew or of the servants on board the vessel, including stewards, waiters, "cafedji," etc. The term is to be construed in this sense wherever employed in the present convention.

In the case of vessels in ballast this operation shall be performed as soon as possible before taking on cargo.

ART. 22. Vessels *suspected of plague* shall be subjected to the measures indicated under Nos. 1, 4, and 5 of Article 21.

Moreover, the crew and passengers may be subjected to a surveillance not to exceed five days from the arrival of the vessel. The landing of the crew may be forbidden during the same period except in connection with the service.

It is recommended that the rats on the vessel be destroyed. This destruction should be effected before or after the discharge of cargo as rapidly as possible, and at all events within a maximum period of forty-eight hours, avoiding injury to the merchandise, plating, and engines.

In case of vessels in ballast this operation shall be performed, if there is occasion for it, as soon as possible and at all events before taking on cargo.

ART. 23. Vessels *uninfected with plague* shall be granted pratique immediately, whatever be the nature of their bill of health.

The only measures which the authority of the port of arrival may prescribe with regard to them shall be the following:

1. Medical inspection.

2. Disinfection of the soiled linen, wearing apparel, and other articles of the crew and passengers, but only in exceptional cases when the health authority has special reason to believe that they are contaminated.

3. Although not to be adopted as a general rule, the health authority may subject vessels coming from a contaminated port to an operation designed to destroy the rats on board, either before or after the discharge of the cargo. This operation should take place as soon as possible and should not in any event last more than twenty-four hours, avoiding injury to the cargo, plating, and engines, and avoiding hindrance to the movement of the passengers and crew between the vessel and the shore. In case of vessels in ballast this operation, if there is occasion for it, should take place as soon as possible and at all events before taking on cargo.

When a vessel hailing from a contaminated port has been subjected to an operation for the destruction of rats, this operation shall not be repeated unless the vessel has stopped and moored at a wharf in a contaminated port, or unless the presence of dead or diseased rats is discovered on board.

The crew and passengers may be subjected to a surveillance not to exceed five days from the date on which the vessel left the contaminated port. The landing of the crew may also be forbidden during the same time except in connection with the service.

The competent authority of the port of arrival may always demand an affidavit from the ship's physician, or, in default of such physician, from the captain, to the effect that there has not been a case of plague on the vessel since its departure and that no unusual mortality among the rats has been observed.

ART. 24. When rats have been recognized as plague-stricken on board an *uninfected* vessel as a result of a bacteriological examination, or when an unusual mortality has been discovered among these rodents, the following measures shall be applied:

I. Vessels with plague-stricken rats:

a) Medical inspection.

b) The rats shall be destroyed either before or after the discharge of the cargo as rapidly as possible, and at all events within a maximum period of forty-eight hours, avoiding injury to the cargo, plating, and engines. On vessels in ballast this operation shall be performed as soon as possible and at all events before taking on cargo.

c) The parts of the vessel and the articles which the health authority considers to be contaminated shall be disinfected.

d) The passengers and crew may be subjected to a surveillance whose duration shall not exceed five days from the date of arrival, save exceptional cases, in which the health authority may prolong the surveillance to a maximum of ten days.

II. Vessels on which an unusual mortality among rats is discovered:

a) Medical inspection.

b) An examination of the rats with regard to the plague shall be made as far and as quickly as possible.

c) If the destruction of the rats is deemed necessary, it shall take place under the conditions indicated above for vessels with plague-stricken rats.

d) Until all suspicion is removed, the passengers and the crew may be subjected to a surveillance whose duration shall not exceed five days from the date of arrival, save exceptional cases, in which the health authority may prolong the surveillance to a maximum of ten days.

ART. 25. The health authority of the port shall deliver to the captain or to the shipowner or his agent, whenever demanded, a certificate to the effect that the measures for the destruction of rats have been applied, and stating the reasons for their application.

ART. 26. Vessels *infected* with cholera shall be subjected to the following measures:

1. Medical inspection.
2. The patients shall be immediately landed and isolated.
3. The other persons shall likewise be landed, if possible, and subjected, from the date of arrival of the vessel, to an observation or a surveillance whose duration shall vary according to the sanitary condition of the vessel and the date of the last case, without, however, exceeding five days.
4. The soiled linen, wearing apparel, and other articles of the crew and passengers which are considered by the health authority of the port as being contaminated shall be disinfected.
5. The parts of the vessel which have been occupied by cholera patients or which are considered by the health authority as being contaminated shall be disinfected.
6. The bilge water shall be discharged after disinfection.

The health authority may order the substitution of good drinking water for that stored on board.

It may be forbidden to throw human excrements or allow them to run into the water of a port unless they are previously disinfected.

ART. 27. Vessels *suspected of cholera* shall be subjected to the measures prescribed under Nos. 1, 4, 5, and 6 of Article 26.

The crew and passengers may be subjected to a surveillance not to exceed five days from the arrival of the vessel. It is recommended that the landing of the crew be prevented during the same period except for purposes connected with the service.

ART. 28. Vessels *uninfected with cholera* shall be granted pratique immediately, whatever be the nature of their bill of health.

The only measures to which they may be subjected by the health authority of the port of arrival shall be those provided under Nos. 1, 4, and 6 of Article 26.

With regard to the state of their health, the crew and passengers may be subjected to a surveillance not to exceed five days from the date on which the vessel left the contaminated port.

It is recommended that the landing of the crew be forbidden during the same period except for purposes connected with the service.

The competent authority of the port of arrival may always demand an affidavit from the ship's physician, or, in the absence of such, from the captain, to the effect that there has not been a case of cholera on board since the vessel sailed.

ART. 29. In order to apply the measures indicated in Articles 21 to 28, the competent authority shall take account of the presence of a physician and of disinfecting apparatuses (chambers) on board the vessels of the three categories mentioned above.

In regard to plague, he shall likewise take account of the installation on board of apparatus for the destruction of rats.

The health authorities of nations which may deem it suitable to reach an understanding on this point may excuse from the medical inspection and other measures those uninfected vessels which have on board a physician specially commissioned by their country.

ART. 30. Special measures may be prescribed in regard to crowded vessels, especially emigrant vessels or any others presenting bad hygienic conditions.

ART. 31. Any vessel not desiring to submit to the obligations imposed by the authority of the port by virtue of the stipulations of the present convention shall be free to put to sea again.

It may be permitted to land its cargo after the necessary precautions have been taken, viz.:

1. Isolation of the vessel, crew, and passengers.

2. In regard to plague, inquiry as to the existence of an unusual mortality among the rats.

3. In regard to cholera, the discharge of the bilge water after disinfection and the substitution of good drinking water for that stored on board the vessel.

It may also be permitted to land passengers who so request, upon condition that they submit to the measures prescribed by the local authority.

ART. 32. Vessels hailing from a contaminated port, which have been disinfected and subjected to sanitary measures applied in an efficient manner, shall not undergo the same measures a second time upon their arrival in a new port, provided that no case has appeared since the disinfection took place and that they have not touched at a contaminated port in the meantime.

When a vessel lands only passengers and their baggage, or the mails, without having been in communication with the mainland, it is not to be considered as having touched at the port.

ART. 33. Passengers arriving on an infected vessel shall have the right to demand a certificate of the health authority of the port, showing the date of their arrival and the measures to which they and their baggage have been subjected.

ART. 34. Coasting vessels shall be subjected to special measures to be established by mutual agreement among the countries concerned.

ART. 35. Without prejudice to the right which governments possess to agree upon the organization of common sanitary stations, each country shall provide at least one port upon each of its seaboards with an organization and equipment sufficient to receive a vessel, whatever may be its sanitary condition.

When an uninfected vessel hailing from a contaminated port arrives in a large maritime port, it is recommended that she be not sent back to another port for the purpose of having the prescribed sanitary measures executed.

In every country, ports open to the arrival of vessels from ports infected with plague or cholera shall be equipped in such a manner that uninfected vessels may, immediately upon their arrival, undergo the prescribed measures and not be sent for this purpose to another port.

The governments shall make known the ports which are open in their territories to arrivals from ports infected with plague or cholera.

ART. 36. It is recommended that there be established in large maritime ports:

a) A regular medical service of the port and a permanent medical surveillance of the sanitary conditions of the crews and the inhabitants of the port.

b) Places set apart for the isolation of the sick and the observation of suspected persons.

c) The necessary plants for efficient disinfection, and bacteriological laboratories.

d) A supply of drinking water beyond suspicion for the use of the port, and a system affording all possible security for the carrying off of refuse and sewage.

Section IV. Measures on Land Frontiers; Travelers; Railroads; Frontier Zones; River Routes

ART. 37. Land quarantines shall no longer be established.

Persons showing symptoms of plague or cholera shall alone be detained at frontiers.

This principle shall not bar the right of each nation to close a part of its frontier in case of necessity.

ART. 38. It is important that travelers be subjected to a surveillance on the part of railroad employees, with a view to determining the state of their health.

ART. 39. Medical interference is limited to an examination of the passengers and the care to be given to the sick. If such an examination is made, it should be combined as far as possible with the customhouse inspection, to the end that travelers may be detained as short a time as possible. Only persons who are obviously ill shall be subjected to a thorough medical examination.

ART. 40. As soon as travelers coming from an infected locality shall have arrived at their destination, it would be of the greatest utility to subject them to a surveillance which should not exceed ten or five days from the date of departure, according to whether it is a question of plague or cholera.

ART. 41. The governments reserve the right to take special measures in regard to certain categories of persons, notably gypsies, vagabonds, emigrants, and persons traveling or crossing the frontier in troops.

ART. 42. Cars used for the conveyance of passengers, mail, and baggage shall not be detained at frontiers.

If it should happen that one of these cars is contaminated or has been occupied by a plague or cholera patient, it shall be detached from the train and disinfected as soon as possible.

The same rule shall apply to freight cars.

ART. 43. The measures concerning the crossing of frontiers by railroad and postal employees shall be determined by the companies or departments concerned, and shall be so arranged as not to hinder the service.

ART. 44. The regulation of frontier traffic and questions pertaining thereto, as well as the adoption of exceptional measures of surveillance, shall be left to special arrangements between the contiguous nations.

ART. 45. It is the province of the governments of the riparian nations to regulate the sanitary conditions of river routes by means of special arrangements.

TITLE II. SPECIAL PROVISIONS APPLICABLE TO COUNTRIES SITUATED OUTSIDE OF EUROPE

CHAPTER I. ARRIVALS BY SEA

Section I. Measures in Contaminated Ports upon the Departure of Vessels

ART. 46. It shall be incumbent upon the competent authority to take effectual measures to prevent the embarkation of persons showing symptoms of plague or cholera.

Every person taking passage on board a vessel shall, at the time of embarkation, be examined individually in the daytime on shore, for the necessary length of time, by a physician delegated by the authorities. The consular officer of the nation to which the ship belongs may be present at this examination.

As an exception to this stipulation, the medical examination may take place on shipboard at Alexandria and Port Said, when the local health authority deems it expedient, provided that the third-class passengers shall not be permitted to leave the vessel. This medical examination may be made at night in the case of first- and second-class passengers, but not of third-class passengers.

ART. 47. It shall be incumbent upon the competent authorities to take effectual measures:

1. To prevent the exportation of merchandise or any articles which they may consider as contaminated, and which have not been previously disinfected on shore under the supervision of the physician delegated by the public authorities.

2. In case of plague, to prevent the access of rats to the vessel.

3. In case of cholera, to see that the drinking water taken on board is wholesome.

Section II. Measures with Respect to Ordinary Vessels hailing from Contaminated Northern Ports and appearing at the Entrance of the Suez Canal or in Egyptian Ports

ART. 48. Ordinary *uninfected* vessels hailing from a plague- or cholera-infected port of Europe or the basin of the Mediterranean and presenting themselves for passage through the Suez Canal shall be allowed to pass through in quarantine. They shall continue their route under observation of five days.

ART. 49. Ordinary uninfected vessels wishing to make a landing in Egypt may stop at Alexandria or Port Said, where the passengers shall complete the observation period of five days either on shipboard or in a sanitary station, according to the decision of the local health authority.

ART. 50. The measures to which *infected* or *suspected* vessels shall be subjected which hail from a plague- or cholera-infected port of Europe or the shores of the Mediterranean, and which desire to effect a landing in one of the Egyptian ports or to pass through the Suez Canal, shall be determined by the board of health of Egypt in conformity with the stipulations of the present convention.

The regulations containing these measures shall, in order to become effective, be accepted by the various Powers represented on the board; they shall determine the measures to which vessels, passengers, and merchandise are to be subjected and shall be presented within the shortest possible period.

Section III. Measures in the Red Sea

A. MEASURES WITH RESPECT TO ORDINARY VESSELS HAILING FROM THE SOUTH AND APPEARING IN PORTS OF THE RED SEA OR BOUND TOWARD THE MEDITERRANEAN

ART. 51. Independently of the general provisions contained in Section III, Chapter II, Title I, concerning the classification of and the measures applicable to infected, suspected, or uninfected vessels, the special provisions contained in the ensuing articles are applicable to ordinary vessels coming from the south and entering the Red Sea.

ART. 52. *Uninfected* vessels must have completed or shall be required to complete an observation period of five full days from the time of their departure from the last infected port.

They shall be allowed to pass through the Suez Canal in quarantine and shall enter the Mediterranean, continuing the aforesaid observation period of five days. Ships having a physician and a disinfecting chamber on board shall not undergo disinfection until the passage through in quarantine begins.

ART. 53. Suspected vessels shall be treated differently, according to whether they have a physician and a disinfecting apparatus (chamber) on board or not.

a) Vessels having a physician and a disinfecting apparatus (chamber) on board and fulfilling the necessary conditions shall be permitted to pass through the Suez Canal in quarantine under conditions prescribed by the regulations for the passage through.

b) Other suspected vessels having neither physician nor disinfecting apparatus (chamber) on board shall, before being permitted to pass through in quarantine, be detained at Suez or Moses Spring a sufficient length of time to carry out the disinfecting measures prescribed and to ascertain the sanitary condition of the vessel.

In the case of mail vessels or of packets specially utilized for the transportation of passengers and having no disinfecting apparatus (chamber), but having a physician on board, if the local authority is assured by an official declaration that the measures of sanitation and disinfection have been suitably carried out either at the point of departure or during the voyage, the passage through in quarantine shall be allowed.

In the case of mail vessels or of packets specially utilized for the transportation of passengers and having no disinfecting apparatus (chamber), but having a physician on board, if the last case of plague or cholera dates back longer than seven days and if the sanitary condition of the vessel is satisfactory, pratique may be granted at Suez when the operations prescribed by the regulations are completed.

When a vessel has had a run of less than seven days without infection, the passengers destined for Egypt shall be landed at an establishment designated by the board of health of Alexandria and isolated a sufficient length of time to complete the observation period of five days. Their soiled linen and wearing apparel shall be disinfected. They shall then receive pratique.

Vessels having had a run of less than seven days without infection and desiring to obtain pratique in Egypt shall be detained in an establishment designated by the board of health of Alexandria for a sufficient length of time to complete the observation period of five days. They shall undergo the measures prescribed for suspected vessels.

When plague or cholera has appeared exclusively among the crew, only the soiled linen of the latter shall be disinfected, but it shall all be disinfected, including that in the living quarters of the crew.

ART. 54. Infected vessels are divided into vessels with a physician and a disinfecting apparatus (chamber) on board, and vessels without a physician and a disinfecting apparatus (chamber).

a) Vessels without a physician and a disinfecting apparatus (chamber) shall be stopped at Moses Spring; [1] persons showing symptoms of plague or cholera shall be landed, and isolated in a hospital. The disinfection shall be carried out in a thorough manner. The other passengers shall be landed and isolated in groups

[1] The patients shall as far as possible be landed at Moses Spring. The other persons may undergo the observation in a sanitary station designated by the Sanitary, Maritime, and Quarantine Board of Egypt (pilots' lazaretto).

composed of as few persons as possible, so that the whole number may not be infected by a particular group if the plague or cholera should develop. The soiled linen, wearing apparel, and clothing of the crew and passengers, as well as the vessel, shall be disinfected.

It is to be distinctly understood that there shall be no discharge of cargo but simply a disinfection of the part of the vessel which has been infected.

The passengers shall remain for five days in an establishment designated by the Sanitary, Maritime, and Quarantine Board of Egypt. When the cases of plague or cholera date back several days, the length of the isolation shall be diminished. This length shall vary according to the date of the cure, death, or isolation of the last patient. Thus when the last case of plague or cholera has terminated six days before by a cure or death, or when the last patient has been isolated for six days, the observation shall last one day; if only five days have elapsed, the observation period shall be two days; if only four days have elapsed, the observation period shall be three days; if only three days have elapsed, the observation period shall be four days; if only two days or one day have elapsed, the observation period shall be five days.

b) Vessels with a physician and a disinfecting apparatus (chamber) on board shall be stopped at Moses Spring. The ship's physician must declare, under oath, what persons on board show symptoms of plague or cholera. These patients shall be landed and isolated.

After the landing of these patients the soiled linen of the rest of the passengers, which the health authority may consider as dangerous, as well as that of the crew, shall undergo disinfection on board.

When plague or cholera shall have appeared exclusively among the crew, the disinfection of the linen shall be limited to the soiled linen of the crew and the linen of the living apartments of the crew.

The ship's physician shall indicate also, under oath, the part or compartment of the vessel and the section of the hospital in which the patient or patients have been transported. He shall also declare, under oath, what persons have been in contact with the plague or cholera patient since the first manifestation of the disease, either directly or through contact with objects which might be contaminated. Such persons alone shall be considered as suspects.

The part or compartment of the vessel and the section of the hospital in which the patient or patients shall have been transported shall be thoroughly disinfected. By the "part of the ship" shall be understood the cabin of the patient, the neighboring cabins, the corridor upon which these cabins are located, the deck, and the parts of the deck where the patients may have stayed.

If it is impossible to disinfect the part or compartment of the vessel which has been occupied by the persons stricken with plague or cholera without landing the persons declared as suspects, these persons shall be either placed in another vessel specially designated for this purpose or landed and lodged in the sanitary establishment without coming in contact with the patients, who should be placed in the hospital.

The duration of this stay on the vessel or on shore for disinfection shall be as short as possible and shall not exceed twenty-four hours.

The suspects shall undergo, either on their vessel or on the vessel designated for this purpose, an observation period whose duration shall vary according to the cases and under the conditions provided in the third paragraph of subdivision *a*).

The time taken up by the prescribed operations shall be comprised in the duration of the observation period.

The passage through in quarantine may be allowed before the expiration of the periods indicated above if the health authority deems it possible. It shall at all events be granted when the disinfection has been completed, if the vessel leaves behind not only its patients but also the persons indicated above as "suspects."

A disinfecting chamber placed on a lighter may come alongside the vessel in order to expedite the disinfecting operations.

Infected vessels requesting pratique in Egypt shall be detained at Moses Spring five days; they shall, moreover, undergo the same measures as those adopted for infected vessels arriving in Europe.

B. MEASURES WITH RESPECT TO ORDINARY VESSELS HAILING FROM THE INFECTED PORTS OF HEDJAZ DURING THE PILGRIMAGE SEASON

ART. 55. If plague or cholera prevails in Hedjaz during the time of the Mecca pilgrimage, vessels coming from Hedjaz or from any other part of the Arabian coast of the Red Sea without having embarked there any pilgrims or similar masses of persons, and which have not had any suspicious occurrence on board during the voyage, shall be placed in the category of ordinary suspected vessels. They shall be subjected to the preventive measures and to the treatment imposed on such vessels.

If they are bound for Egypt, they shall undergo, in a sanitary establishment designated by the Sanitary, Maritime, and Quarantine Board, an observation of five days from the date of departure, for cholera as well as for plague. They shall be subjected, moreover, to all the measures prescribed for suspected vessels (disinfection, etc.), and shall not be granted pratique until they have passed a favorable medical examination.

It shall be understood that if the vessels have had suspicious occurrences during the voyage, they shall pass the observation period at Moses Spring, which shall last five days whether it be a question of plague or cholera.

Section IV. Organization of the Surveillance and of the Disinfection at Suez and Moses Spring

ART. 56. The medical inspection prescribed by the regulations shall be made on each vessel arriving at Suez by one or more of the physicians of the station, being made in the daytime on vessels hailing from ports infected with plague or cholera. It may, however, be made at night on vessels which present themselves in order to pass through the canal, if they are lighted by electricity, and whenever the local health authority is satisfied that the lighting facilities are adequate.

ART. 57. The physicians of the Suez station shall be at least seven in number, — one chief physician and six others. They must possess a regular diploma and shall be chosen preferably from among physicians who have made special practical studies in epidemiology and bacteriology. They shall be appointed by the minister of the interior upon the recommendation of the Sanitary, Maritime, and Quarantine Board of Egypt. They shall receive a salary which shall begin at 8000 francs and may progressively rise to 12,000 francs for the six physicians, and which shall vary from 12,000 to 15,000 francs for the chief physician.

If the medical service should still prove inadequate, recourse may be had to the surgeons of the navies of the several nations, who shall be placed under the authority of the chief physician of the sanitary station.

ART. 58. A corps of sanitary guards shall be intrusted with the surveillance and the execution of the prophylactic measures applied in the Suez Canal, at the establishment at Moses Spring, and at Tor.

ART. 59. This corps shall comprise ten guards.

It shall be recruited from among former noncommissioned officers of the European and Egyptian armies and navies.

After their competence has been ascertained by the board, the guards shall be appointed in the manner provided by Article 14 of the khedival decree of June 19, 1893.

ART. 60. The guards shall be divided into two classes, the first class comprising four guards and the second class comprising six guards.

ART. 61. The annual compensation allowed to the guards shall be:

For the first class, from £160 Eg. to £200 Eg.;

For the second class, from £120 Eg. to £168 Eg.;

With a progressive increase until the maximum is reached.

ART. 62. The guards shall be invested with the character of officers of the public peace, with the right to call for assistance in case of infractions of the sanitary regulations.

They shall be placed under the immediate orders of the director of the Suez or the Tor bureau.

They shall be instructed in all the methods and operations of disinfection in vogue, and must understand the manipulation of the substances and the handling of the instruments employed for this purpose.

ART. 63. The disinfection and isolation station of Moses Spring is placed under the authority of the chief physician of Suez.

If patients are landed there, two of the physicians of Suez shall be interned there, one to take care of plague or cholera patients, the other to care for the persons not stricken with plague or cholera.

In case there are plague and cholera patients and other sick at the same time, the number of interned physicians shall be increased to three, one for the plague patients, one for the cholera patients, and the third for those sick with other ailments.

ART. 64. The disinfection and isolation station at Moses Spring shall comprise:

1. Three disinfecting chambers, one being placed on a lighter, and the necesssary apparatus for the destruction of rats.

2. Two isolation hospitals with twelve beds each, one for plague patients and persons suspected of plague, the other for persons stricken with or suspected of

cholera. These hospitals shall be so arranged that the patients, the suspects, the men, and the women shall be isolated from one another in each of them.

3. Huts, hospital tents, and ordinary tents for the landed persons.

4. Bath tubs and shower baths in sufficient number.

5. The necessary buildings for the ordinary services, the medical staff, the guards, etc., a store, and a laundry.

6. A tank of water.

7. The various buildings shall be so arranged as to render impossible all contact among the patients, the infected or suspicious objects, and the other persons.

ART. 65. A machinist shall be specially intrusted with the care of the disinfecting chambers installed at Moses Spring.

Section V. Passage through the Suez Canal in Quarantine

ART. 66. The health authority of Suez shall grant the passage through in quarantine, and the board shall be immediately informed thereof.

In doubtful cases the decision shall be reached by the board.

ART. 67. As soon as the permit provided for in the preceding article is granted, a telegram shall be sent to the authority designated by each Power, the dispatch of the telegram being at the expense of the vessel.

ART. 68. Each Power shall establish penalties against vessels which abandon the route indicated by the captain and unduly approach one of the ports within its territory, cases of *vis major* and enforced sojourn being excepted.

ART. 69. Upon a vessel's being spoken, the captain shall be obliged to declare whether he has on board any gangs of native stokers or of wage-earning employees of any description who are not inscribed on the crew list or the register kept for this purpose.

The following questions in particular shall be asked the captains of all vessels arriving at Suez from the south, and shall be answered under oath:

"Have you any helpers (stokers or other workmen) not inscribed on your crew list or on the special register? What is their nationality? Where did you embark them?"

The sanitary physicians should ascertain the presence of these helpers, and if they discover that any of them are missing, they should carefully seek the cause of their absence.

ART. 70. A health officer and two sanitary guards shall board the vessel and accompany her to Port Said. Their duty shall be to prevent communications and see to the execution of the prescribed measures during the passage through the canal.

ART. 71. All embarkations, landings, and transshipments of passengers or cargo are forbidden during the passage through the Suez Canal to Port Said.

However, passengers may embark at Port Said in quarantine.

ART. 72. Vessels passing through in quarantine shall make the trip from Suez to Port Said without putting into dock.

In case of stranding or of being compelled to put into dock, the necessary operations shall be performed by the personnel on board, all communication with the employees of the Suez Canal Company being avoided.

ART. 73. When troops are conveyed through the canal on suspicious or infected vessels passing through in quarantine, the trip shall be made in the daytime only. If it is necessary to stop at night in the canal, the vessels shall anchor in Lake Timsah or the Great Lake.

ART. 74. Vessels passing through in quarantine are forbidden to stop in the harbor of Port Said except in the cases contemplated in Articles 71 (paragraph 2) and 75.

The supply and preparation of food on board vessels shall be effected with the means at hand on the vessels.

Stevedores or any other persons who may have gone on board shall be isolated on the quarantine lighter. Their clothing shall there undergo disinfection as per regulations.

ART. 75. When it is absolutely necessary for vessels passing through in quarantine to take on coal at Port Said, they shall perform this operation in a locality affording the necessary facilities for isolation and sanitary surveillance, to be selected by the board of health. When it is possible to maintain a strict supervision on board the vessel and to prevent all contact with the persons on board, the coaling of the vessel by the workmen of the port may be permitted. At night the place where the coaling is done should be illuminated by electric lights.

ART. 76. The pilots, electricians, agents of the company, and sanitary guards shall be put off at Port Said, outside of the port between the jetties, and thence conducted directly to the quarantine lighter, where their clothing shall undergo disinfection when deemed necessary.

ART. 77. The war vessels hereinafter specified shall enjoy the benefits of the following provisions when passing through the Suez Canal:

They shall be recognized by the quarantine authority as uninfected upon the production of a certificate issued by the physicians on board, countersigned by the commanding officer, and affirming under oath:

a) That there has not been any case of plague or cholera on board either at the time of departure or during the passage.

b) That a careful examination of all persons on board, without any exception, has been made less than twelve hours before the arrival in the Egyptian port, and that it revealed no case of these diseases.

These vessels shall be exempted from the medical examination and immediately receive pratique, provided a period of five full days has elapsed since their departure from the last infected port.

In case the required period has not elapsed, the vessels may pass through the canal in quarantine without undergoing the medical examination, provided they present the above-mentioned certificate to the quarantine authorities.

The quarantine authorities shall, nevertheless, have the right to cause their agents to perform the medical examination on board war vessels whenever they deem it necessary.

Suspicious or infected war vessels shall be subjected to the regulations in force.

Only fighting units shall be considered as war vessels, transports and hospital ships falling under the category of ordinary vessels.

ART. 78. The maritime and quarantine board of Egypt is authorized to organize the transit through Egyptian territory by rail of the mails and ordinary passengers coming from infected countries in quarantine trains, under the conditions set forth in Annex I.

Section VI. Sanitary Measures Applicable to the Persian Gulf

ART. 79. Vessels shall be spoken at the sanitary establishment of the Island of Ormuz before entering the Persian Gulf. According to their sanitary condition and their port of departure, they shall be subjected to the measures prescribed by Section III, Chapter II, Title I.

However, vessels which are to go up the Chat-el-Arab shall, if the observation period is not terminated, be permitted to continue their voyage upon condition of passing through the Persian Gulf and up the Chat-el-Arab in quarantine. A chief guard and two sanitary guards, taken on board at Ormuz, shall watch the vessel as far as Bassorah, where a second medical examination shall be made and the necessary disinfections performed.

Pending the organization of the sanitary station of Ormuz, sanitary guards taken from the provisional post established in accordance with Article 82, paragraph 2, shall accompany the vessels passing in quarantine into the Chat-el-Arab and to the establishment situated in the neighborhood of Bassorah.

Vessels which are to touch at Persian ports in order to land passengers and cargo there may perform these operations at Bender-Bouchir.

It is distinctly understood that a vessel which remains uninfected at the expiration of five days from the date on which it left the last port infected with plague or cholera, shall obtain pratique in the ports of the gulf after it has been ascertained, upon its arrival, that it is uninfected.

ART. 80. Articles 20 to 28 of the present convention are applicable with regard to the classification of the vessels and the measures to be applied to them in the Persian Gulf, with the three following exceptions:

1. The surveillance of the passengers and crew shall always be superseded by an observation of the same duration.

2. Uninfected vessels shall only obtain pratique upon condition that five full days have elapsed since the time of their departure from the last infected port.

3. In regard to suspected vessels the period of five days for the observation of the crew and passengers shall begin as soon as there is no case of plague or cholera on board.

Section VII. Sanitary Establishments in the Persian Gulf

ART. 81. Sanitary establishments shall be constructed under the direction of the board of health of Constantinople and at its expense, one on the Island of Ormuz and the other in the neighborhood of Bassorah, at a place to be determined upon.

At the sanitary station of the Island of Ormuz there shall be at least two physicians, sanitary agents, sanitary guards, and a complete set of appliances for disinfection and the destruction of rats. A small hospital shall be built.

At the station in the neighborhood of Bassorah there shall be constructed a large lazaretto suitable for a medical service composed of several physicians, and apparatus for the disinfection of merchandise.

ART. 82. The Superior Board of Health of Constantinople, which has the sanitary establishment of Bassorah under its control, shall exercise the same power over that of Ormuz.

Pending the construction of the sanitary establishment of Ormuz, a sanitary post shall be established there under the direction of the Superior Board of Health of Constantinople.

CHAPTER II. ARRIVALS BY LAND

Section I. General Rules

ART. 83. The measures taken on land routes against arrivals from regions infected with plague or cholera shall conform to the sanitary principles formulated by the present convention.

Modern disinfecting methods shall be substituted for land quarantines. To this end disinfecting chambers and other disinfecting appliances shall be installed at well-chosen points along the routes followed by travelers.

The same means shall be employed on railroad lines already built or to be built.

Freight shall be disinfected according to the principles of the present convention.

ART. 84. Each government shall be free to close, when necessary, a part of its frontiers against passengers and freight at places where the organization of a sanitary supervision is attended with difficulties.

Section II. Turkish Land Frontiers

ART. 85. The Superior Board of Health of Constantinople shall, without delay, organize the sanitary establishments of Hanikin and Kisil Dizie, near Bayazid, on the Turko-Persian and Turko-Russian frontiers.

TITLE III. PROVISIONS SPECIALLY APPLICABLE TO PILGRIMAGES

CHAPTER I. GENERAL PROVISIONS

ART. 86. The provisions of Articles 46 and 47 of Title II are applicable to persons and objects to be embarked on a pilgrim ship sailing from a port of the Indian Ocean and Oceania, even if the port is not infected with plague or cholera.

ART. 87. When cases of plague or cholera exist in the port, no embarkation shall be made on pilgrim ships until after the persons, assembled in a group, have been subjected to an observation for the purpose of ascertaining that none of them is stricken with plague or cholera.

It shall be understood that, in executing this measure, each government may take into account the local circumstances and possibilities.

ART. 88. If local circumstances permit, the pilgrims shall be obliged to prove that they possess the means absolutely necessary to complete the pilgrimage, especially a round-trip ticket.

ART. 89. Steamships shall alone be permitted to engage in the long-voyage transportation of pilgrims, all other vessels being forbidden to engage in this traffic.

ART. 90. Pilgrim ships engaged in coasting trade and used in making the conveyances of short duration called "coasting voyages" shall be subject to the provisions contained in the special regulations applicable to the Hedjaz pilgrimage, which shall be published by the board of health of Constantinople in accordance with the principles announced in the present convention.

ART. 91. A vessel which does not embark a greater proportion of pilgrims of the lowest class than one per hundred tons gross burden, in addition to its ordinary passengers (among whom pilgrims of the higher classes may be included), shall not be considered as a pilgrim ship.

ART. 92. Every pilgrim ship, upon entering the Red Sea or the Persian Gulf, must conform to the provisions contained in the special regulations applicable to the Hedjaz pilgrimage, which shall be published by the board of health of Constantinople in accordance with the principles set forth in the present convention.

ART. 93. The captain shall be obliged to pay all the sanitary taxes collectible from the pilgrims, which shall be comprised in the price of the ticket.

ART. 94. As far as possible, the pilgrims who land or embark at the sanitary stations should not come in contact with one another at the points of debarkation.

After landing their pilgrims the vessels shall change their anchorage in order to reëmbark them.

The pilgrims who are landed shall be sent to the encampment in as small groups as possible.

They must be furnished with good drinking water, whether it is found on the spot or obtained by distillation.

ART. 95. When there is plague or cholera in Hedjaz, the provisions carried by the pilgrims shall be destroyed if the health authority deems it necessary.

CHAPTER II. PILGRIM SHIPS. SANITARY ARRANGEMENTS

Section I. General Arrangement of Vessels

ART. 96. The vessel must be able to lodge pilgrims between decks.

Outside of the crew, the vessel shall furnish to every individual, whatever be his age, a surface of 1.5 square meters (16 English square feet), with a height between decks of about 1.8 meters.

On vessels engaged in coasting trade each pilgrim shall have at his disposal a space of at least two meters wide along the gunwales of the vessel.

ART. 97. On each side of the vessel, on deck, there shall be reserved a place screened from view and provided with a hand pump so as to furnish sea water for the needs of the pilgrims. One such place shall be reserved exclusively for women.

ART. 98. In addition to the water-closets for the use of the crew, the vessel shall be provided with latrines flushed with water or provided with a stopcock, in the proportion of at least one latrine for every 100 persons embarked.

There shall be latrines reserved exclusively for women.

There shall be no water-closets between decks or within the hold.

ART. 99. The vessel shall have two places arranged for private cooking by the pilgrims, who shall be forbidden to make a fire elsewhere and especially on deck.

ART. 100. An infirmary regularly fitted up and properly arranged with regard to safety and sanitary conditions shall be reserved for lodging the sick.

It must be able to receive at least 5 per cent of the pilgrims embarked, allowing at least 3 square meters per head.

ART. 101. The vessel shall be provided with the means of isolating persons who show symptoms of plague or cholera.

ART. 102. Every vessel shall have on board the medicines, disinfectants, and articles necessary for the care of the sick. The regulations made for this kind of vessels by each government shall determine the nature and quantity of the medicines.[1] The care and the remedies shall be furnished gratuitously to the pilgrims.

ART. 103. Every vessel embarking pilgrims shall have on board a physician holding a regular diploma and commissioned by the government of the country to which the vessel belongs, or by the government of the port in which the vessel takes pilgrims on board. A second physician shall be embarked as soon as the number of pilgrims carried by the vessel exceeds 1000.

ART. 104. The captain shall be obliged to have handbills posted on board in a position which is conspicuous and accessible to those interested. They shall be in the principal languages of the countries inhabited by the pilgrims embarked, and show:

1. The destination of the vessel.
2. The price of the tickets.
3. The daily ration of water and food allowed to each pilgrim.
4. A price list of victuals not comprised in the daily ration and to be paid for extra.

ART. 105. The heavy baggage of the pilgrims shall be registered, numbered, and placed in the hold. The pilgrims shall keep with them only such articles as are absolutely necessary, the regulations made by each government for its vessels determining the nature, quantity, and dimensions thereof.

ART. 106. The provisions of Chapters I, II (Sections I, II, and III), and III of the present title shall be posted, in the form of regulations, in the language of the nationality of the vessel, as well as in the principal languages of the countries inhabited by the pilgrims embarked, in a conspicuous and accessible place on each deck and between decks on every vessel carrying pilgrims.

[1] It is desirable that each vessel be provided with the principal immunizing agents (antiplague serum, Haffkine vaccine, etc.).

Section II. Measures to be taken before Departure

ART. 107. At least three days before departure the captain, or in the absence of the captain the owner or agent, of every pilgrim ship must declare his intention to embark pilgrims to the competent authority of the port of departure. In ports of call the captain, or in the absence of the captain the owner or agent, of every pilgrim ship must make this same declaration twelve hours before the departure of the vessel. This declaration must indicate the intended day of sailing and the destination of the vessel.

ART. 108. Upon the declaration prescribed by the preceding article being made, the competent authority shall proceed to the inspection and measurement of the vessel at the expense of the captain. The consular officer of the country to which the vessel belongs may be present at this inspection.

The inspection only shall be made if the captain is already provided with a certificate of measurement issued by the competent authority of his country, unless it is suspected that the document no longer corresponds to the actual state of the vessel.[1]

ART. 109. The competent authority shall not permit the departure of a pilgrim ship until he has ascertained:

a) That the vessel has been put in a state of perfect cleanliness and, if necessary, disinfected.

b) That the vessel is in a condition to undertake the voyage without danger; that it is properly equipped, arranged, and ventilated; that it is provided with an adequate number of small boats; that it contains nothing on board which is or might become detrimental to the health or safety of the passengers, and that the deck is of wood or of iron covered over with wood.

c) That, in addition to the provisions for the crew, there are provisions and fuel of good quality on board, suitably stored and in sufficient quantity for all the pilgrims and for the entire anticipated duration of the voyage.

d) That the drinking water taken on board is of good quality and from a source protected against all contamination; that there is a sufficient quantity thereof; that the tanks of drinking water on board are protected against all contamination and closed in such a way that the water can only be let out through the stopcocks or pumps. The devices for letting water out, called "suckers," are absolutely forbidden.

e) That the vessel has a distilling apparatus capable of producing at least five liters of water per head each day for every person embarked, including the crew.

f) That the vessel has a disinfecting chamber whose safety and efficiency have been ascertained by the health authority of the port of embarkation of the pilgrims.

[1] The competent authority is at present: in British India, an officer designated for this purpose by the local government (Native Passenger Ships Act, 1887, Art. 7); in Dutch India, the master of the port; in Turkey, the health authority; in Austria-Hungary, the authority of the port; in Italy, the captain of the port; in France, Tunis, and Spain, the health authority; in Egypt, the quarantine and health authority, etc.

g) That the crew comprises a physician holding a diploma and commissioned [1] either by the government of the country to which the vessel belongs or by the government of the port where the vessel takes on pilgrims, and that the vessel has a supply of medicines, all in conformity with Articles 102 and 103.

h) That the deck of the vessel is free from all cargo and other incumbrances.

i) That the arrangements of the vessel are such that the measures prescribed by Section III hereinafter may be executed.

ART. 110. The captain shall not sail until he has in his possession:

1. A list viséed by the competent authority and showing the name, sex, and total number of the pilgrims whom he is authorized to embark.

2. A bill of health setting forth the name, nationality, and tonnage of the vessel, the name of the captain and of the physician, the exact number of persons embarked (crew, pilgrims, and other passengers), the nature of the cargo, and the port of departure.

The competent authority shall indicate upon the bill of health whether the number of pilgrims allowed by the regulations is reached or not, and, in case it is not reached, the additional number of passengers which the vessel is authorized to embark in subsequent ports of call.

Section III. Measures to be taken during the Passage

ART. 111. The deck shall remain free from encumbering objects during the voyage and shall be reserved day and night for the persons on board and be placed gratuitously at their service.

ART. 112. Every day the space between decks should be cleaned carefully and scrubbed with dry sand, mixed with disinfectants, while the pilgrims are on deck.

ART. 113. The latrines intended for passengers, as well as those for the crew, should be kept neat and be cleansed and disinfected three times a day.

ART. 114. The excretions and dejections of persons showing symptoms of plague or cholera shall be collected in vessels containing a disinfecting solution. These vessels shall be emptied into the latrines, which shall be thoroughly disinfected after each flushing.

ART. 115. Articles of bedding, carpets, and clothing which have been in contact with the patients mentioned in the preceding article shall be immediately disinfected. The observance of this rule is especially enjoined with regard to the clothing of persons who come near to these patients and who may have become contaminated.

Such of the articles mentioned above as have no value shall either be thrown overboard, if the vessel is neither in a port nor a canal, or else destroyed by fire. The others shall be carried to the disinfecting chamber in impermeable sacks washed with a disinfecting solution.

ART. 116. The quarters occupied by the patients and referred to in Article 100 shall be rigorously disinfected.

[1] Exception is made for governments which have no commissioned physicians.

ART. 117. Pilgrim ships shall be compelled to submit to disinfecting operations in conformity with the regulations in force on the subject in the country whose flag they fly.

ART. 118. The quantity of drinking water allowed daily to each pilgrim free of charge, whatever be his age, shall be at least five liters.

ART. 119. If there is any doubt about the quality of the drinking water or any possibility of its contamination either at the place of its origin or during the course of the voyage, the water shall be boiled or otherwise sterilized, and the captain shall be obliged to throw it overboard at the first port in which a stop is made and in which he is able to procure a better supply.

ART. 120. The physician shall examine the pilgrims, attend the patients, and see that the rules of hygiene are observed on board. He shall especially:

1. Satisfy himself that the provisions dealt out to the pilgrims are of good quality, that their quantity is in conformity with the obligations assumed, and that they are suitably prepared.

2. Satisfy himself that the requirements of Article 118 relative to the distribution of water are observed.

3. If there is any doubt about the quality of the drinking water, remind the captain in writing of the provisions of Article 119.

4. Satisfy himself that the vessel is maintained in a constant state of cleanliness, and especially that the latrines are cleansed in accordance with the provisions of Article 113.

5. Satisfy himself that the lodgings of the pilgrims are maintained in a healthful condition, and that, in case of transmissible disease, they are disinfected in conformity with Articles 116 and 117.

6. Keep a diary of all the sanitary incidents occurring during the course of the voyage and present this diary to the competent authority of the port of arrival.

ART. 121. The persons intrusted with the care of the plague or cholera patients shall alone have access to them and shall have no contact with the other persons on board.

ART. 122. In case of a death occurring during the voyage, the captain shall make note of the death opposite the name on the list viséed by the authority of the port of departure, besides entering on his journal the name of the deceased person, his age, where he comes from, the presumable cause of his death according to the physician's certificate, and the date of the death.

In case of death by a transmissible disease, the body shall be wrapped in a shroud saturated with a disinfecting solution and thrown overboard.

ART. 123. The captain shall see that all the prophylactic measures executed during the voyage are recorded in the ship's journal. This journal shall be presented by him to the competent authority of the port of arrival.

In each port of call the captain shall have the list prepared in accordance with Article 110 viséed by the competent authority.

In case a pilgrim is landed during the course of the voyage, the captain shall note the fact on the list opposite the name of the pilgrim.

In case of an embarkation, the persons embarked shall be mentioned on this list in conformity with the aforementioned Article 110, and before it is viséed again by the competent authority.

ART. 124. The bill of health delivered at the port of departure shall not be changed during the course of the voyage.

It shall be viséed by the health authority of each port of call, who shall note thereon:

1. The number of passengers landed or embarked in the port.

2. The incidents occurring at sea and affecting the health or life of the persons on board.

3. The sanitary condition of the port of call.

Section IV. Measures to be taken on the Arrival of Pilgrims in the Red Sea

A. SANITARY MEASURES APPLICABLE TO MUSSULMAN-PILGRIM SHIPS HAILING FROM AN INFECTED PORT AND BOUND FROM THE SOUTH TOWARD HEDJAZ

ART. 125. Pilgrim ships hailing from the south and bound for Hedjaz shall first stop at the sanitary station of Camaran, where they shall be subjected to the measures prescribed by Articles 126 to 128.

ART. 126. Vessels recognized as *uninfected* after a medical inspection shall obtain pratique when the following operations are completed:

The pilgrims shall be landed, take a shower or sea bath, and their soiled linen and the part of their wearing apparel and baggage which appears suspicious in the opinion of the health authority shall be disinfected. The duration of these operations, including debarkation and embarkation, shall not exceed forty-eight hours.

If no real or suspected case of plague or cholera is discovered during these operations, the pilgrims shall be reëmbarked immediately and the vessel shall proceed toward Hedjaz.

For plague, the provisions of Articles 23 and 24 shall be applied with regard to the rats which may be found on board the vessels.

ART. 127. *Suspicious* vessels on board of which there were cases of plague or cholera at the time of departure, but on which there has been no new case of plague or cholera for seven days, shall be treated in the following manner:

The pilgrims shall be landed, take a shower or sea bath, and their soiled linen and the part of their wearing apparel and baggage which appears suspicious in the opinion of the health authority shall be disinfected.

In time of cholera the bilge water shall be changed.

The parts of the vessel occupied by the patients shall be disinfected. The duration of these operations, including debarkation and embarkation, shall not exceed forty-eight hours.

If no real or suspected case of plague or cholera is discovered during these operations, the pilgrims shall be reëmbarked immediately and the vessel shall proceed to Djeddah, where a second medical inspection shall take place on board. If the result thereof is favorable, and on the strength of a written affidavit by the ship's physician to the effect that there has been no case of plague or cholera during the passage, the pilgrims shall be immediately landed.

If, on the contrary, one or more real or suspected cases of plague or cholera have been discovered during the voyage or at the time of arrival, the vessel shall be sent back to Camaran, where it shall undergo anew the measures applicable to infected vessels.

For plague, the provisions of Article 22, third paragraph, shall be applied with regard to the rats which may be found on board the vessels.

ART. 128. *Infected vessels*, that is, those having cases of plague or cholera on board, or having had cases of plague or cholera within seven days, shall undergo the following treatment:

The persons stricken with plague or cholera shall be landed and isolated in the hospital. The other passengers shall be landed and isolated in groups comprising as few persons as possible, so that the whole number may not be infected by a particular group if plague or cholera should develop therein.

The soiled linen, wearing apparel, and clothing of the crew and passengers, as well as the vessel, shall be disinfected in a thorough manner.

However, the local health authority may decide that the discharge of the heavy baggage and the cargo is not necessary, and that only a part of the vessel need be disinfected.

The passengers shall remain at the Camaran establishment seven or five days, according to whether it is a question of plague or cholera. When cases of plague or cholera date back several days, the length of the isolation may be diminished. This length may vary according to the date of appearance of the last case and the decision of the health authority.

The vessel shall then proceed to Djeddah, where an individual and rigorous medical inspection shall be made. If the result thereof is favorable, the vessel shall obtain pratique. If, on the contrary, real cases of plague or cholera have appeared on board during the voyage or at the time of arrival, the vessel shall be sent back to Camaran, where it shall undergo anew the treatment applicable to infected vessels.

For plague, the measures prescribed by Article 21 shall be applied with regard to the rats which may be found on board the vessels.

1. *The Camaran Station*

ART. 129. The following conditions shall exist at the Camaran station:

The island shall be completely vacated by its inhabitants.

In order to insure the safety and facilitate the movement of vessels in the bay of Camaran Island:

1. Buoys and beacons shall be installed in sufficient number.

2. A mole or quay shall be constructed to land passengers and baggage.

3. A separate flying bridge shall be arranged for the embarkation of the pilgrims of each camp.

4. A steam tug and a sufficient number of barges shall be provided in order to land and embark the pilgrims.

ART. 130. The landing of the pilgrims from infected vessels shall be effected with the means on board. If these means are inadequate, the persons and the barges which have assisted in the landing must undergo the same treatment as the pilgrims and the infected vessel.

ART. 131. The sanitary station shall comprise the following installations and equipment:

1. A system of railway tracks connecting the landing places with the administrative and disinfecting quarters as well as with the buildings used for the various services and with the camps.

2. Quarters for the administrative office and for the personnel of the sanitary and other services.

3. Buildings for the disinfection and washing of wearing apparel and other articles.

4. Buildings in which the pilgrims shall be subjected to shower or sea baths while their clothing in use is being disinfected.

5. Hospitals separated for the two sexes and completely isolated:

a) For the observation of suspects;

b) For plague patients;

c) For cholera patients;

d) For patients stricken with other contagious diseases;

e) For those sick with ordinary diseases.

6. Camps suitably separated from one another, the distance between them being as great as possible. The lodgings intended for pilgrims shall be constructed on the best hygienic principles and shall not contain over twenty-five persons.

7. A well-situated cemetery, remote from all habitations, without contact with any sheet of underground water, and drained half a meter below the level of the graves.

8. Steam disinfecting chambers in sufficient number and combining all the elements of safety, efficiency, and rapidity. Apparatuses for the destruction of rats.

9. Atomizers, disinfecting chambers, and the appliances necessary for chemical disinfection.

10. Machines for distilling water, apparatus for the sterilization of water by heat, and machines for manufacturing ice. For the distribution of the drinking water: pipes and closed, tight tanks capable of being emptied only by stopcocks or pumps.

11. A bacteriological laboratory with the necessary personnel.

12. A set of movable night-soil cans for receiving the previously disinfected fecal matters and spreading them over one of the most distant parts of the island from the camps, care being taken that these dumping grounds are properly managed from a hygienic standpoint.

13. All dirty water shall be removed from the camps and shall neither be allowed to stagnate nor be used in preparing food. The waste waters coming from hospitals shall be disinfected.

ART. 132. The health authority shall provide a building for the food supplies and one for the fuel in each camp.

The schedule of prices fixed by the competent authority shall be posted up in several places in the camp in the principal languages of the countries inhabited by the pilgrims.

The camp physician shall each day inspect the quality of the victuals and see that there is a sufficient supply thereof.

Water shall be furnished free of charge.

2. *Stations of Abou-Ali, Abou-Saad, Djeddah, Vasta, and Yambo*

ART. 133. The sanitary stations of Abou-Ali, Abou-Saad, and Vasta, as well as those of Djeddah and Yambo, shall fulfill the following conditions:

1. At Abou-Ali there shall be established four hospitals — two for plague patients (male and female) and two for cholera patients (male and female).
2. At Vasta a hospital for ordinary patients shall be created.
3. At Abou-Saad and Vasta stone lodgings with a capacity of fifty persons each shall be constructed.
4. Three disinfecting chambers shall be located at Abou-Ali, Abou-Saad, and Vasta, with laundries, accessories, and apparatus for the destruction of rats.
5. Shower baths shall be established at Abou-Saad and Vasta.
6. On each of the islands of Abou-Saad and Vasta there shall be installed distilling apparatus capable of furnishing altogether fifteen tons of water a day.
7. The measures with regard to fecal matters and dirty water shall be regulated in accordance with the rules adopted for Camaran.
8. A cemetery shall be established in one of the islands.
9. The sanitary arrangements at Djeddah and Yambo provided for in Article 150 shall be installed, and especially the disinfecting chambers and other means of disinfection for pilgrims leaving Hedjaz.

ART. 134. The rules prescribed for Camaran with regard to food supplies and water shall be applicable to the camps of Abou-Ali, Abou-Saad, and Vasta.

B. SANITARY MEASURES APPLICABLE TO MUSSULMAN-PILGRIM SHIPS HAILING FROM THE NORTH AND BOUND TOWARD HEDJAZ

ART. 135. If plague or cholera is not known to exist in the port of departure or its neighborhood, and if no case of plague or cholera has occurred during the passage, the vessel shall be immediately granted pratique.

ART. 136. If plague or cholera is known to exist in the port of departure or its vicinity, or if a case of plague or cholera has occurred during the voyage, the vessel shall be subjected at Tor to the rules established for vessels coming from the south and stopping at Camaran. The vessels shall thereupon be granted pratique.

Section V. Measures to be taken upon the Return of Pilgrims

A. PILGRIM SHIPS RETURNING NORTHWARD

ART. 137. Every vessel bound for Suez or for a Mediterranean port, having on board pilgrims or similar masses of persons, and hailing from a port of Hedjaz or from any other port on the Arabian coast of the Red Sea, must repair to Tor in order to undergo there the observation and the sanitary measures indicated in Articles 141 to 143.

ART. 138. Vessels bringing Mussulman pilgrims back toward the Mediterranean shall pass through the canal in quarantine only.

ART. 139. The agents of navigation companies and captains are warned that, after completing their observation period at the sanitary station of Tor, the Egyptian pilgrims will alone be permitted to leave the vessel permanently in order to return thereupon to their homes.

Only those pilgrims will be recognized as Egyptians or as residents of Egypt who are provided with a certificate of residence issued by an Egyptian authority and conforming to the established model. Samples of this certificate shall be deposited with the consular and health authorities of Djeddah and Yambo, where the agents and captains of vessels can examine them.

Pilgrims other than Egyptians, such as Turks, Russians, Persians, Tunisians, Algerians, Moroccans, etc., cannot be landed in an Egyptian port after leaving Tor. Consequently navigation agents and captains are warned that the transshipment of pilgrims not residents of Egypt at Tor, Suez, Port Said, or Alexandria is forbidden.

Vessels having on board pilgrims who belong to the nationalities mentioned in the foregoing paragraph shall be subject to the rules applicable to these pilgrims and shall not be received in any Egyptian port of the Mediterranean.

ART. 140. Before being granted pratique Egyptian pilgrims shall undergo an observation of three days and a medical examination at Tor, Souakim, or any other station designated by the board of health of Egypt.

ART. 141. If plague or cholera is known to exist in Hedjaz or in the port from which the vessel hails, or if it has existed in Hedjaz during the course of the pilgrimage, the vessel shall be subjected at Tor to the rules adopted at Camaran for infected vessels.

The persons stricken with plague or cholera shall be landed and isolated in the hospital. The other passengers shall be landed and isolated in groups composed of as few persons as possible, so that the whole number may not be infected by a particular group if the plague or cholera should develop therein.

The soiled linen, wearing apparel, and clothing of the crew and passengers, as well as the baggage and cargo suspected of contamination, shall be landed and disinfected. Their disinfection as well as that of the vessel shall be thorough.

However, the local health authority may decide that the unloading of the heavy baggage and the cargo is not necessary, and that only a part of the vessel need undergo disinfection.

The measures provided by Articles 21 and 24 shall be applied with regard to the rats which may be found on board.

All the pilgrims shall be subjected to an observation of seven full days from the day on which the disinfecting operations are completed, whether it be a question of plague or of cholera. If a case of plague or cholera has appeared in one section, the period of seven days shall not begin for this section until the day on which the last case was discovered.

ART. 142. In the case contemplated in the preceding article, the Egyptian pilgrims shall be subjected, besides, to an additional observation of three days.

ART. 143. If plague or cholera is not known to exist either in Hedjaz or in the port from which the vessel hails, and has not been known to exist in Hedjaz during the course of the pilgrimage, the vessel shall be subjected at Tor to the rules adopted at Camaran for uninfected vessels.

The pilgrims shall be landed and take a shower or sea bath, and their soiled linen or the part of their wearing apparel and baggage which may appear suspicious in the opinion of the health authority shall be disinfected. The duration of these operations, including the debarkation and embarkation, shall not exceed seventy-two hours.

However, a pilgrim ship belonging to one of the nations which have adhered to the stipulations of the present and the previous conventions, if it has had no plague or cholera patients during the course of the voyage from Djeddah to Yambo or Tor, and if the individual medical examination made at Tor after debarkation establishes the fact that it contains no such patients, may be authorized by the board of health of Egypt to pass through the Suez Canal in quarantine, even at night, when the four following conditions are fulfilled:

1. Medical attendance shall be given on board by one or several physicians commissioned by the government to which the vessel belongs.

2. The vessel shall be provided with disinfecting chambers, and it shall be ascertained that the soiled linen has been disinfected during the course of the voyage.

3. It shall be shown that the number of pilgrims does not exceed that authorized by the pilgrimage regulations.

4. The captain shall bind himself to repair directly to a port of the country to which the vessel belongs.

The medical examination shall be made as soon as possible after debarkation at Tor.

The sanitary tax to be paid to the quarantine administration shall be the same as the pilgrims would have paid had they remained in quarantine three days.

ART. 144. A vessel which has had a suspicious case on board during the voyage from Tor to Suez shall be sent back to Tor.

ART. 145. The transshipment of pilgrims is strictly forbidden in Egyptian ports.

ART. 146. Vessels leaving Hedjaz and having on board pilgrims who are bound for a port on the African shore of the Red Sea shall be authorized to proceed directly to Souakim or to such other place as the board of health of Alexandria may determine, where they shall submit to the same quarantine procedure as at Tor.

ART. 147. Vessels hailing from Hedjaz or from a port on the Arabian coast of the Red Sea with a clean bill of health, having no pilgrims or similar groups of people on board, and which have had no suspicious occurrence during the voyage, shall be granted pratique at Suez after a favorable medical inspection.

ART. 148. When plague or cholera shall have been proven to exist in Hedjaz:

1. Caravans composed of Egyptian pilgrims shall, before going to Egypt, undergo at Tor a rigid quarantine of seven days in case of cholera or plague. They shall then undergo an observation of three days at Tor, after which they

shall not be granted pratique until a favorable medical inspection has been made and their belongings have been disinfected.

2. Caravans composed of foreign pilgrims who are about to return to their homes by land routes shall be subjected to the same measures as the Egyptian caravans and shall be accompanied by sanitary guards to the edge of the desert.

ART. 149. When plague or cholera has not been observed in Hedjaz, the caravans of pilgrims coming from Hedjaz by way of Akaba or Moila shall, upon their arrival at the canal or at Nakhel, be subjected to a medical examination and their soiled linen and wearing apparel shall be disinfected.

B. PILGRIMS RETURNING SOUTHWARD

ART. 150. Sufficiently complete sanitary arrangements shall be installed in the ports of embarkation of Hedjaz in order to render possible the application, to pilgrims who have to travel southward in order to return to their homes, of the measures which are obligatory by virtue of Articles 46 and 47 at the moment of departure of these pilgrims in the ports situated beyond the Straits of Bab-el-Mandeb.

The application of these measures is optional; that is, they are only to be applied in those cases in which the consular officer of the country to which the pilgrim belongs, or the physician of the vessel on which he is about to embark, deems them necessary.

CHAPTER III. PENALTIES

ART. 151. Every captain convicted of not having conformed, in the distribution of water, provisions, or fuel, to the obligations assumed by him, shall be liable to a fine of two Turkish pounds.[1] This fine shall be collected for the benefit of the pilgrim who shall have been the victim of the default, and who shall prove that he has vainly demanded the execution of the agreement made.

ART. 152. Every infraction of Article 104 shall be punished by a fine of thirty Turkish pounds.

ART. 153. Every captain who has committed or who has knowingly permitted any fraud whatever concerning the list of pilgrims or the bill of health provided for in Article 110 shall be liable to a fine of fifty Turkish pounds.

ART. 154. Every captain of a vessel arriving without a bill of health from the port of departure, or without a visé from the ports of call, or who is not provided with the list required by the regulations and regularly kept in accordance with Articles 110, 123, and 124, shall be liable in each case to a fine of twelve Turkish pounds.

ART. 155. Every captain convicted of having or having had on board more than 100 pilgrims without the presence of a commissioned physician in conformity with the provisions of Article 103 shall be liable to a fine of thirty Turkish pounds.

[1] The Turkish pound is worth 22 francs and 50 centimes.

ART. 156. Every captain convicted of having or having had on board a greater number of pilgrims than that which he is authorized to embark in conformity with the provisions of Article 110 shall be liable to a fine of five Turkish pounds for each pilgrim in excess.

The pilgrims in excess of the regular number shall be landed at the first station at which a competent authority resides, and the captain shall be obliged to furnish the landed pilgrims with the money necessary to pursue their voyage to their destination.

ART. 157. Every captain convicted of having landed pilgrims at a place other than their destination, except with their consent or excepting cases of *vis major*, shall be liable to a fine of twenty Turkish pounds for each pilgrim wrongfully landed.

ART. 158. All other infractions of the provisions relative to pilgrim ships are punishable by a fine of from 10 to 100 Turkish pounds.

ART. 159. Every violation proven in the course of a voyage shall be noted on the bill of health as well as on the list of pilgrims. The competent authority shall draw up a report thereof and deliver it to the proper party.

ART. 160. In Ottoman ports violations of the provisions concerning pilgrim ships shall be proven and the fine imposed by the competent authority in conformity with Articles 173 and 174.

ART. 161. All agents called upon to assist in the execution of the provisions of the present convention with regard to pilgrim ships are liable to punishment in conformity with the laws of their respective countries in case of faults committed by them in the application of the said provisions.

TITLE IV. SURVEILLANCE AND EXECUTION

I. THE SANITARY, MARITIME, AND QUARANTINE BOARD OF EGYPT

ART. 162. The stipulations of Annex III of the Sanitary Convention of Venice of January 30, 1892, concerning the composition, rights and duties, and operation of the Sanitary, Maritime, and Quarantine Board of Egypt, are confirmed as they appear in the decrees of his Highness the Khedive under date of June 19, 1893, and December 25, 1894, as well as in the ministerial decision of June 19, 1894.

The said decrees and decision are annexed to the present convention.

ART. 163. The ordinary expenses resulting from the provisions of the present convention, especially those relating to the increase of the personnel belonging to the Sanitary, Maritime, and Quarantine Board of Egypt, shall be covered by means of an annual supplementary payment by the Egyptian government of the sum of 4000 Egyptian pounds, which may be taken from the surplus revenues from the lighthouse service remaining at the disposal of said government.

However, the proceeds of a supplementary quarantine tax of ten tariff dollars per pilgrim, to be collected at Tor, shall be deducted from this sum.

In case the Egyptian government should find difficulty in bearing this share of the expenses, the Powers represented in the board of health shall reach an understanding with the khedival government in order to insure the participation of the latter in the expenses contemplated.

ART. 164. The Sanitary, Maritime, and Quarantine Board of Egypt shall undertake the task of bringing the provisions of the present convention into conformity with the regulations at present enforced by it in regard to the plague, cholera, and yellow fever, as well as with the regulations relative to arrivals from the Arabian ports of the Red Sea during the pilgrim season.

To the same end it shall, if necessary, revise the general regulations of the sanitary, maritime, and quarantine police at present in force.

These regulations, in order to become effective, must be accepted by the various Powers represented on the board.

II. THE SUPERIOR BOARD OF HEALTH OF CONSTANTINOPLE

ART. 165. The Superior Board of Health of Constantinople shall decide on the measures to be adopted in order to prevent the introduction of epidemic diseases into the Ottoman empire and their transmission to foreign countries.

ART. 166. The number of Ottoman delegates to the Superior Board of Health who shall take part in the voting of the board is fixed at four members, namely:

The president of the board, or, in his absence, the person presiding over the meeting. They shall not take part in the voting except in case of a tie.

The inspector general of the sanitary services.

The service inspector.

The delegate acting as intermediary between the board and the Sublime Porte, called Mouhassebedgi.

ART. 167. The appointment of the inspector general, of the service inspector, and of the aforementioned delegate, who are designated by the board, shall be ratified by the Ottoman government.

ART. 168. The high contracting parties recognize the right of Roumania, as a maritime power, to be represented on the board by one delegate.

ART. 169. The delegates of the various nations shall be physicians holding regular diplomas from a European faculty of medicine and citizens or subjects of the country which they represent, or consular officers of the grade of vice consul at least or an equivalent grade.

The delegates shall have no connection of any kind with the local authorities or with a maritime company.

These provisions do not apply to the present incumbents.

ART. 170. The decisions of the Superior Board of Health, reached by a majority of the members who compose it, are of an executory character and without appeal.

The signatory governments agree that their representatives at Constantinople shall be instructed to notify the Ottoman government of the present convention and to endeavor to obtain its accession thereto.

ART. 171. The enforcement and surveillance of the provisions of the present convention with regard to pilgrimages and to measures against the invasion and propagation of plague and cholera are intrusted, within the scope of the jurisdiction of the Superior Board of Health of Constantinople, to a committee appointed entirely from among the members of this board and composed of representatives of the various Powers which shall have adhered to the present convention.

The number of representatives of Turkey on this committee shall be three, one of them being president thereof. In case of a tie in voting, the president shall have the casting vote.

ART. 172. A corps of diplomaed physicians, disinfectors, and skilled mechanics, as well as of sanitary guards recruited from among persons who have performed military service as officers or noncommissioned officers, shall be created for the purpose of insuring the proper operation, under the direction of the superior Board of Health of Alexandria, of the various sanitary establishments enumerated in and instituted by the present convention.

ART. 173. The health authority of the Ottoman port of call or arrival who discovers a violation of the regulations, shall draw up a report thereof, on which the captain may enter his observations. A certified copy of this report shall be transmitted, at the port of call or arrival, to the consular officer of the country whose flag the vessel flies. The latter officer shall see that the fine is deposited with him. In the absence of a consul, the health authority shall receive this fine on deposit. The fine shall not be finally credited to the Superior Board of Health of Constantinople until the consular commission referred to in the following article has pronounced upon the validity of the fine.

A second copy of the certified report shall be transmitted by the health authority who has discovered the violation to the president of the board of health of Constantinople, who shall communicate the document to the consular commission.

A minute shall be made on the bill of health by the health or consular authority, noting the violation discovered and the deposit of the fine.

ART. 174. At Constantinople there shall be created a consular commission to pass judgment upon the contradictory declarations of the health officer and the captain under charge. It shall be appointed each year by the consular corps. The health department may be represented by an agent acting as public prosecutor. The consul of the nation interested shall always be summoned and shall be entitled to vote.

ART. 175. The expenses of the establishment, within the jurisdiction of the Superior Board of Health of Constantinople, of the permanent and temporary sanitary posts contemplated by the present convention, shall be borne by the Ottoman government as far as the construction of buildings is concerned. The Superior Board of Health of Constantinople is authorized, if there is urgent need, to advance the necessary sums out of the reserve fund; these sums shall be furnished it upon demand by "the mixed commission in charge of the revision of the sanitary tariff." It shall, in this case, see to the construction of these establishments.

The Superior Board of Health of Constantinople shall organize without delay the sanitary establishments of Hanikin and Kisil-Dizie, near Bayazid, upon the Turko-Persian and Turko-Russian frontiers, by means of the funds which are henceforth placed at its disposal.

The other expenses arising, within the jurisdiction of the said board, in connection with the measures prescribed by the present convention, shall be divided between the Ottoman government and the Superior Board of Health of Constantinople, in conformity with the understanding reached between the government and the Powers represented on this board.

III. The International Health Board of Tangier

Art. 176. In the interest of public health, the high contracting parties agree that their representatives in Morocco shall again invite the attention of the International Health Board of Tangier to the necessity of enforcing the provisions of the sanitary conventions.

IV. Miscellaneous Provisions

Art. 177. Each government shall determine the means to be employed for disinfection and for the destruction of rats.[1]

Art. 178. The proceeds from the sanitary taxes and fines shall in no case be employed for objects other than those within the scope of the boards of health.

[1] The following modes of disinfection are given by way of suggestion:

Old clothing, old rags, infected materials used in dressing wounds, paper, and other objects without value should be destroyed by fire.

Wearing apparel, bedding, and mattresses contaminated by plague bacilli are positively disinfected —

By passing them through a disinfecting chamber using steam under pressure, or through a chamber with flowing steam at 100° C.

By exposure to vapors of formol.

Objects which may, without damage, be immersed in antiseptic solutions (bed covers, underclothes, sheets) may be disinfected by means of solutions of sublimate in the proportion of 1 per 1000, of phenic acid in the proportion of 3 per 100, of lysol and commercial cresyl in the proportion of 3 per 100, of formol in the proportion of 1 per 100 (one part of the commercial solution of formaldehyde in the proportion of 40 per 100), or by means of alkaline hypochlorites (of soda, potassium) in the proportion of 1 per 100, — that is, one part of the usual commercial hypochlorite.

It goes without saying that the time of contact should be long enough to allow dried-up germs to be penetrated by the antiseptic solutions, four to six hours being sufficient.

For the destruction of rats three methods are at present employed:

1. That using sulphurous acid mixed with a small quantity of sulphuric anhydride, which is forced under pressure into the holds, stirring the air up. This causes the death of the rats and insects, and destroys the plague bacilli at the same time when the content of sulphuro-sulphuric anhydride is sufficiently great.

2. The process by which a noncombustible mixture of carbon monoxide and carbon dioxide is sent into the holds.

3. The process which utilizes carbonic acid in such a way that the content of this gas in the air of the vessel is about 30 per cent.

The last two procedures cause the death of the rodents, but are not claimed to kill the insects and plague bacilli.

The technical committee of the Paris sanitary conference of 1903 suggested the following three remedies — viz., a mixture of sulphuro-sulphuric anhydride, a mixture of carbon monoxide and carbonic acid, and carbonic acid, — as being among those to which the governments might have recourse, and it was of opinion that, in case they were not used by the health department itself, the latter ought to supervise each operation and ascertain that the rats have been destroyed.

ART. 179. The high contracting parties agree to have a set of instructions prepared by their health departments for the purpose of enabling captains of vessels, especially when there is no physician on board, to enforce the provisions contained in the present convention with regard to plague and cholera, as well as the regulations relative to yellow fever.

V. THE PERSIAN GULF

ART. 180. The expenses of construction and maintenance of the sanitary station whose creation at the Island of Ormuz is provided for by Article 81 of the present convention shall be borne by the Superior Board of Health of Constantinople. The mixed committee of revision of the said board shall meet as soon as possible in order to furnish it, upon its demand, the necessary funds from the available reserves.

VI. AN INTERNATIONAL HEALTH BUREAU

ART. 181. The conference having taken note of the annexed conclusions of its committee on ways and means regarding the creation of an international health bureau at Paris, the French government shall, when it judges it opportune, submit propositions to this effect through diplomatic channels to the nations represented at the conference.

TITLE V. YELLOW FEVER

ART. 182. It is recommended that the countries interested modify their sanitary regulations so as to bring them into accord with the latest scientific data regarding the mode of transmission of yellow fever, and especially regarding the part played by mosquitoes as vehicles of the germs of the disease.

TITLE VI. ADHESIONS AND RATIFICATIONS

ART. 183. The governments which have not signed the present convention shall be permitted to adhere thereto upon request. Notice of this adhesion shall be given through diplomatic channels to the government of the French republic and by the latter to the other signatory governments.

ART. 184. The present convention shall be ratified and the ratifications thereof deposited at Paris as soon as possible.

It shall be enforced as soon as it shall have been proclaimed in conformity with the legislation of the signatory nations. In the respective relations of the Powers which shall have ratified it, it shall supersede the international sanitary conventions signed January 30, 1892; April 15, 1893; April 3, 1894; and March 19, 1897.

The previous arrangements enumerated above shall remain in force with regard to the Powers which, having signed or adhered to them, may not ratify or accede to the present act.

In witness whereof the respective plenipotentiaries have signed the present convention and affixed thereto their seals.

Done at Paris on December 3, 1903, in a single copy which shall remain deposited in the archives of the government of the French republic, and of which certified copies shall be transmitted through diplomatic channels to the contracting Powers.

[Signatures]

PROCÈS-VERBAL OF THE DEPOSIT OF THE RATIFICATIONS OF THE INTERNATIONAL SANITARY CONVENTION SIGNED AT PARIS, DECEMBER 3, 1903

In execution of Article 184 of the international sanitary convention of December 3, 1903, the undersigned, representatives of the cosignatory Powers, to wit, [names follow], met in the ministry of foreign affairs at Paris in order to deposit the ratifications of the high contracting Powers with the government of the French republic.

The undersigned note that:

I. The governments of Greece and Servia having given notice, by means of two communications delivered to the legations of the French republic at Athens and Belgrade on May 16 and July 14, 1904, that they did not adhere to the said convention, it follows that Greece and Servia, whose delegates signed this act *ad referendum*, cannot be considered as contracting parties.

II. The ratification of the President of the United States of America is deposited with the following declaration, to wit: "That it is necessary to substitute 'observation' for 'surveillance' in the United States in the cases contemplated by Articles 21 et seq., on account of the peculiar legislation of the different states of the Union."

III. The ratification of his Majesty the King of the United Kingdom of Great Britain and Ireland, Emperor of India, is deposited with the following declarations:

"1. That the establishment of a sanitary station on the Island of Ormuz by the Superior Board of Health of Constantinople shall not take place until the said board shall have been reorganized in conformity with the provisions of the convention of December 3, 1903, and until the mixed tariff commission shall have placed funds at the disposal of the said board for this purpose by a unanimous decision.

"2. That the stipulations of the said convention shall not be applicable to the colonies, possessions, or protectorates of his Britannic Majesty until after notification to this effect shall have been sent by the representative of his Britannic Majesty at Paris to the minister of foreign affairs of the French republic in the name of such colony, possession, or protectorate."

IV. The ratification of his Majesty the Shah of Persia is deposited with the following declaration, to wit: "That it shall be understood that the flag which is to fly over the sanitary station of Ormuz shall be the Persian flag, and that the armed guards who may be necessary to insure the observance of the sanitary measures shall be furnished by the Persian government."

V. The signatory Powers have made the following double declaration, which is, moreover, in conformity with the stipulations contained in the convention of Venice of March 19, 1897, viz.: "That the contracting Powers reserve the right to agree with one another with regard to the introduction of modifications in the text of the present convention, and that each of these Powers preserves the right to denounce the present convention, which denunciation shall not have effect except with regard to it."

VI. The deposit of the instrument of the ratifications of the Egyptian government is made through the medium of the government of the republic in compliance with a request made in a letter of the minister of foreign affairs of his Highness the Khedive under date of October 25, 1906.

The undersigned also declare that their governments agree to grant to Spain and Portugal, whose parliaments have not yet acted on the convention of December 3, 1903, the privilege of depositing their ratifications later, and within the shortest period possible.

The government of the republic shall take note of these ratifications and shall advise the other ratifying Powers of the deposit of the ratifications of the two Powers above mentioned.

Whereupon, all the ratifications having been presented and found, upon examination, to be in good and due form, they are confided to the government of the republic to be deposited in the archives of the department of foreign affairs of the French republic.

In witness whereof the present *procès-verbal* has been drawn up, and a certified copy thereof shall be transmitted, through the government of the French republic, to each of the Powers which ratified the sanitary convention of December 3, 1903.

Done at Paris, April 6, 1907.

[Signatures]

CHAPTER XI

PROTECTION OF INDUSTRIAL PROPERTY

For the protection of industrial property, a convention and final protocol were concluded on March 20, 1883, at Paris, between Belgium, Brazil, France, Guatemala, Italy, the Netherlands, Portugal, Salvador, Servia, Spain, and the Swiss Confederation. Salvador withdrew on August 17, 1887. Other Powers gave their adhesion afterward; namely, Great Britain, Tunis, the Dominican republic, Norway, Sweden, the United States, Austria, Cuba, Germany, Japan, Mexico, Ceylon, and New Zealand. By the terms of the convention, certain enumerated colonies and possessions of France, Portugal, and Spain, were included. The official title of the organization formed by the agreement of the Powers is "The Union for the Protection of Industrial Property." The number and rank of the Powers adhering is sufficient to give their collective will the force of world law, and the convention is therefore placed in the code. The purpose of the Powers is expressed officially as follows:

Equally animated by the desire to assure, by common accord, a complete and efficacious protection to the industry and commerce of the subjects of the respective states, and to contribute to the safeguard of the rights of inventors, and to the loyalty of commercial transactions, (the original contracting Powers) have resolved to include a convention to that effect.

This convention, now become a chapter of world law, is as follows, — according to the official translation from the French language, published by the state department of the United States, — with amendments incorporated which were made by supplementary conventions of 1891 and 1900.

ART. 1. The governments of Belgium, of Brazil, of Spain, of France, of Guatemala, of Italy, of the Netherlands, of Portugal, of Salvador, of Servia, and of Switzerland, have constituted themselves into a state of union for the protection of industrial property.

ART. 2. The subjects or citizens of each of the contracting states shall enjoy, in all the other states of the union, so far as concerns patents for inventions, trade or commercial marks, and the commercial name, the advantages that the respective laws thereof at present accord, or shall afterwards accord, to subjects or citizens.

In consequence they shall have the same protection as these latter, and the same legal recourse against all infringements of their rights, under reserve of complying with the formalities and conditions imposed upon subjects or citizens by the domestic legislation of each state.

ART. 3. There are assimilated to the subjects or citizens of the contracting states, the subjects or citizens of states not forming part of the union, who are domiciled or have bona fide industrial or commercial establishments upon the territory of one of the states of the union.

ART. 4. Any one who shall have regularly deposited an application for a patent of invention of an industrial model, or design, of a trade or commercial mark, in one of the contracting states, shall enjoy, for the purpose of making the deposit in the other states, and under reserve of the rights of third parties, a right of priority during the periods hereinafter determined.

In consequence, the deposit subsequently made in one of the other states of the union before the expiration of these periods cannot be invalidated by acts performed in the interval, especially by another deposit, by the publication of the invention or its working, by the sale of copies of the design or model, by the employment of the mark.

The periods of priority above mentioned shall be 12 months for patents of invention and four months for designs or industrial models, as well as for trade or commercial marks.

ART. 4 *bis*. Patents applied for in the different contracting states by persons admitted to the benefit of the convention under the terms of Articles 2 and 3 shall be independent of the patents obtained for the same invention in the other states adherent or nonadherent to the union.

This provision shall apply to patents existing at the time of its going into effect.

The same rule applies, in the case of adhesion of new states, to patents already existing on both sides at the time of the adhesion.

ART. 5. The introduction by the patentee into countries where the patent has been granted, of articles manufactured in any other of the states of the union, shall not entail forfeiture.

The patentee, however, shall be subject to the obligation of working his patent conformably to the laws of the country into which he has introduced the patented articles.

ART. 6. Every trade or commercial mark regularly deposited in the country of origin shall be admitted to deposit and so protected in all the other countries of the union.

The country where the depositor has his principal establishment shall be considered as country of origin.

If this principal establishment is not situated in one of the countries of the union, that shall be considered as country of origin to which the depositor belongs.

The deposit may be refused if the object for which it is asked is considered contrary to morals and to public order.

ART. 7. The nature of the production upon which the trade or commercial mark is to be affixed cannot in any case be an obstacle to the deposit of the mark.

ART. 8. The commercial name shall be protected in all the countries of the union without obligation of deposit, whether it forms part or not of a trade or commercial mark.

ART. 9. Every production bearing, unlawfully, a trade or commercial mark, or a commercial name, may be seized upon importation into those of the states of the union in which such mark or such commercial name has a right to legal protection.

The seizure shall take place either at the instance of the public prosecutor or of the interested party, conformably to the domestic legislation of each state.

In the states whose legislation does not admit of seizure on importation, such seizure may be replaced by prohibition of importation.

The authorities shall not be required to make the seizure in case of transit.

ART. 10. The provisions of the preceding article shall be applicable to every production bearing falsely, as indication of origin, the name of a stated locality, when this indication shall be joined to a fictitious commercial name or a name borrowed with fraudulent intention.

Every producer, manufacturer, or trader engaged in the production, the manufacture, or the sale of this production when established either in the locality falsely indicated as place of origin or in the region where that locality is situated, is a reputed interested party.

ART. 10 *bis*. Those entitled of right under the convention (Articles 2 and 3) shall enjoy, in all the states of the union, the protection accorded to citizens or subjects against unfair competition.

ART. 11. The high contracting parties shall accord, conformably to the legislation of each country, a temporary protection to patentable inventions, to industrial designs, or models, as well as to trademarks for the productions which shall be shown at official or officially recognized international expositions organized upon the territory of one of them.

ART. 12. Each one of the high contracting parties engages to establish a special service of industrial property and a central depot, for giving information to the public concerning patents of invention, industrial designs or models, and trade or commercial marks.

ART. 13. An international office shall be organized under the title of "International Bureau of the Union for the Protection of Industrial Property."

This bureau, the cost of which shall be supported by the governments of all the contracting states, shall be placed under the high authority of the superior administration of the Swiss Confederation, and shall work under its supervision. Its powers shall be determined by common accord between the states of the union.

ART. 14. The present convention shall be submitted to periodical revisions for the purpose of introducing improvements calculated to perfect the system of the union.

With this object, conferences shall take place successively in one of the contracting states between the delegates of said states.

ART 15. It is understood that the high contracting parties respectively reserve the right to make, separately, between themselves, special arrangements for the protection of industrial property so far as these arrangements shall not interfere with the provisions of the present convention.

ART. 16. The states that have not taken part in the present convention shall be admitted to adhere to the same upon their application.

This adhesion shall be notified through the diplomatic channel to the govern ment of the Swiss Confederation, and by the latter to all the others.

It shall convey of full right accession to all the clauses, and admission to all the advantages stipulated by the present convention, and shall go into force a month after the sending of the notification given by the Swiss government to the unionist states, unless a later date shall have been indicated by the adhering state.

ART. 17. The execution of the reciprocal engagements contained in the present convention is subordinated, so far as needful, to the accomplishment of the formalities and rules established by the constitutional laws of such of the high contracting parties as are bound to ask the application thereof, which they agree to do with the shortest delay possible.

ART. 18. The present convention shall be put into execution within a month after exchange of ratifications, and shall remain in force during a period of time not determined, until the expiration of one year from the day upon which the denunciation shall be made.

This denunciation shall be addressed to the government empowered to receive adhesions. It shall only produce its effect as regards the state making it, the convention remaining executory for the other contracting parties.

ART. 19. The present convention shall be ratified and the ratifications shall be exchanged at Paris, within the period of one year at the latest.

In witness whereof the respective plenipotentiaries have signed it and affixed to it their seals.

Done at Paris the 20th of March, 1883.

[Signatures]

FINAL PROTOCOL

On proceeding to the signature of the convention concluded this day between the governments of Belgium, Brazil, Spain, France, Guatemala, Italy, the Netherlands, Portugal, Salvador, Servia, and Switzerland, for the protection of industrial property, the undersigned plenipotentiaries have agreed on the following:

1. The words "industrial property" are to be understood in their widest acceptation, in the sense that they apply not only to the productions of industry properly so called, but equally to the productions of agriculture (wines, grains, fruits, cattle, etc.) and to mineral productions used in commerce (mineral waters, etc.).

2. Under the name "patents of invention" are included the various classes of industrial patents granted by the laws of the contracting states, such as patents of importation, patents of improvement, etc.

3. It is understood that the final provision of Article 2 of the convention shall in no respect infringe upon the laws of any of the contracting states, so far as concerns the procedure before the courts and the competence of the said courts.

3. *bis.* The patentee, in each country, shall not suffer forfeiture because of nonworking until after a minimum period of three years, to date from the

deposit of the application in the country concerned, and in the case where the patentee shall not justify the reasons of his inaction.

4. Paragraph 1 of Article 6 is to be understood in the sense that no trade or commercial mark shall be excluded from protection, in any of the states of the union, by the mere fact that it may not satisfy, in respect to the signs composing it, the conditions of the laws of this state, provided that it does satisfy, in this regard, the laws of the country of origin, and that it has been in this latter country duly deposited. Saving this exception, which concerns only the form of the mark, and under reservation of the provisions of the other articles of the convention, the domestic legislation of each of the states shall receive its due application.

In order to avoid all misinterpretation, it is understood that the use of public armorial bearings and decorations may be considered contrary to public order in the sense of the final paragraph of Article 6.

5. The organization of a special service of industrial property mentioned in Article 12 shall include, as far as is possible, the publication in each state of an official periodical.

6. The expenses of the international bureau instituted by Article 13 shall be supported by the contracting states in common. They cannot in any event exceed the sum of 60,000 francs per annum.

In order to determine the contributory share of each of the states in this sum total of expenses, the contracting states, and those which may hereafter adhere to the union, shall be divided into six classes, each contributing in the proportion of a certain number of units, namely:

1st class	25 units
2d class	20 units
3d class	15 units
4th class	10 units
5th class	5 units
6th class	3 units

These coefficients shall be multiplied by the number of the states of each class, and the sum of the products thus obtained shall furnish the number of units by which the total expense is to be divided. The quotient will give the amount of the unit of expense.

The contracting states are classified as follows in respect to the division of the expenses:

1st class	France, Italy
2d class	Spain
3d class	Belgium, Brazil, Portugal, Switzerland
4th class	Netherlands
5th class	Servia
6th class	Guatemala, Salvador

The Swiss government shall supervise the expenditure of the international bureau, make the necessary advances, and state the annual account, which shall be communicated to all the other governments.

The international bureau shall collect information of every kind relating to the protection of industrial property, and shall compile from it general statistics, which shall be transmitted to all the governments. It shall occupy itself with examinations of general utility which may be of interest to the union, and shall publish, with the assistance of the documents put at its disposal by the various governments, a periodical in the French language on questions which concern the object of the union.

The numbers of this periodical and all the documents published by the international bureau shall be partitioned among the governments of the states of the union in the proportion of the number of contributory units above mentioned.

The copies and supplementary documents which may be requested, either by the said governments or by corporations or private persons, shall be paid for separately.

The international bureau must always hold itself at the disposal of the members of the union, in order to furnish them, on questions relating to the international service of industrial property, with such special information as they may need.

The government of the country where the next conference is to be held shall prepare, with the assistance of the international bureau, the work of the said conference.

The director of the international bureau shall be present at the sessions of the conferences, and shall take part in the discussions without voting.

He shall make an annual report on its management, which shall be communicated to all the members of the union.

The official language of the international bureau shall be the French language.

7. The present final protocol, which shall be ratified at the same time as the convention concluded this day, shall be considered as forming an integral part of that convention, and shall have the same force, value, and duration.

In faith whereof the undersigned plenipotentiaries have drawn up the present protocol.

[Signatures]

CHAPTER XII

PROTECTION OF SUBMARINE CABLES

For the protection of submarine cables a convention was concluded at Paris on March 14, 1884, between the United States, Germany, the Argentine Confederation, Austria-Hungary, Belgium, Brazil, Costa Rica, Denmark, the Dominican republic, Spain, the United States of Colombia, France, Great Britain, Guatemala, Greece, Italy, Turkey, the Netherlands, Persia, Portugal, Roumania, Russia, Salvador, Servia, Sweden and Norway, and Uruguay, with provision for admitting the following colonies of Great Britain: Canada, Newfoundland, the Cape of Good Hope, Natal, New South Wales, Victoria, Queensland, Tasmania, South Australia, West Australia, and New Zealand. The convention became operative on January 15, 1886. It was not ratified by Persia nor the United States of Colombia. Japan adhered April 12, 1884. The purpose of the convention was "to secure the maintenance of telegraphic communication by means of submarine cables." Manifestly the will of such an array of Powers is entitled to rank as world law, and the convention is therefore given as a chapter of the code as follows:

ART. 1. The present convention shall be applicable, outside of the territorial waters, to all legally established submarine cables landed in the territories, colonies, or possessions of one or more of the high contracting parties.

ART. 2. The breaking or injury of a submarine cable, done willfully or through culpable negligence, and resulting in the total or partial interruption or embarrassment of telegraphic communication, shall be a punishable offense, but the punishment inflicted shall be no bar to a civil action for damages.

This provision shall not apply to ruptures or injuries when the parties guilty thereof have become so simply with the legitimate object of saving their lives or their vessels, after having taken all necessary precautions to avoid such ruptures or injuries.

ART. 3. The high contracting parties agree to insist, as far as possible, when they shall authorize the landing of a submarine cable, upon suitable conditions of safety, both as regards the track of the cable and its dimensions.

ART. 4. The owner of a cable who, by the laying or repairing of that cable, shall cause the breaking or injury of another cable, shall be required to pay the cost of the repairs which such breaking or injury shall have rendered necessary, but such payment shall not bar the enforcement, if there be ground therefor, of Article 2 of this convention.

ART. 5. Vessels engaged in laying or repairing submarine cables must observe the rules concerning signals that have been or shall be adopted, by common consent, by the high contracting parties, with a view to preventing collisions at sea.

When a vessel engaged in repairing a cable carries the said signals, other vessels that see or are able to see those signals shall withdraw or keep at a distance of at least one nautical mile from such vessel, in order not to interfere with its operations.

Fishing gear and nets shall be kept at the same distance.

Nevertheless, a period of twenty-four hours at most shall be allowed to fishing vessels that perceive or are able to perceive a telegraph ship carrying the said signals, in order that they may be enabled to obey the notice thus given, and no obstacle shall be placed in the way of their operations during such period.

The operations of telegraph ships shall be finished as speedily as possible.

ART. 6. Vessels that see or are able to see buoys designed to show the position of cables when the latter are being laid, are out of order, or are broken, shall keep at a distance of one quarter of a nautical mile at least from such buoys.

Fishing nets and gear shall be kept at the same distance.

ART. 7. Owners of ships or vessels who can prove that they have sacrificed an anchor, a net, or any other implement used in fishing, in order to avoid injuring a submarine cable, shall be indemnified by the owner of the cable.

In order to be entitled to such indemnity, one must prepare, whenever possible, immediately after the accident, in proof thereof, a statement supported by the testimony of the men belonging to the crew; and the captain of the vessel must, within twenty-four hours after arriving at the first port of temporary entry, make his declaration to the competent authorities. The latter shall give notice thereof to the consular authorities of the nation to which the owner of the cable belongs.

ART. 8. The courts competent to take cognizance of infractions of this convention shall be those of the country to which the vessel on board of which the infraction has been committed belongs.

It is, moreover, understood that, in cases in which the provision contained in the foregoing paragraph cannot be carried out, the repression of violations of this convention shall take place, in each of the contracting states, in the case of its subjects or citizens, in accordance with the general rules of penal competence established by the special laws of those states, or by international treaties.

ART. 9. Prosecutions on account of the infractions contemplated in Articles 2, 5, and 6 of this convention, shall be instituted by the state or in its name.

ART. 10. Evidence of violations of this convention may be obtained by all methods of securing proof that are allowed by the laws of the country of the court before which a case has been brought.

When the officers commanding the vessels of war or the vessels specially commissioned for that purpose, of one of the high contracting parties, shall have reason to believe that an infraction of the measures provided for by this convention has been committed by a vessel other than a vessel of war, they may require the captain or master to exhibit the official documents furnishing evidence of the nationality of the said vessel. Summary mention of such exhibition shall at once be made on the documents exhibited.

Reports may, moreover, be prepared by the said officers, whatever may be the nationality of the inculpated vessel. These reports shall be drawn up in the form and in the language in use in the country to which the officer drawing them up belongs; they may be used as evidence in the country in which they shall be invoked, and according to the laws of such country. The accused parties and the witnesses shall have the right to add or to cause to be added thereto, in their own language, any explanations that they may deem proper; these declarations shall be duly signed.

ART. 11. Proceedings and trial in cases of infractions of the provisions of this convention shall always take place as summarily as the laws and regulations in force will permit.

ART. 12. The high contracting parties engage to take or to propose to their respective legislative bodies the measures necessary in order to secure the execution of this convention, and especially in order to cause the punishment, either by fine or imprisonment, or both, of such persons as may violate the provisions of Articles 2, 5, and 6.

ART. 13. The high contracting parties shall communicate to each other such laws as may already have been or as may hereafter be enacted in their respective countries, relative to the subject of this convention.

ART. 14. States that have not taken part in this convention shall be allowed to adhere thereto, on their requesting to do so. Notice of such adhesion shall be given, diplomatically, to the government of the French republic, and by the latter to the other signatory governments.

ART. 15. It is understood that the stipulations of this convention shall in no wise affect the liberty of action of belligerents.

ART. 16. This convention shall take effect on such day as shall be agreed upon by the high contracting parties.

It shall remain in force for five years from that day, and, in case none of the high contracting parties shall have given notice, twelve months previously to the expiration of the said period of five years, of its intention to cause its effects to cease, it shall continue in force for one year, and so on from year to year.

In case one of the signatory Powers shall give notice of its desire for the cessation of the effects of the convention, such notice shall be effective as regards that Power only.

ART. 17. This convention shall be ratified; its ratifications shall be exchanged at Paris as speedily as possible, and within one year at the latest.

In testimony whereof the respective plenipotentiaries have signed it, and have thereunto affixed their seals.

Done in twenty-six copies, at Paris, this 14th day of March, 1884.

[Signatures]

Additional Article

The stipulations of the convention concluded this day for the protection of submarine cables shall be applicable, according to Article 1, to the colonies and possessions of her Britannic Majesty with the exception of those named below, to wit: Canada, Newfoundland, The Cape, Natal, New South Wales, Victoria, Queensland, Tasmania, South Australia, West Australia, New Zealand.

Nevertheless, the stipulations of the said convention shall be applicable to one of the above-named colonies or possessions if, in their [its?] name, a notification to that effect has been addressed by the representative of her Britannic Majesty at Paris to the minister of foreign affairs of France.

Each of the above-named colonies or possessions that shall have adhered to the said convention, shall have the privilege of withdrawing in the same manner as the contracting Powers. In case one of the colonies or possessions in question shall desire to withdraw from the convention, a notification to that effect shall be addressed by her Britannic Majesty's representative at Paris to the minister of foreign affairs of France.

Done in twenty-six copies at Paris, this 14th day of March, 1884.

[Signatures]

A declaration and final protocol explaining certain terms of the preceding convention were signed at Paris on December 1, 1886, as follows:

DECLARATION

The undersigned, plenipotentiaries of the signatory governments of the convention of March 14, 1884, for the protection of submarine cables, having recognized the expediency of defining the sense of the terms of Articles 2 and 4, of the said convention, have prepared by common accord the following declaration:

Certain doubts having arisen as to the meaning of the word "willfully" inserted in Article 2 of the convention of the 14th of March, 1884, it is understood that the imposition of penal responsibility, mentioned in the said article, does not apply to cases of breaking or of injuries occasioned accidentally or necessarily in repairing a cable, when all precautions have been taken to avoid such breakings or damages.

It is likewise understood that Article 4 of the convention has no other object and is to have no other effect than to charge the competent tribunals of each country with the determination, conformably to their laws and according to circumstances, of the question of the civil responsibility of the owner of a cable, who, by the laying or repairing of such cable, causes the breaking or injury of another cable, and also of the consequences of that responsibility, if it is found to exist.

Done at Paris, December 1, 1886, and March 23, 1887, for Germany.

[Signatures]

FINAL PROTOCOL

The undersigned, plenipotentiaries of the governments, parties to the convention of March 14, 1884, for the protection of submarine cables, having met at Paris for the purpose of fixing, in pursuance of Article 16 of that international instrument, a date for putting the said convention into execution, have agreed upon the following:

I. The international convention of March 14, 1884, for the protection of submarine cables, shall go into operation on the 1st day of May, 1888, provided, however, that at that date those of the contracting governments that have not yet adopted the measures provided for by Article 12 of the said international instrument shall have conformed to that stipulation.

II. The measures which shall have been taken by the said states in execution of Article 12 aforesaid, shall be made known to the other contracting Powers through the French government, which is charged with the examination of the said measures.

III. The government of the French republic is likewise charged with the examination of the similar legislative and reglementary provisions which are to be adopted, in their respective countries, in pursuance of Article 12, by such states as have not taken part in the convention, and as may desire to avail themselves of the privilege of accession, for which provision is made in Article 14.

In testimony whereof, the undersigned plenipotentiaries have adopted this final protocol, which shall be considered as forming an integral part of the international convention of March 14, 1884.

Done at Paris, July 7, 1887.

[Signatures]

CHAPTER XIII

REPRESSION OF THE SLAVE TRADE AND RESTRICTION OF CERTAIN IMPORTATIONS INTO AFRICA

A general act for the repression of the African slave trade and the restriction of the importation into, and sale in, a certain defined zone of Africa of firearms, ammunition, and spirituous liquors, was signed at Brussels on July 2, 1890, by plenipotentiaries of the United States, Germany, Austria-Hungary, Belgium, Denmark, Spain, the Independent State of the Congo, France, Great Britain, Italy, the Netherlands, Persia, Portugal, Russia, Sweden and Norway, Turkey, and Zanzibar. The purpose was expressed as follows, as given in the translation from the French original published officially by the United States: "Being equally actuated by the firm intention of putting an end to the crimes and devastations engendered by the traffic in African slaves, of efficiently protecting the aboriginal population of Africa, and of securing for that vast continent the benefits of peace and civilization; wishing to give fresh sanction to the decisions already adopted in the same sense and at different times by the Powers, to complete the results secured by them and to draw up a body of measures guaranteeing the accomplishment of the work which is the object of their common solicitude,—[the powers named] have resolved, in pursuance of the invitation addressed to them by the government of his Majesty the King of the Belgians, in agreement with the government of her Majesty the Queen of Great Britain and Ireland, Empress of India, to convene for this purpose a conference at Brussels."

A protocol was signed at Brussels on January 2, 1892, by the plenipotentiaries of the above-named Powers, providing for the partial ratification of the general act by France. The protocol and the general act were duly ratified by the Powers named and were duly proclaimed and took effect on April 2, 1892. This general act is as follows, by the official translation of the United States from the French original, and worthily takes its place in the code of world law:

Chapter I. Slave-trade Countries. Measures to be taken in the Places of Origin

Art. 1. The Powers declare that the most effective means of counteracting the slave trade in the interior of Africa are the following:

1. Progressive organization of the administrative, judicial, religious, and military services in the African territories placed under the sovereignty or protectorate of civilized nations.

2. The gradual establishment in the interior, by the Powers to which the territories are subject, of strongly occupied stations, in such a way as to make their protective or repressive action effectively felt in the territories devastated by slave hunting.

3. The construction of roads, and in particular of railways, connecting the advanced stations with the coast, and permitting easy access to the inland waters, and to such of the upper courses of the rivers and streams as are broken by rapids and cataracts, with a view to substituting economical and rapid means of transportation for the present system of carriage by men.

4. Establishment of steamboats on the inland navigable waters and on the lakes, supported by fortified posts established on the banks.

5. Establishment of telegraphic lines, insuring the communication of the posts and stations with the coast and with the administrative centers.

6. Organization of expeditions and flying columns, to keep up the communication of the stations with each other and with the coast, to support repressive action, and to insure the security of high roads.

7. Restriction of the importation of firearms, at least of those of modern pattern, and of ammunition throughout the entire extent of the territory in which the slave trade is carried on.

Art. 2. The stations, the inland cruisers organized by each Power in its waters, and the posts which serve as ports of register for them shall, independently of their principal task, which is to prevent the capture of slaves and intercept the routes of the slave trade, have the following subsidiary duties:

1. To support and, if necessary, to serve as a refuge for the native population, whether placed under the sovereignty or the protectorate of the state to which the station is subject, or independent, and temporarily for all other natives in case of imminent danger; to place the population of the first of these categories in a position to coöperate for their own defense; to diminish intestine wars between tribes by means of arbitration; to initiate them in agricultural labor and in the industrial arts so as to increase their welfare; to raise them to civilization and bring about the extinction of barbarous customs, such as cannibalism and human sacrifices.

2. To give aid and protection to commercial enterprises; to watch over their legality by especially controlling contracts for service with natives, and to prepare the way for the foundation of permanent centers of cultivation and of commercial settlements.

3. To protect, without distinction of creed, the missions which are already or that may hereafter be established.

4. To provide for the sanitary service and to extend hospitality and help to explorers and to all who take part in Africa in the work of repressing the slave trade.

ART. 3. The Powers exercising a sovereignty or a protectorate in Africa confirm and give precision to their former declarations, and engage to proceed gradually, as circumstances may permit, either by the means above indicated or by any other means that they may consider suitable, with the repression of the slave trade, each state in its respective possessions and under its own direction. Whenever they consider it possible, they shall lend their good offices to such Powers as, with a purely humanitarian object, may be engaged in Africa in the fulfillment of a similar mission.

ART. 4. The states exercising sovereign Powers or protectorates in Africa may in all cases delegate to companies provided with charters all or a portion of the engagements which they assume in virtue of Article 3. They remain, nevertheless, directly responsible for the engagements which they contract by the present act, and guarantee the execution thereof. The Powers promise to encourage, aid, and protect such national associations and enterprises due to private initiative as may wish to coöperate in their possessions in the repression of the slave trade, subject to their receiving previous authorization, such authorization being revocable at any time, subject also to their being directed and controlled, and to the exclusion of the exercise of rights of sovereignty.

ART. 5. The contracting Powers pledge themselves, unless this has already been provided for by laws in accordance with the spirit of the present article, to enact or propose to their respective legislative bodies, in the course of one year at the latest from the date of the signing of the present general act, a law rendering applicable, on the one hand, the provisions of their penal laws concerning grave offenses against the person, to the organizers and abetters of slave hunting, to those guilty of mutilating male adults and children, and to all persons taking part in the capture of slaves by violence; and, on the other hand, the provisions relating to offenses against individual liberty, to carriers and transporters of, and into dealers in, slaves.

The accessories and accomplices of the different categories of slave captors and dealers above specified shall be punished with penalties proportionate to those incurred by the principals.

Guilty persons who may have escaped from the jurisdiction of the authorities of the country where the crimes or offenses have been committed shall be arrested either on communication of the incriminating evidence by the authorities who have ascertained the violation of the law, or on production of any other proof of guilt by the Power in whose territory they may have been discovered, and shall be kept, without other formality, at the disposal of the tribunals competent to try them.

The Powers shall communicate to one another, with the least possible delay, the laws or decrees existing or promulgated in execution of the present article.

ART. 6. Slaves liberated in consequence of the stoppage or dispersion of a convoy in the interior of the continent, shall be sent back, if circumstances permit, to their country of origin; if not, the local authorities shall facilitate, as much as possible, their means of living, and if they desire it, help them to settle on the spot.

ART. 7. Any fugitive slave claiming, on the continent, the protection of the signatory Powers, shall receive it, and shall be received in the camps and stations officially established by said Powers, or on board of the vessels of the state plying on the lakes and rivers. Private stations and boats are only permitted to exercise the right of asylum subject to the previous consent of the state.

ART. 8. The experience of all nations that have intercourse with Africa having shown the pernicious and preponderating part played by firearms in operations connected with the slave trade as well as in internal wars between the native tribes; and this same experience having clearly proved that the preservation of the African population, whose existence it is the express wish of the Powers to protect, is a radical impossibility if measures restricting the trade in firearms and ammunition are not adopted, the Powers decide, so far as the present state of their frontiers permits, that the importation of firearms, and especially of rifles and improved weapons, as well as of powder, ball, and cartridges, is, except in the cases and under the conditions provided for in the following article, prohibited in the territories comprised between the 20th parallel of north latitude and the 22d parallel of south latitude, and extending westward to the Atlantic Ocean and eastward to the Indian Ocean and its dependencies, including the islands adjacent to the coast within 100 nautical miles from the shore.

ART. 9. The introduction of firearms and ammunition, when there shall be occasion to authorize it in the possessions of the signatory Powers that exercise rights of sovereignty or of protectorate in Africa, shall be regulated, unless identical or stricter regulations have already been enforced, in the following manner in the zone defined in Article 8:

All imported firearms shall be deposited, at the cost, risk, and peril of the importers, in a public warehouse under the supervision of the state government. No withdrawal of firearms or imported ammunition shall take place from such warehouses without the previous authorization of the said government. This authorization shall, except in the cases hereinafter specified, be refused for the withdrawal of all arms for accurate firing, such as rifles, magazine guns, or breechloaders, whether whole or in detached pieces, their cartridges, caps, or other ammunition intended for them.

In seaports, and under conditions affording the needful guarantees, the respective governments may permit private warehouses, but only for ordinary powder and for flintlock muskets, and to the exclusion of improved arms and ammunition therefor.

Independently of the measures directly taken by governments for the arming of the public force and the organization of their defense, individual exceptions may be allowed in the case of persons furnishing sufficient guarantees that the weapon and ammunition delivered to them shall not be given, assigned, or sold to third parties, and for travelers provided with a declaration of their government stating that the weapon and ammunition are intended for their personal defense exclusively.

All arms, in the cases provided for in the preceding paragraph, shall be registered and marked by the supervising authorities, who shall deliver to the persons in question permits to bear arms, stating the name of the bearer and showing the stamp with which the weapon is marked. These permits shall be revocable in case proof is furnished that they have been improperly used, and shall be issued for five years only, but may be renewed.

The above rule as to warehousing shall also apply to gunpowder.

Only flintlock guns, with unrifled barrels, and common gunpowder known as trade powder, may be withdrawn from the warehouses for sale. At each withdrawal of arms and ammunition of this kind for sale, the local authorities shall determine the regions in which such arms and ammunition may be sold. The regions in which the slave trade is carried on shall always be excluded. Persons authorized to take arms or powder out of the public warehouses shall present to the state government, every six months, detailed lists indicating the destinations of the arms and powder sold, as well as the quantities still remaining in the warehouses.

ART. 10. The governments shall take all such measures as they may deem necessary to insure as complete a fulfillment as possible of the provisions respecting the importation, sale, and transportation of firearms and ammunition, as well as to prevent either the entry or exit thereof via their inland frontiers, or the passage thereof to regions where the slave trade is rife.

The authorization of transit within the limits of the zone specified in Article 8 shall not be withheld when the arms and ammunition are to pass across the territory of the signatory or adherent Power occupying the coast, towards inland territories under the sovereignty or protectorate of another signatory or adherent Power, unless this latter Power have direct access to the sea through its own territory. If this access be wholly interrupted, the authorization of transit cannot be withheld. Any application for transit must be accompanied by a declaration emanating from the government of the Power having the inland possessions, and certifying that the said arms and ammunition are not intended for sale, but are for the use of the authorities of such Power, or of the military forces necessary for the protection of the missionary or commercial stations, or of persons mentioned by name in the declaration. Nevertheless, the territorial Power of the coast retains the right to stop, exceptionally and provisionally, the transit of improved arms and ammunition across its territory, if, in consequence of inland disturbances or other serious danger, there is ground for fearing lest the dispatch of arms and ammunition may compromise its own safety.

ART. 11. The Powers shall communicate to one another information relating to the traffic in firearms and ammunition, the permits granted, and the measures of repression in force in their respective territories.

ART. 12. The Powers engage to adopt or to propose to their respective legislative bodies the measures necessary everywhere to secure the punishment of infringers of the prohibitions contained in Articles 8 and 9, and that of their accomplices, besides the seizure and confiscation of the prohibited arms and ammunition, either by fine or imprisonment, or by both of these penalties, in proportion to the importance of the infraction and in accordance with the gravity of each case.

ART. 13. The signatory Powers that have possessions in Africa in contact with the zone specified in Article 8, bind themselves to take the necessary measures for preventing the introduction of firearms and ammunition across their inland frontiers into the regions of said zone, at least that of improved arms and cartridges.

Art. 14. The system stipulated in Articles 8 to 13 shall remain in force for twelve years. In case none of the contracting parties shall have given notice, twelve months before the expiration of this period, of its intention to put an end to it, or shall have demanded its revision, it shall remain obligatory for two years longer, and shall thus continue in force from two years to two years.

Chapter II. Caravan Routes and Transportation of Slaves by Land

Art. 15. Independently of the repressive or protective action which they exercise in the centers of the slave trade, it shall be the duty of the stations, cruisers, and posts, whose establishment is provided for in Article 2, and of all other stations established or recognized by Article 4, by each government in its possessions, to watch, so far as circumstances shall permit, and in proportion to the progress of their administrative organization, the roads traveled in their territory by slave dealers, to stop convoys on their march, or to pursue them wherever their action can be legally exercised.

Art. 16. In the regions of the coasts known to serve habitually as places of passage or terminal points for slave traffic coming from the interior, as well as at the points of intersection of the principal caravan routes crossing the zone contiguous to the coast already subject to the control of the sovereign or protective Powers, posts shall be established under the conditions and with the reservations mentioned in Article 3, by the authorities to which the territories are subject, for the purpose of intercepting the convoys and liberating the slaves.

Art. 17. A strict watch shall be organized by the local authorities at the ports and places near the coast, with a view to preventing the sale and shipment of slaves brought from the interior, as well as the formation and departure landwards of bands of slave hunters and dealers.

Caravans arriving at the coast or in its vicinity, as well as those arriving in the interior at a locality occupied by the territorial Power, shall, on their arrival, be subjected to a minute inspection as to the persons composing them. Any such person being ascertained to have been captured or carried off by force, or mutilated, either in his native place or on the way, shall be set free.

Art. 18. In the possessions of each of the contracting Powers it shall be the duty of the government to protect liberated slaves, to return them, if possible, to their country, to procure means of subsistence for them, and, in particular, to take charge of the education and subsequent employment of abandoned children.

Art. 19. The penal arrangements provided for by Article 5 shall be applicable to all offenses committed in the course of operations connected with the transportation of and traffic in slaves on land whenever such offenses may be ascertained to have been committed.

Any person having incurred a penalty in consequence of an offense provided for by the present general act, shall incur the obligation of furnishing security before being able to engage in any commercial transaction in countries where the slave trade is carried on.

CHAPTER III. REPRESSION OF THE SLAVE TRADE BY SEA

Section I. General Provisions

ART. 20. The signatory Powers recognize the desirability of taking steps in common for the more effective repression of the slave trade in the maritime zone in which it still exists.

ART. 21. This zone extends, on the one hand, between the coasts of the Indian Ocean (those of the Persian Gulf and of the Red Sea included), from Baluchistan to Cape Tangalane (Quilimane); and, on the other hand, a conventional line which first follows the meridian from Tangalane till it intersects the 26th degree of south latitude; it is then merged in this parallel, then passes round the island of Madagascar by the east, keeping 20 miles off the east and north shore, till it intersects the meridian at Cape Ambre. From this point the limit of the zone is determined by an oblique line, which extends to the coast of Baluchistan, passing 20 miles off Cape Ras el Hadd.

ART. 22. The signatory Powers of the present general act — among whom exist special conventions for the suppression of the slave trade — have agreed to restrict the clauses of those conventions concerning the reciprocal right of visit, of search, and of seizure of vessels at sea, to the above-mentioned zone.

ART. 23. The same Powers also agree to limit the above-mentioned right to vessels whose tonnage is less than 500 tons. This stipulation shall be revised as soon as experience shall have shown the necessity thereof.

ART. 24. All other provisions of the conventions concluded for the suppression of the slave trade between the aforesaid Powers shall remain in force provided they are not modified by the present general act.

ART. 25. The signatory Powers engage to adopt efficient measures to prevent the unlawful use of their flag, and to prevent the transportation of slaves on vessels authorized to fly their colors.

ART. 26. The signatory Powers engage to adopt all measures necessary to facilitate the speedy exchange of information calculated to lead to the discovery of persons taking part in operations connected with the slave trade.

ART. 27. At least one international bureau shall be created; it shall be established at Zanzibar. The high contracting parties engage to forward to it all the documents specified in Article 41, as well as all information of any kind likely to assist in the suppression of the slave trade.

ART. 28. Any slave who has taken refuge on board a ship of war bearing the flag of one of the signatory Powers shall be immediately and definitively set free. Such freedom, however, shall not withdraw him from the competent jurisdiction if he has been guilty of any crime or offense at common law.

ART. 29. Any slave detained against his will on board of a native vessel shall have the right to demand his liberty. His release may be ordered by any agent of any of the signatory Powers on whom the present general act confers the right of ascertaining the status of persons on board of such vessels, although such release shall not withdraw him from the competent jurisdiction if he has committed any crime or offense at common law.

Section II. Regulation concerning the Use of the Flag and Supervision by Cruisers

I. RULES FOR GRANTING THE FLAG TO NATIVE VESSELS, AND AS TO CREW LISTS AND MANIFESTS OF BLACK PASSENGERS ON BOARD

ART. 30. The signatory Powers engage to exercise a strict surveillance over native vessels authorized to carry their flag in the zone mentioned in Article 21, and over the commercial operations carried on by such vessels.

ART. 31. The term "native vessel" applies to vessels fulfilling one of the following conditions:

1. It shall present the outward appearance of native build or rigging.

2. It shall be manned by a crew of whom the captain and the majority of the seamen belong by origin to one of the countries on the coast of the Indian Ocean, the Red Sea, or the Persian Gulf.

ART. 32. The authorization to carry the flag of one of the said Powers shall in future be granted only to such native vessels as shall satisfy at the same time the three following conditions:

1. Fitters-out or owners of ships must be either subjects of or persons protected by the Power whose flag they ask to carry.

2. They shall be obliged to prove that they possess real estate situated in the district of the authority to whom their application is addressed, or to furnish bona fide security as a guaranty of the payment of such fines as may be incurred.

3. The above-named fitters-out or owners of ships, as well as the captain of the vessel, shall prove that they enjoy a good reputation, and that in particular they have never been sentenced to punishment for acts connected with the slave trade.

ART. 33. This authorization granted shall be renewed every year. It may at any time be suspended or withdrawn by the authorities of the Power whose colors the vessel carries.

ART. 34. The act of authorization shall contain the statements necessary to establish the identity of the vessel. The captain shall have the keeping thereof. The name of the native vessel and the amount of its tonnage shall be cut and painted in Latin characters on the stern, and the initial or initials of the name of the port of registry, as well as the registration number in the series of the numbers of that port, shall be printed in black on the sails.

ART. 35. A list of the crew shall be issued to the captain of the vessel at the port of departure by the authorities of the Power whose colors it carries. It shall be renewed at every fresh venture of the vessel, or, at the latest, at the end of a year, and in accordance with the following provisions:

1. The list shall be visaed at the departure of the vessel by the authority that has issued it.

2. No negro can be engaged as a seaman on a vessel without having previously been questioned by the authority of the Power whose colors it carries, or, in default thereof, by the territorial authority, with a view to ascertaining the fact of his having contracted a free engagement.

3. This authority shall see that the proportion of seamen and boys is not out of proportion to the tonnage or rigging.

4. The authorities who shall have questioned the men before their departure shall enter them on the list of the crew in which they shall be mentioned with a summary description of each of them alongside his name.

5. In order the more effectively to prevent any substitution, the seamen may, moreover, be provided with a distinctive mark.

ART. 36. When the captain of a vessel shall desire to take negro passengers on board, he shall make his declaration to that effect to the authority of the Power whose colors he carries, or in default thereof, to the territorial authority. The passengers shall be questioned, and after it has been ascertained that they embarked of their own free will, they shall be entered in a special manifest, bearing the description of each of them alongside of his name, and specially sex and height. Negro children shall not be taken as passengers unless they are accompanied by their relations, or by persons whose respectability is well known. At the departure, the passenger roll shall be visaed by the aforesaid authority after it has been called. If there are no passengers on board, this shall be specially mentioned in the crew list.

ART. 37. At the arrival at any port of call or of destination, the captain of the vessel shall show to the authority of the Power whose flag he carries, or, in default thereof, to the territorial authority, the crew list, and, if need be, the passenger roll previously delivered. The authority shall check the passengers who have reached their destination or who are stopping in a port of call, and shall mention their landing in the roll. At the departure of the vessel the same authority shall affix a fresh *visé* to the list and roll, and call the roll of the passengers.

ART. 38. On the African coast and on the adjacent islands, no negro passengers shall be taken on board of a native vessel, except in localities where there is a resident authority belonging to one of the signatory Powers.

Throughout the extent of the zone mentioned in Article 21 no negro passenger shall be landed from a native vessel except at a place in which there is a resident officer belonging to one of the high contracting Powers, and unless such officer is present at the landing.

Cases of *vis major* that may have caused an infraction of these provisions shall be examined by the authority of the Power whose colors the vessel carries, or, in default thereof, by the territorial authority of the port at which the vessel in question calls.

ART. 39. The provisions of Articles 35, 36, 37, and 38 are not applicable to vessels only partially decked, having a crew not exceeding ten men, and fulfilling one of the two following conditions:

1. That it be exclusively used for fishing within the territorial waters.

2. That it be occupied in the petty coasting trade between the different ports of the same territorial Power, without going further than five miles from the coast.

These different boats shall receive, as the case may be, a special license from the territorial or consular authority, which shall be renewed every year, and subject to revocation as provided in Article 40, the uniform model of which license is annexed to the present general act and shall be communicated to the international information office.

ART. 40. Any act or attempted act connected with the slave trade that can be legally shown to have been committed by the captain, fitter-out, or owner of a ship authorized to carry the flag of one of the signatory Powers, or having procured the license provided for in Article 39, shall entail the immediate withdrawal of the said authorization or license. All violations of the provisions of Section 2 of Chapter III shall render the person guilty thereof liable to the penalties provided by the special laws and ordinances of each of the contracting Powers.

ART. 41. The signatory Powers engage to deposit at the international information office the specimen forms of the following documents:

1. License to carry the flag;
2. The crew list;
3. The negro passenger list.

These documents, the tenor of which may vary according to the different regulations of each country, shall necessarily contain the following particulars, drawn up in one of the European languages:

1. As regards the authorization to carry the flag:

(*a*) The name, tonnage, rig, and the principal dimensions of the vessel;

(*b*) The register number and the signal letter of the port of registry;

(*c*) The date of obtaining the license, and the office held by the person who issued it.

2. As regards the list of the crew:

(*a*) The name of the vessel, of the captain, and of the fitter-out or owner;

(*b*) The tonnage of the vessel;

(*c*) The register number and the port of registry, its destination, as well as the particulars specified in Article 25.

3. As regards the list of negro passengers:

The name of the vessel which conveys them, and the particulars indicated in Article 36, for the proper identification of the passengers.

The signatory Powers shall take the necessary measures so that the territorial authorities or their consuls may send to the same office certified copies of all authorizations to carry their flag as soon as such authorizations shall have been granted, as well as notices of the withdrawal of any such authorization.

The provisions of the present article have reference only to papers intended for native vessels.

2. THE STOPPING OF SUSPECTED VESSELS

ART. 42. When the officers in command of war vessels of any of the signatory Powers have reason to believe that a vessel whose tonnage is less than 500 tons, and which is found navigating in the above-named zone, is engaged in the slave trade or is guilty of the fraudulent use of a flag, they may examine the ship's papers.

The present article does not imply any change in the present state of things as regards jurisdiction in territorial waters.

ART. 43. To this end, a boat commanded by a naval officer in uniform may be sent to board the suspected vessel after it has been hailed and informed of this intention.

The officers sent on board of the vessel which has been stopped shall act with all possible consideration and moderation.

ART. 44. The examination of the ship's papers shall consist of the examination of the following documents:

1. As regards native vessels, the papers mentioned in Article 41.

2. As regards other vessels, the documents required by the different treaties or conventions that are in force.

The examination of the ship's papers only authorizes the calling of the roll of the crew and passengers in the cases and in accordance with the conditions provided for in the following article.

ART. 45. The examination of the cargo or the search can only take place in the case of vessels sailing under the flag of one of the Powers that have concluded, or may hereafter conclude, the special conventions provided for in Article 22, and in accordance with the provisions of such conventions.

ART. 46. Before leaving the detained vessel, the officer shall draw up a minute according to the forms and in the language in use in the country to which he belongs.

This minute shall be dated and signed by the officer, and shall recite the facts.

The captain of the detained vessel, as well as the witnesses, shall have the right to cause to be added to the minutes any explanations they may think expedient.

ART. 47. The commander of a man-of-war who has detained a vessel under a foreign flag shall, in all cases, make a report thereof to his own government, and state the grounds upon which he has acted.

ART. 48. A summary of this report, as well as a copy of the minute drawn up by the officer on board of the detained vessel, shall be sent, as soon as possible, to the international information office, which shall communicate the same to the nearest consular or territorial authority of the Power whose flag the vessel in question has shown. Duplicates of these documents shall be kept in the archives of the bureau.

ART. 49. If, in performing the acts of supervision mentioned in the preceding articles, the officer in command of the cruiser is convinced that an act connected with the slave trade has been committed on board during the passage, or that irrefutable proofs exist against the captain, or fitter-out, for accusing him of fraudulent use of the flag, or fraud, or participation in the slave trade, he shall conduct the arrested vessel to the nearest port of the zone where there is a competent magistrate of the Power whose flag has been used.

Each signatory Power engages to appoint in the zone, and to make known to the international information office, the territorial or consular authorities or special delegates who are competent in the above-mentioned cases.

A suspected vessel may also be turned over to a cruiser of its own nation, if the latter consents to take charge of it.

3. OF THE EXAMINATION AND TRIAL OF VESSELS SEIZED

ART. 50. The magistrate referred to in the preceding article, to whom the arrested vessel has been turned over, shall proceed to make a full investigation according to the laws and rules of his country, in the presence of an officer belonging to the foreign cruiser.

ART. 51. If it is proved by the inquiry that the flag has been fraudulently used, the arrested vessel shall remain at the disposal of its captor.

ART. 52. If the examination shows an act connected with the slave trade, proved by the presence on board of slaves destined for sale, or any other offense connected with the slave trade for which provision is made by special convention, the vessel and cargo shall remain sequestrated in charge of the magistrate who shall have conducted the inquiry.

The captain and crew shall be turned over to the tribunals designated by Articles 54 and 56. The slaves shall be set at liberty as soon as judgment has been pronounced.

In the cases provided for by this article, liberated slaves shall be disposed of in accordance with the special conventions concluded, or to be concluded, between the signatory Powers. In default of such conventions, the said slaves shall be turned over to the local authority, to be sent back, if possible, to their country of origin; if not, this authority shall facilitate to them, in so far as may be in its power, the means of livelihood, and, if they desire it, of settling on the spot.

ART. 53. If it shall be proved by the inquiry that the vessel has been illegally arrested, there shall be clear title to an indemnity in proportion to the damages suffered by the vessel's being taken out of its course.

The amount of this indemnity shall be fixed by the authority that has conducted the inquiry.

ART. 54. In case the officer of the capturing vessel does not accept the conclusions of the inquiry held in his presence, the matter shall be turned over to the tribunal of the nation whose flag the captured vessel has borne.

No exception shall be made to this rule, unless the disagreement arises in respect of the amount of the indemnity stipulated in Article 53, and this shall be fixed by arbitration, as specified in the following article.

ART. 55. The capturing officer and the authority which has conducted the inquiry shall each appoint a referee within forty-eight hours, and the two arbitrators shall have twenty-four hours to choose an umpire. The arbitrators shall, as far as possible, be chosen from among the diplomatic, consular, or judicial officers of the signatory Powers. Natives in the pay of the contracting governments are formally excluded. The decision shall be by a majority of votes, and be considered as final.

If the court of arbitration is not constituted in the time indicated, the procedure in respect of the indemnity, as in that of damages, shall be in accordance with the provisions of Article 58, paragraph 2.

ART. 56. The cases shall be brought with the least possible delay before the tribunal of the nation whose flag has been used by the accused. However, the consuls or any other authority of the same nation as the accused, specially commissioned to this end, may be authorized by their government to pronounce judgment instead of the tribunal.

ART. 57. The procedure and trial of violations of the provisions of Chapter III shall always be conducted in as summary a manner as is permitted by the laws and regulations in force in the territories subject to the authority of the signatory Powers.

ART. 58. Any decision of the national tribunal or authorities referred to in Article 56, declaring that the seized vessel did not carry on the slave trade, shall be immediately enforced, and the vessel shall be at perfect liberty to continue on its course.

In this case, the captain or owner of any vessel that has been seized without legitimate ground of suspicion, or subjected to annoyance, shall have the right of claiming damages, the amount of which shall be fixed by agreement between the governments directly interested, or by arbitration, and shall be paid within a period of six months from the date of the judgment acquitting the captured vessel.

ART. 59. In case of condemnation, the sequestered vessel shall be declared lawfully seized for the benefit of the captor.

The captain, crew, and all other persons found guilty shall be punished according to the gravity of the crimes or offenses committed by them, and in accordance with Article 5.

ART. 60. The provisions of Articles 50 to 59 do not in any way affect the jurisdiction or procedure of existing special tribunals, or of such as may hereafter be formed to take cognizance of offenses connected with the slave trade.

ART. 61. The high contracting parties engage to make known to one another, reciprocally, the instructions which they shall give, for the execution of the provisions of Chapter III, to the commanders of their men-of-war navigating the seas of the zone referred to.

CHAPTER IV. COUNTRIES TO WHICH SLAVES ARE SENT, WHOSE INSTITUTIONS RECOGNIZE THE EXISTENCE OF DOMESTIC SLAVERY

ART. 62. The contracting Powers whose institutions recognize the existence of domestic slavery, and whose possessions, in consequence thereof, in or out of Africa, serve, in spite of the vigilance of the authorities, as places of destination for African slaves, pledge themselves to prohibit their importation, transit, and departure, as well as the trade in slaves. The most active and the strictest supervision shall be enforced at all places where the arrival, transit, and departure of African slaves take place.

ART. 63. Slaves set free under the provisions of the preceding article shall, if circumstances permit, be sent back to the country from whence they came. In all cases they shall receive letters of liberation from the competent authorities, and shall be entitled to their protection and assistance for the purpose of obtaining means of subsistence.

ART. 64. Any fugitive slave arriving at the frontier of any of the Powers mentioned in Article 62 shall be considered free, and shall have the right to claim letters of release from the competent authorities.

ART. 65. Any sale or transaction to which the slaves referred to in Articles 63 and 64 may have been subjected through circumstances of any kind whatsoever, shall be considered as null and void.

ART. 66. Native vessels carrying the flag of one of the countries mentioned in Article 62, if there is any indication that they are employed in operations connected with the slave trade, shall be subjected by the local authorities in the ports frequented by them to a strict examination of their crews and passengers both on arrival and departure. If African slaves are found on board, judicial proceedings shall be instituted against the vessel and against all persons who may be implicated. Slaves found on board shall receive letters of release through the authorities who have seized the vessels.

ART. 67. Penal provisions similar to those provided for by Article 5 shall be enacted against persons importing, transporting, and trading in African slaves, against the mutilators of male children or adults, and those who traffic in them, as well as against their associates and accomplices.

ART. 68. The signatory Powers recognize the great importance of the law respecting the prohibition of the slave trade sanctioned by his Majesty the Emperor of the Ottomans on the 4th (16th) of December, 1889 (22 Rebi-ul-Akhir, 1307), and they are assured that an active surveillance will be organized by the Ottoman authorities, especially on the west coast of Arabia and on the routes which place that coast in communication with the other possessions of his Imperial Majesty in Asia.

ART. 69. His Majesty the Shah of Persia consents to organize an active surveillance in the territorial waters and those off the coast of the Persian Gulf and Gulf of Oman which are under his sovereignty, and on the inland routes which serve for the transportation of slaves. The magistrates and other authorities shall, to this effect, receive the necessary powers.

ART. 70. His Highness the Sultan of Zanzibar consents to give his most effective support to the repression of crimes and offenses committed by African slave traders on land as well as at sea. The tribunals created for this purpose in the sultanate of Zanzibar shall rigorously enforce the penal provisions mentioned in Article 5. In order to render more secure the freedom of liberated slaves, both in virtue of the provisions of the present general act and of the decrees adopted in this matter by his Highness and his predecessors, a liberation office shall be established at Zanzibar.

ART. 71. The diplomatic and consular agents and the naval officers of the contracting Powers shall, within the limits of existing conventions, give their assistance to the local authorities in order to assist in repressing the slave trade where it still exists. They shall be entitled to be present at trials for slave trading brought about at their instance, without, however, being entitled to take part in the deliberations.

ART. 72. Liberation offices, or institutions in lieu thereof, shall be organized by the governments of the countries to which African slaves are sent, for the purposes specified by Article 18.

ART. 73. The signatory Powers having undertaken to communicate to one another all information useful for the repression of the slave trade, the governments which the present chapter concerns shall periodically exchange with the other governments statistical data relating to slaves intercepted and liberated, and to the legislative and administrative measures which have been taken for suppressing the slave trade.

CHAPTER V. INSTITUTIONS INTENDED TO INSURE THE EXECUTION OF THE GENERAL ACT

Section I. Of the International Maritime Office

ART. 74. In accordance with the provisions of Article 27, an international office shall be instituted at Zanzibar, in which each of the signatory Powers may be represented by a delegate.

ART. 75. The office shall be constituted as soon as three Powers have appointed their representatives.

It shall draw up regulations fixing the manner of exercising its functions. These regulations shall immediately be submitted to the approval of such signatory Powers as shall have signified their intention of being represented in this office. They shall decide in this respect within the shortest possible time.

ART. 76. The expenses of this institution shall be divided in equal parts among the signatory Powers mentioned in the preceding article.

ART. 77. The object of the office at Zanzibar shall be to centralize all documents and information of a nature to facilitate the repression of the slave trade in the maritime zone. For this purpose the signatory Powers engage to forward within the shortest time possible:

1. The documents specified in Article 41;
2. Summaries of the reports and copies of the minutes referred to in Article 48;
3. The list of the territorial or consular authorities and special delegates competent to take action as regards vessels seized according to the terms of Article 49;
4. Copies of judgments and condemnations in accordance with Article 58;
5. All information that may lead to the discovery of persons engaged in the slave trade in the above-mentioned zone.

ART. 78. The archives of the office shall always be open to the naval officers of the signatory Powers authorized to act within the limits of the zone defined by Article 21, as well as to the territorial or judicial authorities, and to consuls specially designated by their governments.

The office shall supply to foreign officers and agents authorized to consult its archives, translations into a European language of documents written in an Oriental language.

It shall make the communications provided for in Article 48.

ART. 79. Auxiliary offices in communication with the office at Zanzibar may be established in certain parts of the zone, in pursuance of a previous agreement between the interested Powers.

They shall be composed of delegates of these Powers, and established in accordance with Articles 75, 76, and 78.

The documents and information specified in Article 77, so far as they may relate to a part of the zone specially concerned, shall be sent to them directly by the territorial and consular authorities of the region in question, but this shall not exempt the latter from the duty of communicating the same to the office at Zanzibar, as provided by the same article.

ART. 80. The office at Zanzibar shall prepare in the first two months of every year a report of its own operations, and of those of the auxiliary offices, during the past twelve months.

Section II. Of the Exchange between the Governments of Documents and Information relating to the Slave Trade

ART. 81. The Powers shall communicate to one another, to the fullest extent and with the least delay that they shall consider possible:

1. The text of the laws and administrative regulations existing or enacted by application of the clauses of the present general act;

2. Statistical information concerning the slave trade, slaves arrested and liberated, and the traffic in firearms, ammunition, and alcoholic liquors.

ART. 82. The exchange of these documents and information shall be centralized in a special office attached to the foreign office at Brussels.

ART. 83. The office at Zanzibar shall forward to it every year the report mentioned in Article 80 concerning its operations during the past year, and concerning those of the auxiliary offices that may have been established in accordance with Article 79.

ART. 84. The documents and information shall be collected and published periodically, and addressed to all the signatory Powers. This publication shall be accompanied every year by an analytical table of the legislative, administrative, and statistical documents mentioned in Articles 81 and 83.

ART. 85. The office expenses, as well as those incurred in correspondence, translation, and printing, shall be shared by all the signatory Powers, and shall be collected through the agency of the department of the foreign office at Brussels.

Section III. Of the Protection of Liberated Slaves

ART. 86. The signatory Powers having recognized the duty of protecting liberated slaves in their respective possessions, engage to establish, if they do not already exist, in the ports of the zone determined by Article 21, and in such parts of their said possessions as may be places for the capture, passage, and arrival of African slaves, such offices and institutions as may be deemed sufficient by them, whose business shall specially consist in liberating and protecting them in accordance with the provisions of Articles 6, 18, 52, 63, and 66.

ART. 87. The liberation offices, or the authorities charged with this service, shall deliver letters of release and shall keep a register thereof.

In case of the denunciation of an act connected with the slave trade, or one of illegal detention, or on application of the slaves themselves, the said offices or authorities shall exercise all necessary diligence to insure the release of the slaves and the punishment of the offenders.

The delivery of letters of release shall in no case be delayed if the slave be accused of a crime or offense against the common law. But after the delivery of the said letters an investigation shall be proceeded with in the form established by the ordinary procedure.

ART. 88. The signatory Powers shall favor, in their possessions, the foundation of establishments of refuge for women and of education for liberated children.

ART. 89. Freed slaves may always apply to the offices for protection in the enjoyment of their freedom.

Whoever shall have used fraudulent or violent means to deprive a freed slave of his letters of release or of his liberty, shall be considered as a slave dealer.

CHAPTER VI. MEASURES TO RESTRICT THE TRAFFIC IN SPIRITUOUS LIQUORS

ART. 90. Being justly anxious concerning the moral and material consequences to which the abuse of spirituous liquors subjects the native population, the signatory Powers have agreed to enforce the provisions of Articles 91, 92, and 93 within a zone extending from the 20th degree of north latitude to the 22d degree of south latitude, and bounded on the west by the Atlantic Ocean and on the east by the Indian Ocean and its dependencies, including the islands adjacent to the mainland within 100 nautical miles from the coast.

ART. 91. In the districts of this zone where it shall be ascertained that, either on account of religious belief or from some other causes, the use of distilled liquors does not exist or has not been developed, the Powers shall prohibit their importation. The manufacture of distilled liquors shall be likewise prohibited there.

Each Power shall determine the limits of the zone of prohibition of alcoholic liquors in its possessions or protectorates, and shall be bound to make known the limits thereof to the other Powers within the space of six months.

The above prohibition can only be suspended in the case of limited quantities intended for the consumption of the non-native population and imported under the régime and conditions determined by each government.

ART. 92. The Powers having possessions or exercising protectorates in those regions of the zone which are not subjected to the régime of the prohibition, and into which alcoholic liquors are at present either freely imported or pay an import duty of less than 15 francs per hectoliter at 50 degrees centigrade, engage to levy on such alcoholic liquors an import duty of 15 francs per hectoliter at 50 degrees centigrade, for three years after the present general act comes into force. At the expiration of this period the duty may be increased to 25 francs during a fresh period of three years. At the end of the sixth year it shall be submitted to revision, the average results produced by these tariffs being taken as a basis, for the purpose of then fixing, if possible, a minimum duty throughout the whole extent of the zone where the prohibition referred to in Article 91 is not in force.

The Powers retain the right of maintaining and increasing the duties beyond the minimum fixed by the present article in those regions where they already possess that right.

ART. 93. Distilled liquors manufactured in the regions referred to in Article 92, and intended for inland consumption, shall be subject to an excise duty.

This excise duty, the collection of which the Powers engage to secure, as far as possible, shall not be less than the minimum import duty fixed by Article 92.

ART. 94. The signatory Powers having possessions in Africa contiguous to the zone specified in Article 90 engage to adopt the necessary measures for preventing the introduction of spirituous liquors within the territories of the said zone via their inland frontiers.

ART. 95. The Powers shall communicate to one another, through the office at Brussels, and according to the terms of Chapter 5, information relating to the traffic in alcoholic liquors within their respective territories.

CHAPTER VII. FINAL PROVISIONS

ART. 96. The present general act repeals all contrary stipulations of conventions previously concluded between the signatory Powers.

ART. 97. The signatory Powers, without prejudice to the stipulations contained in Articles 14, 23, and 92, reserve the right of introducing into the present general act, hereafter and by common consent, such modifications or improvements as experience may prove to be useful.

ART. 98. Powers which have not signed the present general act shall be allowed to adhere to it.

The signatory Powers reserve the right to impose such conditions as they may deem necessary to their adhesion.

If no conditions shall be stipulated, adhesion implies acceptance of all the obligations and admission to all the advantages stipulated by the present general act.

The Powers shall agree among themselves as to the steps to be taken to secure the adhesion of states whose coöperation may be necessary or useful in order to insure complete execution of the general act.

Adhesion shall be effected by a separate act. Notice thereof shall be given through the diplomatic channel to the government of the king of the Belgians, and by that government to all the signatory and adherent states.

ART. 99. The present general act shall be ratified within the shortest possible period, which shall not in any case exceed one year.

Each Power shall address its ratification to the government of the king of the Belgians, which shall give notice thereof to all the other Powers that have signed the present general act.

The ratifications of all the Powers shall remain deposited in the archives of the kingdom of Belgium.

As soon as all the ratifications shall have been furnished, or at the latest one year after the signature of the present general act, their delivery shall be recorded in a protocol which shall be signed by the representatives of all the Powers that have ratified.

A certified copy of this protocol shall be forwarded to all the Powers interested.

ART. 100. The present general act shall come into force in all the possessions of the contracting Powers on the sixtieth day, reckoned from the day on which the protocol provided for in the preceding article shall have been drawn up.

In witness whereof the respective plenipotentiaries have signed the present general act, and have thereto affixed their seals.

Done at Brussels the 2d day of the month of July, 1890.

[Signatures]

On June 8, 1899, a convention for the regulation of the importation of spirituous liquors into certain regions of Africa was signed at Brussels by the plenipotentiaries of Germany, Belgium, Spain, the Independent State of the Congo, France, Great Britain, Italy, the Netherlands, Portugal, Russia, Sweden and Norway, and Turkey. Adhesions were afterward given by Denmark, Persia, Austria-Hungary, Liberia, and the United States. That convention was superseded by the one given below.

On November 3, 1906, there was signed at Brussels a convention revising the duties imposed by the Brussels convention of June 8, 1899, on spirituous liquors imported into certain regions of Africa, by the plenipotentiaries of Germany, Belgium, Spain, the Independent State of the Congo, France, Great Britain, Italy, the Netherlands, Portugal, Russia, and Sweden. Adhesion was afterward given by the United States. The revision is as follows:

ART. 1. From the putting into operation of this convention, the import duty on spirits shall be advanced throughout the zone wherein the prohibition régime contemplated in Article 91 of the general act of Brussels, to the rate of 100 francs per hectoliter at 50 centesimal degrees.

It is however agreed in regard to Erythrea that the duty may be not more than 70 francs per hectoliter at 50 centesimal degrees, the excess being in a general and continuous way represented by the aggregate of other duties existing in that colony.

The import duty shall be proportionally increased for each degree above 50 centesimal degrees; it may be proportionally decreased for each degree below 50 centesimal degrees.

The Powers retain the right to maintain and advance the tax beyond the minimum fixed by this article in the regions where they now have that right.

ART. 2. As a consequence of Article 93 of the general act of Brussels, distilled beverages made within the regions contemplated in Article 92 of the said general act and intended for consumption therein, shall be subjected to an excise duty.

This excise duty which the Powers engage to collect as far as practicable shall not be less than the minimum import duty fixed by Article 1 of this convention.

It is however agreed, in regard to Angola, that the Portuguese government will be at liberty, with a view to effect the gradual and complete transformation of distilleries into sugar factories, to take out of the proceeds of the said 100 francs duty a sum of 30 francs which would be allowed to the producers on condition that they shall, under the Portuguese government's supervision, carry out the said transformation.

If the Portuguese government should avail itself of this liberty, the number of distilleries in operation and the producing power of each should not be greater than the number and power ascertained on the 31st of October, 1906.

ART. 3. The provisions of this convention are established for a term of ten years.

At the expiration of that period, the import duty fixed by Article 1 shall be subject to revision on the basis of the results produced by the preceding rates.

Each one of the contracting Powers will, however, be at liberty to move the revision of the duty at the expiration of the eighth year.

The Power availing itself of this liberty should give notice of its intention, six months before the said expiration, to the other Powers through the Belgian government, which would then undertake to call the conference within the above stated term of six months.

ART. 4. It is agreed that the Powers that have signed the general act of Brussels or adhered thereto, and are not represented at this conference, retain the right of adhering to this convention.

ART. 5. This convention shall be ratified and the ratification shall be deposited at the ministry of foreign affairs at Brussels with as little delay as possible and in no case shall the term exceed one year.

A certified copy of the *procès-verbal* of deposit shall be addressed by the Belgian government to all the Powers concerned.

ART. 6. This convention shall go into effect in all the possessions of the contracting Powers within the zone defined by Article 90 of the general act of Brussels on the thirtieth day after that on which the *procès-verbal* of deposit contemplated in the foregoing article shall have been closed.

From that date the convention relative to regulations affecting spirits in Africa, signed at Brussels on the 8th of June, 1889, shall cease and determine.

In witness whereof the respective plenipotentiaries have signed this convention and affixed their seals thereto.

Done in a single copy at Brussels the 3d day of the month of November, 1906.

[Signatures]

CHAPTER XIV

TRADE IN WHITE WOMEN

There was signed at Paris on May 18, 1904, by the governments of Germany, Belgium, Denmark, Spain, France, Great Britain, Italy, the Netherlands, Portugal, Russia, Sweden, Norway, and the Swiss Federal Council a formal agreement for the suppression of the white slave traffic. Adhesions were afterward given by Austria-Hungary, Brazil, and the United States, thus making such a proportion of the body of the nations of the world as to make the agreement worthy of standing as a chapter in world law. The introduction to the agreement set forth that the sovereigns of the countries which were represented in the Paris conference, "being desirous to assure to women who have attained their majority and are subjected to deception or constraint, as well as minor women and girls, an efficacious protection against the criminal traffic known under the name of trade in white women, have resolved to conclude an arrangement with a view to concert proper measures to attain this purpose, and have appointed as their plenipotentiaries [the names follow], who, having exchanged their full powers, found in good and due form, have agreed upon the following provisions:"

ART. 1. Each of the contracting governments agrees to establish or designate an authority who will be directed to centralize all information concerning the procuration of women or girls both in a view to their debauchery in a foreign country; that authority shall have the right to correspond directly with the similar service established in each of the other contracting states.

ART. 2. Each of the governments agrees to exercise a supervision for the purpose of finding out, particularly in the stations, harbors of embarkation, and on the journey, the conductors of women or girls intended for debauchery. Instructions shall be sent for that purpose to the officials or to any other qualified persons, in order to procure, within the limits of the laws, all information of a nature to discover a criminal traffic.

The arrival of persons appearing evidently to be the authors, the accomplices, or the victims of such a traffic will be notified, in each case, either to the authorities of the place of destination or to the interested diplomatic or consular agents, or to any other competent authorities.

ART. 3. The governments agree to receive, in each case, within the limits of the laws, the declarations of women and girls of foreign nationality who surrender themselves to prostitution, with a view to establish their identity and their civil status and to ascertain who has induced them to leave their country. The information received will be communicated to the authorities of the country of origin of the said women or girls, with a view to their eventual return.

The governments agree, within the limits of the laws and as far as possible, to confide, temporarily and with a view to their eventual return, the victims of criminal traffic, when they are without any resources, to some institutions of public or private charity or to private individuals furnishing the necessary guaranties.

The governments agree also, within the limits of the laws, to return to their country of origin those of those women or girls who ask their return or who may be claimed by persons having authority over them. Return will be made only after reaching an understanding as to their identity and nationality, as well as to the place and date of their arrival at the frontiers. Each of the contracting parties will facilitate the transit on his territory.

The correspondence relative to the return will be made, as far as possible, through the direct channel.

ART. 4. In case the woman or girl to be sent back cannot herself pay the expenses of her transportation, and she has neither husband, nor relations, nor guardian to pay for her the expenses occasioned by her return, they shall be borne by the country on the territory of which she resides, as far as the nearest frontier or port of embarkation in the direction of the country of origin, and by the country of origin for the remainder.

ART. 5. The provisions of the above Articles 3 and 4 shall not infringe upon the provisions of special conventions which may exist between the contracting governments.

ART. 6. The contracting governments agree, within the limits of the laws, to exercise, as far as possible, a supervision over the bureaus or agencies which occupy themselves with finding places for women or girls in foreign countries.

ART. 7. The nonsignatory states are admitted to adhere to the present arrangement. For this purpose, they shall notify their intention, through the diplomatic channel, to the French government, which shall inform all the contracting states.

ART. 8. The present arrangement shall take effect six months after the date of the exchange of ratifications. In case one of the contracting parties shall denounce it, that denunciation shall take effect only as regards that party and then twelve months only from the date of the day of the said denunciation.

ART. 9. The present arrangement shall be ratified and the ratifications shall be exchanged at Paris, as soon as possible.

In faith whereof the respective plenipotentiaries have signed the present agreement, and thereunto affixed their seals.

Done at Paris, the 18th May, 1904, in single copy, which shall be deposited in the archives of the ministry of foreign affairs of the French republic, and of which one copy, certified correct, shall be sent to each contracting party.

[Signatures]

CHAPTER XV

INTERNATIONAL INSTITUTE OF AGRICULTURE

Following widespread discussion of the advantages of an international institute of agriculture, there was signed at Rome on June 7, 1905, a convention for the creation and maintenance of such an institute. The signing countries were the United States of America, Italy, Montenegro, Russia, Argentine Republic, Roumania, Servia, Belgium, Salvador, Portugal, the United Mexican States, Luxemburg, the Swiss Confederation, Persia, Japan, Ecuador, Bulgaria, Denmark, Spain, France, Sweden, the Netherlands, Greece, Uruguay, Germany, Cuba, Austria-Hungary, Norway, Egypt, Great Britain, Guatemala, Ethiopia, Nicaragua, Brazil, Costa Rica, Chile, Peru, China, Paraguay, and Turkey. San Marino gave adherence subsequently. The convention stands worthily as a chapter of world law, and is as follows:

ART. 1. There is hereby created a permanent international institute of agriculture, having its seat at Rome.

ART. 2. The international institute of agriculture is to be a government institution, in which each adhering Power shall be represented by delegates of its choice.

The institute shall be composed of a general assembly and a permanent committee, the composition and duties of which are defined in the ensuing articles.

ART. 3. The general assembly of the institute shall be composed of the representatives of the adhering governments. Each nation, whatever be the number of its delegates, shall be entitled to a number of votes in the assembly, which shall be determined according to the group to which it belongs and to which reference will be made in Article 10.

ART. 4. The general assembly shall elect for each session from among its members a president and two vice presidents.

The sessions shall take place on dates fixed by the last general assembly and according to a program proposed by the permanent committee and adopted by the adhering governments.

ART. 5. The general assembly shall exercise supreme control over the international institute of agriculture.

It shall approve the projects prepared by the permanent committee regarding the organization and internal workings of the institute. It shall fix the total amount of expenditures and audit and approve the accounts.

It shall submit to the approval of the adhering governments modifications of any nature involving an increase in expenditure or an enlargement of the functions of the institute. It shall set the date for holding the sessions. It shall prepare its regulations.

The presence at the general assemblies of delegates representing two thirds of the adhering nations shall be required in order to render the deliberations valid.

ART. 6. The executive power of the institute is intrusted to the permanent committee, which, under the direction and control of the general assembly, shall carry out the decisions of the latter and prepare propositions to submit to it.

ART. 7. The permanent committee shall be composed of members designated by the respective governments. Each adhering nation shall be represented in the permanent committee by one member. However, the representation of one nation may be intrusted to a delegate of another adhering nation, provided that the actual number of members shall not be less than fifteen.

The conditions of voting in the permanent committee shall be the same as those indicated in Article 3 for the general assemblies.

ART. 8. The permanent committee shall elect from among its members for a period of three years a president and a vice president, who may be reëlected. It shall prepare its internal regulations, vote the budget of the institute within the limits of the funds placed at its disposal by the general assembly, and appoint and remove the officials and employees of its office.

The general secretary of the permanent committee shall act as secretary of the assembly.

ART. 9. The institute, confining its operations within an international sphere, shall —

(a) Collect, study, and publish as promptly as possible statistical, technical, or economic information concerning farming, both vegetable and animal products, the commerce in agricultural products, and the prices prevailing in the various markets;

(b) Communicate to parties interested, also as promptly as possible, all the information just referred to;

(c) Indicate the wages paid for farm work;

(d) Make known the new diseases of vegetables which may appear in any part of the world, showing the territories infected, the progress of the disease, and, if possible, the remedies which are effective in combating them;

(e) Study questions concerning agricultural coöperation, insurance, and credit, in all their aspects; collect and publish information which might be useful in the various countries in the organization of works connected with agricultural coöperation, insurance, and credit;

(f) Submit to the approval of the governments, if there is occasion for it, measures for the protection of the common interests of farmers and for the improvement of their condition, after having utilized all the necessary sources of information, such as the wishes expressed by international or other agricultural congresses or congresses of sciences applied to agriculture, agricultural societies, academies, learned bodies, etc.

All questions concerning the economic interests, the legislation, and the administration of a particular nation shall be excluded from the consideration of the institute.

ART. 10. The nations adhering to the institute shall be classed in five groups, according to the place which each of them thinks it ought to occupy.

The number of votes which each nation shall have and the number of units of assessment shall be established according to the following gradations:

Groups of nations	Numbers of votes	Units of assessment
I	5	16
II	4	8
III	3	4
IV	2	2
V	1	1

In any event the contribution due per unit of assessment shall never exceed a maximum of 2500 francs.

As a temporary provision the assessment for the first two years shall not exceed 1500 francs per unit.

Colonies may, at the request of the nations to which they belong, be admitted to form part of the institute on the same conditions as the independent nations.

ART. 11. The present convention shall be ratified and the ratifications exchanged as soon as possible by depositing them with the Italian government.

In faith whereof the respective plenipotentiaries have signed the present convention and have hereunto affixed their seals.

Done at Rome the 7th of June, 1905, in a single original, deposited with the ministry of foreign affairs of Italy, of which certified copies shall be sent through the diplomatic channel to the contracting states.

[Signatures]

CHAPTER XVI

THE INTERNATIONAL RED CROSS

Following the Geneva convention of 1864 for the amelioration of the condition of the wounded and the sick of armies in the field, which was a sequence of the Crimean War and the war between France and Italy, occurred revisions of the famous agreement and adherences to it by other nations. The last revision was signed at Geneva on July 6, 1906, by plenipotentiaries of the United States of America, Germany, the Argentine Republic, Austria-Hungary, Belgium, Bulgaria, Chile, China, the Congo Free State, Denmark, Spain, Brazil, Mexico, France, Great Britain, Greece, Guatemala, Honduras, Italy, Japan, Luxemburg, Montenegro, Norway, the Netherlands, Peru, Persia, Portugal, Roumania, Russia, Servia, Siam, Sweden, Switzerland, and Uruguay. Afterward Colombia, Cuba, Nicaragua, Turkey, and Venezuela gave their adherence to the convention. The preliminary part of the document says that the heads of these respective countries, "being equally animated by the desire to lessen the inherent evils of warfare as far as is within their power, and wishing for this purpose to improve and supplement the provisions agreed upon at Geneva on August 22, 1864, for the amelioration of the condition of the wounded in armies in the field, have decided to conclude a new convention to that effect," etc. The convention becomes the will of the world, practically, and thus rises to the rank of world law. It is as follows:

Chapter I. The Sick and Wounded

Art. 1. Officers, soldiers, and other persons officially attached to armies, who are sick or wounded, shall be respected and cared for, without distinction of nationality, by the belligerent in whose power they are.

A belligerent, however, when compelled to leave his wounded in the hands of his adversary, shall leave with them, so far as military conditions permit, a portion of the personnel and matériel of his sanitary service to assist in caring for them.

Art. 2. Subject to the care that must be taken of them under the preceding article, the sick and wounded of an army who fall into the power of the other belligerent become prisoners of war, and the general rules of international law in respect to prisoners become applicable to them.

The belligerents remain free, however, to mutually agree upon such clauses, by way of exception or favor, in relation to the wounded or sick as they may deem proper. They shall especially have authority to agree:

1. Mutually to return the sick and wounded left on the field of battle after an engagement.

2. To send back to their own country the sick and wounded who have recovered, or who are in a condition to be transported and whom they do not desire to retain as prisoners.

3. To send the sick and wounded of the enemy to a neutral state, with the consent of the latter and on condition that it shall charge itself with their internment until the close of hostilities.

ART. 3. After every engagement the belligerent who remains in possession of the field of battle shall take measures to search for the wounded and to protect the wounded and dead from robbery and ill treatment.

He will see that a careful examination is made of the bodies of the dead prior to their interment or incineration.

ART. 4. As soon as possible each belligerent shall forward to the authorities of their country or army the marks or military papers of identification found upon the bodies of the dead, together with a list of names of the sick and wounded taken in charge by him.

Belligerents will keep each other mutually advised of internments and transfers, together with admissions to hospitals and deaths which occur among the sick and wounded in their hands. They will collect all objects of personal use, valuables, letters, etc., which are found upon the field of battle, or have been left by the sick or wounded who have died in sanitary formations or other establishments, for transmission to persons in interest through the authorities of their own country.

ART. 5. Military authority may make an appeal to the charitable zeal of the inhabitants to receive and, under its supervision, to care for the sick and wounded of the armies, granting to persons responding to such appeals special protection and certain immunities.

CHAPTER II. SANITARY FORMATIONS AND ESTABLISHMENTS

ART. 6. Mobile sanitary formations (i.e. those which are intended to accompany armies in the field) and the fixed establishments belonging to the sanitary service shall be protected and respected by belligerents.

ART. 7. The protection due to sanitary formations and establishments ceases if they are used to commit acts injurious to the enemy.

ART. 8. A sanitary formation or establishment shall not be deprived of the protection accorded by Article 6 by the fact:

1. That the personnel of a formation or establishment is armed and uses its arms in self-defense or in defense of its sick and wounded.

2. That in the absence of armed hospital attendants, the formation is guarded by an armed detachment or by sentinels acting under competent orders.

3. That arms or cartridges, taken from the wounded and not yet turned over to the proper authorities, are found in the formation or establishment.

Chapter III. Personnel

Art. 9. The personnel charged exclusively with the removal, transportation, and treatment of the sick and wounded, as well as with the administration of sanitary formations and establishments, and the chaplains attached to armies, shall be respected and protected under all circumstances. If they fall into the hands of the enemy they shall not be considered as prisoners of war.

These provisions apply to the guards of sanitary formations and establishments in the case provided for in section 2 of Article 8.

Art. 10. The personnel of volunteer aid societies, duly recognized and authorized by their own governments, who are employed in the sanitary formations and establishments of armies, are assimilated to the personnel contemplated in the preceding article, upon condition that the said personnel shall be subject to military laws and regulations.

Each state shall make known to the other, either in time of peace or at the opening or during the progress of hostilities, and in any case before actual employment, the names of the societies which it has authorized to render assistance, under its responsibility, in the official sanitary service of its armies.

Art. 11. A recognized society of a neutral state can only lend the services of its sanitary personnel and formations to a belligerent with the prior consent of its own government and the authority of such belligerent. The belligerent who has accepted such assistance is required to notify the enemy before making any use thereof.

Art. 12. Persons described in Articles 9, 10, and 11 will continue in the exercise of their functions, under the direction of the enemy, after they have fallen into his power.

When their assistance is no longer indispensable they will be sent back to their army or country, within such period and by such route as may accord with military necessity. They will carry with them such effects, instruments, arms, and horses as are their private property.

Art. 13. While they remain in his power the enemy will secure to the personnel mentioned in Article 9 the same pay and allowances to which persons of the same grade in his own army are entitled.

Chapter IV. Matériel

Art. 14. If mobile sanitary formations fall into the power of the enemy, they shall retain their matériel, including the teams, whatever may be the means of transportation and the conducting personnel. Competent military authority, however, shall have the right to employ it in caring for the sick and wounded. The restitution of the matériel shall take place in accordance with the conditions prescribed for the sanitary personnel, and, as far as possible, at the same time.

ART. 15. Buildings and matériel pertaining to fixed establishments shall remain subject to the laws of war, but cannot be diverted from their use so long as they are necessary for the sick and wounded. Commanders of troops engaged in operations, however, may use them, in case of important military necessity, if, before such use, the sick and wounded who are in them have been provided for.

ART. 16. The matériel of aid societies admitted to the benefits of this convention, in conformity to the conditions therein established, is regarded as private property and, as such, will be respected under all circumstances, save that it is subject to the recognized right of requisition by belligerents in conformity to the laws and usages of war.

CHAPTER V. CONVOYS OF EVACUATION

ART. 17. Convoys of evacuation shall be treated as mobile sanitary formations subject to the following special provisions:

1. A belligerent intercepting a convoy may, if required by military necessity, break up such convoy, charging himself with the care of the sick and wounded whom it contains.

2. In this case the obligation to return the sanitary personnel, as provided for in Article 12, shall be extended to include the entire military personnel employed, under competent orders, in the transportation and protection of the convoy.

The obligation to return the sanitary matériel, as provided for in Article 14, shall apply to railway trains and vessels intended for interior navigation which have been especially equipped for evacuation purposes, as well as to the ordinary vehicles, trains, and vessels which belong to the sanitary service.

Military vehicles, with their teams, other than those belonging to the sanitary service, may be captured.

The civil personnel and the various means of transportation obtained by requisition, including railway matériel and vessels utilized for convoys, are subject to the general rules of international law.

CHAPTER VI. DISTINCTIVE EMBLEM

ART. 18. Out of respect to Switzerland the heraldic emblem of the red cross on a white ground, formed by the reversal of the federal colors, is continued as the emblem and distinctive sign of the sanitary service of armies.

ART. 19. This emblem appears on flags and brassards, as well as upon all matériel appertaining to the sanitary service, with the permission of the competent military authority.

ART. 20. The personnel protected in virtue of the first paragraph of Article 9, and Articles 10 and 11, will wear attached to the left arm a brassard bearing a red cross on a white ground, which will be issued and stamped by competent military authority, and accompanied by a certificate of identity in the case of persons attached to the sanitary service of armies who do not have military uniform.

ART. 21. The distinctive flag of the convention can only be displayed over the sanitary formations and establishments which the convention provides shall be respected, and with the consent of the military authorities. It shall be accompanied by the national flag of the belligerent to whose service the formation or establishment is attached.

Sanitary formations which have fallen into the power of the enemy, however, shall fly no other flag than that of the Red Cross so long as they continue in that situation.

ART. 22. The sanitary formations of neutral countries which, under the conditions set forth in Article 11, have been authorized to render their services, shall fly, with the flag of the convention, the national flag of the belligerent to which they are attached. The provisions of the second paragraph of the preceding article are applicable to them.

ART. 23. The emblem of the red cross on a white ground and the words "Red Cross" or "Geneva Cross" may only be used, whether in time of peace or war, to protect or designate sanitary formations and establishments, the personnel and matériel protected by the convention.

CHAPTER VII. APPLICATION AND EXECUTION OF THE CONVENTION

ART. 24. The provisions of the present convention are obligatory only on the contracting Powers, in case of war between two or more of them. The said provisions shall cease to be obligatory if one of the belligerent Powers should not be signatory to the convention.

ART. 25. It shall be the duty of the commanders in chief of the belligerent armies to provide for the details of execution of the foregoing articles, as well as for unforeseen cases, in accordance with the instructions of their respective governments, and conformably to the general principles of this convention.

ART. 26. The signatory governments shall take the necessary steps to acquaint their troops, and particularly the protected personnel, with the provisions of this convention, and to make them known to the people at large.

CHAPTER VIII. REPRESSION OF ABUSES AND INFRACTIONS

ART. 27. The signatory Powers whose legislation may not now be adequate engage to take, or recommend to their legislatures, such measures as may be necessary to prevent the use, by private persons or by societies other than those upon which this convention confers the right thereto, of the emblem or name of the Red Cross or Geneva Cross, particularly for commercial purposes by means of trade-marks or commercial labels.

The prohibition of the use of the emblem or name in question shall take effect from the time set in each act of legislation, and at the latest five years after this convention goes into effect. After such going into effect, it shall be unlawful to use a trade-mark or commercial label contrary to such prohibition.

ART. 28. In the event of their military penal laws being insufficient, the signatory governments also engage to take, or to recommend to their legislatures, the necessary measures to repress, in time of war, individual acts of robbery and ill treatment of the sick and wounded of the armies, as well as to punish, as usurpations of military insignia, the wrongful use of the flag and brassard of the Red Cross by military persons or private individuals not protected by the present convention.

They will communicate to each other through the Swiss Federal Council the measures taken with a view to such repression, not later than five years from the ratification of the present convention.

General Provisions

Art. 29. The present convention shall be ratified as soon as possible. The ratifications will be deposited at Berne.

A record of the deposit of each act of ratification shall be prepared, of which a duly certified copy shall be sent, through diplomatic channels, to each of the contracting Powers.

Art. 30. The present convention shall become operative, as to each Power, six months after the date of deposit of its ratification.

Art. 31. The present convention, when duly ratified, shall supersede the convention of August 22, 1864, in the relations between the contracting states.

The convention of 1864 remains in force in the relations between the parties who signed it but who may not also ratify the present convention.

Art. 32. The present convention may, until December 31, proximo, be signed by the Powers represented at the conference which opened at Geneva on June 11, 1906, as well as by the Powers not represented at the conference which have signed the convention of 1864.

Such of these Powers as shall not have signed the present convention on or before December 31, 1906, will remain at liberty to accede to it after that date. They shall signify their adherence in a written notification addressed to the Swiss Federal Council, and communicated to all the contracting Powers by the said council.

Other Powers may request to adhere in the same manner, but their request shall only be effective if, within the period of one year from its notification to the Federal Council, such council has not been advised of any opposition on the part of any of the contracting Powers.

Art. 33. Each of the contracting parties shall have the right to denounce the present convention. This denunciation shall only become operative one year after a notification in writing shall have been made to the Swiss Federal Council, which shall forthwith communicate such notification to all the other contracting parties.

This denunciation shall only become operative in respect to the Power which has given it.

In faith whereof the plenipotentiaries have signed the present convention and affixed their seals thereto.

Done at Geneva, the 6th day of July, 1906, in a single copy, which shall remain in the archives of the Swiss Confederation and certified copies of which shall be delivered to the contracting parties through diplomatic channels.

[Signatures follow]

CHAPTER XVII

BUREAU OF WEIGHTS AND MEASURES

Early in the era of joint action by a large number of nations was recognized the need of uniform standards for use in trade. Accordingly an international gathering was held in Paris, which concluded, May 20, 1875, the convention which established the international bureau of weights and measures. The countries which were represented in the gathering were the United States, Germany, Austria-Hungary, Belgium, Brazil, the Argentine Confederation, Denmark, Spain, France, Italy, Peru, Portugal, Russia, Sweden and Norway, Switzerland, Turkey, and Venezuela. The official reason for their joint action was that they, "desiring international uniformity and precision in standards of weights and measures, have resolved to conclude a convention to this effect, and have named as their plenipotentiaries the following." Although some important nations are not included in this list above, it is still reasonable to include this convention in the body of world law. It is as follows, with appendixes:

ART. 1. The high contracting parties engage to establish and maintain, at their common expense, a scientific and permanent international bureau of weights and measures, the location of which shall be at Paris.

ART. 2. The French government shall take all the necessary measures to facilitate the purchase, or, if expedient, the construction, of a building which shall be especially devoted to this purpose, subject to the conditions stated in the regulations which are subjoined to this convention.

ART. 3. The operation of the international bureau shall be under the exclusive direction and supervision of an international committee of weights and measures, which latter shall be under the control of a general conference for weights and measures, to be composed of the delegates of all the contracting governments.

ART. 4. The general conference for weights and measures shall be presided over by the president for the time being of the Paris Academy of Sciences.

ART. 5. The organization of the bureau, as well as the formation and the powers of the international committee, and of the general conference for weights and measures, are established by the regulations subjoined to this convention.

ART. 6. The international bureau of weights and measures shall be charged with the following duties:

1st. All comparisons and verifications of the new prototypes of the meter and kilogram.

2d. The custody of the international prototypes.

3d. The periodical comparison of the national standards with the international prototypes and with their test copies, as well as comparisons of the standard thermometers.

4th. The comparison of the prototypes with the fundamental standards of non-metrical weights and measures used in different countries for scientific purposes.

5th. The sealing and comparison of geodetic measuring bars.

6th. The comparison of standards and scales of precision, the verification of which may be requested by governments or by scientific societies, or even by constructors or men of science.

ART. 7. The persons composing the bureau shall be a director, two assistants, and the necessary number of employees. When the comparisons of the new prototypes shall have been finished, and when these prototypes shall have been distributed among the different states, the number of persons composing the bureau shall be reduced so far as may be deemed expedient.

The governments of the high contracting parties will be informed by the international committee of the appointment of the persons composing this bureau.

ART. 8. The international prototypes of the meter and of the kilogram, together with the test copies of the same, shall be deposited in the bureau, and access to them shall be allowed to the international committee only.

ART. 9. The entire expense of the construction and outfit of the international bureau of weights and measures, together with the annual cost of its maintenance and the expenses of the committee, shall be defrayed by contributions from the contracting states, the amount of which shall be computed in proportion to the actual population of each.

ART. 10. The amounts representing the contributions of each of the contracting states shall be paid at the beginning of each year, through the ministry of foreign affairs of France, into the *Caisse de dépôts et consignations* at Paris, whence they may be drawn as occasion may require, upon the order of the director of the bureau.

ART. 11. Those governments which may take advantage of the privilege, open to every state, of acceding to this convention, shall be required to pay a contribution, the amount of which shall be fixed by the committee on the basis established in Article 9, and which shall be devoted to the improvement of the scientific apparatus of the bureau.

ART. 12. The high contracting parties reserve to themselves the power of introducing into the present convention, by common consent, any modifications the propriety of which may have been shown by experience.

ART. 13. At the expiration of twelve years this convention may be abrogated by any one of the high contracting parties, so far as it is concerned.

Any government which may avail itself of the right of terminating this convention, so far as it is concerned, shall be required to give notice of its intentions one year in advance, and by so doing shall renounce all rights of joint ownership in the international prototypes and in the bureau.

ART. 14. This convention shall be ratified according to the constitutional laws of each state, and the ratifications shall be exchanged in Paris within six months, or sooner, if possible.

It shall take effect on the first day of January, 1876.

In testimony whereof the respective plenipotentiaries have attached their signatures and have hereunto affixed their seals of arms.

Done at Paris, May 20, 1875. [Signatures follow]

APPENDIX NO. 1

REGULATIONS

ART. 1. The international bureau of weights and measures shall be established in a special building possessing all the necessary safeguards of stillness and stability.

It shall comprise, in addition to the vault, which shall be devoted to the safe keeping of the prototypes, rooms for mounting the comparators and balances; a laboratory, a library, a room for the archives, workrooms for the employees, and lodgings for the watchmen and attendants.

ART. 2. It shall be the duty of the international committee to acquire and fit up the aforesaid building and to set in operation the work for which it was designed.

In case of the committee's inability to obtain a suitable building, one shall be built under its directions and in accordance with its plans.

ART. 3. The French government shall, at the request of the international committee, take the necessary measures to cause the bureau to be recognized as an establishment of public utility.

ART. 4. The international committee shall cause the necessary instruments to be constructed, such as comparators for the standards of line and end measures, apparatus for the determination of absolute dilatations, balances for weighing in air and in vacuo, comparators for geodetic measuring bars, etc.

ART. 5. The entire expense incurred in the purchase or construction of the building, and in the purchase and placing of the instruments and apparatus, shall not exceed 400,000 francs.

ART. 6. The estimate of annual expenditures is as follows:

A. For the first period, — during the construction and comparison of the new prototypes:

(*a*) Salary of the director	15,000 fr.
Salary of two adjuncts, at 6000 fr. each	12,000
Salary of four assistants, at 3000 fr. each	12,000
Pay of doorkeeper (mechanic)	3,000
Wages of two office boys, at 1500 fr. each	3,000
Total for salaries	45,000
(*b*) Compensation to men of science and artists who, by direction of the committee, may be employed to perform special duties, keeping of the building in proper order, purchase and repair of apparatus, fuel, light, and office expenses	24,000
(*c*) Compensation of the secretary of the international committee of weights and measures	6,000
Total	75,000

The annual budget of the bureau may be modified by the international committee as necessity may require at the suggestion of the director, but it shall in no case exceed the sum of 100,000 francs.

The contracting governments shall be notified of any modifications that the committee may think proper to make within these limits, in the annual budget fixed by the present regulations.

The committee may authorize the director, at his request, to make transfers from one subdivision of the allotted budget to another.

B. For the period subsequent to the distribution of the prototypes:

(*a*) Salary of the director	15,000 fr.
Salary of one adjunct	6,000
Pay of a doorkeeper (mechanic)	3,000
Wages of an office boy	1,500
	25,500
(*b*) Office expenses	18,500
(*c*) Compensation of secretary, international committee	6,000
Total	50,000

ART. 7. The general conference mentioned in Article 3 of this convention shall be at Paris, upon the summons of the international committee, at least once every six years.

It shall be its duty to discuss and initiate measures necessary for the dissemination and improvement of the metrical system, and to pass upon such new fundamental metrological determinations as may have been made during the time when it was not in session. It shall receive the report of the international committee concerning the work that has been accomplished, and shall replace one half of the international committee by secret ballot.

The voting in the general conference shall be by states; each state shall be entitled to one vote.

Each of the members of the international committee shall be entitled to a seat at the meetings of the conference. They may at the same time be delegates of their governments.

ART. 8. The international committee mentioned in Article 3 of the convention shall be composed of fourteen members, who shall belong to different states.

It shall consist, at first, of the twelve members of the former permanent committee of the international commission of 1872, and of the two delegates who, at the time of the appointment of that permanent committee, received the largest number of votes next to the members who were elected.

At the time of the renewal of one half of the international committee, the retiring members shall be, first, those who, in cases of vacancy, may have been elected provisionally during the interval occurring between two sessions of the conference. The others shall be designated by lot.

The retiring members shall be reëligible.

ART. 9. The international committee shall direct the work connected with the verification of the new prototypes, and, in general, all the metrological labors, as the high contracting parties may decide to have performed at the common expense. It shall, moreover, exercise supervision over the safe keeping of the international prototype.

ART. 10. The international committee shall choose its chairman and secretary by secret ballot. The governments of the high contracting parties shall be notified of the result of such elections.

The chairman and secretary of the committee, and the director of the bureau, must belong to different countries.

After having been formed, the committee shall hold no new elections and make no new appointments until three months after notice thereof shall have been given to all the members by the bureau of the committee.

ART. 11. Until the new prototypes shall have been finished and distributed, the committee shall meet at least once a year. After that time its meetings shall be held at least biennially.

ART. 12. Questions upon which a vote is taken in the committee shall be decided by a majority of the votes cast. In case of a tie, the vote of the chairman shall decide. No resolution shall be considered to have been duly adopted unless the number of members present be at least equal to a majority of the members composing the committee.

This condition being fulfilled, absent members shall have the right to authorize members who are present to vote for them, and the members thus authorized shall furnish proper evidence of their authorization. The same shall be the case in elections by secret ballot.

ART. 13. During the interval occurring between two sessions, the committee shall have the right to discuss questions by correspondence.

In such cases, in order that its resolutions may be considered to have been adopted in due form, it shall be necessary for all the members of the committee to have been called upon to express their opinions.

ART. 14. The international committee for weights and measures shall provisionally fill such vacancies as may occur in it; these elections shall take place by correspondence, each of the members being called upon to take part therein.

ART. 15. The international committee shall prepare detailed regulations for the organization and the labors of the bureau, and shall fix the amounts to be paid for the performance of the extraordinary duties provided for in Article 6 of this convention.

Such amounts shall be applied to the improvement of the scientific apparatus of the bureau.

ART. 16. All communications from the international committee to the governments of the high contracting parties shall take place through the diplomatic representatives of such countries at Paris.

For all matters requiring the attention of the French authorities, the committees shall have recourse to the ministry of foreign affairs of France.

ART. 17. The director of the bureau and the adjuncts shall be chosen by the international committee by secret ballot.

The employees shall be appointed by the director.

The director shall have a right to take part in the deliberations of the committee.

ART. 18. The director of the bureau shall have access to the place of deposit of the international prototypes of the meter and the kilogram only in pursuance of a resolution of the committee and in the presence of two of its members.

The place of deposit of the prototypes shall be opened only by means of three keys, one of which shall be in possession of the director of the archives of France, the second in that of the chairman of the committee, and the third in that of the director of the bureau.

The standards of the class of national prototypes alone shall be used for the ordinary comparing work of the bureau.

ART. 19. The director of the bureau shall annually furnish to the committee: 1st, a financial report concerning the accounts of the preceding year, which shall be examined, and, if found correct, a certificate to that effect shall be given him; 2d, a report on the condition of the apparatus; 3d, a general report concerning the work accomplished during the course of the year just closed.

The international committee shall make to each of the governments of the high contracting parties an annual report concerning all its scientific, technical, and administrative operations, and concerning those of the bureau. The chairman of the committee shall make a report to the general conference concerning the work that has been accomplished since its last session.

The reports and publications of the committee shall be in the French language. They shall be printed and furnished to the governments of the high contracting parties.

ART. 20. The contributions referred to in Article 9 of the convention shall be paid according to the following scale:

The number representing the population, expressed in millions, shall be multiplied by the coefficient three for states in which the use of the metrical system is obligatory;

by the coefficient two for those in which it is optional;

by the coefficient one for other states.

The sum of the products thus obtained will furnish the number of units by which the total expense is to be divided. The quotient will give the amount of the unit of expense.

ART. 21. The expense of constructing the international prototypes, and the standards and test copies which are to accompany them, shall be defrayed by the high contracting parties in accordance with the scale fixed in the foregoing article.

The amounts to be paid for the comparison and verification of standards required by states not represented at this convention shall be regulated by the committee in conformity with the rates fixed in virtue of Article 15 of the regulations.

ART. 22. These regulations shall have the same force and value as the convention to which they are annexed.

[Signatures follow]

APPENDIX NO. 2

Transient Provisions

Art. 1. All states which were represented at the international meter commission which met at Paris in 1872, whether they are contracting parties to the present convention or not, shall receive the prototypes that they may have ordered, which shall be delivered to them in the condition guaranteed by the said international commission.

Art. 2. The principal object of the first meeting of the general conference of weights and measures shall be to sanction these new prototypes, and to distribute them among the states which shall have expressed a desire to receive them.

In consequence, the delegates of all the governments which were represented in the international commission of 1872, as likewise the members of the French section, shall, of right, form part of this first meeting for the sanction of the prototypes.

Art. 3. It shall be the duty of the international committee mentioned in Article 3 of the convention, and composed as provided in Article 8 of the regulations, to receive and compare the new prototypes one with the other, in accordance with the scientific decisions of the international commission of 1872, and of its permanent committee. Such modifications may, however, be made as may in future be suggested by experience.

Art. 4. The French section of the international commission of 1872 shall continue to have charge of the labors intrusted to it in the construction of the new prototypes, with the coöperation of the international committee.

Art. 5. The cost of manufacturing the metrical standards prepared by the French section shall be reimbursed by the governments interested, according to the cost price per unit which shall be fixed by the said section.

Art. 6. The immediate formation of the international committee is authorized, and that body, when formed, is hereby empowered to make all necessary preparatory examinations for the carrying into effect of the convention, without, however, incurring any expense before the exchange of the ratifications of the said convention.

[Signatures follow]

CHAPTER XVIII

WIRELESS TELEGRAPHY

On November 3, 1906, there was concluded between nearly all of the nations of the world a convention in regard to the use and management of wireless telegraphy. In the order in which the signatures of their delegates are printed, the nations were the following: Germany, the United States, Argentina, Austria-Hungary, Belgium, Brazil, Bulgaria, Chile, Denmark, Spain, France, Great Britain, Greece, Italy, Japan, Mexico, Monaco, Norway, the Netherlands, Persia, Portugal, Roumania, Russia, Sweden, Turkey, and Uruguay. Their convention, which may properly be added to the code of world law, on the assumption that, in due time, it will be ratified by a sufficient number of nations, is as follows:

The undersigned, plenipotentiaries of the governments of the countries enumerated above, having met in conference at Berlin, have agreed on the following convention, subject to ratification:

ART. 1. The high contracting parties bind themselves to apply the provisions of the present convention to all wireless telegraph stations open to public service between the coast and vessels at sea — both coastal stations and stations on shipboard — which are established or worked by the contracting parties.

They further bind themselves to make the observance of these provisions obligatory upon private enterprises authorized either to establish or work coastal stations for wireless telegraphy open to public service between the coast and vessels at sea, or to establish or work wireless telegraph stations, whether open to general public service or not, on board of vessels flying their flag.

ART. 2. By "coastal stations" is to be understood every wireless telegraph station established on shore or on board a permanently moored vessel used for the exchange of correspondence with ships at sea.

Every wireless telegraph station established on board any vessel not permanently moored is called a "station on shipboard."

ART. 3. The coastal stations and the stations on shipboard shall be bound to exchange wireless telegrams without distinction of the wireless telegraph system adopted by such stations.

ART. 4. Notwithstanding the provisions of Article 3, a station may be reserved for a limited public service determined by the object of the correspondence or by other circumstances independent of the system employed.

ART. 5. Each of the high contracting parties undertakes to connect the coastal stations to the telegraph system by special wires, or, at least, to take other measures which will insure a rapid exchange between the coastal stations and the telegraph system.

ART. 6. The high contracting parties shall notify one another of the names of coastal stations and stations on shipboard referred to in Article 1, and also of all data necessary to facilitate and accelerate the exchange of wireless telegrams, as specified in the regulations.

ART. 7. Each of the high contracting parties reserves the right to prescribe or permit at the stations referred to in Article 1, apart from the installation the data of which are to be published in conformity with Article 6, the installation and working of other devices for the purpose of establishing special wireless communication without publishing the details of such devices.

ART. 8. The working of the wireless telegraph stations shall be organized as far as possible in such manner as not to disturb the service of other wireless stations.

ART. 9. Wireless telegraph stations are bound to give absolute priority to calls of distress from ships, to answer similarly such calls, and to take such action with regard thereto as may be required.

ART. 10. The total charge for wireless telegrams shall comprise:

1. The charge for the maritime transmission, that is:

(a) The coastal rate, which shall fall to the coastal station;

(b) The shipboard rate, which shall fall to the shipboard station.

2. The charge for transmission over the lines of the telegraph system, to be computed according to the general regulations.

The coastal rate shall be subject to the approval of the government on which the coastal station is dependent, and the shipboard rate to the approval of the government whose flag the ship is flying.

Each of these rates shall be fixed in accordance with the tariff per word, pure and simple, with an optional minimum rate per wireless telegram, on the basis of an equitable remuneration for the wireless work. Neither rate shall exceed a maximum to be fixed by the high contracting parties.

However, each of the high contracting parties shall be at liberty to authorize higher rates than such maximum in the case of stations of ranges exceeding 800 kilometers or of stations whose work is exceptionally difficult owing to physical conditions in connection with the installation or working of the same.

For wireless telegrams proceeding from or destined for a country and exchanged directly with the coastal stations of such country, the high contracting parties shall advise one another of the rates applicable to the transmission over the lines of their telegraph system. Such rates shall be those resulting from the principle that the coastal station is to be considered as the station of origin or of destination.

ART. 11. The provisions of the present convention are supplemented by regulations, which shall have the same force and go into effect at the same time as the convention.

The provisions of the present convention and of the regulations relating thereto may at any time be modified by the high contracting parties by common consent.

Conferences of plenipotentiaries or simply administrative conferences, according as the convention or the regulations are affected, shall take place from time to time; each conference shall fix the time and place of the next meeting.

ART. 12. Such conferences shall be composed of delegates of the governments of the contracting countries.

In the deliberations each country shall have but one vote.

If a government adheres to the convention for its colonies, possessions, or protectorates, subsequent conferences may decide that such colonies, possessions, or protectorates, or a part thereof, shall be considered as forming a country as regards the application of the preceding paragraph. But the number of votes at the disposal of one government, including its colonies, possessions, or protectorates, shall in no case exceed six.

ART. 13. An international bureau shall be charged with collecting, coördinating, and publishing information of every kind relating to wireless telegraphy, examining the applications for changes in the convention or regulations, promulgating the amendments adopted, and generally performing all administrative work referred to it in the interest of international wireless telegraphy.

The expenses of such institution shall be borne by all the contracting countries.

ART. 14. Each of the high contracting parties reserves to itself the right of fixing the terms on which it will receive wireless telegrams proceeding from or intended for any station, whether on shipboard or coastal, which is not subject to the provisions of the present convention.

If a wireless telegram is received, the ordinary rates shall be applicable to it.

Any wireless telegram proceeding from a station on shipboard and received by a coastal station of a contracting country, or accepted in transit by the administration of a contracting country, shall be forwarded.

Any wireless telegram intended for a vessel shall also be forwarded if the administration of the contracting country has accepted it originally or in transit from a noncontracting country, the coastal station reserving the right to refuse transmission to a station on shipboard subject to a noncontracting country.

ART. 15. The provisions of Articles 8 and 9 of this convention are also applicable to wireless telegraph installations other than those referred to in Article 1.

ART. 16. Governments which are not parties to the present convention shall be permitted to adhere to it upon their request. Such adherence shall be communicated through diplomatic channels to the contracting government in whose territory the last conference shall have been held, and by the latter to the remaining governments.

The adherence shall carry with it to the fullest extent acceptance of all the clauses of this convention and admission to all the advantages stipulated therein.

ART. 17. The provisions of Articles 1, 2, 3, 5, 6, 7, 8, 11, 12, and 17 of the international telegraph convention of St. Petersburg of July 10–22, 1875, shall be applicable to international wireless telegraphy.

ART. 18. In case of disagreement between two or more contracting governments regarding the interpretation or execution of the present convention or of the regulations referred to in Article 11, the question in dispute may, by mutual agreement, be submitted to arbitration. In such case each of the governments concerned shall choose another government not interested in the question at issue.

The decision of the arbiters shall be arrived at by the absolute majority of votes.

In case of a division of votes, the arbiters shall choose, for the purpose of settling the disagreement, another contracting government which is likewise a stranger to the question at issue. In case of failure to agree on a choice, each arbiter shall propose a disinterested contracting government, and lots shall be drawn between the governments proposed. The drawing of the lots shall fall to the government within whose territory the international bureau provided for in Article 13 shall be located.

ART. 19. The high contracting parties bind themselves to take, or propose to their respective legislatures, the necessary measures for insuring the execution of the present convention.

ART. 20. The high contracting parties shall communicate to one another any laws already framed, or which may be framed, in their respective countries relative to the object of the present convention.

ART. 21. The high contracting parties shall preserve their entire liberty as regards wireless telegraph installations other than provided for in Article 1, especially naval and military installations, which shall be subject only to the obligations provided for in Articles 8 and 9 of the present convention.

However, when such installations are used for general public service they shall conform, in the execution of such service, to the provisions of the regulations as regards the mode of transmission and rates.

ART. 22. The present convention shall go into effect on the 1st day of July, 1908, and shall remain in force for an indefinite period or until the expiration of one year from the day when it shall be denounced by any of the contracting parties.

Such denunciation shall affect only the government in whose name it shall have been made. As regards the other contracting Powers, the convention shall remain in force.

ART. 23. The present convention shall be ratified and the ratifications exchanged at Berlin with the least possible delay.

In witness whereof the respective plenipotentiaries have signed one copy of the convention, which shall be deposited in the archives of the imperial government of Germany, and a copy of which shall be transmitted to each party.

Done at Berlin, November 3, 1906.

[Signatures follow]

SUPPLEMENTARY AGREEMENT

The undersigned plenipotentiaries of the governments of Germany, the United States of America, Argentina, Austria-Hungary, Belgium, Brazil, Bulgaria, Chile, Denmark, Spain, France, Greece, Monaco, Norway, the Netherlands, Roumania, Russia, Sweden, Turkey, and Uruguay, bind themselves mutually, from the date of the going into effect of the convention, to conform to the provisions of the following supplementary articles:

I. Each station on shipboard referred to in Article 1 of the convention shall be bound to correspond with any other station on shipboard without distinction of the wireless telegraph system adopted by such stations respectively.

II. The governments which have not adhered to the foregoing article may at any time signify, by following the procedure prescribed by Article 16 of the convention, that they bind themselves to conform to its provisions.

Those which have adhered to the foregoing article may at any time, under the same conditions as provided for in Article 22, signify their intention to cease conforming to its provisions.

III. This agreement shall be ratified and the ratifications exchanged at Berlin with the least possible delay.

In witness whereof the respective plenipotentiaries have signed one copy of the present agreement, which shall be deposited in the archives of the imperial government of Germany, and a copy of which shall be transmitted to each of the parties.

Done at Berlin, November 3, 1906.

[Signatures follow]

FINAL PROTOCOL

At the moment of signing the convention adopted by the international wireless telegraph conference of Berlin, the undersigned plenipotentiaries have agreed as follows:

I. The high contracting parties agree that at the next conference the number of votes to which each country is entitled (Article 12 of the convention) shall be decided at the beginning of the deliberations, so that the colonies, possessions, or protectorates admitted to the privilege of voting may exercise their right to vote during the entire course of the proceedings of such conference.

This decision shall be of immediate effect and remain in force until amended by a subsequent conference.

As regards the next conference, applications for the admission of new votes in favor of colonies, possessions, or protectorates which may have adhered to the convention shall be addressed to the international bureau at least six months prior to the date of the convening of such conference. Notice of such applications shall at once be given to the remaining contracting governments, which may, within the period of two months from the receipt of the notice, formulate similar applications.

II. Each contracting government may reserve the right to designate, according to circumstances, certain coastal stations to be exempted from the obligation imposed by Article 3 of the convention, provided that, as soon as this measure goes into effect, there shall be opened within its territory one or several stations subject to the obligations of Article 3, insuring, within the region where the exempted stations are located, such wireless telegraph service as will satisfy the needs of the public service. The governments desiring to reserve this right shall give notice thereof in the form provided for in the second paragraph of Article 16 of the convention, not later than three months before the convention goes into effect, or, in case of subsequent adhesion, at the time of such adhesion.

The countries whose names follow below declare now that they will not reserve such right: Germany, United States, Argentina, Austria-Hungary, Belgium, Brazil, Bulgaria, Chile, Greece, Mexico, Monaco, Norway, the Netherlands, Roumania, Russia, Sweden, Uruguay.

III. The manner of carrying out the provisions of the foregoing article shall be at the discretion of the government which takes advantage of the right of exemption; such government shall be at liberty to decide from time to time, in its own judgment, how many stations and what stations shall be exempted. Such government shall likewise be at liberty as regards the manner of carrying out the provision relative to the opening of other stations subject to the obligations of Article 3, insuring, within the region where the exempted stations are located, such wireless telegraph service as will satisfy the needs of the public service.

IV. It is understood that, in order not to impede scientific progress, the provisions of Article 3 of the convention shall not prevent the eventual employment of a wireless telegraph system incapable of communicating with other systems, provided, however, that such incapacity shall be due to the specific nature of such system and that it shall not be the result of devices adopted for the sole purpose of preventing intercommunication.

V. The adherence to the convention by the government of a country having colonies, possessions, or protectorates shall not carry with it the adherence of its colonies, possessions, or protectorates, unless a declaration to that effect is made by such government. Such colonies, possessions, and protectorates as a whole, or each of them separately, may form the subject of a separate adherence or a separate denunciation within the provisions of Articles 16 and 22 of the convention.

It is understood that the stations on board of vessels whose headquarters is a port in a colony, possession, or protectorate may be deemed as subject to the authority of such colony, possession, or protectorate.

VI. Note is taken of the following declaration:

The Italian delegation in signing the convention does so with the reservation that the convention cannot be ratified on the part of Italy until the date of the expiration of her contracts with Mr. Marconi and his company, or at an earlier date if the government of the king of Italy shall succeed in fixing such date by negotiations with Mr. Marconi and his company.

VII. In case one or several of the high contracting parties shall not ratify the convention, it shall nevertheless be valid as to the parties which shall have ratified it.

In witness whereof the undersigned plenipotentiaries have drawn up the present final protocol, which shall be of the same force and effect as though the provisions thereof had been embodied in the text of the convention itself to which it has reference, and they have signed one copy of the same, which shall be deposited in the archives of the imperial government of Germany, and a copy of which shall be transmitted to each of the parties.

Done at Berlin, November 3, 1906.

[Signatures follow]

SERVICE REGULATIONS ANNEXED TO THE INTERNATIONAL WIRELESS TELEGRAPH CONVENTION

1. Organization of Wireless Telegraph Stations

I. The choice of wireless apparatus and devices to be used by the coastal stations and stations on shipboard shall be unrestricted. The installation of such stations shall as far as possible keep pace with scientific and technical progress.

II. Two wave lengths, one of 300 meters and the other of 600 meters, are authorized for general public service. Every coastal station opened to such service shall use one or the other of these two wave lengths. During the whole time that a station is open to service it shall be in condition to receive calls according to its wave length, and no other wave length shall be used by it for the service of general public correspondence. Each government may, however, authorize in coastal stations the employment of other wave lengths designed to insure long-range service or any service, other than for general public correspondence, established in conformity with the provisions of the convention, provided such wave lengths do not exceed 600 meters, or that they do exceed 1600 meters.

III. 1. The normal wave length for stations on shipboard shall be 300 meters. Every station on shipboard shall be installed in such manner as to be able to use this wave length. Other wave lengths may be employed by such stations provided they do not exceed 600 meters.

2. Vessels of small tonnage which are unable to have plants on board insuring a wave length of 300 meters may be authorized to use a shorter wave length.

IV. 1. The international bureau shall be charged with drawing up a list of wireless telegraph stations of the class referred to in Article 1 of the convention. Such list shall contain for each station the following data:

(1) Name, nationality, and geographical location in the case of coastal stations; name, nationality, distinguishing signal of the international code, and name of ship's home port in the case of stations on shipboard;

(2) Call letters (the calls shall be distinguishable from one another and each must be formed of a group of three letters);

(3) Normal range;

(4) Wireless telegraph system;

(5) Class of receiving apparatus (recording, acoustic, or other apparatus);

(6) Wave lengths used by the station (the normal wave length to be underscored);

(7) Nature of service carried on by the station:

General public correspondence;

Limited public correspondence (correspondence with vessels . . .; correspondence with shipping lines . . .; correspondence with ships fitted with apparatus of the . . . system, etc.);

Long-range public correspondence;

Correspondence of private interest;

Special correspondence (exclusively official correspondence); etc.

(8) Hours during which the station is open;

(9) Coastal rate or shipboard rate.

2. The list shall also contain such data relating to wireless telegraph stations other than those specified in Article 1 of the convention as may be communicated to the international bureau by the management of the wireless telegraph service ("administration") to which such stations are subject.

V. The exchange of superfluous signals and words is prohibited to stations of the class referred to in Article 1 of the convention. Experiments and practice will be permitted in such stations in so far as they do not interfere with the service of other stations.

VI. 1. No station on shipboard shall be established or worked by private enterprise without authority from the government to which the vessel is subject. Such authority shall be in the nature of a license issued by said government.

2. Every station on shipboard that has been so authorized shall comply with the following requirements:

(a) The system employed shall be a syntonized system;

(b) The rate of transmission and reception, under normal conditions, shall not be less than twelve words a minute, words to be counted at the rate of five letters each;

(c) The power transmitted to the wireless telegraph apparatus shall not, under normal conditions, exceed one kilowatt. Power exceeding one kilowatt may be employed when the vessel finds it necessary to correspond while more than 300 kilometers distant from the nearest coastal station, or when, owing to obstructions, communication can be established only by means of an increase of power.

3. The service of the station on shipboard shall be carried on by a telegraph operator holding a certificate issued by the government to which the vessel is subject. Such certificate shall attest the professional efficiency of the operator as regards:

(a) Adjustment of the apparatus;

(b) Transmission and acoustic reception at the rate of not less than 20 words a minute;

(c) Knowledge of the regulations governing the exchange of wireless telegraph correspondence.

4. The certificate shall furthermore state that the government has bound the operator to secrecy with regard to the correspondence.

VII. 1. If the management of the wireless telegraph service of a country has knowledge of any infraction of the convention or of the regulations committed in any of the stations authorized by it, it shall ascertain the facts and fix the responsibility.

In the case of stations on shipboard, if the operator is responsible for such infraction, the management of the wireless telegraph service shall take the necessary measures and, if the necessity should arise, withdraw the certificate. If it is ascertained that the infraction is the result of the condition of the apparatus or of instructions given the operator, the same method shall be pursued with regard to the license issued to the vessel.

2. In cases of repeated infractions chargeable to the same vessel, if the representations made to the wireless telegraph management of the country to which

the vessel is subject by that of another country remain without effect, the latter shall be at liberty, after giving due notice, to authorize its coastal stations not to accept communications proceeding from the vessel at fault. In case of disagreement between the managements of the wireless telegraph service of two countries, the question shall be submitted to arbitration at the request of either of the two governments at issue. The procedure in such case shall be the same as indicated in Article 18 of the convention.

2. Hours of Service of Coastal Stations

VIII. 1. The service of coastal stations shall, as far as possible, be constant, day and night, without interruption.

Certain coastal stations, however, may have a service of limited duration. The management of the wireless telegraph service of each country shall fix the hours of service.

2. The coastal stations whose service is not constant shall not close before having transmitted all their wireless telegrams to the vessels which are within their radius of action, nor before having received from such vessels all the wireless telegrams of which notice has been given. This provision is likewise applicable when vessels signal their presence before the actual cessation of work.

3. Form and Posting of Wireless Telegrams

IX. If the route of a wireless telegram is partly over telegraph lines, or through wireless telegraph stations subject to a noncontracting government, such telegram may be transmitted provided the managements of the wireless telegraph service to which such lines or stations are subject have declared that, if the occasion should arise, they will comply with such provisions of the convention and of the regulations as are indispensable to the regular transmission of wireless telegrams and that the payment of charges is insured.

X. 1. Wireless telegrams shall show in the preamble that the service is "wireless" ("radio").

2. In the transmission of wireless telegrams of shipboard stations to coastal stations, the date and hour of posting may be omitted in the preamble.

Upon reforwarding a wireless telegram over the telegraph system, the coastal station shall show thereon its own name as the office of origin, followed by that of the vessel, and shall state, as the hour of posting, the hour when the telegram was received by it.

XI. The address of wireless telegrams intended for ships at sea shall be as complete as possible. It shall embrace the following:

(a) The name of the addressee, with additional designations if any;

(b) The name of the vessel as it appears in the list, supplemented by her nationality and, if necessary, by her distinguishing signal of the international code, in case there are several vessels of the same name;

(c) The name of the coastal station as it appears in the list.

4. Rates

XII. The coastal rates shall not exceed 60 centimes (11.6 cents) a word, and the shipboard rate shall not exceed 40 centimes (7.7 cents) a word.

A minimum rate per telegram, not to exceed the coastal rate or shipboard rate for a wireless telegram of ten words, may be imposed as coastal or shipboard rate.

XIII. The country within whose territory a coastal station is established which serves as intermediary for the exchange of wireless telegrams between a station on board ship and another country shall be considered, so far as the application of telegraph rates is concerned, as the country of origin or of destination of such telegrams, and not as the country of transit.

5. Collection of Charges

XIV. The total charge for wireless telegrams shall be collected of the sender.

Stations on shipboard shall to that end have the necessary tariffs. They shall be at liberty, however, to obtain information from coastal stations on the subject of rates for wireless telegrams for which they do not possess all the necessary data.

6. Transmission of Wireless Telegrams

a. *Signals of Transmission*

XV. The signals to be employed are of the Morse International Code.

XVI. Ships in distress shall use the following signal:

• • • — — — • • •

repeated at brief intervals.

As soon as a station perceives the signal of distress it shall cease all correspondence and not resume it until after it has made sure that the correspondence to which the call for assistance has given rise is terminated.

In case the ship in distress adds at the end of the series of her calls the call letters of a particular station the answer to the call shall be incumbent upon that station alone. If the call for assistance does not specify any particular station, every station perceiving such call shall be bound to answer it.

XVII. 1. The call letters following the letters

• — — • • — • — • • •

"P R B" signify that the vessel or station making the call desires to communicate with the station called, by means of the international signal code.

The combination of the letters "P R B" as a service signal for any other purpose than that specified above is prohibited.

2. Wireless telegrams may be framed with the aid of the international signal code.

Those addressed to a wireless telegraph station with a view to being forwarded by it are not to be translated by such station.

b. *Order of Transmission*

XVIII. Between two stations wireless telegrams of the same order shall be transmitted one by one, by the two stations alternately, or in series of several telegrams, as the coastal station may indicate, provided the duration of the transmission of each series does not exceed twenty minutes.

c. *Method of calling Wireless Stations and Transmission of Wireless Telegrams*

XIX. 1. As a general rule, it shall be the shipboard station that calls the coastal station.

2. The call should be made, as a general rule, only when the distance of the vessel from the coastal station is less than 75 per cent of the normal range of the latter.

3. Before proceeding to a call, the station on shipboard shall adjust its receiving apparatus to its maximum sensibility and make sure that the coastal station which it wishes to call up is not in correspondence with any other station. If it finds that any transmission is in progress, it shall wait for the first pause.

4. The shipboard station shall use for calling the normal wave of the coastal station.

5. If in spite of these precautions the public exchange of wireless telegrams is impeded at any place, the call shall cease upon the first request from a coastal station open to public correspondence. The latter station shall in such case indicate the approximate length of time it will be necessary to wait.

XX. 1. The call shall comprise the signal

— • — • —

the call letters of the station called repeated three times, the word "from" ("*de*") followed by the call letters of the sending station repeated three times.

2. The called station shall answer by making the signal

— • — • —

followed by the call letters of the corresponding station repeated three times, the word "from," its own call letters, and the signal

— • —

XXI. If a station called does not answer the call (Article XX) repeated three times at intervals of two minutes, the call shall not be resumed until after an interval of half an hour, the station issuing the call having first made sure that no wireless telegraph correspondence is in progress.

XXII. 1. As soon as the coastal station has answered, the shipboard station shall make known to it:

(a) The distance of the vessel from the coastal station in nautical miles;
(b) Her true bearing in degrees counted from 0 to 360;
(c) Her true course in degrees counted from 0 to 360;
(d) Her speed in nautical miles;
(e) The number of words she has to transmit.

2. The coastal station shall answer, stating the number of words to be transmitted to the vessel.

3. If the transmission cannot take place immediately, the coastal station shall inform the station on shipboard of the approximate length of time that it will be necessary to wait.

XXIII. When a coastal station receives calls from several shipboard stations, the coastal station shall decide the order in which the shipboard stations shall be admitted to exchange their messages.

In fixing this order the coastal station shall be guided exclusively by the necessity of permitting each station concerned to exchange the greatest possible number of wireless telegrams.

XXIV. Before beginning the exchange of correspondence the coastal station shall advise the shipboard station whether the transmission is to be effected in the alternate order or by series (Article XVIII); it shall then begin the transmission or follow up the preliminaries with the signal

— · —

(invitation to transmit).

XXV. The transmission of the wireless telegram shall be preceded by the signal

— · — · —

and terminated by the signal

· — · — ·

followed by the name of the sending station.

XXVI. When a wireless telegram to be transmitted contains more than 40 words, the sending station shall interrupt the transmission after each series of about 20 words by an interrogation point

· · — — · ·

and shall not resume it until after it has obtained from the receiving station a repetition of the last word duly received, followed by an interrogation point.

In the case of transmission by series, acknowledgment of receipt shall be made after each wireless telegram.

XXVII. 1. When the signals become doubtful every possible means shall be resorted to to finish the transmission. To this end the wireless telegram shall be repeated at the request of the receiving station, but not to exceed three times. If in spite of such triple repetition the signals are still unreadable the wireless telegram shall be canceled. If no acknowledgment of receipt is received the transmitting station shall again call up the receiving station. If no reply is made after three calls the transmission shall not be followed up any further.

2. If in the opinion of the receiving station the wireless telegram, although imperfectly received, is nevertheless capable of transmission, said station shall enter the words "reception doubtful" at the end of the preamble and let the wireless telegram follow.

XXVIII. All stations are bound to carry on the service with as little expense of energy as may be necessary to insure safe communication.

d. *Acknowledgment of Receipt and Conclusion of Work*

XXIX. 1. Receipt shall be acknowledged in the form prescribed by the international telegraph regulations, preceded by the call letters of the transmitting station and followed by those of the receiving station.

2. The conclusion of a correspondence between two stations shall be indicated by each station by means of the signal

• • • — • —

followed by its call letters.

e. *Directions to be followed in sending Wireless Telegrams*

XXX. 1. In general, the shipboard stations shall transmit their wireless telegrams to the nearest coastal station.

2. A sender on board a vessel shall, however, have the right to designate the coastal station through which he desires to have his wireless telegram transmitted.

3. The station on shipboard shall then wait until such coastal station shall be the nearest. If this cannot be done, the wishes of the sender are to be complied with only if the transmission can be effected without interfering with the service of other stations.

7. Delivery of Wireless Telegrams at their Destination

XXXI. When for any cause whatever a wireless telegram proceeding from a vessel at sea cannot be delivered to the addressee, a notice of nondelivery shall be issued. Such notice shall be transmitted to the vessel if possible. When a wireless telegram received by a shipboard station cannot be delivered, the station shall notify the office of origin by official notice. Such notice shall be transmitted, whenever practicable, to the coastal station through which the wireless telegram has passed in transit; otherwise, to the nearest coastal station.

XXXII. If the ship for which a wireless telegram is intended has not signaled her presence to the coastal station within the period designated by the sender, or, in the absence of such designation, by the morning of the 29th day following, the coastal station shall notify the sender.

The latter shall have the right to ask, by a paid official notice, sent by either telegraph or mail and addressed to the coastal station, that his wireless telegram be held for a further period of 30 days for transmission to the vessel, and so on. In the absence of such request, the wireless telegram shall be put aside as not transmissible at the end of the 30th day (exclusive of the day of posting).

If, however, the coastal station has positive information that the vessel has left its radius of action before it has been able to transmit to her the wireless message, such station shall so notify the sender.

8. Special Telegrams

XXXIII. The following telegrams shall not be accepted for transmission:

(a) Telegrams with answer prepaid;

(b) Money-order telegrams;

(c) Telegrams calling for repetition of message (for purposes of verification);

(d) Telegrams calling for acknowledgment of receipt;

(e) Telegrams to be forwarded (if addressee is not found at the address given);

(f) Paid service telegrams, except in so far as transmission over the lines of the telegraph system is concerned;

(g) Urgent telegrams, except in so far as transmission over the lines of the telegraph system is concerned, subject to the application of the provisions of the international telegraph regulations;

(h) Telegrams to be delivered by express or mail.

9. Files

XXXIV. The originals of wireless telegrams and the documents relating thereto retained by the managements of the wireless telegraph service or by private enterprises shall be kept for a period of at least twelve months, beginning with the month following that of the posting of the wireless telegram, with all the necessary precautions as regards secrecy.

Such originals and documents shall, as far as practicable, be sent at least once a month by the shipboard stations to the management of the wireless telegraph service to which they are subject.

10. Rebates and Reimbursements

XXXV. 1. With regard to rebates and reimbursements, the provisions of the international telegraph regulations shall be applicable, taking into account the restrictions specified in Article XXXIII of the present regulations and subject to the following reservations:

The time employed in the transmission of wireless telegrams and the time that wireless telegrams remain in a coastal station or station on shipboard shall not be counted as delays as regards rebates or reimbursements.

Reimbursements shall be borne by the different managements of the wireless telegraph service or private enterprises which have taken part in the transmission of the wireless telegram, each management or private enterprise relinquishing its share of the rate. Wireless telegrams to which Articles 7 and 8 of the convention of St. Petersburg are applicable shall remain subject, however, to the provisions of the international telegraph regulations, except when the acceptance of such telegrams is the result of an error made by the telegraph service.

2. When the acknowledgment of receipt of a wireless telegram has not reached the station which has transmitted the telegram, the charges shall be refunded only if the fact has been established that the wireless telegram is entitled to reimbursement.

11. Accounts and Payment of Charges

XXXVI. 1. The coastal and shipboard charges shall not enter into the accounts provided for by the international telegraph regulations.

The accounts regarding such charges shall be liquidated by the managements of the wireless telegraph service of the countries concerned. They shall be drawn up by the wireless telegraph management to which the coastal stations are subject, and communicated by them to the wireless telegraph managements concerned.

2. For transmission over the lines of the telegraph system wireless telegrams shall be treated, so far as the payment of rates is concerned, in conformity with the international telegraph regulations.

3. For wireless telegrams proceeding from ships, the wireless telegraph management to which the shipboard station is subject shall be charged by the wireless telegraph management to which the coastal station is subject with the coastal and ordinary telegraph rates charged on board of vessels.

For wireless telegrams intended for ships, the wireless telegraph management which has collected the fees shall be charged directly by the wireless telegraph management to which the coastal station is subject with the coastal and shipboard rates. The latter shall credit the wireless telegraph management to which the vessel is subject with the shipboard rate.

In case the wireless telegraph management which has collected the charges is the same, however, as the one to which the shipboard station is subject, the shipboard rate shall not be charged by the wireless telegraph management to which the coastal station is subject.

4. The monthly accounts serving as a basis for the special accounts of wireless telegrams shall be made out for each telegram separately, with all the necessary data, within a period of six months from the month to which they refer.

5. The governments reserve the right to enter into special agreements among themselves and with private enterprises (parties operating wireless telegraph stations, shipping companies, etc.) with a view of adopting other provisions with regard to accounts.

12. International Bureau

XXXVII. The international bureau of telegraphs shall be intrusted with the duties specified in Article 13 of the convention, subject to the consent of the government of the Swiss Confederation and the approval of the telegraph union.

The additional expenses resulting from the work of the international bureau so far as wireless telegraphy is concerned shall not exceed 40,000 francs a year, exclusive of the special expenses arising from the convening of the international conference.

These expenses shall form the subject of a special account, and the provisions of the international telegraph regulations shall be applicable to them. Before the convening of the next conference, however, each contracting government shall notify the international bureau of the class in which it desires to be entered.

XXXVIII. The management of the wireless telegraph service of the different countries shall forward to the international bureau a table in conformity with the annexed blank, containing the data enumerated in said table for stations such as referred to in Article IV of the regulations. Changes occurring and additional data shall be forwarded by the wireless telegraph managements to the international bureau between the 1st and 10th day of each month. With the aid of such data the international bureau shall draw up a list which it shall keep up to date. The list and the supplements thereto shall be printed and distributed to the wireless telegraph managements of the countries concerned; they may also be sold to the public at the cost price.

The international bureau shall see to it that the same call letters for several wireless telegraph stations shall not be adopted.

13. Miscellaneous Provisions

XXXIX. The managements of the wireless telegraph service shall give to agencies of maritime information such data regarding losses and casualties at sea, or other information of general interest to navigation, as the coastal stations may properly report.

XL. The exchange of correspondence between shipboard stations such as referred to in Article 1 of the convention shall be carried on in such a manner as not to interfere with the service of the coastal stations, the latter, as a general rule, being accorded the right of priority for the public service.

XLI. 1. In the absence of special agreements between the parties concerned, the provisions of the present regulations shall be applicable analogously to the exchange of wireless telegrams between two vessels at sea, subject to the following exceptions:

(a) To Article XIV. The shipboard rate falling to the transmitting ship shall be collected from the sender, and that falling to the receiving ship shall be collected from the addressee;

(b) To Article XVIII. The order of transmission shall be regulated in each case by mutual agreement between the corresponding stations.

(c) To Article XXXVI. The rates for the wireless telegrams in question shall not enter into the accounts provided for in that article, such charges falling to the wireless telegraph managements which have collected them.

2. Retransmission of wireless telegrams exchanged between vessels at sea shall be subject to special agreements between the parties concerned.

XLII. The provisions of the international telegraph regulations shall be applicable analogously to wireless telegraph correspondence in so far as they are not contrary to the provisions of the present regulations.

In conformity with Article 11 of the convention of Berlin, these regulations shall go into effect on the first day of July, 1908.

In witness whereof the respective plenipotentiaries have signed one copy of the present regulations, which shall be deposited in the archives of the imperial government of Germany, and a copy of which shall be transmitted to each of the parties.

Done at Berlin, November 3, 1906.

[Signatures follow]

EXTRACT FROM THE INTERNATIONAL TELEGRAPH CONVENTION, SIGNED AT ST. PETERSBURG, JULY 10–22, 1875

[See Article 17 of the convention]

Art. 1. The high contracting parties concede to all persons the right to correspond by means of the international telegraphs.

Art. 2. They bind themselves to take all the necessary measures for the purpose of insuring the secrecy of the correspondence and its safe transmission.

ART. 3. They declare, nevertheless, that they accept no responsibility as regards the international telegraph service.

ART. 5. Telegrams are classed in three categories:

1. State telegrams: those emanating from the head of the nation, the ministers, the commanders in chief of the army and naval forces, and the diplomatic or consular agents of the contracting governments, as well as the answers to such telegrams.

2. Service telegrams: those which emanate from the managements of the telegraph service of the contracting states and which relate either to the international telegraph service or to subjects of public interest determined jointly by such managements.

3. Private telegrams.

In the transmission, the state telegrams shall have precedence over other telegrams.

ART. 6. State telegrams and service telegrams may be issued in secret language, in any communications.

Private telegrams may be exchanged in secret language between two states which admit of this mode of correspondence.

The states which do not admit of private telegrams in secret language, upon the expedition or arrival of the same, shall allow them to pass in transit, except in the case of suspension defined in Article 8.

ART. 7. The high contracting parties reserve the right to stop the transmission of any private telegram which may appear dangerous to the safety of the state, or which may be contrary to the laws of the country, to public order or good morals.

ART. 8. Each government also reserves the right to suspend the international telegraph service for an indefinite period, if deemed necessary by it, either generally, or only over certain lines and for certain classes of correspondence, of which such government shall immediately notify all the other contracting governments.

ART. 11. Telegrams relating to the international telegraph service of the contracting states shall be transmitted free of charge over the entire systems of such states.

ART. 12. The high contracting parties shall render accounts to one another of the charges collected by each of them.

ART. 17. The high contracting parties reserve respectively the right to enter among themselves into special arrangements of any kind with regard to points of the service which do not interest the states generally.

CHAPTER XIX

EXCHANGE OF DOCUMENTS

Of a minor character, and including only a small number of nations, is an agreement which may suitably be extended to include all the nations, and which is for the promotion of information in each regarding the official action of the others, including their scientific and literary publications. These conventions are therefore included in this compilation. On March 15, 1886, there was concluded at Brussels, between the United States, Belgium, Brazil, Italy, Portugal, Servia, and Spain a convention for "the immediate exchange of the official journal, as well as of the parliamentary annals and documents, of their respective states." This convention was as follows:

ART. 1. Independently of the obligations which result from Article 2 of the general convention of this day, relative to the exchange of official documents and of scientific and literary publications, the respective governments undertake to have transmitted to the legislative chambers of each contracting state, as fast as their publication, a copy of the official journal, as well as of the parliamentary annals and documents which are given publicity.

ART. 2. The states which have not taken part in the present convention are admitted to adhere thereto on their request.

This adhesion will be notified diplomatically to the Belgian government, and by that government to all the other signatory states.

ART. 3. The present convention will be ratified and the ratifications will be exchanged at Brussels as soon as practicable. It is concluded for ten years from the day of the exchange of the ratifications and it will remain in force beyond that time, so long as one of the governments shall not have declared six months in advance that it renounces it.

In witness whereof, the respective plenipotentiaries have signed it, and have thereunto affixed their seals.

Done at Brussels, in seven copies, the 15th of March, 1886.

[Signatures follow]

On March 15, 1886, there was concluded a convention between the United States, Belgium, Brazil, Italy, Portugal, Servia, Spain, and Switzerland for "a system of international exchanges of the official documents and of the scientific and literary publications of their respective states," as follows:

ART. 1. There shall be established in each of the contracting states a bureau charged with the duty of the exchanges.

ART. 2. The publications which the contracting states agree to exchange are the following:

1st. The official documents, parliamentary and administrative, which are published in the country of their origin.

2nd. The works executed by order and at the expense of the government.

ART. 3. Each bureau shall cause to be printed a list of the publications that it is able to place at the disposal of the contracting states.

This list shall be corrected and completed each year and regularly addressed to all the bureaus of exchange.

ART. 4. The bureaus of exchange will arrange between themselves the number of copies which they may be able eventually to demand and furnish.

ART. 5. The transmissions shall be made directly from bureau to bureau. Uniform models and formulas will be adopted for the memoranda of the contents of the cases, as well as for all the administrative correspondence, requests, acknowledgments of reception, etc.

ART. 6. For exterior transmissions, each state assumes the expense of packing and transportation to the place of destination. Nevertheless, when the transmissions shall be made by sea, special arrangements will regulate the share of each state in the expense of transportation.

Art. 7. The bureaus of exchange will serve, in an official capacity, as intermediaries between the learned bodies and literary and scientific societies, etc., of the contracting states for the reception and transmission of their publications.

It remains, however, well understood that, in such case, the duty of the bureaus of exchange will be confined to the free transmission of the works exchanged, and that these bureaus will not in any manner take the initiative to bring about the establishment of such relations.

ART. 8. These provisions apply only to the documents and works published after the date of the present convention.

ART. 9. The states which have not taken part in the present convention are admitted to adhere to it on their request.

This adhesion will be notified diplomatically to the Belgian government and by that government to all the other signatory states.

ART. 10. The present convention will be ratified, and the ratifications will be exchanged at Brussels, as soon as practicable. It is concluded for ten years, from the day of the exchange of ratifications, and it will remain in force beyond that time, so long as one of the governments shall not have declared six months in advance that it renounces it.

In witness whereof, the respective plenipotentiaries have signed it, and have thereunto affixed their seals.

Done at Brussels, in eight copies, the 15th of March, 1886.

[Signatures follow]

CHAPTER XX

THE WORLD JUDICIARY

After the Hague court of arbitration had been established by act of the Hague peace conference of 1899, it seemed as if that court might possibly be the germ from which would be developed the world judiciary. Here was a body whose official name was "Court." By it was to be dispensed justice to both sides of a controversy. It is true that in reality the court of arbitration is a department of the world executive, as a state board of arbitration is a part of the state executive department, not of the judicial. But the use of the word "Court," and the circumstances amid which the court is to act, made it plausible that here was a germ of the world judiciary.

But much sooner than any such germ could grow appreciably by the addition of true judicial functions came the action of the delegates of all the nations assembled in the second peace conference at The Hague, in 1907. In the proposition before that conference for the establishment of an international prize court was the germ of a true world judiciary. The proposition was fruitful, and in the list of conventions adopted by the second conference and submitted to the nations for ratification is that "relative to the establishment of an international prize court." This international court is to be a court of appeals from the decisions of national prize courts. But it appears clearly that, for the first time, there is a formal establishment of a true world judiciary; for the language used in the preamble to the articles includes these words: "the institution of an international court, whose jurisdiction and procedure would be carefully defined." In the articles of this convention there is true world law whereby this "international court," with "jurisdiction and procedure . . . carefully defined," is established. The subjects of its jurisdiction are specified by this law of all the nations. The nations, furthermore, when they ratify this convention, fix the methods whereby this world court of appeals shall act. The lack of a world executive power with strength to compel is recognized; and what is really a higher power than a world police or a world army, for honorable nations, is brought in,—namely, the solemn pledge of each nation. Read Article 9 again: "The contracting Powers undertake to submit in good faith to the decisions of the international prize court, and to carry them out with the least possible delay." There is the sufficient substitute for a world army to enforce the decisions of world courts. Those few words have a mighty historical pertinence in questions which will surely arise in the development of the single organic government of the world.

Still further, this convention, or chapter of world law, prescribes how the international prize court shall be constituted. Full provision is made for the procedure of the court. Details are duly provided for, even to the formality whereby the life of this judicial germ may itself be destroyed,—a catastrophe to the world which should never occur, unless some better form of judicial proceedings is substituted whereby the development of the world judiciary may be carried forward upon better conditions.

This convention for the establishment of an international prize court might fitly be included in this chapter regarding the judicial department of the world; but it is retained in its place with other conventions of the Second Hague Conference in order that the results of that body may appear as a historic whole.

Some of the nations which took part in the conference of 1907 were not satisfied with the method of practice proposed for the international prize court. In order that some code might be agreed upon before any case should be presented, the international naval conference was held in London, beginning December 4, 1908, upon the invitation of Great Britain, to draft a convention and formulate rules in accordance with Article 7, paragraph 2, of the convention relating to the creation of an international prize court, which was signed at The Hague in 1907. This Article 7, paragraph 2, is as follows: "In the absence of such provisions, the court shall apply the rules of international law. If no generally recognized rule exists, the court shall give judgment in accordance with the general principles of justice and equity." Because of the vagueness of such a basis of procedure, fearing detriment to immense commercial interests, Great Britain called the conference.

To that conference were invited the United States, France, the Netherlands, Spain, Germany, Italy, Austria-Hungary, Russia, and

Japan. These are the chief maritime powers of the world. By meeting by themselves they avoided complications which would have been possible by the presence of a large number of small Powers, each with an equal vote, according to the precedents of previous conferences, if all the nations had been invited which were represented at the conference at The Hague in 1907. Furthermore, it is hoped that a sufficient number of the other Powers to include practically the will of the world will adhere to the convention adopted by this conference. The action of the conference is of high historical value, for its convention, signed at London, February 26, 1909, constitutes the first body of world law ever framed distinctly and designedly as such for the purpose of a world court. Here stands, beyond question, the formal beginning, as such, of a code of world law. At this particular spot the stake is to be driven to mark the place where the body of world law, which will doubtless grow rapidly in official standing, emerged from the concurrent judgment of delegates of the nations and gave definite date for the beginning of the new era of unspeakable benefit to the peace and prosperity of all the nations. To this culmination events had been tending with increasing clearness and rapidity. This first formal body of world law is as follows:

The London naval conference, called together by his Britannic Majesty's government, assembled at the foreign office on the 4th December, 1908, with the object of laying down the generally recognized principles of international law in accordance with Article 7 of the convention signed at The Hague on the 18th October, 1907, for the establishment of an international prize court.

The Powers enumerated below took part in this conference, at which they appointed as their representatives the following delegates:

[List of Powers and delegates follows]

In a series of sittings held from the 4th December, 1908, to the 26th February, 1909, the conference has drawn up for signature by the plenipotentiaries, the *declaration concerning the laws of naval war*, the text of which is annexed to the present protocol.

Furthermore, the following wish has been recorded by the delegates of those Powers which have signed or expressed the intention of signing the convention of The Hague of the 18th October, 1907, for the establishment of an international prize court:

The delegates of the Powers represented at the naval conference which have signed or expressed the intention of signing the convention of The Hague of the 18th October, 1907, for the establishment of an international prize court, having regard to the difficulties of a constitutional nature which, in some states, stand in the way of the ratification of that convention in its present form, agree to call the attention of their respective governments to the advantage of concluding an arrangement under which such states would have the power, at the time of depositing their ratifications, to add thereto a reservation to the effect that resort to the international prize court in respect of decisions of their national tribunals shall take the form of a direct claim for compensation, provided always that the effect of this reservation shall not be such as to impair the rights secured under the said convention either to individuals or to their governments, and that the terms of the reservation shall form the subject of a subsequent understanding between the Powers signatory of that convention.

In faith whereof the plenipotentiaries and the delegates representing those plenipotentiaries who have already left London have signed the present protocol.

Done at London the twenty-sixth day of February, one thousand nine hundred and nine, in a single original, which shall be deposited in the archives of the British government, and of which duly certified copies shall be sent through the diplomatic channel to the Powers represented at the naval conference.

[Names follow]

DECLARATION CONCERNING THE LAWS OF NAVAL WAR

His Majesty the German Emperor, King of Prussia; the President of the United States of America; his Majesty the Emperor of Austria, King of Bohemia, etc., and Apostolic King of Hungary; his Majesty the King of Spain; the President of the French Republic; his Majesty the King of the United Kingdom of Great Britain and Ireland and of the British Dominions beyond the Seas, Emperor of India; his Majesty the King of Italy; his Majesty the Emperor of Japan; her Majesty the Queen of the Netherlands; his Majesty the Emperor of all the Russias;

Having regard to the terms in which the British government invited various Powers to meet in conference in order to arrive at an agreement as to what are the generally recognized rules of international law within the meaning of Article 7 of the convention of 18th October, 1907, relative to the establishment of an international prize court;

Recognizing all the advantages which an agreement as to the said rules would, in the unfortunate event of a naval war, present, both as regards peaceful commerce and as regards the belligerents and their diplomatic relations with neutral governments;

Having regard to the divergence often found in the methods by which it is sought to apply in practice the general principles of international law;

Animated by the desire to insure henceforward a greater measure of uniformity in this respect;

Hoping that a work so important to the common welfare will meet with general approval;

Have appointed as their plenipotentiaries, that is to say:

[Names follow]

Who, after having communicated their full powers, found to be in good and due form, have agreed to make the present declaration:

PRELIMINARY PROVISION

The signatory Powers are agreed that the rules contained in the following chapters correspond in substance with the generally recognized principles of international law.

CHAPTER I. BLOCKADE IN TIME OF WAR

ART. 1. A blockade must not extend beyond the ports and coasts belonging to or occupied by the enemy.

ART. 2. In accordance with the declaration of Paris of 1856, a blockade, in order to be binding, must be effective, — that is to say, it must be maintained by a force sufficient really to prevent access to the enemy coast line.

ART. 3. The question whether a blockade is effective is a question of fact.

ART. 4. A blockade is not regarded as raised if the blockading force is temporarily withdrawn on account of stress of weather.

ART. 5. A blockade must be applied impartially to the ships of all nations.

ART. 6. The commander of a blockading force may give permission to a warship to enter, and subsequently to leave, a blockaded port.

ART. 7. In circumstances of distress, acknowledged by an officer of the blockading force, a neutral vessel may enter a place under blockade and subsequently leave it, provided that she has neither discharged nor shipped any cargo there.

ART. 8. A blockade, in order to be binding, must be declared in accordance with Article 9, and notified in accordance with Articles 11 and 16.

ART. 9. A declaration of blockade is made either by the blockading Power or by the naval authorities acting in its name.

It specifies

(1) The date when the blockade begins;

(2) The geographical limits of the coast line under blockade;

(3) The period within which neutral vessels may come out.

ART. 10. If the operations of the blockading Power, or of the naval authorities acting in its name, do not tally with the particulars, which, in accordance with Article 9, (1) and (2), must be inserted in the declaration of blockade, the declaration is void, and a new declaration is necessary in order to make the blockade operative.

ART. 11. A declaration of blockade is notified:

(1) To neutral Powers, by the blockading Power by means of a communication addressed to the governments direct, or to their representatives accredited to it;

(2) To the local authorities, by the officer commanding the blockading force. The local authorities will, in turn, inform the foreign consular officers at the port or on the coast line under blockade as soon as possible.

ART. 12. The rules as to declaration and notification of blockade apply to cases where the limits of a blockade are extended, or where a blockade is reëstablished after having been raised.

ART. 13. The voluntary raising of a blockade, as also any restriction in the limits of a blockade, must be notified in the manner prescribed by Article 11.

ART. 14. The liability of a neutral vessel to capture for breach of blockade is contingent on her knowledge, actual or presumptive, of the blockade.

ART. 15. Failing proof to the contrary, knowledge of the blockade is presumed if the vessel left a neutral port subsequently to the notification of the blockade to the Power to which such port belongs, provided that such notification was made in sufficient time.

ART. 16. If a vessel approaching a blockaded port has no knowledge, actual or presumptive, of the blockade, the notification must be made to the vessel itself by an officer of one of the ships of the blockading force. This notification should be entered in the vessel's log book, and must state the day and hour, and the geographical position of the vessel at the time.

If through the negligence of the officer commanding the blockading force no declaration of blockade has been notified to the local authorities, or if in the declaration, as notified, no period has been mentioned within which neutral vessels may come out, a neutral vessel coming out of the blockaded port must be allowed to pass free.

ART. 17. Neutral vessels may not be captured for breach of blockade except within the area of operations of the warships detailed to render the blockade effective.

ART. 18. The blockading forces must not bar access to neutral ports or coasts.

ART. 19. Whatever may be the ulterior destination of a vessel or of her cargo, she cannot be captured for breach of blockade, if, at the moment, she is on her way to a nonblockaded port.

ART. 20. A vessel which has broken blockade outwards, or which has attempted to break blockade inwards, is liable to capture so long as she is pursued by a ship of the blockading force. If the pursuit is abandoned, or if the blockade is raised, her capture can no longer be effected.

ART. 21. A vessel found guilty of breach of blockade is liable to condemnation. The cargo is also condemned, unless it is proved that at the time of the shipment of the goods the shipper neither knew nor could have known of the intention to break the blockade.

CHAPTER II. CONTRABAND OF WAR

ART. 22. The following articles may, without notice, be treated as contraband of war, under the name of absolute contraband:

(1) Arms of all kinds, including arms for sporting purposes, and their distinctive component parts.

(2) Projectiles, charges, and cartridges of all kinds, and their distinctive component parts.

(3) Powder and explosives specially prepared for use in war.

(4) Gun mountings, limber boxes, limbers, military wagons, field forges, and their distinctive component parts.

(5) Clothing and equipment of a distinctively military character.

(6) All kinds of harness of a distinctively military character.

(7) Saddle, draft, and pack animals suitable for use in war.

(8) Articles of camp equipment, and their distinctive component parts.

(9) Armor plates.

(10) Warships, including boats, and their distinctive component parts of such a nature that they can only be used on a vessel of war.

(11) Implements and apparatus designed exclusively for the manufacture of munitions of war, for the manufacture or repair of arms, or war material for use on land or sea.

ART. 23. Articles exclusively used for war may be added to the list of absolute contraband by a declaration, which must be notified.

Such notification must be addressed to the governments of other Powers, or to their representatives accredited to the Power making the declaration. A notification made after the outbreak of hostilities is addressed only to neutral Powers.

ART. 24. The following articles, susceptible of use in war as well as for purposes of peace, may, without notice, be treated as contraband of war, under the name of conditional contraband:

(1) Foodstuffs.

(2) Forage and grain, suitable for feeding animals.

(3) Clothing, fabrics for clothing, and boots and shoes, suitable for use in war.

(4) Gold and silver in coin or bullion; paper money.

(5) Vehicles of all kinds available for use in war, and their component parts.

(6) Vessels, craft, and boats of all kinds; floating docks, parts of docks, and their component parts.

(7) Railway material both fixed and rolling stock, and material for telegraphs, wireless telegraphs, and telephones.

(8) Balloons and flying machines, and their distinctive component parts, together with accessories and articles recognizable as intended for use in connection with balloons and flying machines.

(9) Fuel; lubricants.

(10) Powder and explosives not specially prepared for use in war.

(11) Barbed wire, and implements for fixing and cutting the same.

(12) Horseshoes and shoeing materials.

(13) Harness and saddlery.

(14) Field glasses, telescopes, chronometers, and all kinds of nautical instruments.

ART. 25. Articles susceptible of use in war as well as for purposes of peace, other than those enumerated in Articles 22 and 24, may be added to the list of conditional contraband by a declaration, which must be notified in the manner provided for in the second paragraph of Article 23.

ART. 26. If a Power waives, so far as it is concerned, the right to treat as contraband of war an article comprised in any of the classes enumerated in Articles 22 and 24, such intention shall be announced by a declaration, which must be notified in the manner provided for in the second paragraph of Article 23.

ART. 27. Articles which are not susceptible of use in war may not be declared contraband of war.

ART. 28. The following may not be declared contraband of war:

(1) Raw cotton, wool, silk, jute, flax, hemp, and other raw materials of the textile industries, and yarns of the same.

(2) Oil seeds and nuts; copra.

(3) Rubber, resins, gums, and lacs; hops.

(4) Rawhides and horns, bones, and ivory.

(5) Natural and artificial manures, including nitrates and phosphates for agricultural purposes.

(6) Metallic ores.

(7) Earths, clays, lime, chalk, stone, including marble, bricks, slates, and tiles.

(8) Chinaware and glass.

(9) Paper and paper-making materials.

(10) Soap, paint, and colors, including articles exclusively used in their manufacture, and varnish.

(11) Bleaching powder, soda ash, caustic soda, salt cake, ammonia, sulphate of ammonia, and sulphate of copper.

(12) Agricultural, mining, textile, and printing machinery.

(13) Precious and semiprecious stones, pearls, mother-of-pearl, and coral.

(14) Clocks and watches, other than chronometers.

(15) Fashion and fancy goods.

(16) Feathers of all kinds, hairs, and bristles.

(17) Articles of household furniture and decoration; office furniture and requisites.

ART. 29. Likewise the following may not be treated as contraband of war:

(1) Articles serving exclusively to aid the sick and wounded. They can, however, in case of urgent military necessity and subject to the payment of compensation, be requisitioned, if their destination is that specified in Article 30.

(2) Articles intended for the use of the vessel in which they are found, as well as those intended for the use of her crew and passengers during the voyage.

ART. 30. Absolute contraband is liable to capture if it is shown to be destined to territory belonging to or occupied by the enemy, or to the armed forces of the enemy. It is immaterial whether the carriage of the goods is direct or entails transshipment or a subsequent transport by land.

ART. 31. Proof of the destination specified in Article 30 is complete in the following cases:

(1) When the goods are documented for discharge in an enemy port, or for delivery to the armed forces of the enemy.

(2) When the vessel is to call at enemy ports only, or when she is to touch at an enemy port or meet the armed forces of the enemy before reaching the neutral port for which the goods in question are documented.

ART. 32. Where a vessel is carrying absolute contraband, her papers are conclusive proof as to the voyage on which she is engaged, unless she is found clearly out of the course indicated by her papers and unable to give adequate reasons to justify such deviation.

ART. 33. Conditional contraband is liable to capture if it is shown to be destined for the use of the armed forces or of a government department of the enemy state, unless in this latter case the circumstances show that the goods cannot in fact be used for the purposes of the war in progress. This latter exception does not apply to a consignment coming under Article 24, (4).

ART. 34. The destination referred to in Article 33 is presumed to exist if the goods are consigned to enemy authorities, or to a contractor established in the enemy country who, as a matter of common knowledge, supplies articles of this kind to the enemy. A similar presumption arises if the goods are consigned to a fortified place belonging to the enemy, or other place serving as a base for the armed forces of the enemy. No such presumption, however, arises in the case of a merchant vessel bound for one of these places if it is sought to prove that she herself is contraband.

In cases where the above presumptions do not arise, the destination is presumed to be innocent.

The presumptions set up by this article may be rebutted.

ART. 35. Conditional contraband is not liable to capture, except when found on board a vessel bound for territory belonging to or occupied by the enemy, or for the armed forces of the enemy, and when it is not to be discharged in an intervening neutral port.

The ship's papers are conclusive proof both as to the voyage on which the vessel is engaged and as to the port of discharge of the goods, unless she is found clearly out of the course indicated by her papers, and unable to give adequate reasons to justify such deviation.

ART. 36. Notwithstanding the provisions of Article 35, conditional contraband, if shown to have the destination referred to in Article 33, is liable to capture in cases where the enemy country has no seaboard.

ART. 37. A vessel carrying goods liable to capture as absolute or conditional contraband may be captured on the high seas or in the territorial waters of the belligerents throughout the whole of her voyage, even if she is to touch at a port of call before reaching the hostile destination.

ART. 38. A vessel may not be captured on the ground that she has carried contraband on a previous occasion if such carriage is in point of fact at an end.

ART. 39. Contraband goods are liable to condemnation.

ART. 40. A vessel carrying contraband may be condemned if the contraband, reckoned either by value, weight, volume, or freight, forms more than half the cargo.

ART. 41. If a vessel carrying contraband is released, she is liable for the costs and expenses incurred by the captor in respect of the proceedings in the national prize court and the custody of the ship and cargo during the proceedings.

ART. 42. Goods which belong to the owner of the contraband and are on board the same vessel are liable to condemnation.

ART. 43. If a vessel is encountered at sea while unaware of the outbreak of hostilities or of the declaration of contraband which applies to her cargo, the contraband cannot be condemned except on payment of compensation; the vessel herself and the remainder of the cargo are not liable to condemnation or to the costs and expenses referred to in Article 41. The same rule applies if the master, after becoming aware of the outbreak of hostilities, or of the declaration of contraband, has had no opportunity of discharging the contraband.

A vessel is deemed to be aware of the existence of a state of war, or of a declaration of contraband, if she left a neutral port subsequently to the notification to the Power to which such port belongs of the outbreak of hostilities or of the declaration of contraband respectively, provided that such notification was made in sufficient time. A vessel is also deemed to be aware of the existence of a state of war if she left an enemy port after the outbreak of hostilities.

ART. 44. A vessel which has been stopped on the ground that she is carrying contraband, and which is not liable to condemnation on account of the proportion of contraband on board, may, when the circumstances permit, be allowed to continue her voyage if the master is willing to hand over the contraband to the belligerent warship.

The delivery of the contraband must be entered by the captor on the log book of the vessel stopped, and the master must give the captor duly certified copies of all relevant papers.

The captor is at liberty to destroy the contraband that has been handed over to him under these conditions.

CHAPTER III. UNNEUTRAL SERVICE

ART. 45. A neutral vessel will be condemned and will, in a general way, receive the same treatment as a neutral vessel liable to condemnation for carriage of contraband:

(1) If she is on a voyage specially undertaken with a view to the transport of individual passengers who are embodied in the armed forces of the enemy, or with a view to the transmission of intelligence in the interest of the enemy.

(2) If, to the knowledge of either the owner, the charterer, or the master, she is transporting a military detachment of the enemy, or one or more persons who, in the course of the voyage, directly assist the operations of the enemy.

In the cases specified under the above heads, goods belonging to the owner of the vessel are likewise liable to condemnation.

The provisions of the present article do not apply if the vessel is encountered at sea while unaware of the outbreak of hostilities, or if the master, after becoming aware of the outbreak of hostilities, has had no opportunity of disembarking the passengers. The vessel is deemed to be aware of the existence of a state of war if she left an enemy port subsequently to the outbreak of hostilities, or a neutral port subsequently to the notification of the outbreak of hostilities to the Power to which such port belongs, provided that such notification was made in sufficient time.

ART. 46. A neutral vessel will be condemned and, in a general way, receive the same treatment as would be applicable to her if she were an enemy merchant vessel:

(1) If she takes a direct part in the hostilities;

(2) If she is under the orders or control of an agent placed on board by the enemy government;

(3) If she is in the exclusive employment of the enemy government;

(4) If she is exclusively engaged at the time either in the transport of enemy troops or in the transmission of intelligence in the interest of the enemy.

In the cases covered by the present article, goods belonging to the owner of the vessel are likewise liable to condemnation.

ART. 47. Any individual embodied in the armed forces of the enemy who is found on board a neutral merchant vessel, may be made a prisoner of war, even though there be no ground for the capture of the vessel.

CHAPTER IV. DESTRUCTION OF NEUTRAL PRIZES

ART. 48. A neutral vessel which has been captured may not be destroyed by the captor; she must be taken into such port as is proper for the determination there of all questions concerning the validity of the capture.

ART. 49. As an exception, a neutral vessel which has been captured by a belligerent warship, and which would be liable to condemnation, may be destroyed if the observance of Article 48 would involve danger to the safety of the warship or to the success of the operations in which she is engaged at the time.

ART. 50. Before the vessel is destroyed all persons on board must be placed in safety, and all the ship's papers and other documents which the parties interested consider relevant for the purpose of deciding on the validity of the capture must be taken on board the warship.

ART. 51. A captor who has destroyed a neutral vessel must, prior to any decision respecting the validity of the capture, establish that he only acted in the face of an exceptional necessity of the nature contemplated in Article 49. If he fails to do this, he must compensate the parties interested and no examination shall be made of the question whether the capture was valid or not.

ART. 52. If the capture of a neutral vessel is subsequently held to be invalid, though the act of destruction has been held to have been justifiable, the captor must pay compensation to the parties interested, in place of the restitution to which they would have been entitled.

ART. 53. If neutral goods not liable to condemnation have been destroyed with the vessel, the owner of such goods is entitled to compensation.

ART. 54. The captor has the right to demand the handing over, or to proceed himself to the destruction of, any goods liable to condemnation found on board a vessel not herself liable to condemnation, provided that the circumstances are such as would, under Article 49, justify the destruction of a vessel herself liable to condemnation. The captor must enter the goods surrendered or destroyed in the log book of the vessel stopped, and must obtain duly certified copies of all relevant papers. When the goods have been handed over or destroyed and the formalities duly carried out, the master must be allowed to continue his voyage.

The provisions of Articles 51 and 52 respecting the obligations of a captor who has destroyed a neutral vessel are applicable.

CHAPTER V. TRANSFER TO A NEUTRAL FLAG

ART. 55. The transfer of an enemy vessel to a neutral flag, effected before the outbreak of hostilities, is valid, unless it is proved that such transfer was made in order to evade the consequences to which an enemy vessel, as such, is exposed. There is, however, a presumption, if the bill of sale is not on board a vessel which has lost her belligerent nationality less than sixty days before the outbreak of hostilities, that the transfer is void. This presumption may be rebutted.

Where the transfer was effected more than thirty days before the outbreak of hostilities, there is an absolute presumption that it is valid if it is unconditional, complete, and in conformity with the laws of the countries concerned, and if its effect is such that neither the control of, nor the profits arising from the employment of, the vessel remain in the same hands as before the transfer. If, however, the vessel lost her belligerent nationality less than sixty days before the outbreak of hostilities, and if the bill of sale is not on board, the capture of the vessel gives no right to compensation.

ART. 56. The transfer of an enemy vessel to a neutral flag, effected after the outbreak of hostilities, is void unless it is proved that such transfer was not made in order to evade the consequences to which an enemy vessel, as such, is exposed.

There is, however, an absolute presumption that a transfer is void:

(1) If the transfer has been made during a voyage or in a blockaded port;

(2) If a right to repurchase or recover the vessel is reserved to the vendor;

(3) If the requirements of the municipal law governing the right to fly the flag under which the vessel is sailing, have not been fulfilled.

CHAPTER VI. ENEMY CHARACTER

ART. 57. Subject to the provisions respecting transfer to another flag, the neutral or enemy character of a vessel is determined by the flag which she is entitled to fly.

The case where a neutral vessel is engaged in a trade which is closed in time of peace, remains outside the scope of, and is in no wise affected by, this rule.

ART. 58. The neutral or enemy character of goods found on board an enemy vessel is determined by the neutral or enemy character of the owner.

ART. 59. In the absence of proof of the neutral character of goods found on board an enemy vessel, they are presumed to be enemy goods.

ART. 60. Enemy goods on board an enemy vessel retain their enemy character until they reach their destination, notwithstanding any transfer effected after the outbreak of hostilities while the goods are being forwarded.

If, however, prior to the capture, a former neutral owner exercises, on the bankruptcy of an existing enemy owner, a recognized legal right to recover the goods, they regain their neutral character.

Chapter VII. Convoy

Art. 61. Neutral vessels under national convoy are exempt from search. The commander of a convoy gives, in writing, at the request of the commander of a belligerent warship, all information as to the character of the vessels and their cargoes, which could be obtained by search.

Art. 62. If the commander of the belligerent warship has reason to suspect that the confidence of the commander of the convoy has been abused, he communicates his suspicions to him. In such a case it is for the commander of the convoy alone to investigate the matter. He must record the result of such investigation in a report, of which a copy is handed to the officer of the warship. If, in the opinion of the commander of the convoy, the facts shown in the report justify the capture of one or more vessels, the protection of the convoy must be withdrawn from such vessels.

Chapter VIII. Resistance to Search

Art. 63. Forcible resistance to the legitimate exercise of the right of stoppage, search, and capture, involves in all cases the condemnation of the vessel. The cargo is liable to the same treatment as the cargo of an enemy vessel. Goods belonging to the master or owner of the vessel are treated as enemy goods.

Chapter IX. Compensation

Art. 64. If the capture of a vessel or of goods is not upheld by the prize court, or if the prize is released without any judgment being given, the parties interested have the right to compensation, unless there were good reasons for capturing the vessel or goods.

FINAL PROVISIONS

Art. 65. The provisions of the present declaration must be treated as a whole, and cannot be separated.

Art. 66. The signatory Powers undertake to insure the mutual observance of the rules contained in the present declaration in any war in which all the belligerents are parties thereto. They will therefore issue the necessary instructions to their authorities and to their armed forces, and will take such measures as may be required in order to insure that it will be applied by their courts, and more particularly by their prize courts.

Art. 67. The present declaration shall be ratified as soon as possible.

The ratifications shall be deposited in London.

The first deposit of ratifications shall be recorded in a protocol signed by the representatives of the Powers taking part therein, and by his Britannic Majesty's principal secretary of state for foreign affairs.

The subsequent deposits of ratifications shall be made by means of a written notification addressed to the British government, and accompanied by the instrument of ratification.

A duly certified copy of the protocol relating to the first deposit of ratifications, and of the notifications mentioned in the preceding paragraph, as well as of the instruments of ratification which accompany them, shall be immediately sent by the British government, through the diplomatic channel, to the signatory Powers. The said government shall, in the cases contemplated in the preceding paragraph, inform them at the same time of the date on which it received the notification.

ART. 68. The present declaration shall take effect, in the case of the Powers which were parties to the first deposit of ratifications, sixty days after the date of the protocol recording such deposit, and, in the case of the Powers which shall ratify subsequently, sixty days after the notification of their ratification shall have been received by the British government.

ART. 69. In the event of one of the signatory Powers wishing to denounce the present declaration, such denunciation can only be made to take effect at the end of a period of twelve years, beginning sixty days after the first deposit of ratifications, and, after that time, at the end of successive periods of six years, of which the first will begin at the end of the period of twelve years.

Such denunciation must be notified in writing, at least one year in advance, to the British government, which shall inform all the other Powers.

It will only operate in respect of the denouncing Power.

ART. 70. The Powers represented at the London naval conference attach particular importance to the general recognition of the rules which they have adopted, and therefore express the hope that the Powers which were not represented there will accede to the present declaration. They request the British government to invite them to do so.

A Power which desires to accede shall notify its intention in writing to the British government, and transmit simultaneously the act of accession, which will be deposited in the archives of the said government.

The said government shall forthwith transmit to all the other Powers a duly certified copy of the notification, together with the act of accession, and communicate the date on which such notification was received. The accession takes effect sixty days after such date.

In respect of all matters concerning this declaration, acceding Powers shall be on the same footing as the signatory Powers.

ART. 71. The present declaration, which bears the date of the 26th February, 1909, may be signed in London up till the 30th June, 1909, by the plenipotentiaries of the Powers represented at the naval conference.

In faith whereof the plenipotentiaries have signed the present declaration, and have thereto affixed their seals.

Done at London, the twenty-sixth day of February, one thousand nine hundred and nine, in a single original, which shall remain deposited in the archives of the British government, and of which duly certified copies shall be sent through the diplomatic channel to the Powers represented at the naval conference.

[Names follow]

A much stronger case for the world judiciary exists in fact than appears from the official record of what has been accomplished. The principle of a regular court of justice for all the nations was formally approved by the second peace conference at The Hague, but it was found impossible to reach an agreement regarding the method of securing the judges. Therefore the establishment of such a court, apart from war, does not appear in the conventions adopted by that conference, although the larger nations were in agreement and it was the smaller ones, fearful of conceding too much for their welfare, which prevented the success of the effort at that time.

But the movement has advanced since then. On October 18, 1909, Secretary of State Knox, at Washington, sent to the Powers an identic note, suggesting an extension of the jurisdiction of the international prize court so as to include cases of difference between nations other than those growing out of war. The matter rests, as far as its official status is concerned, at the time of publication, with the receipt of many encouraging replies. But there is no doubt that the world judiciary is in vital process of evolution, and its development to a stage of efficiency seems to be near.

CHAPTER XXI

THE WORLD EXECUTIVE

If the political organization of all the world were an act consummated at a particular time, or within a brief and well-defined period, like the formation of the Constitution of the United States of North America and its ratification by the several states whose delegates had made it, then all the departments would begin existence simultaneously in definite form. The legislative, the executive, and the judicial departments would begin action together, and the wheels of governmental machinery would go around in every nation of the earth in harmony.

But the nations are coming into the unity of political organization in a different way. It has already been shown how the world legislature is on its way into fully developed being; the sprouting of the germ of the world judiciary has become a historical fact, already noticed. It is pertinent here to show, for the benefit of those who may not have turned their attention to the wonderful movement of modern times toward the political unity of all the nations, that the world executive department is already in progress of development. In the author's little book entitled "World Organization," in the chapter on The World Constitution, and other chapters severally upon the legislative, the executive, and the judicial departments, the whole matter is treated in detail as a political proposition and as a historic development. For the purposes of this book, for the rounding out of the scheme of a unit of political organization, for the information of those who are not familiar with the previous work, it seems best to give here sufficient to show that the world executive is already here, has come to stay, and is on the way upward to a stronger and clearer existence in the international life of the nations. At present the germs — for there are more than one — are so feeble as to attract little notice. But several offices already exist, whose incumbents have specified executive duties assigned to them by the will of the nations which participated in international conferences, of such high rank that their acts are to be regarded as acts of world legislation. These offices, therefore, are in reality a part of an executive department of the world, and the officials are true world executive officials.

First in importance of these is the permanent secretary of the Universal Postal Union, who has a regular office in Berne, Switzerland. Compared with the possible development of the world chief executive, following the analogy of the chief executive of the union of the states of North America, of Switzerland, or other national federations, this office is very humble; but its inconspicuous function does not at all change its nature as an executive office, serving all the world and subject to the will of the world as expressed by delegates of the nations assembled in official conference.

Again, a germ of the world executive is found in the international committee on weights and measures, an executive board always in existence, with an agent who is director of the international bureau of weights and measures. This was established by a convention which was agreed to May 20 by seventeen of the nineteen nations which met in the diplomatic metrical conference in Paris in 1875.

Executive functions are characteristic of the Hague court of arbitration. An executive department of the court is the permanent administrative council, which has true world executive duties to perform. It is "charged with the establishment and organization of the international bureau, which shall remain under its direction and control. . . . It shall decide all administrative questions which may arise relating to the working of the court." Subordinate to this permanent administrative council is the international bureau. It is given, formally, the rank of a clerk's office in connection with the court. Here, then, are several phases of executive power in connection with the court, all of them established by the will of the adhering Powers, which may rightly be called world legislation.

By the international sanitary conference of 1881 there were established at Vienna and Havana respectively permanent international sanitary agencies of notification, and the right was specified to establish a third in Asia. The conference also established a temporary scientific sanitary commission. All of these bodies were truly executive in nature, subject and responsible not to any one Power, but only to the high contracting Powers acting as one world Power.

By the convention of March 20, 1883, for the protection of industrial property, an international bureau was established, whose cost should be paid by the governments of all the contracting states, and which should work under the supervision of the superior administration of the Swiss Confederation. Here is another international body with executive functions, created by the will of the nations represented.

By the Brussels convention of July 2, 1890, for the suppression of the slave trade in Africa, certain executive duties for all the signatory Powers were imposed upon the foreign office at Brussels, which thus had somewhat of the character of a world executive put upon it, rather than have a separate office for the service created. But the character of the work is none the less that of executive service for all of the signatory Powers, defined by the will of the world, as far as those nations represented civilization.

Again, by the convention adopted at Rome on June 7, 1905, establishing the international institute of agriculture, it is provided that "the executive power of the institute is intrusted to the permanent committee, which, under the direction and control of the general assembly, shall carry out the decisions of the latter and prepare propositions to submit to it." Here, then, is another germ of the world executive department.

Finally, by the convention regarding wireless telegraphy adopted at Berlin, November 3, 1906, an international bureau was established with executive functions covering "all administrative work referred to it in the interest of international wireless telegraphy."

Here are nine different international bodies, established by the will of the world, as far as the several signatory Powers represented the world, having executive duties. They are none the less true world executives because they are of comparatively humble rank. Wherever there has been a temporary commission, charged with doing certain administrative service, there has been also a true illustration of the executive department of the united world. It is not necessary to have a world president, or a world emperor, or a world despot, as the beginning of the world executive department. Rather, the humble beginning points to a culmination when the world chief executive will be a commissioner in general, the coördinating official who shall, in an administrative way, see that all departments are working together harmoniously,— responsible to the people of the world, rather than an autocrat of any degree of irresponsible power.

CHAPTER XXII

PEACE AND GOOD WILL

Into the history of mankind the world court now enters. " Court " implies justice and righteousness. Justice will carry with it, as one consequence, international peace. Only dishonorable nations will refuse to abide by the just decision of the world court, and resort to war rather than yield what seems possible of conquest by force. Against such nations it is possible that the entire military strength of the other nations might be exerted, if necessary to prevent acts hostile to the common welfare of mankind. Certainly such nations would forfeit the respect of mankind. But the good opinion of the world would be a treasure of higher value than gold or conquered territory or the forced submission of sullen and unwilling peoples, and no nation would be likely to sacrifice the greater for the less. National honor could not drive a people into war against the judgment of the world court, for national honor would involve a high place in the good opinion of the world; and it is inevitable that the world should have a higher opinion of the nation which, for the sake of peace, should accept a decision which it felt to be unjust, rather than violate the judgment of the world expressed in the decision of the world court, by refusing to accept that decision and going to war. National honor is possible, in the broad and valuable sense of being a recognition of worth by other people than one's own, only with the good opinion of the world. It is therefore a safe reliance when it is said that the decisions of the world court will be accepted without resort to arms to enforce them. It is true, in a sense, that national honor is not dependent upon the good opinion of the world, as a person's character does not depend upon what other persons think of him. But if any nation, seeking to realize the highest honor to itself, tries with the full national strength and national enthusiasm to do what its conscience commands, it may be safely trusted not to violate the peace of the world and commit serious injustice by war.

In its beginning the world judiciary has taken the form of an international prize court. This court will have for its function the determination of the lawfulness, by the laws of war, of the capture of vessels in time of war. That is, war is a necessary condition for the operation of the new world court. Yet it is the function of a court superior to nations to do justice between them, and thereby to remove occasions for war.

A great historic monument, therefore, has been erected by the world to its own barbaric stage of development in this twentieth century of time, as the world reckons time from the coming of the Prince of Peace. A world court, an institution for the peace of the world, for the establishment of justice between all nations, is created under such conditions that it shall be inoperative except in case of war. What a monstrous self-contradiction! What a powerful demonstration of the brute stage in which the most advanced nations are yet lingering! Yet, also, what an irrefutable proof that the brute has at last opened his eyes to the heinousness of his own brutality, and that he is groping upward into that light which he is sure to attain when brutality shall have become spirituality, and the strength of unarmed truth shall be mightier than all the armies and navies of the world!

Manifestly this primary form of the judicial department of the world must be very transient. That it shall never become operative must be the strong desire of every right-minded man in every nation. Yet the fact of the establishment of such a world court, with all that it implies of judgment with justice and world peace, immediately points the way to a higher level which must be reached at once if the world judiciary is to become a practical reality.

Higher than the function of a court to determine the rightfulness of captures of vessels in time of war is the function of determining whether a nation has committed injustice toward another and so has provoked a national resentment and inflamed the fighting temper so as to make war imminent. Immediately there is demonstrated, beyond doubt, the need of a body of world law for the fixing of the relations and duties of nations to each other under world conditions, and the need of a world court which shall have power to adjudicate, upon appeal to it by one or both parties, what world law demands, whether or not it has been infringed, if so, how, and what would be reasonable reparation on the part of the offending nation. This present establishment of the world judiciary, therefore, is so transient a device that it must be followed, as soon as the nations can attend to the matter, by the further establishment of a world court to pass upon violations by nations of conditions of international peace.

This, in turn, implies for its ideal realization a formal codification of present international law and its enactment into genuine world law, or the formally ratified will of the nations of the earth. Evidently this immense and valuable service to mankind is to be realized by means of one or more international conferences which shall formulate for the nations the propositions which are to be ratified. When the ratification shall have been made by a sufficient number of the nations, then the body of world law for the guidance of the world court in the establishment of world peace will have been put into formal operation, and it will be reasonable for the world from that time forward to expect to settle international differences by the court and not by arms. From that time on, armies and navies will be ridiculously out of keeping with the spirit of the times, and the nation which maintains them will advertise both its folly and its barbarism.

When that development of the world court shall have been reached, mankind will have done its noblest work possible in way of the organization of the human race. One man may compile, more or less imperfectly, the First Book of World Law; but the subject matter of the compilation embodies the highest achievements of the greatest statesmen of the world up to that date, in establishing the formal relations of the nations to each other and in recognizing the fundamental unity of mankind. When the Second Book of World Law, however, shall come into being, if it proves to be in the main a codification of existing international law plus the insertion of new principles by which nations shall be guided in affairs of peace rather than of war, and by which higher progress in pioneer civilization shall be attained,—then it will be the direct work of the best legal and political sense of all the nations combined. It will be, it is perhaps right to say, the greatest single achievement of the human race. It will be the expressed essence of the mind of man recognizing its own relation as an organic entity and adapting itself to the conditions of its most rapid and substantial progress. All development of world law from that time will be built on that foundation.

Such, then, is the mighty achievement, imperative for the progress of mankind, which confronts us in the near future. The faith and the ability which have brought the nations to this crisis will surely carry them through it; and then will come the unending era of universal peace and the unprecedented prosperity of mankind, materially, intellectually, and spiritually.

Doubters may say that the existence of the world court will not prevent the nations from flying at each other's throats. Perhaps they are right. It will take a long time to outgrow the brute in human nature. But within a few years the world has made wonderful progress. Most encouraging of all the signs is the fact that mankind is getting its eyes open to its own brutality. To the minds of a rapidly increasing number of influential men and women this brutality is not to be excused or tolerated, much less encouraged. Once let any particular policy be recognized by the conscience of the nations as an outcropping of the ancient brute, whether of the tiger, the hog, the fox, or the snake, and it is immediately left without a defender among all who appreciate the higher ideals of the race. The movements for world peace and for world organization unite in stimulating the tendency to bring the world court into action as soon as possible.

Given a world court whereby each nation will feel absolutely sure that it will secure so much of justice that it will prefer to accept the court's award rather than go to war for what it does not get; given a public opinion among the nations that their honor and their interests both lie in making use of the world court for securing justice, rather than in making use of armies and navies; and given also such a preponderance of world opinion that the backward nations will not fight counter to the combined judgment of the advanced nations, — and there will be a permanent status of peace which will tend mightily to eradicate the fighting disposition between the nations.

It is a reasonable prediction, in view of the wonderful progress of the world organization movement within the last few years, to say that the world legislature will, by means of the ratifications of the nations, establish a body of world law for the guidance and interpretation of the world court, whereby all the essential rights of the great and the small nations will be equally secured. Half of the difficulty is in getting the world to see the problem clearly and to have it take form in the consciousness of mankind. That is the process which is now going on. Statesmen in the leading nations realize more than ever — and the recommendation for a third Hague conference is ample demonstration — that the getting together of the nations must be promoted and hastened, that international law must be codified and enacted into world law, that there must be a world court on a higher and more practical plane than a court of appeals in the case of prizes captured in war, and that it is only the persistence of brutality in the nations which prevents them from a speedy enjoyment of universal peace. The problem will be half solved when it shall have been clearly comprehended by the leading men of the world. Then will follow quickly the determination to solve it wholly and to put the solution into practice. A few years ago it seemed as if this solution were perhaps hundreds of years in the future. To-day it is no stretch of probability to say that men now living will see the world court in successful operation; and then wars between nations will be as popularly abhorred and condemned, and as much a thing of the past, as the duel between individuals is to-day in the United States.

World progress hitherto justifies prediction of world progress hereafter. How much of the past progress has been due to resistless cosmic forces which are as much beyond the will of man as the mighty pressures which bend granite rocks like paper, and how much is due to human origination and energy, may be left for philosophers in that field to determine; but no one will deny that cosmic forces which have wrought for progress since man appeared on the earth will continue to act to the same end, while the originating power in man in the past is sufficient warrant for predicting that this will continue for at least a few years more. Given both of these resistless forces working in unison for even a comparatively few years more, as historic periods are counted, and there is no more doubt of the great consummation of world political unity being in sight than there is doubt of the revolution of the earth around the sun. Forces which act upon the human intellect and upon the human conscience are rapidly bringing the days when the formal political organization of the nations as a world unit will be complete, and will be a practical, constant reliance, as truly as are the legislatures, the courts, and the executives of the states of our United States to-day.

By the world legislature world laws will surely be enacted, not only to regulate the relations of nations to each other so that differences which have led in the past to war shall hereafter be referred to the several branches of the world court with as much certainty of justice as now obtains in the courts of any nation for its own citizens, but far more will be accomplished. Settlement of quarrels between nations in order to avoid war is a very crude function for a court. Legislation merely to provide for justice between litigants marks a barbaric stage of civilization. Not less legislation, but more, will surely mark the world development of the nations as truly as it marks the advance of the most progressive states in our union.

Nor will this legislation be remedial legislation only for the evils inherited from the past. It will be organizing and constructive legislation, to bring into the service of mankind forces which are to be developed for the progress of the future. Crime alone is comparatively a small subject of our legislation to-day. Civil quarrels, in addition, form by no means the only subject of the remainder of our lengthening codes. The chief feature of our laws to-day is their organizing and constructive function for the development of human society. Organic humanity is slowly coming into the rightful possession and operation of the vast mass of raw material in the shape of human beings which characterizes the savage and the barbaric stages of progress, in distinction from those stages which have some claim to be called civilized.

This is the meaning of the resistless tendency toward centralization which so many champions of local rights deplore, — and rightly deplore, so far as it is an unjust invasion upon local right and lawful development under the laws imposed upon society by a Power higher than man. This is the meaning of the harnessing of the forces of the human race for the collective service of the race. This is the meaning of that growing protest against the exploitation of the race by powerful favored interests, which aggrandize themselves at the expense of the masses, out of whom they take wealth more than is measured by what they give. This is the meaning of the establishment of different departments of organic activity in business fields, whereby national and state commissions, presumably composed of the most expert professional ability, are set to guard the interests of the whole people, who are inexpert and occupied with their daily toil, in the various productive, financial, educational, sanitary, transportation, insurance, and other fields.

This forecast includes legislation by the world legislature to regulate business forces, so that world monopolies shall be as specifically regulated when hostile to public policy as they are within the limits of any of our states in the United States. Not merely interstate commerce laws, but world commerce laws will save all the nations from a predatory combination of transportation interests beyond the scope of any merely national laws. World sanitary legislation will rise to a sphere higher than national laws can cover, and be as necessary to the health of all the nations severally as health laws in the several states of our nation are necessary in addition to the rules and regulations of local boards of health. Organization and progress will be the fruitful field of the world legislature in its normal activity, bringing the mass of mankind into a united whole pressing on to higher and better things, — rather than deliberation over the details of national quarrels and misunderstandings. Organization, with the reliable activity of world courts, will reduce national quarrels to as negligible a feature of world life as lawsuits are a comparatively negligible feature in the transactions of thousands of millions of dollars' worth of business in our country yearly without thought of lawsuits. Law and peace make business possible without highwaymen or crime to any material percentage of the business of the nations; and so world law and world peace will make such a permanent status for business transactions that healthful activity for the satisfaction of humanity's desires will bear an overwhelming ratio to whatever activity is necessary for the settlement of differences between nations.

Such is the reasonable development which is already in sight. If the progress of the last few years can be maintained for a generation, the most essential features of all the departments will have been established and the nations will be far beyond the stage where armies and navies will have become needless and discreditable.

In the midst of the immense war preparations of to-day, therefore, it is only a calm and reasonable proposition to put before fearful statesmen and ambitious warriors,—the fact that their fears are groundless and their ambition sure to be thrown violently against the wall by collision with the locomotive of human progress. Standing armies — with their magnificent field maneuvers as a training for war and a spectacle for the vanity of pugnacious men and silly women, with their destruction of profitable production, their prodigious financial burden and their moral rottenness — will cease to be tolerated. Great navies — now provoking admiration in world-encircling trips — will no longer be constructed by nations which are throwing off needless weights in the real race for the higher rewards and standards of civilization. Inventors will turn their fertile brains to other devices than those for the wholesale destruction of their brother men by fighting-machines on the ground, under the sea, or in the air. Military and naval schools will be discontinued because young men have something better to learn than the scientific destruction of human life, and because they will be needless on an earth where the world court's decrees are obeyed by force of a moral public opinion mightier than any force which ever formed a battle line. Justice to all so far as human power can secure it, safety to all industrial and commercial enterprises, and fresh stimulus to every activity of hand and brain, — from the roughest manual labor to the highest level of art and science, — will force far into the background all necessity or thought of fighting by arms. Such will be the world's attainment in no distant future by the operation of forces now active and in sight. Armies and navies are doomed in the presence of organized humanity, and the rule of the world court will bring universal peace, order, and good will.

ANNOUNCEMENTS